Johan Herman Bavinck
(1895-1964)

HEART FOR THE GOSPEL, HEART FOR THE WORLD

The Life and Thought of a Reformed Pioneer Missiologist

Johan Herman Bavinck, 1895-1964

By

Paul Jan Visser

Wipf and Stock Publishers
199 West 8th Avenue, Eugene, OR 97401

HEART FOR THE GOSPEL, HEART FOR THE WORLD
The Life and Thought of a Reformed Pioneer Missiologist
Johan Herman Bavinck, 1895-1964
by Paul Jan Visser
Copyright © 2003

ISBN:1-59244-275-7
ISBN: 978-1-49824-711-5

Wipf and Stock Publishers
199 West 8th Avenue
Eugene, OR 97401

Table of Contents

List of Abbreviations

General

CHDDP/FUA	Center for the Historical Documentation of Dutch Protestantism from 1800 Onward, Free University, Amsterdam
DHB	*De Heerbaan*
DM	*De Macedoniër*
DMC	Dutch Missionary Council
DWME	Division of World Mission and Evangelism
FUQ	*Free University Quarterly*
GKN	Gereformeerde Kerken in Nederland
GTT	*Gereformeerd Theologisch Tijdschrift*
GW	*Gereformeerd Weekblad*
HZB	*Het Zendingsblad*
IBMR	*International Bulletin of Missionary Research*
IMC	International Missionary Council
IRM	*International Review of Mission*
KJV	King James Version of the Bible
NHK	Nederlandse Hervormde Kerk
NRC	Netherlands Reformed Church (Nederlandse Hervormde Kerk)
NRSV	New Revised Standard Version of the Bible
NTT	*Nederlands Theologisch Tijdschrift*
RCN	Reformed Churches in the Netherlands (Gereformeerde Kerken in Nederland)
WCC	World Council of Churches
WZ	*Wereld en Zending*

Bavinck's Books and Monographs

AWW	*Alzo wies het Woord* (And Thus the Word Grew and Increased, 1941)
BBO	*De Bijbel: Het boek der ontmoetingen* (The Bible: The Book of Encounters, 1942)
BCNCR	*De boodschap van Christus en de niet-christelijke religies* (The Message of Christ and Non-Christian Religions, 1940)
CBTM	*The Church Between the Temple and Mosque* (1966)
CMO	*Christus en de mystiek van het Oosten* (Christ and Eastern Mysticism, 1934)
CPVW	*Christusprediking in de volkerenwereld* (Preaching Christ to the Nations, 1939)

CWS   *Christus en de wereldstorm* (Christ and the World
               Storm, 1944)
DAC   *De absoluutheid van het christendom* (The
               Absoluteness of Christianity, n.d.)
DMN   *De mens van nu* (Contemporary Man, 1967)
DTK   *De toekomst van onze kerken* (The Future of Our
               Churches, 1943)
EGAHS   *Der Einfliss des Gefühls auf das Assoziationsleben bei
               Heinrich von Suso* (The Influence of Feeling on the
               Process of Association in the Work of Heinrich von
               Suso, 1919)
EVWE   *En voort wentelen de eeuwen: Gedachten over het boek
               der Openbaring van Johannes* (And Age Follows Upon
               Age: Reflections on John's Book of Revelation, 1952)
FF   *Flitsen en fragmenten*, (Flashes and Fragments,
                       1959).
GGNT   *Geschiedenis der Godsopenbaring II: Het Nieuwe
               Testament* (History of Divine Revelation II: The New
               Testament, 1938)
IBD   *In de ban der demonen* (Under the Spell of
                       Demons, 1950)
ICNCW   *The Impact of Christianity on the Non-Christian World*
               (1948)
IGHG   *Ik geloof in de Heilige Geest* (I Believe in the Holy
               Spirit, 1963)
ISM   *An Introduction to the Science of Missions*
                       (1960)
IZK   *Inleiding in de zielkunde* (Introduction to
                       Psychology, 1935^2)
IZW   *Inleiding in de zendingswetenschap*
                       (Introduction to the Science of Mission, 1954)
LV   *Levensvragen* (Questions of Life, 1927)
OKZK   *Onze kerk, zendingskerk* (Our Church: Missionary
               Church, 1948)
OZB   *Ons zendingsboek* (Our Missionary Book,
                       1941)
MZW   *De mensch en zijn wereld* (Man and His World, 1946)
PO   *De psychologie van den Oosterling* (The
                       Psychology of Eastern Peoples, 1942)
PPRAO   *Het probleem van de pseudo-religie en de algemene
               openbaring* (The Problem of Pseudoreligion and
               General Revelation, n.d.)
PWB   *Persoonlijkheid en wereldbeschouwing* (Personality
               and World View, 1928)
RBCG   *Religieus besef en christelijk geloof* (Religious
               Consciousness and Christian Faith, 1949, 1989^2)
ROL   *Het raadsel van ons leven* (The Riddle of Our
                       Life, 1940)

RPW	*Het rassenvraagstuk, problem van wereldformaat* (The Race Question: A World Problem, 1956)
RWBOT	*Religies en wereldbeschouwingen in onze tijd* (Religions and World Views in Our Day, 1958)
WW	*Het Woord voor de wereld* (Word for the World, 1950)
ZKO	*Zielkundige opstellen* (Essays on Psychology, 1925)
ZWN	*Zending in een wereld in nood* (Mission in a World in Need, 1946)

FOREWORD

It gives me great pleasure that now, after encouraging requests from various parties, especially Calvin Theological Seminary, an English edition appears of my Ph. D. study, done under Prof. dr. Jan A. B. Jongeneel from the University of Utrecht in the Netherlands.

Special thanks for a beautiful and perfect translation goes to Prof. Jerry Gort, from the Free University of Amsterdam, the Netherlands. Thanks to his work, many quotes, which appeared in the Dutch version in the footnotes, are now included in the text. The result is a greater familiarity with the thinking of Johan H. Bavinck.

It is my firm conviction that the missionary theology of Johan H. Bavinck has not lost its relevance- it is not for nothing that Johan Verkuyl called him a modern classic-and it is my sincere wish that many will be enriched through his theological inheritance.

Paul J. Visser
The Hague, Netherlands
July 2003

PREFACE

When Paul Visser asked me to write a preface for his book on the life and missionary theology of J.H.Bavinck, I was pleased. Because although I never met J.H. Bavinck, nor sat in his classroom, through his writings he shaped my missiological thinking more than any other person. It is unfortunate that many of Bavinck's important writings have not yet been translated into English, and the few titles that have appeared are out of print. Therefore, I am delighted that Visser's broad and comprehensive study of Bavinck's life and ideas has become available in the English language through what I consider to be a wonderful translation from the Dutch.

As I read through the manuscript, I was impressed by the relevance of Bavinck's missiology for contemporary readers and the issues facing us today. Names and circumstances have changed, but the basic issues remain the same. I found especially helpful Visser's account of how Bavinck dealt with the question of the uniqueness of Jesus Christ and the ultimacy of the gospel over against other religions. This is a subject that will surely receive major attention on the part of missiologists throughout the 21st century.

In this connection, Visser uncovers a change in Bavinck's thinking, a "reversal of thought" he calls it, of which I had been previously unaware. It has to do with the question of whether unregenerate persons possess a natural seed of desire for God, and whether they in fact genuinely seek for God. In his later life, Bavinck rejected the more positive position he had taken earlier. He concluded that from the biblical standpoint, the unregenerate do not, and cannot, seek after God. For in the integral core of their beings they are sinners, rebels who at the deepest level of their nature are afraid of God, avoid Him, push Him away and resist Him entirely. For those who agree with him, Bavinck's position on this subject has enormous implications for the presuppositions with which they start in inter-religious dialogue.

Visser observes that every step Bavinck took removed him further from psychological speculation and philosophical considerations, and toward a deeper biblical-theological rooting of his missiology. For this we can all be grateful.

Visser's book appears at a time when amazing changes are occurring in Christian missions. The momentum is shifting from North to South, and from West to East. In growing numbers, missionaries are sent out from churches in countries that not long ago were called "mission fields." Departments of Missiology are being developed in schools and seminaries in places like Seoul (South Korea), Manila (Philippines), Sao Paulo (Brazil), San Jose (Costa Rica), Nairobi (Kenya), and Dehra Dun (India). A younger generation of missiologists is rising up. They are developing new, contextualized approaches to Christian witness, while at the same time building on what they regard as the best of western Missiology. They will benefit greatly from Visser's study of Bavinck's missionary theology as they explore new frontiers in this ever-expanding field.

This leads me to suggest that still another book ought to be written, one that will be shorter, easier to read, and will translate Bavinck's ideas from the arena of high academia to the levels where, globally speaking, the greatest number of pastors, missionaries and students operate. Visser's book is a scholarly work, rich in important insights for advanced students of theology and missions. Someday soon, however, a writer needs to arise who has the education and mental capacity to understand Bavinck thoroughly, has a deep sensitivity to the needs of thousands of students, pastors and evangelists in Asia, Africa and Latin America who come from different cultural and educational backgrounds, who struggle with English, cannot afford big books published in the West, and nevertheless need to understand the issues that Bavinck addressed and the biblical insights he applied to them. When such a person appears, he or she will be deeply indebted to Paul Visser's monumental study of one of the 20th century's greatest missiologists, Johan Herman Bavinck.

Roger S. Greenway
Calvin Theological Seminary
Grand Rapids, Michigan 49546

CHAPTER ONE

Background and Early Years

"In reality it is impossible to write a person's biography, for what we call a person's life constitutes only half of that person's existence: what he has done, thought, sought, what sins he has committed. A truly biographical sketch would require seeing the other half of a person's 'life' as well: God's dealings with him, God's boundless concern for him, God's gracious watchfulness over him." (*IGHG*, 73)

1. Family Heritage

The biographical details of Bavinck's career testify to the indissoluble connection between his life and his historical background. The Bavinck family was intellectually and spiritually rooted in the Dutch Reformed church schism of 1834 (*Afscheiding*), which was characterized by an emphasis on personal piety and faith experience. Engagement in the life of the church and in Reformed theology took on an important place among Bavinck's immediate relatives, preeminently in the persons of his grandfather, Jan Bavinck, and his father, Coenraad, both of whom were Reformed pastors, and his uncle, the gifted dogmatician Herman Bavinck. The following paragraphs outlining the more recent history of the Bavinck family are meant to provide insight into the spiritual and theological environment in which Johan Herman grew up.

1.1. Jan Bavinck (1826-1909)

The Bavincks came from the county of Bentheim,[1] an area in Germany bordering on the eastern Dutch provinces of Drenthe and Overijssel. It was there that Jan Bavinck, too, first saw the light of day on February 5, 1826, the fifth child and only son of Hermanus Bavinck (1781-1829) and Fenna Niehaus ((1795-1858). Jan's father died three years later, leaving his mother, a widow of 33 years, to care for six children. Despite the deep sorrow she felt at the loss of her husband, Fenna devoted herself wholly to the care of her family. Jan wrote of her:

> Our good mother lived and worked to the best of her ability for her children, who were her pride and joy. She did her utmost to

---

[1] Genealogical records compiled by members of the family reveal that the name Bavinck appears in Bentheim as early as 1594.

provide us with a good upbringing, for which task she had received a number of gifts and the necessary tact. She watched over us carefully and was at pains to see that we didn't get into the wrong company, reminding us constantly to avoid things that are bad or mean. She had us attend school faithfully, took us to church on the day of rest, and sent us to catechism. We were not allowed to miss even one time. In short, we had a good and faithful mother, to whom we owe a great deal.[2]

During his youth Jan underwent a spiritual development that would prove to be of decisive significance for his own later life and his posterity. The nature of that development is illustrated by a few striking passages in his biography. After describing his solid upbringing and the dedicated allegiance of his family to the *Reformierte Kirche* van Bentheim, he writes:

I had a decent middle-class, religious upbringing, but despite this, in my younger years I never heard anything about 'inward Christianity' or about the things of salvation that can not be known by reason but are apprehended through personal experience by God's children. As far as I can remember, I was never called to faith and conversion and neither did anyone ever urge me to bend my knees before Jesus and to seek and desire Him as my Lord and Savior.[3]

Both in family and church, religious life consisted in "the observation of external religious duties,"[4] he writes, and continues as follows.

Though I grew up in an environment in which godliness and piety were not a matter of everyday parlance, I was concerned from my youth with the things of eternity. . . . Now and then, when I was alone, I bent my knees before God and poured out my heart to Him, sometimes with a flood of tears, praying and begging for mercy.[5]

Meanwhile a dissenting church came into being in Bentheim under the leadership of Jan B. Sundag, which was closely affiliated with the Dutch church that emerged from the ecclesiastical schism of 1834 (*Afscheiding*) in the Netherlands. At sixteen years of age Jan became involved with this *Alt-Reformierte Kirche* through his uncle Harm Niehaus. The conversion of his uncle and that of his cousin made a deep impression upon him. He visited them regularly and participated in their family worship services. He writes:

Under the guidance of my uncle the Lord caused me to become ever more aware of my own deep depravity and on the other hand of the salvation to be found in Christ Jesus. Through God's grace I surrendered myself to the Savior and made a conscious

---

[2]J. Bavinck, *Korte schets van mijn leven*, 3.

[3]*Ibid.*, 4.

[4]*Ibid.*

[5]*Ibid.*

decision to follow, cling to and serve Him.[6]

From then on he began attending the church services led by Sundag. That this was not an easy decision is made clear by the following passage.

> If one stops to consider that I was just a boy of sixteen years and that I was the only young person from Bentheim who went to the meetings of the Cocksians,[7] and if one takes further into account that the Cocksians were deeply despised and hated, that they were considered to be scum and garbage, it is not hard to see how and why I too came to be on the receiving end of the calumnious abuse heaped upon the *Afscheiding*.[8]

Still more difficult was the decision to break definitively with the *Reformierte Kirche* and to join the *Alt Reformierte Kirche*. Fear of sectarianism and separatism caused him to hesitate for a long time. He wanted to stay within the Reformed (*Gereformeerde*) fold. Finally, after a great deal of inner struggle, his decision was made: he transferred his membership. "I can say open heartedly that in order to remain Reformed (*Gereformeerd*), I left the *Reformierte Kirche* and affiliated myself with the *Alt-Reformierte Kirche*."[9]

Even long before his separation from his former church, Jan had "a deep, burning desire" to become a minister. But because his mother simply did not have the financial means to make this possible,[10] he apprenticed himself to the spinning wheel maker (*Drechsel-Wieldraier*), J..B. Krabbe, in 1842. This was more of a choice for Krabbe, who also belonged to the separatists, than for the trade he practiced. He soon felt at home in the Krabbe household, where Sundag also happened to be lodging at the time, which allowed for daily contact between the young ministerial aspirant and the experienced dissident preacher. At a certain point it became clear that Sundag's preaching responsibilities in the various separatist congregations had become too much for him, and the decision was taken to look around for young men capable of being trained for the gospel ministry. Of the five candidates who came forward, one was to be chosen. Jan Bavinck had also applied, in the hope that perhaps now his fondest wish would be fulfilled.

On January 17, 1845 twenty-two office bearers from the various separatist congregations met in the town of Brandlegt to decide which applicant should be selected. When the vote was tallied, it appeared that 11 ballots had been cast for one, Frederik Huisken, and 11 for Jan Bavinck. How was this impasse to be

---

[6]*Ibid.*, 10

[7]The ecclesiastical party or group named after Rev. Hendrik de Cock (1801-1842), who was the leader of the 1834 church schism (*Afscheiding*) in the Netherlands.

[8]J. Bavinck, *Korte schets van mijn leven*, 12.

[9]*Ibid.*, 13.

[10]*Ibid.*, 19.

resolved? After joining in prayer, it was decided to settle the issue by lot.[11] A servant girl was enlisted to draw one of the two names. On the slip she drew was written: Jan Bavinck.[12] About this he writes:

> So it came about that the way to training as servant of the Word was opened for me. One may think whatever one wishes to concerning the manner in which this came about; as far as I am concerned, I saw God's hand in it, the answer to my many prayers and an initial fulfilment of my heart's fervent desire.[13]

At that time there were three theological schools in the Netherlands where ministerial candidates of the Christian Separatist Reformed Church (*Christelijk Afgescheiden Gereformeerde Kerk*) received their training: one in Arnhem under the leadership of Rev. Anthonie Brummelkamp, one in Groningen headed by Rev. Tamme F. De Haan, and one in Bergen, a community near Ruinerwold in the province of Drenthe, led by Rev. Wolter A. Kok. It was decided that Jan would attend the school in Bergen. Jan and his ten fellow students received instruction from Kok and a converted Jewish scholar named Rozensweigh, who taught them history and classical languages. In 1846 Kok accepted a call to the congregation in Hoogeveen and the school automatically moved along with him. Jan was a bright student and worked hard. When Rozensweigh unexpectedly accepted an appointment in The Hague, Jan was designated, at Kok's suggestion and with the approval of his fellow students but much to his own amazement, to take over Rozensweigh's teaching duties. He himself called it "an emergency choice in needful circumstances" and added that he "had received a special passion from the Lord for the study of languages."[14] Even after the completion of his studies he continued his substitute teaching up to the time of the establishment of Kampen Theological Seminary in 1854.

On August 9, 1848 the 23-year old Jan was ordained to the ministry in the *Alt-Reformierte Kirche* in Beneden-Graafschap by his teacher Rev. Kok, who chose 2 Timothy 4:5 as the text for his sermon: "But you, keep your head in all situations, endure hardship, do the work of an evangelist, discharge all the duties of your ministry."[15] Jan wrote concerning this occasion, "As for me, I was aware, deeply aware, of the weight and gravity of the task that had been laid upon my shoulders."[16] The text he preached on at his installation was Colossians 1:8: "[You learned it

---

[11]This was the second time in this meeting that the participants had to resort to the casting of lots. The vote was also split on the earlier question of whether a person should be *chosen* to be trained for the ministry.

[12]J. Bavinck, *Korte schets van mijn leven*, 20-22.

[13]*Ibid.*, 23.

[14]*Ibid.*, 27.

[15]Unless otherwise indicated Scripture quotations are taken from *The Holy Bible, New International Version*, Copyright © 1973, 1978, 1984 International Bible Society. Used by permission of Zondervan Bible Publishers.

[16]J. Bavinck, *Korte schets van mijn leven*, 33.

from Epaphras,...] who also told us of your love in the Spirit." Even this choice of sermon text reflected the deep bond of solidarity he felt with Sundag. He now began serving the congregations in Veldhausen, Ülsen, Wilsum, and Emlichheim. Later his ministerial and pastoral responsibilities were limited to Ülsen and Wilsum. Initially, the civil authorities did everything they could to hinder *Alt-Reformierte* gatherings, but as time went on they became more and more tolerant of them.[17] On the advice of his church council, which also acted as intermediary, Jan became engaged to Gesina Magdelena Holland (1827-1900), a vigorous and plucky woman from the town of Vriezenveen, whom he married on April 27, 1850.

In subsequent years Jan was confronted with two difficult decisions. First, he was requested by Rev. Kok to consider a call to become associate pastor of the church in Hoogeveen. This call was issued not only owing to the size of the congregation in Hoogeveen but also with a view to the organizational improvement of the theological education for which the two of them bore responsibility in that region. At that moment, the students had to pursue the first part of their studies with Jan Bavinck and then go to Hoogeveen to complete them.[18] Kok thought it would be better for the students if their theological training were concentrated in a single locality once again. But Jan could not bring himself to leave Beneden-Graafschap. After some time, however, the congregation in Hoogeveen decided to call him anyway, which led to a great inner struggle on his part. He writes:

> I will not mention here what it cost me to make a final decision but only
> say that after much hesitation and doubt I finally resolved to leave
> Beneden-Graafschap and move to Hoogeveen.[19]

Nevertheless, even after he had taken the decision, doubts remained in his mind, and more than once the idea arose that he should have remained where he was. In the end, however, he was confident that the choice was according to God's will and that God would go and be with him. On May 16, 1853 he preached his farewell sermon on Acts 20:32: "Now I commend you to God and to the word of His grace, which is able to build you up and to give you the inheritance among all those who are sanctified."

A year later the General Synod of Zwolle decided to establish a theological seminary in Kampen,[20] with an initial staff of four instructors: Simon Van Velzen, Anthonie Brummelkamp, Tamme F. De Haan, and Jan Bavinck, then just 28 years old. His appointment took him by surprise:

> No! That, I truly could not have imagined.... This appointment
> seemed to me to carry such great weight that I considered turning
> it down right there on the spot at the meeting. How could I take
> my place and work alongside men who had the benefit of an

---

[17]*Ibid.*, 36-39. Here he gives a detailed report of the measures the civil authorities took against the *Alt-Reformierte Kirche.*

[18]More information about this theological training can be found in J.Kok, 171-180.

[19]J. Bavinck, *Korte schets van mijn leven,* 42.

[20]For details about this decision cf. J. Bosch, 154-156, and H. Algra, 152-156.

academic education?[21]

He was urged from many quarters, however, to accept the appointment, and he was becoming gradually convinced in his own mind that he should. But modest doubt with respect to his own abilities prevented him from answering the call in a wholeheartedly affirmative manner. He finally wrote two letters: one in which he accepted and another in which he declined the seminary position. The he had one of his students, J. Moolhuizen, who happened to be with him at the time, pick one of the letters out and mail it. It was the letter of declination. "No," he wrote, "I won't make any mention of how I felt and what went on inside me...when I learned [which of the letters had been sent]. I will say only this: that I had no peace with the matter, neither then nor for a long time afterward." [22] In this connection, he admitted to being one of "those weak souls who usually think very little of themselves, who have insufficient self-confidence, and who therefore shy away from taking the action called for in a given situation."[23] He tried to reverse his decision, but his efforts were rejected by the seminary Board of Trustees.[24] When 28 years later his son Herman, who was born in 1854, was appointed professor at Kampen Seminary, he wrote, "As for me, I saw the hand of the Lord in this, and I thanked Him for allowing my son - I wouldn't say to 'succeed' me but - to occupy the position I didn't dare to accept through lack of faith."[25]

In 1857 Jan Bavinck accepted a call to Bunschoten, where he served for five happy years. In 1862 he moved on to the congregation of Almkerk and Emmikhoven, where he and his wife had to come to terms with one great sorrow after another: within a period of five years, from 1863 to 1868, three of their children succumbed to death. But they also experienced the joy of the birth of three sons during this period in Almkerk, among whom was J.H. Bavinck's father, Coenraad Bernardus. In 1873 Jan accepted a call to the church in Kampen. Though he hadn't dared earlier to accept an appointment as instructor at the theological seminary, now "as shepherd and teacher" he would be able "if only indirectly, to contribute something to [the students'] training and spiritual upliftment after all."[26] In Kampen, too, the Bavincks were dealt a number of heavy blows: in 1896 their youngest son, a brilliant doctoral student, died at age 24, and four years later Gesina Magdelena herself passed away at age 73, after a marriage of more than fifty years. This was a very great loss for Jan, who, unable to bear the loneliness after his wife's death, moved in for good with his son Herman, who had become professor at the seminary in 1882. After 54 years of faithful service in the

---

[21]J. Bavinck, *Korte schets van mijn leven*, 48-49.

[22]*Ibid.*, 51.

[23]*Ibid.*

[24]Bavinck does not mention this in his biography, but the matter is recorded in the published minutes of the Board of Trustees, *Handelingen der Curatoren 1854.* Cf. R.H. Bremmer, *Herman Bavinck en zijn tijdgenoten*, 14.

[25]J. Bavinck, *Korte schets van mijn leven*, 51.

[26]*Ibid.*, 69.

ministry, Jan preached his farewell sermon in Kampen on January 25, 1903, using 1 Thessalonians 5:23 as his text: "May God himself, the God of peace, sanctify you through and through, may your whole spirit, soul and body be kept blameless at the coming of our Lord Jesus Christ." He received royal recognition for his life's work and was named Knight in the Order of Orange Nassau by Queen Wilhelmina.[27] Towards the end of his life he moved to Amsterdam with Herman, who had meanwhile been appointed professor of dogmatics at the Free University. After a long and difficult illness which confined him to his bed, he passed away on November 20, 1909.

Jan Bavinck was greatly loved and esteemed for his preaching abilities. This is reflected in the following words from the *In Memoriam* for him published in the church yearbook of 1910: "He spoke so clearly and lucidly from the pulpit that even the simplest folk could follow him; and yet he was a man of deep insight into God's Word and was possessed of a rich dogmatic erudition."[28] But this admiration is also borne out by the fact that, at the urging of many, a goodly number of his sermons appeared in print throughout the years. His first book of sermons, entitled *Stemmen des heils* (Voices of Salvation), was published in 1863, followed in subsequent years by three additional volumes containing sermons delivered on the various holy days of the Christian calendar.

Though Jan Bavinck remained a local pastor all his life, he was active in the church at a broader level as well. He was a member of the Board of Trustees of Kampen Seminary from 1859 to 1900, for example, and also served repeatedly between 1854 and 1892 as delegate to the synodical gatherings of his church. Nor could he belie his academic bent. In 1868, together with a colleague, Rev. Helenius de Cock, he initiated the establishment and publication of a new journal entitled *De Getuigenis* (The Witness). In the first issue he explained that despite initial hesitation, they had decided to go ahead with the project because among all the existing journals there was not one that was edited by ministers or members of the dissenting church, though it had already been in existence for thirty years. The principles on which the new journal was based were clearly defined: acceptance of Holy Scripture as absolute norm, and loyal commitment to the confessions of the Dutch Reformed tradition: the Heidelberg Catechism, the Dutch Confession of Faith, and the Canons of Dort.[29]

The expressed aim of the journal was the defense and spread of the doctrine of truth. This could be accomplished, it was thought, by nurturing commitment to the gospel among young people as a shield against the spirit of the times; by propagating Reformed (*Gereformeerd*) thought as an alternative to the many other contemporary denominational and secular apprehensions of reality; and by demonstrating, in the face of accusations of isolationism and narrow-mindedness, "that we too know what we believe and that we dare to express and defend our

---

[27]Cf. "In memoriam ds. J. Bavinck," *Handboek van de Gereformeerde Kerken in Nederland*, 22 (1910), 311-312.

[28]*Ibid.*, 312.

[29]These confessions, it was added, were to be tested constantly on the touchstone of Scripture and accepted unequivocally unless they proved to be unbiblical.

faith."[30] The articles published in the journal evince a concern on the part of the editors and authors to produce writing of a genuinely theological nature. Jan Bavinck contributed fairly deep-going theological essays to the journal on a regular basis. He also wrote a two-volume interpretive commentary on the Heidelberg Catechism in 1903,[31] which bears witness to careful research and mature theological learning.

In summary it can be concluded that Jan Bavinck had a generous and very unassuming character, was possessed of a keen mind, and was a man of great diligence and ardent faith.

1.2. Herman Bavinck (1854-1921)

It was by dint of the assiduous study and hard work of Jan Bavinck's eldest son, Herman,[32] that the Bavinck name would become a household word in Dutch theological circles. After graduating from the high school for classical studies (*gymnasium*) in Zwolle, Herman himself had a keen desire to enroll in the faculty of theology at the state university in Leyden. He was motivated in this choice by the wish to acquire a firsthand knowledge of modern theology and to obtain a more academic schooling than was possible in Kampen at the time. At the urging of his parents, however, he registered himself as a student at Kampen Seminary in 1873. Partly at the instigation of Rev. Johannes H. Donner Sr., then pastor in Leyden, Herman left Kampen for Leyden on completion of his first year of study at the seminary. Naturally this raised a lot of eyebrows in Kampen. That the son of a Kampen pastor would leave the safety of this bulwark of Reformed orthodoxy to study under the modernist, liberal professors of theology at Leyden University was shocking and incomprehensible to many. Even Brummelkamp, the most open-minded of the Kampen Seminary instructors, said to Jan Bavinck : "You are entrusting your son to a den of lions."[33] Herman's studies in Leyden went extremely well and his intellectual brilliance did not go unnoticed there. He passed all of his examinations with honors and capped his university studies with a doctoral dissertation dealing with the ethical thought of Ulrich Zwingli, for which he was awarded a PhD degree *cum laude* in June 1880.

After completing his graduate studies, his one desire was to put the learning he had acquired to work for the dissident church to which he belonged. And with this in mind he applied for admittance to the ecclesiastical examination for ministerial candidates in 1880, which he subsequently sustained with good results. After his trial sermon was approved, he was declared eligible for call as minister in the Christian Reformed Church in the Netherlands (*Christelijk Gereformeerde Kerk*). On March 13, 1881 Herman was ordained in the church in

---

[30]*De Getuigenis*, 1 (1868), 1-2.

[31]Entitled, *De Heidelbergse Catechismus in 60 leerredenen verklaard.*

[32]Detailed biographical information on H. Bavinck can be found in R.H. Bremmer, *Herman Bavinck en zijn tijdgenoten*, and in V. Hepp, *Dr. Herman Bavinck.*

[33]H. Algra, 267.

the Frisian town of Franeker in a service led by his father, who used Isaiah 52:7 as the text for his sermon: "How beautiful on the mountains are the feet of those who bring good news, who proclaim peace, who bring good tidings, who proclaim salvation, who say to Zion, 'Your God reigns!' " For his inaugural sermon on this occasion Herman chose 1 Thessalonians 2:4 as text: "We speak as men approved by God to be entrusted with the gospel. We are not trying to please men but God, who tests our hearts." Despite his great erudition, as pastor he got along very well with even the humblest of people and they, in turn, with him.[34]

Within a year, however, Herman was granted release from the congregational ministry to make it possible for him to accept an appointment as professor at Kampen Seminary. Earlier that year he had declined an appointment at the Free University in Amsterdam, stating as main reason that he wished first of all to serve his own church. At the seminary he was assigned extensive teaching responsibilities—in the Department of Theology: dogmatics, polemics, ethics, and encyclopedia of theology; in the Department of Literature: antiquities, mythology, philosophy, and Greek. On January 9, 1883 he gave his inaugural address, entitled *De wetenschap der heilige godgeleerdheid* (The Science of Sacred Theology). On July 2, 1891 he married Joanna Adriana Schippers, with whom he had one daughter.

Even though the dissident churches rooted in the two 19th century separatist movements, the *Afscheiding* and the later *Doleantie,* joined to form the Reformed Churches in the Netherlands (RCN)[35] in 1892, their respective theological institutions, Kampen Seminary and the Theological Faculty of the Free University, were averse to their own amalgamation. From the very outset this proved to be a most controversial issue, with the interested parties diametrically opposed to each other. In addition to personal and emotional factors there was an important matter of principle that divided those belonging to the earlier and later dissenting groups. The question was: Does theological education fall under the direct responsibility and supervision of the church, as the party of the *Afscheiding* argued? Or should the study of theology be understood as a free academic discipline pursued in service of the church, as those belonging to the *Doleantie* contended?[36] Resistance to unification of the two institutions was especially strong in Kampen. Herman Bavinck was one of the few there who devoted himself intensively to the cause of their consolidation. His pleas for amalgamation were characterized by careful consideration of the possibilities and potential difficulties of such a merger. When the incorporation of seminary and theological faculty was finally turned down for good at the Synod of Arnhem in 1902, Herman decided the time had come for him to leave Kampen. Relations between him and his colleagues were too badly damaged for him to continue his work there. A few weeks later he accepted an appointment as professor of dogmatics at the Free University in Amsterdam. He departed Kampen with pain in his heart: he had never wanted it to be this way. At the Free University he succeeded Abraham Kuyper, who, as leader of the Christian Anti-Revolutionary Political Party, had become

---

[34]R.H. Bremmer gives a striking example of this in *Herman Bavinck en zijn tijdgenoten,* 38.

[35]Dutch: *Gereformeerde Kerken in Nederland.*

[36]Cf. H.C. Endedijk, *passim*; and H.M. Kuitert, *passim,* who provide an analysis of Abraham Kuyper's views on this matter.

prime minister of the Netherlands. On December 17, 1902 Bavinck delivered his inaugural address in Amsterdam, entitled *Godsdienst en godgeleerdheid* (Religion and Theology). In his person Amsterdam had acquired a fully matured systematic theologian. His monumental study, *Gereformeerde dogmatiek* (Reformed Dogmatics), which appeared in four separate volumes between 1895 and 1901, represented the fruit of years of devoted study in the areas of dogmatics and philosophy during his tenure in Kampen. His extremely industrious life came to an end on July 29, 1921.

R.H. Bremmer depicts Herman Bavinck as a great theologian, who confronted classical Reformed theology with the problems of modernity; as a philosopher, who opposed the positivistic materialism of the 19th century; as a confessor, who did not allow himself to be swept along by the winds of the secularization of faith and theology that were blowing in his day but rather tried to make the thought of Augustine, Aquinas, and Calvin accessible to modern people; in short, as a man who was concerned to lead the dissident movement of which he was a part out of the spiritual backwater in which it found itself into the broader space of the universal church, into the field of tension between church and world.[37]

Herman Bavinck was clearly a gifted theologian, but he was also an unfailingly sensitive pastor. According to Gerard Wisse, who was himself well-versed in homiletics and who as a student regularly heard Herman Bavinck preach, the latter's sermons were both profound and psychologically perceptive.[38] Qualities of this kind are also reflected in his pastoral writings, books such as *De offerande des lofs* (The Offering of Praise) and *De zekerheid des geloofs* (The Certainty of Faith), both of which were published in 1901. The first of these consists of a thoughtful, devotional exposition of the fundamental ideas contained in his earlier four-volume work on dogmatics. In the second, he enters the lists against the all too prevalent tendency in the Reformed Churches to ground the certainty of faith in the hallmarks of the spiritual life rather than in the fixed promises of God. According to Bremmer, these writings are informed by Bavinck's own spiritual struggle.[39]

Wisse states that Herman Bavinck was also a finely tuned, compelling orator.[40] And J.J. Buskes, who was a student under Bavinck at the Free University, wrote:

> During Bavinck's lectures in the tastelessly furnished, unpainted classroom [in Abraham Kuyper's former residence] on the Keizersgracht [in Amsterdam], it sometimes happened that he himself became so overwhelmed by the splendor of God that he forgot us and spoke staring out of the window into the endless distance, perfectly attuned to God's infinite glory; and we sat listening speechlessly while being introduced - for life - to the

---

[37]*Herman Bavinck en zijn tijdgenoten*, 252. Cf. also A. Pos, "Leven en werk van dr. Johan Herman Bavinck," 8.

[38]G. Wisse, *Memoires*, 29.

[39]*Herman Bavinck en zijn tijdgenoten*, 198.

[40]*Memoires,*, 29.

mystery of the salvation of the Eternal and Almighty One, who
in Jesus Christ is our merciful Father.[41]
Young and old alike were eager to listen to him speak. The instructor who taught
Dutch at the high school for classical studies (gymnasium) in Kampen regularly
attended the services in the Burgwal church when Bavinck preached there: "I am
not a Reformed dissenter (*Gereformeerd*), but that Dutch of Bavinck's - it's a joy
to hear, and he speaks it so beautifully."[42]

Finally, Herman Bavinck had very broad interests and possessed an
erudition that reached beyond the field of theology and philosophy. For example,
in 1897 he published a work entitled *Beginselen der psychologie* (Principles of
Psychology), which was the first book to be written in this area of study by an
academic from the dissenting Reformed Churches in the Netherlands (RCN).[43]
Moreover, he was active in matters of school and state. He was a member of the
Upper Chamber of Parliament from 1911 to 1921for the Anti-Revolutionary Party
and served in various capacities related to Christian education.

In conclusion, it can be said that Herman Bavinck inherited from his
father not only a tendency toward hesitancy and diffidence but also a high degree
of intelligence. The combination of these characteristics formed him into a person
more given to deliberation than advocacy. G. Brillenburg Wurth referred to
Bavinck not only as "the unmistakably greatest Dutch dogmatician of the early 20th
century" but also as a modest "sometimes almost self-effacing" person, who was
very much aware of his own limitations and was not easily persuaded to take on
positions of leadership.[44] On the other hand, like his mother, he was enterprising
and practical and did not shrink from taking on large-scale projects. His had
internalized the simple unadorned piety of his childhood home, a piety which later
took on even deeper dimensions as a result of his confrontation with modern
theology and which left such an unforgettable impression on his circle of
acquaintances. Finally, he was a man of immense inner refinement, which made
him into the distinguished and gracious person that he was.

1.3. Coenraad Bernardus Bavinck (1866-1941)

Coenraad Bernardus Bavinck - brother of Herman Bavinck and father of
the subject of this study, Johan Herman Bavinck - followed in the footsteps of his
father, Jan Bavinck. He completed his theological studies in Kampen in 1890 and
was ordained as minister of the Christian Reformed Church (*Christelijke
Gereformeerde Kerk*) in Hazerswoude. In that same year he married Grietje
Bouwes, a cheerful, practical woman. During their four years in Hazerswoude the
Bavincks had three children. In 1894 Coenraad accepted a call to Rotterdam, where
he served as minister until his retirement from office in 1930. In Rotterdam
Coenraad and Grietje were blessed with the birth of an additional five children,

---

[41]*Hoera voor het leven*, 33.

[42]Cited in R.H. Bremmer, *Herman Bavinck en zijn tijdgenoten*, 199.

[43]*Ibid.*

[44]"Herman Bavinck en onze tijd," *Trouw* (Feb. 18, 1961).

among whom was Johan Herman, who came into the world on Nov. 22, 1895. The life of this family, too, was permeated by unaffected piety.

There is little known about the course of Coenraad's life. As theologian he always lived in the shadow of his older brother, Herman. Nevertheless, the existing sources provide enough information to form an idea of the kind of person he was. He was even more modest and socially reserved than his father. Nor was it in his nature to take a leading role in ecclesiastical affairs. This is clearly illustrated by the following passage from his farewell sermon in Rotterdam.

> Especially during the first period of my time in Rotterdam, I often had the feeling that I didn't belong here and that the great majority of the congregation didn't care very much for my preaching. I would had to have been bereft of all feeling for this not to have often caused me, at that time still at the beginning of my career, to become terribly depressed. I still very well remember the call I received at that time from the *Gereformeerde* church in Driesum, where my wife so badly wanted to go. I went to the Consistory and said: "Brothers, you decide for me, but be honest with me, I insist on that. If you judge it to be in the interest of the congregation that I should leave, tell me without beating around the bush. But if it is your judgement that I should stay, tell me that too." The following day the brothers came to inform me of the outcome [of their deliberations]: "It is the true and honest judgement of the Consistory that you should stay." Which I did. And no matter how difficult it often was for me, I continued on my way quietly, with my eyes fixed on God and tried to do my work as best I could. . . . Sometimes it is precisely difficulty that causes character to grow. But I have often had to struggle with bouts of anxiety and have had to wrestle with many weaknesses and much heaviness of mind.[45]

Though inconspicuously, Coenraad was also involved in the broader work of the church. Like his father, he served on the Board of Trustees of Kampen Seminary, from 1923 to 1931. In this same period, from 1923 to 1930, he was a member of the synodical Committee of Deputies charged with the amplification and reformulation of the Reformed confessions. Further, during his Rotterdam years, he served as secretary of the Reformed Churches in the Netherlands (RCN) Committee of Mission Deputies in the province of Zuid Holland. After his death in 1941, the missionary magazine, *Het Zendingsblad*, described him as follows:

> [He was] an accurate, a careful but decisive secretary. His correspondence stood out for its lucidity and liveliness. His judgement in matters both small and great were thoroughly informed by his keen insight and great wisdom.[46]

Coenraad had only a few publications to his name. In 1921 he put out a brochure dealing with the causes of the church divisions among Reformed believers

---

[45]C.B. Bavinck, *Gaat in tot Zijne poorten met lof*, 15-16.

[46]39 (1941), 143.

in the Netherlands.[47] Although he clearly reasons from his own ecclesiastical point of view in this pamphlet, the tone of his argumentation is charitable and generous with respect to other communions, nor does his writing lack in criticism of the denomination to which he belonged.[48] Also characteristic for the way he viewed and did things was his collaboration in the production of the 1926 document, *Ons aller moeder* (Our Every Mother), in which he and four colleagues outlined what they considered to be a balanced solution to the 'Geelkerken Question,'[49] a denominational doctrinal dispute which was raging at that time - a solution "in which neither justice nor truth is shortchanged."

Further, Coenraad, too, had a distinctly studious bent of mind. He was particularly interested in the early church, and then especially in the life and work of St. Augustine.[50] Though he never published the results of his research, it is not entirely inconceivable that his son Johan Herman later made good use of the knowledge his father had acquired in this area, for his own 1934 study, *Christus en de mystiek van het Oosten* (Christ and Eastern Mysticism) relates closely to Augustine's theological thought.

In a word, it can be said that Coenraad B. Bavinck shared the characteristics we noticed earlier in other members of his family: modesty, intelligence, and devoutness. One of J.H. Bavinck's doctoral students, J. van den Berg, who already as a child frequented the Bavinck home, wrote years afterward:

> In my mind's eye I can still see the figure of Rev. C.B. Bavinck
> as I knew him as a child, when he was already in the evening of
> his life: a man totally without pretension and possessed of a deep,
> charitable wisdom built up over a lifetime, purified by the sorrow
> God had brought into his life, deeply thankful for the joy God
> granted him in his children.[51]

---

[47]*Welke zijn de oorzaken van het kerkelijk-gescheiden leven der gereformeerden in Nederland?*

[48]Cf. the review of this brochure by G.H. Kersten in *De Saambinder*, 3, 6 (1922).

[49]In 1926 disciplinary measures were taken by the Reformed Churches in the Netherlands against Rev. J.G. Geelkerken for his interpretation of certain aspects of the biblical account of creation The synod of Assen had required Geelkerken, who was serving a congregation in Amsterdam, to accept its pronouncement that details reported in Genesis 3, such as the speech of the snake, were to be taken literally and understood as "realities perceptible to the senses." Geelkerken refused to do so and was subsequently removed from office, which occasioned the formation of yet another Reformed denomination in the Netherlands, the *Gereformeerde Kerken in Hersteld Verband* (Reestablished Reformed Churches). Cf. J.N. Bakhuizen van den Brink and W.F. Dankbaar, Vol. 4, 233.

[50]A. Pos, "Leven en werk van dr. Johan Herman Bavinck," 8.

[51]"Prof. Bavinck 40 jaar in het ambt," *Centraal Weekblad*, 9, 28 (1961).

1.4. Summary

With respect to J.H. Bavinck's background and the religious climate in which he grew up, the following four points are to be noted in particular.

First, Johan Herman's spiritual background in a broader sense was the church separatist movement (*Afscheiding*) of 1834 with its strong emphasis on biblical-experiential piety. He grew up during the early years of the Reformed Churches in the Netherlands, a time which was characterized by an emphasis on theological reflection and by efforts to perfect the organization of ecclesiastical life.

Second, in a narrower sense his spirituality was informed by the position the Bavinck family occupied within that separatist movement and by the family's distinguishing qualities and traits. Again and again one is struck by the combination of deep personal faith and clear-headed theological reflection that typified the ministerial members of the family. Orientation to classical theology among them always bore an existential character. And they also looked beyond their own closed circle. Good examples of this are Herman Bavinck's decision to pursue his academic studies in Leyden and the breadth of vision exhibited by his theological work.[52]

Third, one can not help but notice the modesty and shy, retiring nature of the Bavincks. On the one hand, this character trait often caused them to be irresolute when it came to making decisions, but on the other hand, coupled with their native intelligence, it also made them deliberate and cautious. They were not given to exaggerated insistence on principle and did not seek out conflict.

Fourth, from whatever nature-nurture source, the Bavincks also inherited a practical bent of mind and a cheerful disposition.

2. Early Years (1895-1938)

J.H. Bavinck's professional history and theological development can be divided into various periods,[53] which together constitute a single cumulative process: these stages were not strictly separated but rather flowed into one another. "Typical for Bavinck was that through time he concentrated his attention on various areas of study, the essence of which was carried along from one phase to a following one,

---

[52]In "Herman Bavinck en onze tijd," G. Brillenburg Wurth wrote: "... though evidencing the same loyalty to the Reformed confession that characterized [Abraham] Kuyper, [Herman Bavinck], starting from the Reformed faith, tried, with a greater degree of openness and, let us say, catholicity [than did Kuyper], to take full [theological] account of contemporary problems in the areas of modern science and culture."

[53]Sources for this history include articles dealing with the life and work of J.H. Bavinck; church and missionary bulletins, magazines and periodicals; the national archives of the RCN in Utrecht; the archives of the *Gereformeerde Kerken* in Heemstede and Delft; the archives of Kampen Theological Seminary; the J.H. Bavinck Archives housed in the CHDDP/FUA; interviews with surviving family members and others who knew Bavinck personally, a number of whom also granted access to written materials in their possession.

there to bear fruit in a new context." [54] Initially, his psychological interest and aptitude led him in the direction of psychology of religion. Later, his ordination as missionary to Java (1929) activated a dormant interest in missiology. His growing fascination with Eastern (Javanese) mysticism and his experience as instructor at the Theological School in Jogjakarta (1934-1938) led him to shift his attention in ever greater measure to issues of a missiological nature. And after his appointment as professor of missions at Kampen Theological Seminary and the Free University of Amsterdam in 1939 and as professor of Practical Theology at the Free University in 1954, both of which will be dealt with in the next chapter, these issues became the object of systematic reflection in his academic work. In the present study the greatest amount of attention is devoted to Bavinck's activities in the fields of mission and missiology.

Especially during the final period of his life and work, in the face of increasing rationalistic and modernistic tendencies, Bavinck urgently appealed for authentic spiritual life as indispensable precondition for the existence of a vital and missionary church. His own work was thoroughly informed by his personal encounter with God in Jesus Christ and his repeated acts of surrender to the Lord.[55] Bavinck's "transparent Christian devotion,"[56] commitment to the cause of the gospel, and "deep sensitivity toward the needs of his fellow human beings,"[57] render it entirely appropriate to use terms such as 'fascination,' 'passion' and 'zeal' in reference to the various stages of his life history.

As a final prefatory note, it should also be pointed out here that though Bavinck worked throughout his entire life within the theological, ecclesiastical and denominational framework of the Reformed Churches in the Netherlands, he received recognition in broader circles through his English-language publications and guest lectureships.

2.1. Youth and Studies: Psychological Fascination (1912-1919)

Born on November 22, 1895 as his parents' fourth child, Bavinck was, as it turned out, prophetically named after his grandfather Jan and his uncle Herman.[58] Profound piety and great erudition would go hand in hand in Johan Herman's life. In preparation for his matriculation at university, Johan attended the Marnix High School for Classical Studies (*Gymnasium*) in Rotterdam.[59] Already then he often

---

[54] J. Veenhof, "Honderd jaar theologie aan de Vrije Universiteit," 81.

[55] Cf. J. Verkuyl, *Contemporary Missiology: An Introduction*, 35-36.

[56] *Ibid.*, 35.

[57] *Ibid.*, 36.

[58] Cf. W. Breukelaar, "Berichten over werkzaamheden van J.H. Bavinck,"*HZB* 36 (1938), 91, and A. Pos, "In memoriam prof. dr. J.H. Bavinck."

[59] W. Breukelaar, "Berichten over werkzaamheden van J.H. Bavinck," *idem.*

spoke to his parents of his desire to become a missionary later on.[60] Meanwhile, he was developing a keen interest in philosophy, and in his free time he loved to peruse the philosophical works he found on the shelves in his father's library.[61]

After successfully completing his secondary education, Johan began studying theology at the Free University in Amsterdam in 1912. Once while at university he became very seriously ill, which, however, only served to deepen his personal faith powerfully. An observer wrote later concerning this bout of sickness: ". . . his parents were afraid that they would lose him, but they were greatly comforted by his testimony that if it was God's will, he was prepared to depart this earth in the hope of eternal life." [62] That he was a very diligent, painstaking student with broad interests is clearly demonstrated by the quality and material diversity of the preserved notebooks he composed during his collegiate years. In two of these collections of written notes, consisting of a total of no less than 239 pages, he traces the history of modern philosophy. Further he produced a handwritten, illustrated volume on the history of art, the content of which shows how impressed he was even at this relatively early stage in his life by the cultural and religious expressions of other peoples.[63] And finally, a number of exegetical annotations dating from his university years, for example those on the gospel of John and Romans 6-8, bespeak his interest not only in philological textual analysis but also in personal encounter with the biblical message and its interpretation.[64]

During his student years Johan was attracted to the Reformed Young People's Movement of that day, which in a positive but critical way was seeking a new identity for itself and the reorientation of Reformed life by fostering the development of a less rigidly dogmatic, antithetical stance, and by attempting to discover a more vitally existential, open form of religious experience. Remarkably, Johan's uncle Herman, unlike many others at the time, did not cast this movement in a negative light.[65] Johan also joined the interdenominational Dutch Student

---

[60]*Ibid.*, 92.

[61]*Ibid.*, 91.

[62]*Ibid.*; cf. also A. Pos, "Het leven en werk van Dr. Johan Herman Bavinck," 11.

[63]This may also be an extract, but, if so, the identity of the book from which the information was taken can not be easily ascertained.

[64]These notebooks are housed in the CHDDP/FUA. In addition to those mentioned in the text above, there are also collections of notes Bavinck made on the theology of the Old Testament, Reformed dogmatics, and the life of the Apostle Paul. Most of these note compilations also contain indices of topics and/or names.

[65]Cf. J. Veenhof, "Geschiedenis van theologie en spiritualiteit in de Gereformeerde Kerken," 30-32. H. Bavinck contributed articles on a regular basis to the periodical, *De Reformatie* (The Reformation), which was established as platform for this movement.

Christian Movement (SCM),[66] chaired by Hendrik Kraemer at that time,[67] which aimed at rethinking the Christian witness to Jesus Christ among the contemporary intelligentsia. In 1918 Johan gave the opening address at the annual conference of this movement.[68] This, too, was indicative of his theological-spiritual stance. The SCM, with no specific ecclesiastical or confessional ties and as counterpart to the Calvinist Student Movement, was not a little suspect within the Reformed Churches in the Netherlands. It was feared that Reformed young people would begin to lean too far toward a moralist theology and that their ecclesiastical awareness would deteriorate if they joined the SCM. With that in mind, the synod of 1920 resolved to "advise strongly against" membership in this student organization. And again, it is interesting to note the protest to that synodical resolution raised by H. Bavinck, who saw possibilities for the enrichment and deepening of one's faith in membership of precisely this kind of movement.[69]

As time went on, Bavinck's interests broadened to include psychology, particularly psychology of religion, in addition to theology and philosophy. This no doubt had to do with the fact that there was a fairly general interest in psychology at the time, but it is also possible that he was led to his new absorption under the influence of his uncle Herman, who, in his Amsterdam period, busied himself with questions of psychology as well as theology and did much to stimulate the academic discipline of psychology of religion. Those years also witnessed a widespread and growing fascination with mysticism, a pursuit and mode of religious experience which appealed to Bavinck personally in a very special way.[70]

After completing his undergraduate work in theology at the Free University in Amsterdam, the gifted Johan left for Germany to continue his studies at the graduate level, first in Giessen and then in Erlangen,[71] where, on July 11,

---

[66]Like its equivalents elsewhere in the world, the Dutch SCM was a national embodiment of the World Student Christian Federation (WSCF), which was founded by John R. Mott and others in 1895; cf. S. Neill, G.H. Anderson and J. Goodwin, 569, 662.

[67]Cf. A.T. van Leeuwen, 11 ff. It was at this time that the first contact was established between Bavinck and Kraemer, a connection which would prove to be of great importance later on.

[68]"Openingsrede NCSV-conferentie 1918," *Eltheto*, 73 (1918): 1-6.

[69]Cf. A.J. van den Berg, *De Nederlandse Christelijke Studenten-Vereniging 1886-1985*, 98ff., and J. Veenhof, "Geschiedenis van theologie en spiritualiteit in de Gereformeerde Kerken," 33-35.

[70]J. van den Berg, "De wetenschappelijke arbeid van Professor Dr. Johan Herman Bavinck," 28.

[71]Bavinck was forced to find a university elsewhere because there was no professor available at the Free University at that time to supervise doctoral studies in his theological discipline of choice. It is not known why he opted for Erlangen. One of the reasons could have been that the university he attended there was an orthodox Lutheran institution, at which other Dutch theologians had also taken their

1919, at 23 years of age, he received a doctor of philosophy degree from Friedrich Alexander University. The main question of his doctoral thesis was whether and to what degree the affective, sensory dimension of human life influences the processes of cognition and association. Do thought and association find their genesis in and develop according to innate causal laws of the mind, as was assumed by the proponents of the widely accepted associationist psychology of that time, or should they rather be understood as personal activities of the individual that are sparked and stimulated by sensation and feeling? He set out to find an answer to this problem by examining the religious life of the medieval mystic, Heinrich von Sumo, and on the basis of this research demonstrated that the processes of thinking and learning, far from occurring autonomously, are closely tied to feeling as intuitive apprehension of given reality. And it is precisely this insight regarding the role played by feeling in the process of human reasoning and the acquirement of knowledge which points to something that associationist psychology ignores: namely, the human self[72]

Bavinck's dissertation shows evidence of both admiration for and disapproval of the mystic life. Johannes van den Berg states that this must be viewed against the backdrop of his warm, vibrant piety, which in the end would constitute a bond between him and the mystics.[73] Johannes Verkuyl adds that the argumentation in Bavinck's dissertation often bespeaks his inner involvement in the struggle between the power of the gospel and the alluring forces of monistic mysticism.[74] Verkuyl quotes Bavinck as saying: "I was born, as it were, with a strong penchant for monistic mystical experience; that's why I can speak of it: I have to fight against it every day."[75] Bavinck never left any doubt, however, that mysticism on the one hand and biblical piety and faith on the other are ultimately two different worlds.[76] In the introduction to one of his earlier books, something of Bavinck's personal struggle against the lure of the mystic way resonates in his reference to St. Augustine: Augustine, he wrote in 1934, "felt the seductive pull of mysticism in his own soul, but, allowing himself to be led by the Word of God, he wrestled himself free from it, albeit with great difficulty."[77] And several years later, in his 1956 farewell address at Kampen Seminary, he said:

> I may not allow myself to be swept away in the storm of the great
> collective life of humanity; at a certain moment I must say 'I.' It

---

graduate degrees.

[72]Cf. *Der Inflows des Gefühls auf das Assoziationsleben bei Heinrich von Sumo*, 25-26.

[73]J. van den Berg, "De wetenschappelijke arbeid van Professor dr. Johan Herman Bavinck," 29.

[74]J. Verkuyl, "In memoriam prof. dr. J.H. Bavinck," 93.

[75]J. Verkuyl, "Woord vooraf," xviii.

[76]This is already clearly indicated in his 1928 book, *PWB*, 150.

[77]*CMO*, 9.

> is not only that I *may* say this, I *must* say it. . . . I am responsible,
> that is to say, I will have to answer, respond to the One who will
> put questions to me.[78]

It is clear from this that Bavinck chose to resist mysticism and was concerned to be a theologian of Epiphany and worship, Question and answer, Revelation and response.[79] Finally, it should be remarked in this connection that his graduate studies laid the foundation for his later missionary work, during which he would delve deeply into Eastern mysticism and the question of the development of religious consciousness. As Abraham Pos wrote in an article memorializing Bavinck's life and work:

> [He] made his own decisions, but at the same time [it was] God's
> providential guidance which selected from a variety of
> possibilities that career and work for him by means of which he
> would best be able to serve the cause of Jesus Christ. The first
> clear lines of this life's journey were plotted here [in Erlangen].[80]

After receiving his doctorate Bavinck returned to the Netherlands without knowing exactly what path he would follow next.

2.2. Ordained Minister: Pastoral Zeal (1919-1929)

2.2.1. Pastor in Medan and Bandung

After the First World War the Reformed Churches in the Netherlands began to intensify their work among Dutch 'people of the dispersion' in Indonesia. This labor was energetically pioneered on the west coast of Sumatra by W. G. Harrenstein, pastor of the RCN congregation in Medan. The work expanded so rapidly that the help of an auxiliary became an urgent necessity. While on leave in the Netherlands, A.A.L. Rutgers, an elder of the church in Medan, approached the young Bavinck and prevailed on him to take up this task.[81] Though Rutgers had acted completely on his own without prior consultation with the Board of synodical Deputies for the People of the Dispersion in the Dutch East Indies, Bavinck made such a good impression when he appeared before this panel that he was appointed forthwith to the position of assistant pastor in Medan,[82] where he commenced his work on January 11, 1920. In Harrenstein, with whom he had already had a good relationship at the Free University, Bavinck found a fatherly friend, who supported him in an unforgettable way during this initial period of practical work. Harrenstein helped his modest and often hesitant young associate to overcome all sorts of

---

[78]"Het evangelie en het mystisch levensgevoel," 158.

[79]Cf. R. van Woudenberg, "Dr. Johan Herman Bavinck (1895-1964): Theoloog van Woord en antwoord," 25.

[80]A. Pos, "Leven en Werk van Dr. Johan Herman Bavinck," 12.

[81]W. Breukelaar, "Berichten over werkzaamheden van J.H. Bavinck," 91.

[82]Cf. A. Algra, *De Gereformeerde Kerken in Nederlands-Indië / Indonesië*, 181.

difficulties, and they developed a lifelong friendship. Bavinck remained forever grateful for this valuable, instructive period of on-the-job pastoral training.[83] But the internship in Medan did not last very long.

On October 25, 1920 the talented assistant pastor received a call to become the regular minister of the RCN congregation in Bandung, "a city whose educational institutions attracted many young people."[84] It was not only Bavinck's obvious gifts that occasioned the move from Medan to Bandung, however, but also the economic malaise that Medan was going through around this time. Many Dutch colonial employees lost their jobs and were forced to return to the Netherlands. In this situation assistant pastors, too, became easily redundant. It took rather a long time before Bavinck could be ordained in Bandung because he had to be examined first by classis,[85] which in that area met only once each year. He had to wait nearly eight months, but finally, on July 3, 1921, he was ordained and installed as pastor of the Bandung congregation by his mentor, Harrenstein.[86] On March 21 of the following year he married Trientje Robers,[87] with whom he had three children and enjoyed more than thirty years of happy wedded life.

During Bavinck's tenure the congregation in Bandung thrived. Soon after his arrival, the congregation moved to its own new church building, for which he had laid the first stone[88] and which was dedicated on December 23, 1921. On this occasion Bavinck preached on Psalm 125:2: "As the mountains surround Jerusalem, so the Lord surrounds his people both now and forevermore." In Bandung his pastoral and homiletical talents were further honed. According to reports, he was a very attentive pastor, who, after first listening calmly and patiently to his parishioners, offered them modest and wise advice, which led to the growth of a great measure of trust between them and him. His sermons were models of simplicity and clarity, and for that very reason were characterized by great spiritual depth. He knew how to express very special things with common, ordinary words. He had a "great gift for making the gospel understandable for both young and old,

---

[83]Cf. A. Pos "Leven en werk van Dr. Johan Herman Bavinck," 12, and W. Breukelaar, "Berichten over werkzaamheden van J.H. Bavinck," 91. This is also apparent from an article Bavinck wrote much later: "Harrenstein als oecumenische gestalte."

[84]J. Verkuyl, *Contemporary Missiology: An Introduction*, 36.

[85]Classes are Reformed ecclesiastical bodies which deal with church matters at the regional level, including evaluation of candidates for ordination to the gospel ministry.

[86]Cf. for this information A. Algra, *De Gereformeerde kerken in Nederlands-Indië*, 161; Algra mistakenly cites 1919 and 1920 as the years for respectively Bavinck's call to Bandung and his ordination there.

[87]Born Feb. 13, 1900; died Jan. 12, 1953.

[88]Cf. J. Verkuyl, *Contemporary Missiology: An Introduction*, 36.

intellectuals and the unschooled, Europeans and Javanese."[89] This explains why not only Dutch colonials but also Dutch-speaking Javanese and Chinese people attended worship services in his church.[90] Moreover, Bavinck had been given a voice which enthralled everyone who ever heard him speak. The anti-colonial leader and later president of Indonesia, Sukarno, who met Bavinck now and then in Bandung prison, once told J. Verkuyl: "I will never forget that mellifluous voice of his."[91] Ever the watchful shepherd, Bavinck kept careful account of the church attendance of his congregants and developed many practical initiatives aimed at the building up of his church.[92] He also spent a great deal of time and effort on youth work.[93] Considering all of this, it was no wonder that the membership of his congregation in Bandung grew in just a few years' time from 180 to 422.[94]

Nevertheless, Bavinck's view embraced more than just his church alone. As early as the spring of 1922 he wrote: "All spiritual work in Indonesia bears a more or less evangelistic character in that it aspires to bring the many who have turned away from the faith back into the fold."[95] With a view to reaching the many secularized Europeans in the area, the congregation in Magelang launched an evangelism magazine, *De Zaaier* (The Sower), to which Bavinck contributed on a regular basis.[96] At that time a plea was also made for the production of tracts and small brochures aimed at this same target group. The first one of these to be written by Bavinck appeared in 1927 and was entitled, *Levensvragen* (Questions of Life). Unfortunately, it was not a great success: after three years less than half of the first

---

[89]A. Algra, *De Gereformeerde kerken in Nederlands-Indië*, 117.

[90]This information regarding the interracial character of Bavinck's audiences was relayed to me by J. Verkuyl during an interview I had with him.

[91]Verkuyl related this in a letter to me, dated Feb. 2, 1990.

[92]Information about these initiatives, often including exact details, can be found in letters and reports from Bavinck that were published in various issues of *De Heraut*, namely, those of April 30 and May 7, 1922, and March 15, 22 and 29, 1925.

[93]Cf., e.g., his article, "De arbeid onder de rijpere jeugd," *De Opwekker*, 68 (1923): 96-101; Bavinck had an enduring interest in work among young people throughout his entire life.

[94]In an interview I had with him, J. Verkuyl reported that there is still a portrait of Bavinck hanging in the consistory room of the church in Bandung— a highly unusual thing in post-colonial Indonesia and indicative of the high esteem in which Bavinck continues to be held among the Christians in that city.

[95]Letter in *De Heraut*, (April 30, 1922).

[96]In 1925 the classis took direct responsibility for this periodical.

edition of 3000 copies had been sold.[97] Notwithstanding these evangelistic activities on behalf of unchurched Dutch people, however, he did not direct his attention to them alone but also to the indigenous population. The missionary interest he had as a boy now began to blossom. This is clearly shown by a striking passage in his 1924 report of activities in Bandung containing the very telling word, *finally*: "A catechism class has finally been organized for Javanese girls. . . . It gives us great satisfaction to be able to participate a little in the work of mission by bringing the children of this land into contact with the gospel."[98] That his early missionary efforts were not bereft of blessing is evinced by what he wrote about the increase in the number of Indonesian members of his congregation in the years prior to the drafting of this report.

In the spring of 1926 Bavinck went back to the Netherlands on leave. When he left Indonesia, it was not clear whether he would return. The last sermon he preached before his departure was on Psalm 90:17: "May the favor of the Lord our God rest upon us; establish the work of our hands for us - yes, establish the work of our hands." In retrospect, this turned out to be a farewell sermon.

2.2.2. Further Study and Ministry in Heemstede

The uncertainty about what to do next with his life was closely tied to his wish to delve further into the other great interest that had occupied him throughout the years alongside theology, namely, (religious) psychology. During his stay in Bandung he continued his study in this area, publishing his findings in a book entitled, *Zielkundige opstellen* (Psychological Essays) in 1925, followed in 1926 by a broadly conceived handbook, *Inleiding in de zielkunde* (Introduction to Psychology). In the foreword to this latter work, he records his purpose in writing it: "[My] chief aim was to try, insofar as possible, to classify and catalogue the phenomena of heart, soul and mind, and to provide insight into the structure of the human inner life." What he writes at the end of the foreword nicely summarizes his views regarding the value and place of psychology.

> It is precisely insight into the structure of the soul that can awaken in us that tender admiration for the soul's Grand Maker. At every point there is a road leading from psychology to theology. Augustine puts it in a nutshell: *Deum et animam scire cupio*, God and my soul I desire to know. Few things in this world are more splendid than being allowed, with faith in God in the heart, to penetrate the depths of the soul.

From these lines it is clear that Bavinck did not wish to see theology eclipsed or absorbed by psychology. He felt that, provided they both took their departure from the scriptural revelation of God, these two fields of study could and should be understood as complementary disciplines, the one subserving the other. He makes this absolutely clear once again on the first page of his handbook on psychology, where he writes as follows concerning the Proverbs of Solomon and the rest of the Bible.

---

[97]A. Algra, *De Gereformeerde kerken in Nederlands-Indië*, 252-253; this brochure was reprinted several times under the title, *Het raadsel van ons leven* (The Riddle of Our Life).

[98]*De Heraut* (March 29, 1925).

What a collection of superb, psychological sayings we find preserved for us in [Proverbs]. Here speaks a psychologist who will never be equaled, whose eyes were enlightened by the Spirit of God to behold the well-springs of the human will and human life. And not only this book but the whole of Scripture is lushly rich with insight into human nature. The Bible teaches us about God but in no lesser degree reveals the human heart to us. It portrays the love of the Father but discloses no less sharply and deeply the essence and extent of human misery. It consists of both Theology and Psychology, [provides] knowledge of both God and man.

In practice, however, the starting point and the elaboration of his thinking were not always entirely congruent. In some of his work theology is overshadowed too much by psychology, particularly in his analyses and descriptions of religious life.

Bavinck's research in psychology was so highly appreciated that, just before he left Bandung to go on leave, he was offered the opportunity to take a few years off to pursue his studies further in this field.[99] He declined to accept this offer immediately, however, because he wished to take advice on it in the Netherlands first and also because he did not consider himself to be at liberty to consider the proposal unless and until he felt it to be a "a call from God."[100] It is no longer possible to determine what was said in the talks Bavinck had with his advisors back at home, but it is not inconceivable that the appointment of a new professor of child development, psychology, pedagogics, and catechetics at the Free University in the middle of 1926 was a determining factor in the decision process. For the time being, there would be no way for him to put the fruits of additional study to productive use within his own circles. Moreover, his book, *Inleiding in de zielkunde* (Introduction to Psychology), had not received an entirely favorable reception in the Dutch Reformed world of that time. There were those who objected to Bavinck's analytical description of the superego or higher self because they thought they detected a tendency toward the idolization of the human person in it.[101] Others censured his views on religion, which he treated as part of the emotional life and defined as, in deepest essence, a longing for communion with God. Basing themselves on the Reformed confessional position that religion always presupposes divine revelation, these critics argued that the act of knowing takes logical precedence over feeling and emotion in religion and that therefore emphasis should be placed on knowledge as its primary element.[102] This turn of events and these negative reactions to his scholarly work could not have been very encouraging to the unassuming, sometimes hesitant, and still relatively young parson.

A call to become the minister of the RCN congregation in the Dutch town of Heemstede, issued in August 1926, made things even more complicated for

---

[99]Cf. *De Heraut*, (June 27, 1926).

[100]*Ibid.*

[101]Cf. J. Stellingwerf, 189.

[102]Cf. T. Hoekstra, *GTT*, 28 (1927): 236 ff., and J. Waterink, *GTT*, 29 (1928): 515 ff.

Bavinck. He declined this call,[103] and the three reasons he gave for doing so give evidence of the great uncertainty he was experiencing in this period: (1) he was still emotionally attached to Bandung, (2) focused pursuance of his scholarly work would be impossible in the parsonage, and (3) he wanted to be certain that he was fully accepted within the church as a whole.[104] The latter demur was no doubt engendered by the discussion on the 'Geelkerken case,'[105] which was raging at that time. Emotions ran high and slurs and imputations pervaded the ecclesiastical atmosphere. One disciplinary action led readily to another. Directly related to this church controversy was another misgiving Bavinck had about accepting the call that had been extended to him: the congregation in Heemstede was deeply divided on the issue of the synodical decisions taken pertaining to 'Geelkerken,' and he did not relish the idea of putting himself in a position where he would be standing between two feuding parties. Toward the end of his leave, in November 1926, he made the decision not to return to Bandung. Heemstede immediately resolved to approach him afresh to sound him out about the possibilities of a new call.[106] After discussions with him on November 17, the consistory, with Bavinck's complete approval, applied to Classis Haarlem for permission to call him for the second time.[107] The day after he received the letter of call, he replied to it as follows.

> I thank God that He took away the misgivings, one by one, that made me decide to decline the first time, and that I now know with full conviction that this is His way. It is my fervent desire and prayer that He may allow me to work long and fruitfully in your midst.[108]

Bavinck was installed in Heemstede by his father on January 9, 1927. Very soon after his inauguration he turned his attention to the dissension in his congregation caused by the controversial 'Geelkerken issue.' True to his irenic nature, he set out to restore unity by means of honest and open talks between the consistory and those

---

[103]To the disappointment of the church consistory, which, according to the Minutes of its meeting on September 7, 1926, received the letter of decline "with deep regret."

[104]These qualms were voiced at a later discussion the consistory held with Bavinck to assess the possibility of extending a second call to him; cf. the Minutes of the consistory meeting of November 17, 1926.

[105]See footnote 49 above.

[106]Cf. the Minutes of the consistory meeting of November 11, 1926.

[107]Cf. the Minutes of the consistory meeting of November 17, 1926; at this session Bavinck also said that, contrary to rumor, he stood behind the decisions of the Synod of Assen with respect to "Geelkerken'; that he no longer regarded the division running through the church in Heemstede as an obstacle to accepting a call there but now considered it to be his calling to try to heal this rift and to prevent a church split; and that he was prepared to make the move to Heemstede "provided the congregation unanimously desired him."

[108]Cited from Bavinck's letter of acceptance, dated December 10, 1926.

who opposed the decisions of synod on this matter. On March 30 the two parties came together for the first time. Bavinck indicated that he thought synod had the right to make a judgement as to whether a given method of exegesis or scriptural interpretation was acceptable or not, and stated further that he agreed with the synod of Assen's decision to disavow the interpretation of the biblical creation account espoused by Geelkerken and his supporters. On the other hand, he said he did not think it right for synod to set itself up as a judge of matters of the heart and to drag people's personal faith into the controversy as it did. The synod, he opined, should have been kinder in its judgments and more charitable in the formulation of its pronouncements. The nine meetings that followed yielded the result Bavinck had hoped for: despite remaining differences of opinion, sufficient mutual confidence had been built up to ensure that the congregation would stay together.[109] Thanks to his appealing preaching and trust-inspiring pastoral activities Bavinck very quickly came to occupy a place of central importance in the church in Heemstede. With an eye to fostering mutual bonds of unity within his growing congregation and nurturing the spiritual maturation of its members Bavinck proposed the establishment of a local church periodical. Though there was some initial opposition to this idea, the paper, entitled, *Kerkblad*, did eventually get off the ground, its first issue appearing in January 1928.

Bavinck's publications dating from this period reveal that he continued to immerse himself in psychology and philosophy. The most extensive work he produced during his time in Heemstede was *Persoonlijkheid en wereldbeschouwing* (Personality and World View), which appeared in 1928 and consisted of a collection of lectures he gave at the Technical College in Delft in the winter of 1927-1928.[110] In this book, the very title of which demonstrates that he linked psychology and philosophy closely together, Bavinck emphasized that behind every world view a personality lies hidden. By characterizing philosophy in this way as revelation of personality, he relativized it as approach to truth. He wanted to make clear that the real fault line in philosophy is conterminous with the fracture running between the presence and absence of inner conviction regarding the truth of the gospel of Jesus Christ. Because of the twisted relation between God and man, he argued, the human heart is split in two: on the one side, every human person seeks God, on the other, everyone flees Him. Every view of life thought up solely in the human brain is characterized by this fundamental brokenness and thus can never fathom reality. It is solely through personal submission to the truth of God that one can secure a world view that bears objectivity in the highest degree, a world view conceived not by us but by God.[111] Although Bavinck would later embrace a more radically biblical anthropology, it is clear from the foregoing that he wanted nothing more than to do all of his work in the areas of philosophy and psychology as a servant of Jesus Christ. He didn't champion ideas but rather upheld those realities

---

[109]The discussions at these meetings are recorded in a separate notebook entitled *Notulen van bespekingen met bezwaarden in 1927,* which can be found in the archives of the RCN congregation in Heemstede.

[110]A.W.F. Idenburg reports in the foreword to this work that these lectures were attended with an extraordinary amount of interest by a large number of students and members of the general public.

[111]Cf. *PWB*, 19-24.

about the truth of which he himself was existentially persuaded. He was concerned to set people in the revealing and saving light of the Truth, Jesus Christ. This desire is perhaps the most important explanation for the switch from psychology to missiology which was to take place in his career erelong.

In April of 1928 H.A. van Andel, pioneer missionary in Solo in central Java, came to the Netherlands to confer with his sending church in Delft[112] about the possibility of commissioning a third missionary servant of the Word for this field, in addition to himself and another colleague who was already there.[113] His proposal was adopted and Delft's partner congregations (see footnote 112) were asked to nominate suitable candidates for this position. The only name submitted was that of J.H. Bavinck, and it was decided unanimously to extend a call to him for this missionary post,[114] and there were good grounds for this consensus. According to a contemporary issue of the Delft church bulletin, Bavinck "had the idea when he returned from Bandung to Holland, that one fine day he would be led back to Indonesia. And he never tried to hide the fact that he was attracted to missionary work."[115] Moreover, because of his great erudition and open attitude, he was considered to be extraordinarily well suited for the work among educated, Dutch-speaking Javanese young people to which he was being called.[116] Thus, it was precisely his psychological-philosophical insight and his mystical instincts that equipped him so perfectly for this missionary task. And this constitutes evidence that the later redirection of his attention from psychology to missiology was due, at least initially, to simple circumstance rather than to the implementation of any conscious, prior plan.

Bavinck found it difficult to make a decision about this call to Solo. He had only been in Heemstede for a year and a half, where he experienced much affection on the part of the members of his church, who "gave thanks to God . . . [for paving] the way for such a good reception of his person and work in the congregation."[117] All the same, he realized from the very beginning that the

---

[112]Pursuant to the decisions of the Synods of Middelburg (1896) and Arnhem (1902) regarding the missionary task of the church, responsibility for carrying out mission had been assigned to the local churches. Because it was impossible for a single congregation to look after all the interests of a mission field on its own, eight regions were formed, each with one sending church which, in association with the other congregations in its region, bore responsibility for the mission field concerned. Delft was designated as the sending church for the northern region of the province of South Holland. Cf. J. Slagboom, 10-14.

[113]Cf. *HZB*, 26 (1928): 48, 98.

[114]Cf. the Minutes of the meeting of the expanded consistory of the RCN congregation in Delft of June 21 and July 5, 1928, in: *Notulenboek Breede Kerkeraad met Diakenen van 15-7-1926 tot 2-11-1935*.

[115]"Varia," *Gereformeerde Kerkbode*, July 7, 1928.

[116]*Idem*, November 10, 1928.

[117]*Kerkblad*, Heemstede, June 9, 1928.

proposed work in Solo, because it was to be directed toward the youth of a people in crisis and would therefore be of decisive importance for the future of that people, was weightier than ecclesiastical service of whatever kind in the Netherlands. That he nonetheless ended up declining the call had to do with the fact that it was a combined appeal, one part emanating from the consistory of Delft for work among Javanese young people, and the other from the consistory of Solo for work among local Chinese immigrants. As he wrote later, he felt that these tasks were too dissimilar and, taken together, too extensive for one person to handle. In any case, he did not consider himself capable of carrying them out simultaneously in any kind of proper way.[118]

A few months after he had turned down the call a message arrived from Solo indicating that the consistory there was prepared to meet Bavinck's objection by dropping their part of the call so that he would be able to devote himself fully to work among Javanese young people, including those who did not speak Dutch. The church in Delft immediately decided to ask Bavinck whether he would consider accepting a second call under these new conditions. Later he described his reaction to this query as follows: "Then we no longer hesitated, having come to understand that, since the very obstacle we saw standing in the way had been removed, we did not have the right to resist any longer. Then we said 'yes.' "[119] On November 8, 1928 a second formal call was extended to Bavinck for the work in Solo.[120] Promptly a day later he answered that he "felt entirely free" to accept the call to "that wonderful and important work."[121] This course of events reveals a lot about Bavinck the man: modest and hesitant, but, if the way became clear, also decisive. And what he wrote to his congregation in Heemstede after he accepted this call is illustrative of his piety, sobriety and levelheadedness.

> Perhaps one or another of you is asking: " But doesn't God provide light? If God by His light led you to decline the first time, can He then suddenly change? Does your reasoning not fail to reckon sufficiently with God's guidance?" Brothers and sisters, during the months in which we had to make our decision, we prayed much for God's light, and in the end we have come to see that God's light does not come to us outside the realm of deliberation but precisely through its agency. God does not send us a voice from heaven, but He does give us insight into the facts, into relationships. When we began to realize the first time around that the composition of the work to which we were called

---

[118]*Idem*, October 13, 1928.

[119]*Ibid.*; cf J.A.C. Rullmann, "Bij het overlijden van prof. dr. J.H. Bavinck," on the course that Bavinck's life took via psychology to missiology: "It went in a roundabout way, but seen in retrospect he was led straight to the place for which he was destined."

[120]Cf. the Minutes of the meeting of the expanded consistory of the RCN congregation in Delft of November 8, 1928, in: *Notulenboek Breede Kerkeraad met Diakenen van 15-7-1926 tot 2-11-1935.*

[121]Cited from Bavinck's letter of acceptance, dated November 11, 1928.

made it impossible for us to accept that call, we saw that as God's guiding light and gave thanks for it. And when the obstacles standing in the way were totally removed, we saw God's light just as certainly in that. God spoke to us clearly in all of these things.[122]

On January 6, 1929 Bavinck preached his farewell sermon in Heemstede on John 4:42: "They said to the woman, 'We no longer believe just because of what you said; now we have heard for ourselves, and we know that this man really is the Savior of the world.' "[123] It was in this light that Bavinck viewed his ministry in the past and in the future.

2.3. Work in Indonesia: Missionary Passion (1929-1938)

2.3.1. Missionary Pastor in Solo

"Leave your country, your people and your father's household and go to the land I will show you" (Genesis 12:1). It was on this text that Bavinck preached his inaugural sermon as missionary of the RCN sending congregation in Delft on January 10, 1929. With regard to this service, it was stated that he "took the opportunity to make clear that Indonesia deserves the best of the best," and further that he "spoke of the power with which this text had touched his soul during the days of deliberation and of the full conviction God had wrought in his heart that this divine command applied to him and his family too." [124] He was commissioned by W.G. Harrenstein,[125] now serving a church in Amsterdam, who chose as his text Acts 13:2-3: "While they were worshiping the Lord and fasting, the Holy Spirit said, 'Set apart for me Barnabas and Saul for the work to which I have called them.' So after they had fasted and prayed, they placed their hands on them and sent them off." On may 2 he successfully sustained his missionary examination before the classis of The Hague, after which he began preparing himself, by means of a program of Javanese-language and other studies at Leyden University and elsewhere, for the task awaiting him in Solo. That Bavinck quickly mastered the Javanese realm of thought is shown by the fact that even before his departure he spoke at a missionary meeting in Delft on the subject of *Solo Adiningrat* (Crown of

---

[122] *Kerkblad*, Heemstede, October 13, 1928.

[123] *Idem*, January 19, 1929; this issue contains a precis of the sermon.

[124] Cf. "Varia," in: *Gereformeerde Kerkbode*, Delft, January 12, 1929, in which it is also reported that while the attendance at the inauguration service was good, it was less than expected because of the radio broadcast of the inauguration of Queen Mother Emma.

[125] In a letter to the consistory of the church in Delft, dated December 3, 1928, Bavinck writes that for various reasons his father didn't feel up to installing him as missionary pastor in this service, "particularly since he installed me last year in Heemstede." It is not clear what was behind this, but it is not impossible that Bavinck's father had problems with his son's departure from Heemstede after such a short period of time.

the Earth). The gist of this vintage-Bavinck lecture was that the goal of mission was to win this Crown of the Earth to Jesus on the grounds that Christ had been given all power in heaven and on earth.[126] On January 8, 1930 Bavinck left for Indonesia for the second time. On the occasion of his departure a colleague wrote about him in the following laudatory terms: "Dr. Bavinck bears a name which has an excellent ring to it in our circles. And he carries that name with honor. Various of his publications have already assured him a place in the company of learned scholars."[127]

At this time Central Java was divided into two ancient princedoms: Surakarta and Jogjakarta, with Solo and Jogja as their respective capitals. Everyday life here still bore the heavy imprint of traditional culture and for that reason these two regions occupied a special place in the hearts of the Javanese: "The Javanese continue to look to the princedoms, to the capitals Jogja and Solo, particularly the latter," wrote a contemporary observer.[128] Central Java, with its 8.5 million people, was a densely populated area. The Reformed Churches in the Netherlands envisaged a special task for themselves here: proclamation of the gospel in the very heart of Javanese indigenous culture. There was a strong feeling among these churches that they had received a God-given mission field that was of importance for the whole of Java.[129] Bavinck wrote in this regard:

> The beautiful and populous island of Java was not freely chosen
> by Holland as area of missionary work. God had to constrain us
> to take up this work there. The mission in Java is thus in the
> most direct sense of the word the fruit of God's dealings with this
> great people.[130]

Bavinck served as missionary pastor from February 1930 to July 1933. His work during this phase was marked by four characteristic features.

1. *Capacity for entering into the Javanese mind.* Bavinck considered immersion in Javanese culture to be his first priority. He described the first stage of evangelism among people of a different culture in the following terms: "A person who carries the gospel to them will have to lean over toward them as far as possible in order to bring them into as close a contact as possible with the crux of the gospel."[131] From time immemorial Javanese culture had been informed by Hinduism and Buddhism and had borne a distinctly mystical character, and later on became influenced by Islam as well. It goes without saying that Bavinck's great adeptness at unraveling psychological processes and his mystical bent were of

---

[126]Cf. *Gereformeerde Kerkbode*, Delft, November 2, 1929.

[127]W. Breukelaar, *HZB*, 27 (1929), 243.

[128]D. Pol, "Vorstenlanden," 648.

[129]Cf. D. Pol, *Midden-Java ten zuiden*, 11-12.

[130]*ZWN*, 141.

[131]"Christendom en cultuuruitingen," 44. Bavinck's personal papers (see footnote 52 above) contain notebooks that witness to the depth of his immersion in the language, culture and mysticism of Java as well as in Buddhism and Islam.

inestimable value in this context. Some twenty years after Bavinck's death, one of his former students, J. van den Berg, wrote: "He [Bavinck] was particularly well qualified in both personality and education to penetrate the subtle and inscrutable world of Javanese mysticism."[132]   And around this same time another observer called attention to the close interplay between knowledge, experience and spirituality that characterized Bavinck's life during this period: his psychological learning "definitely enabled him to enter more deeply into the Eastern soul," which, in turn, "led to an intensification of his own mystical bent and affinity."[133] Thanks to the listening attitude, the respectful stance he invariably assumed toward those holding opinions and convictions differing from his own, he was able to establish good contacts with Javanese mystics and Muslim scholars.[134] He regularly engaged in long conversations with them, the preferred time for which was the middle of the night. He also moved in the court circles of the two Indonesian monarchs who resided in Solo, the more important of whom was the Susuhunan, who lived in the *kraton*, an extensive palace with many entrances and gates, all of which had a religious significance. Bavinck was very desirous of initiation into these secrets and mysteries. He also became engrossed in the *Javanese wayang* puppet shadow plays, and in time came to grasp the religious charge they carried as dramatic representations of mythological events.[135] An important role in all of this was played by the Cultural-Philosophical Study Group set up in Solo in 1931 to meet the need felt by Javanese, Dutch and Chinese to get to know and understand each other better. Bavinck counted it among the most wonderful experiences of his life to have discovered that it was possible to have talks such as these between people of various races in which the tone of trust and mutual appreciation remained wholly intact throughout. The best moments for him were those

> in which our converse rose above all earthly things and turned to the divine world beyond us. Then we no longer thought of ourselves as Chinese, Javanese or Dutch; then, in a certain sense, we all became children standing in the presence of the ineffable greatness of the Eternal One. . . . No, there was no possibility [in these meetings] of expressing our common feelings in terms of a single formula or creed; it was apparent then that there were boundary lines which we could not cross over. And yet,... during these nighttime discourses, we realized, deeply and intensely, how fruitful and wonderful it was that we could speak with one another about these things in such an atmosphere.[136]

In this period Bavinck had a great deal of contact with Hendrik Kraemer of the Netherlands Reformed Church—with whom, as noted earlier, he had already

---

[132]"The Legacy of Johan Herman Bavinck," 7 (1983), 172.

[133]J. van der Linden, *Centraal Weekblad*, 33 (Nov. 29, 1985).

[134]Cf. J. Verkuyl, *Contemporary Missiology: An Introduction*, 38.

[135]In *CMO*, 100, Bavinck provides a succinct, clear explanation of these plays.

[136]"De Cultuur-Wijsgerige Studiekring," 9-11.

become acquainted while at university—who was serving as linguist under the Dutch Bible Society in Solo at the time and, being a specialist in the area of Javanese culture and mysticism, was also a member of the Cultural-Philosophical Study Group.[137] Years later Bavinck wrote of Kraemer: "He was my teacher, the one who initiated me into the secrets of Javanese literature and in particular Javanese mysticism."[138] And Kraemer once told J. Verkuyl: "I have never had a student who came to understand Javanese mysticism more quickly or more thoroughly than Bavinck."[139] By all accounts he absorbed Javanese culture like a sponge. This kind of ability to apprehend the mental and spiritual world of indigenous Javanese culture had never before been witnessed in RCN missionary circles: "Javanese architecture," wrote a contemporary RCN missionary leader, "or Javanese literature and *wayang* plays have seldom if ever been the subject of serious study" among us.[140] The deepest secret behind Bavinck's openness was his unshakable faith in the truth of the gospel.[141] It is also quite possible that Bavinck had contacts with another of his fellow students from university days, Barend M. Schuurman, who at that time was teaching, as a missionary of the Netherlands Reformed Church, at Balé Wiyata Theological College in the eastern Javanese city of Malang. Schuurman, too, was a student of Javanese culture, worked closely with Kraemer, and remained deeply true to his spiritual background.[142]

It should also be pointed out here that these contacts undoubtedly served to reinforce Bavinck's open, ecumenical stance. When Bavinck died, a colleague and friend explained what it was that lay at the base of Bavinck's ecumenicity.

> He was never ultimately concerned with truths; the only thing
> that really mattered to him was *the* Truth. For him Jesus Christ,
> as He comes to us, and His Word were the Truth. This [lack of
> emphasis on truths] explains why he could be genuinely
> ecumenical, seek contacts, consult and cooperate with all who

---

[137]It is a matter of conjecture whether, without these earlier contacts, Kraemer would have influenced Bavinck to the extent he did at the time of the International Missionary Conference in Tambaram in 1938; we will return to this question in chapter 3.

[138]"Dr. Hendrik Kraemer als denker en medewerker," in: R. van Woudenberg, *J.H. Bavinck: Een keuze uit zijn werk*, 161.

[139]J. Verkuyl, *Inleiding in de nieuwere zendingswetenschap*, 63.

[140]H. Bergema, "Over de beteekenis van de kennis der Javaansche cultuur voor het verstaan van het Javaansche levensvisie," 260-261.

[141]Cf. "Protestantisme," 47, where, years later, Bavinck gave expression to this link between faith and openness in terms of a different context: "If we ourselves were more dedicated with heart and soul to what we believe, I'm convinced we would also be more free and open toward the humanists."

[142]Cf. B.M. Schuurman, 9-37, and J.J. Buskes, 92-98.

confessed the same Lord.[143]

As indicated in an article he wrote in the mid-fifties, Bavinck was continually confirmed in his conviction that there were people outside his own circles from whom there was much to learn.

> When we stand together with others on the front line of faith, we come to experience that those belonging to ecclesiastical communions differing from our own, with whose orthodoxy and church order we may and, if justifiable, should find fault, sometimes reveal a surprising depth of religious life that can only put us to shame and make us jealous.[144]

2. *Passion for the further explication of the gospel message.* Bavinck's attempts to get inside the Javanese mind must be perceived in light of his search for possibilities to pass the gospel on in an adequate and effective way. "Bavinck's almost intuitive understanding of Eastern thought did not lead him, however, to any form of syncretism," wrote J. van den Berg.[145] Indeed, quite the contrary was true. Starting from a thorough knowledge of their traditional world, he was at pains to bring the Javanese into contact with the truth of God in Jesus Christ. Illustrative of this is his Javanese-language booklet, *Suksma Supana,*[146] in which he expounded the main points of the gospel in terms of the layout of the *kraton.*[147] He also lectured at the court of the Mangku Nagoro, the other Javanese monarch in Solo, with a view to establishing communication between the gospel and Javanese mysticism in those circles as well.

These efforts were crowned by the appearance of a book in 1934, entitled, *Christus en de mystiek van het Oosten* (Christ and Eastern Mysticism), which Bavinck completed while on home leave in the Netherlands.[148] His approach to other faiths was stamped by his opposition to the concept of 'continuity' which had

---

[143]A. Pos, "Bij het sterven van prof. dr. J.H. Bavinck."

[144]"Apostoliciteit en katholiciteit," 232.

[145]"The Legacy of Johan Herman Bavinck," 172.

[146]This booklet appeared in 1932 under the pseudonym Kjai Martawahana.

[147]According to Bavinck himself, Kraemer helped him with this booklet "from page to page with counsel and aid," *DHB,* XI (1958), 90. Though not everyone at the time found this attempt to articulate the gospel acceptable (cf. J. Verkuyl, *Inleiding in de nieuwere zendingswetenschap,* 63), in 1964 J.A.C. Rullmann wrote that the work was written in such accomplished Javanese "that no one who was made privy to the secret of the pseudonym could believe [this publication] was the product of a Dutchman," *passim.*

[148]Verkuyl termed this work Bavinck's most important publication, cf. *Contemporary Missiology: An Introduction,* 39; it might be better termed his first important work in the area of applied elenctics (for the latter see chapter 6 below); a later book that witnesses equally well to Bavinck's formidable knowledge of the Eastern world is *De psychologie van den Oosterling* (The Psychology of Eastern Peoples), which came out in 1942.

become so deeply instilled in the thinking of that time under the influence of scholars such as Friedrich Heiler, and whose advocates argued for a smooth, seamless attachment of the gospel to existing religions. Yet, Bavinck did not hold to the idea of rigid discontinuity either. That had already become clear from his descriptions of the encounters that took place during the gatherings of the Cultural-Philosophical Study Group. Owing to his strong inner bond with Christ, the Final Answer, he did not give premature answers but instead felt perfectly free to absorb and savor Eastern thought in all openness. He pointed out striking similarities between the gospel and Javanese mysticism, pinpointed elements in Eastern thinking that help us to come to a deeper understanding of the biblical message, and discovered aspects of Eastern experience which formed a point of contact for the proclamation of the gospel. At the same time, however, he always made his position absolutely clear that "life is different and the world is different" from the way they are perceived in Eastern thought, and that "the God of the East is different from the God Who appeared in Christ for our sake."[149] In conclusion he stated:

> I am utterly convinced, thus, that there is only one means by which we can cause the difference to be deeply and truly felt, and that is by confronting the East with the sacred figure of Jesus Christ. Paul, too, shows that he understood this when he wrote: "For I resolved to know nothing while I was with you except Jesus Christ and him crucified" (I Corinthians 2:2). In the final analysis and in the face of all rational arguments, the whole of missionary work consists of nothing more or less than the childlike witness: "Come and see"! (John 1:46)[150]

J. van den Berg rightly points out that in this book Bavinck still dealt with the confrontation and communication between gospel and religion "innocently, as it were. Later, in the period after Tambaram, at which the question of 'continuity or discontinuity' was so hotly debated, he would approach this issue differently."[151]

3. *Special concern for youth work.* The knowledge Bavinck had gained was put to concrete use in his labors among the youth in Solo. The articles he authored on this subject bear consistent witness to his intense involvement in the problems young people in Indonesia faced. In one of his reports he wrote: "The youth of these lands deserve truly special care and commitment, because they have been drawn into exceptionally complicated relationships."[152] These young people were in a very difficult position: undergoing culture shock as a result of their exposure to Western science, they also found themselves standing in the center of the field of tension between old folk beliefs and the Christian faith. Bavinck constantly emphasized the key position occupied by mission schools, pointing to the important role they could and should play in helping the youth to deal with the strong opposite pull of these polarities. In both their intramural and extramural contacts with students, he wrote, instructors were obliged to take careful account of

---

[149]*CMO,* 203, 202.

[150]*Ibid.,* 228-229.

[151]"De wetenschappelijke arbeid van Professor Dr. J.H. Bavinck," 34-35.

[152]*HZB,* 29 (1931), 74.

the conflicts and tensions raised in these youthful hearts by their new situation. Teachers also had the task of showing their students the way to Jesus Christ as the one in whom, "amidst the shaking and jolting of their old faith and world view, rest and strength and stability can be found."[153] After the war in 1945 he wrote: "Education is one of the very best modes of mission, it is an excellent means of showing the Indonesian world that the gospel lays claim to the whole of life, including all science,"[154]

In a review of the 1931 *Report of the Commission on Higher Education in India*, which had been drawn up under the auspices of the International Missionary Council, Bavinck indicated that he subscribed to its recommendations and that he considered them to be of importance for the mission schools in Java as well. There were, he wrote, three main issues to be taken account of in mission-school education: first, that education should be more attuned to Indonesian society; second, it should be developed according to Christian principles; and third, the schools should seek, via closer cooperation with the Christian churches, to strengthen the personal piety of their students and cultivate Christian living among them.[155] Bavinck put these principles into practice at the Christian Teachers College in Solo, where he taught psychology and gave weekly lectures for the whole assembled student body. During these sessions he always provided opportunity for questions and in this way gained insight into what the students were thinking and feeling, which, in turn, made it possible for him to support them effectively in their "agonized heart-searchings." With this same aim in mind a clubhouse was opened in Solo in January 1931 in a Javanese house deliberately purchased in the middle of a Javanese neighborhood in the hope that this would make it more attractive and accessible. This youth center was named *Balé Sudda Sadana*, i.e., House of Deliberation about the Path that Leads to a Higher Goal.[156] Bavinck considered the work among the youth in Solo to be of significance for the whole of Indonesia due to the fact that young people from all parts Java and also from the other islands came there to study. "The broad perspective that keeps opening up here," he wrote, "provides constant reason for joyful hope."[157] It was on this account that he also deemed the youth and youth-leader conferences organized by the RCN mission to be of the utmost value.[158] Those who attended these conferences came from all over Java, the outcome of which was not only that the newly awakened faith of the participants was greatly reinforced during the rallies but also that afterwards the gospel message was, as it were, automatically spread far and wide. Bavinck hoped

---

[153]*Ibid.*, 75.

[154] "De zending nu!," 5.

[155]"De crisis van het zendingsonderwijs in Indië," 97-101,129-133.

[156]Cf. *HZB*, 29 (1931), 76.

[157]*Ibid.*

[158]Accounts of two of these conferences can be found respectively in "Een kamp in een oude koningsstad," *DM*, 36 (1932), 1-8, and "De christelijke jeugdbeweging in Indië," *DM*, 37 (1933), 37-39.

that all of this would give birth to a great movement of faith in Indonesia.

Another aspect of Bavinck's work at this time was his initiative in setting up what he called *pantja saudara*, circles of five.[159] These were Bible-study groups meant to provide young people with undergirding for their personal faith. This kind of support was considered necessary because as soon as students left the mission schools, they found themselves confronted by great difficulties and temptations in the old environments to which they returned. At best they experienced no active opposition at home. These little Bible-study circles, which "had untold influence upon [a number of] young people who would later be called to shoulder heavy responsibilities in a young and independent Indonesia,"[160] endued their participants with an enduring feeling of brotherly and sisterly community. It was not without reason that Bavinck chose 'five' (*pantja*) as the guiding number for these groups. In traditional Javanese culture the figure 'five' had a very special significance: it denoted a multiplicity or quantity that formed an unbreakable unity, like the five fingers of one hand. This link with the local culture spawned a number of favorable effects. The members of these circles themselves kept track of each other's attendance at their meetings, and, in case of illness, ministered to the needs of the absent participant. In this way they broke the common Javanese habit of failing to show up for meetings at appointed times, an unfortunate custom which bore severe negative consequences for club work and the activities of associations and societies in Java. The limited size of these circles also contributed to the development of internal mutual trust, the essential condition for genuine openness among their members. In the weekly meetings of the groups a passage of Scripture was discussed with the aid of study guides written and distributed by Bavinck, the contents of which clearly show that he sought to cultivate not only a better understanding of the biblical message but especially personal commitment to that message. "Sitting in a holy circle, as it were," the members of the groups "learned to discuss, not in some detached fashion, but in deep communal engagement, searching out God's promises and demands."[161] That this type of youth work had become enormously popular can be seen by the fact that before long there was a demand for a thousand of Bavinck's study guides.

Bavinck continued his overall supervision of this work by means of regular meetings with the leaders of the circles of five. This gave them the opportunity to discuss the difficulties they encountered and to exchange ideas on how to meet them. That Bavinck was a person who not only gave but could also receive is shown by what he wrote in respect of these meetings with the group leaders: "The advice we received from these young men and women . . . was often extremely valuable. They frequently had a much better idea than we did of the direction in

---

[159]Cf. J.H. Bavinck, "Jeugdwerk: De kringen van 5," 353-363. The information provided in the sequence is based largely on this article. A concise, clear description of this type of youth work can be found in a letter from Bavinck published in *HZB*, 31 (1933), 13-14.

[160]J. Verkuyl, *Contemporary Missiology: An Introduction*, 38.

[161]*Ibid.*

which we should steer."[162] In addition to these leadership meetings, joint gatherings of all the study groups in Solo were held three times a year in the *Balé Sudda Sadana* clubhouse. Bavinck consciously attuned the structure and setup of these collective assemblies, too, to the Javanese mind, with a view to the development of indigenous forms of Christian religious experience. For instance, these meetings were convened in the *dalem*, the inner chamber of a house where, according to Javanese tradition, the members of a family spent their time together, which gave expression to the idea that the participants could and should view one another as brothers and sisters belonging to the same household. Moreover, Low Javanese was spoken at these gatherings as a sign that social distinctions held no relevance whatsoever in this company. This form of youth work lasted for a decade.[163]

In 1931 the Sower Library was established for the special purpose of facilitating the spiritual equipment of the youth. Each year five booklets were published, dealing with the basic tenets of the Christian faith. Bavinck, too, penned a number of small works during these years.[164] That these booklets met a great need is clearly shown by the fact that 90,000 of them were sold in the space of just four years' time. All biographical sketches devoted to Bavinck emphasize the high esteem in which he was held for the way he shaped and gave leadership to Christian youth work in Central Java during this period. He put his stamp on many young people, and particularly on a large group of teachers who had studied under him at the Teachers Training College in Solo, whereby his influence continued to make itself felt for a very long time.[165] His later publications, too, witness to a lasting interest in youth work in general and education in particular.[166] In 1938 a colleague wrote: "Youth work, for which he was granted singularly special gifts, is very dear to his heart."[167]

---

[162]*DM*, 37 (1933), 358.

[163]The clubs of five flourished until 1942, after which they seemed to die away; in 1951, however, they were revived on a modest scale; cf. *HZB*, 50 (1952), 102-103.

[164]*De tien geboden* (The Ten Commandments), 1932; *Hoe kunnen wij den Heere Jezus vinden?* (How Can We Find the Lord Jesus?), 1933; *Het licht des levens* (The Light of Life), 1934; *Paulus de grote apostel* (Paul, the Great Apostle), 1937.

[165]Cf. A. Pos, "Leven en werk van Dr. Johan Herman Bavinck," 14. According to a contemporary newspaper, *De Rotterdammer*, (6-26-1964) Rev. J.H. Sillevis Smitt said at Bavinck's funeral: "Perhaps his greatest work was the establishment of those little clubs of no more than five persons in Indonesia, in which Javanese and Chinese children met together."

[166]In this connection one can point to various works that appeared in the years 1937, 1939, 1942, 1947, 1949, and 1950; cf. the bibliography of Bavinck's publications compiled by A. Wessels in: A. Pos *et al.*, *Christusprediking in de wereld*, 224-246.

[167]W. Breukelaar, *HZB*, 36 (1938), 92.

4. *Sympathy for rising nationalism and the cognate necessity of establishing the independence of the indigenous churches.* In accordance with the stated principle of the Synod of Middelburg (1896) that no church may be subordinated to another church, the mission agencies of the Reformed Churches in the Netherlands had, from the very beginning, given thought to the issue of the independence of local missionary congregations. That Bavinck had an eye for this matter was, therefore, nothing exceptional. What was unique in his case was that he was pronouncedly sympathetic to the national awakening of Indonesia and did everything he could to stimulate the growth of independence among the Javanese churches. He was deeply aware of an urgent desire among educated indigenous Christians to take over tasks that up till then had belonged to the presumptive bailiwick of the mission. And even though local believers may not always have been completely prepared for such a transition, Bavinck considered it to be of essential importance to create room for the transfer of ecclesiastical authority and pastoral responsibility to them, if for no other reason than to protect the mission from accusations of colonialist power politics and, consequent to that, forfeiture of the trust it had built up through the years. In a different period one might have been inclined to opt for a more gradual path to independence, he said in 1934, but circumstances being what they were, it was better to go along with the times and make an effort to help guide this process along as best as possible.[168] In an article dating from this time Bavinck also dealt at length with the contemporary economic crisis and sought an answer to the question of whether it would be possible to implement a financial cutback of the entire work of mission without doing irreparable damage to vital areas of that work. He warned against taking rash decisions on the basis of financial need alone, particularly any that would adversely affect the growth of independence among the Javanese churches and thereby consign them to an existence characterized by lopsided relationships and colored by foreign customs for a long time to come.[169] Two years earlier he had written in the same vein:

> What can we do for our people? What position should we
> assume with respect to the political, nationalist movements that
> are churning and fermenting among our people? How can we
> Christians escape the ignominy of being lost to the national
> movement? One would have to be blind not to see immediately
> how momentous these questions are in terms of the present phase
> of colonial development.[170]

If the church in Java was to have any future at all, Bavinck maintained, it would have to become a Javanese church.

---

[168]Verkuyl pointed out to me that Kraemer was more radically opposed to colonialism than was Bavinck, who advocated a more gradual development. It is possible that Bavinck assumed the decisive stance he did at this time under the influence of Kraemer's point of view.

[169]Cf. "Zending en crisis," 97-107.

[170]"Een kamp in een oude koningsstad," 7.

In 1933 the church in South-Central Java became independent.[171] Not everyone was equally happy with this development. Many were worried that things had progressed too quickly, but Bavinck tried through the use of sensitive argumentation to overcome their feelings of unease. This is clearly illustrated by the following quotation from a letter addressed by him to the home front.

> Of course [the increasing activity of Javanese Christians] seems a little strange to us at first. We have grown so accustomed to having everything stem from the mission that we have to get used the idea that a new time is dawning, the time of independent, self-reliant activity on the part of the younger churches. And my impression is that there is every reason for us to rejoice [at the nascence of this new era].[172]

Bavinck also realized that if the missionary task was to have any success in a nationalistic climate such as that in Indonesia, it would have to be carried out in increasing measure by local believers. He stated plainly: "Mission work stands or falls, humanly speaking, with the presence or absence of zeal for and love of the gospel among young indigenous Christians."[173]

All in all, it is clear that during these years Bavinck rendered a great service to the progress of mission work in Java. Verkuyl writes:

> Looking back at the way this man immersed himself in the milieu in which he proclaimed the gospel, the only fitting assessment of his work is one that views it as an example that beckons us to emulation even after his death. . . . in terms of mission, Bavinck's stay in Solo was the most fruitful period of his life. It is striking to see the extent to which the influence Bavinck exerted during that time continues to make itself felt in Indonesia.[174]

But it also worked the other way around: as J.A.C. Rullmann pointed out in a newspaper article after Bavinck's death,[175] Bavinck's missionary praxis bore a great deal of significance for himself as well in that it constituted the initial impetus for his later missiological development and reflection.[176]

---

[171]Cf. K.J. Brouwer, *Zending in een gistende wereld*, 12.

[172]*HZB*, 31 (1933), 13-14.

[173]"Zending en crisis," 107.

[174]*Inleiding in de nieuwere zendingswetenschap*, 63-64.

[175]"Bij het overleden van prof. dr. J.H. Bavinck."

[176]Rullmann also pointed out that though Bavinck, according to his own testimony, had "learned a great deal" from his work in Solo, he "never felt completely at home" there, which may have been caused by the general atmosphere in the Dutch Christian community in Solo at the time. J. Verkuyl, *Inleiding in de nieuwere zendingswetenschap*, 63, reports, e.g., that the staff of the missionary bookstore in Solo was instructed not to sell any copy of Bavinck's booklet *Suksma Supana* unless it was accompanied by a Gospel of John.

2.3.2. Teacher of Theology in Jogjakarta

Bavinck's relatively short period of work as missionary youth pastor was ended by his appointment as instructor at the Theological School in Jogjakarta, an academy for the training of Javanese evangelists and ministers. Before proceeding further, it might be well to have some general information about the origin and significance of this educational institution.[177]

The antecedent history of the Theological School goes back to the time of the work of the Netherlands Reformed Missionary Society in Central Java.[178] Already then, missionaries began increasingly to realize how important trained indigenous helpers were for the advancement of the work of mission. With this in mind they founded an educational facility, the Keucheniusschool, in Purworedjo in 1891, at which a number of native Javanese Christians were trained to become teachers and evangelists. After this mission field was taken over by the Reformed Churches in the Netherlands in May, 1894, it was decided at the 1902 RCN Synod of Arnhem to reorganize the Keucheniusschool and move it to Jogjakarta, where it was reopened in new facilities in 1905. The reconstituted school had two divisions: one for training teachers and the other for educating *gurus indjil*, indigenous pastoral adjuncts and missionary evangelists authorized to assist in the ministry of the Word. The latter of these two departments was led by the missionary pastor Dirk Bakker[179] from 1906 until 1911, when the two divisions were turned into separate, independent institutions, whereupon he became director of the newly formed Theological School until his retirement in 1929. In 1923 Frederik L. Bakker was appointed to a teaching post at the School alongside his father, and now, in addition to the existing Javanese-language course of study, a Dutch-language curriculum was introduced to serve the more highly educated Javanese students. Regular efforts were made to improve the educational programs offered, particularly as it became ever more clear that there was a growing need for ordained Javanese ministers, of whom the only viable source at this time was the pool of trained *gurus indjil*. "The Theological School in Jogjakarta is just as important for the mission and the indigenous churches in Central Java as Kampen Seminary and the Theological Faculty of the Free University in Amsterdam are for the churches in the Netherlands."[180]

This being the case, it was not surprising that on the occasion of D. Bakker's farewell in 1929 opportunity was taken to reflect on further ways and

---

[177]These givens are taken mainly from D. Pol, *Midden-Java ten Zuiden*, passim.

[178]This missionary society was founded in October 1859 and began working in North-Central Java in 1861 and in South-Central Java in 1867; cf. D. Pol, *Midden-Java ten Zuiden*, 137.

[179]D. Bakker, the patriarch of a remarkable Dutch missionary family of several generations running, educated some 70 *gurus indjil*, of whom five became ordained ministers in 1929; cf. W. Breukelaar, "De zendingsfamilie Bakker," *HZB*, 27 (1929), 163-168.

[180]W. Breukelaar, *HZB*, 29 (1931), 240.

means of raising the academic level of the School. The duration of the course of study was lengthened from two to three years, and the RCN Mission Deputies took the decision to name two new teachers to fill the vacancy created by Bakker's departure. Abraham Pos, a missionary pastor in Jogjakarta, was appointed in 1930 and, after a period of preparatory study in India, took up his task in 1932. On the recommendation of the Association of Missionary Pastors in Java, Bavinck was appointed in 1931 as third instructor at the Theological School, where he was to concentrate especially on Javanese language studies and the subjects of geography and ethnology. In a letter, dated December 23, 1931, Bavinck wrote that he accepted the appointment. This time there was no evidence of hesitancy. Apparently he had no doubts about his qualifications for this position and felt definitely called of God to serve the cause of His Kingdom in this capacity. Finding it difficult to leave his post in Solo straightaway, however, the more so because his immediate colleague there was going on home leave in 1932,[181] Bavinck arranged to have his appointment postponed until July 1, 1933.[182] Unfortunately, he was felled by a serious illness the last few months of his stay in Solo, and it was feared that he would have to return to the Netherlands for good. Soon it was announced, however, that he was gradually recovering his strength and thus would remain available to take up the position he had accepted.

Although the initial idea was that Bavinck would spend his preparatory year of study in Java, in the end it was decided that he should take early home leave in order to prepare himself at Leyden University, not only because the possibilities for study at Leyden were considered to be better but also because of the fear that if he stayed in Java he would not be able to detach himself sufficiently from the work of the mission, which would place his study in jeopardy. Moreover, by taking early leave he would be able to serve at the Theological School for an unbroken period of six years, which would assure a greater degree of continuity in its academic program.[183] Arriving in the Netherlands in the summer of 1933, Bavinck commenced a year's study at Leyden University, concentrating his efforts in the areas of Old Javanese and traditional Javanese religion. In August 1934 he left for Indonesia for the third time, now as instructor of theology, in which capacity he retained his status as missionary pastor and as such also remained in the service of the sending church in Delft, with continued responsibilities for the work in Solo, his new duties at the Theological School permitting.

Bavinck commenced his work at the Theological School on September 7, 1934 with an inaugural lecture entitled, *De strijd des geloofs* (The Struggle of Faith).[184] He was scheduled for six hours of Dutch-language and five hours of Javanese-language lectures in the areas of ethics, exegesis, theology of the New

---

[181]*Ibid.*, 240-241.

[182]*HZB*, 30 (1932), 32.

[183]*HZB*, 31 (1933), 101.

[184]Though this lecture never appeared in print, a summary report of the inauguration was published in *HZB*, 32 (1934), 172-173.

Testament, and practical theology.[185] From the very beginning Bavinck felt completely at home in this new work, due partly to the fact he and the other two instructors were on such excellent terms with each other. In a letter to the RCN Mission Deputies Bavinck wrote:

> We as teachers are greatly privileged to be able to work together in such a beautiful and harmonious way, feeling ourselves knit together by the bonds of faith and love. Looking back at my first three months of work at the school, I feel thankful to God who has given us this wonderful labor and has also chosen to bless it.[186]

Unfortunately, the various missionary magazines and synodical reports provide little more information about the Theological School than numbers of students and anniversary celebrations. The only thing that can be determined from these sources is that Bavinck helped train nearly 60 *gurus indjil* during these years and that the Theological School occupied a salutary place within the Javanese church.[187] With respect to Bavinck and his special pedagogical gifts, F.L. Bakker wrote several years later: "He understood his students and their thoughts and he brought them close to God, on account of which he had a great influence on the life of the Javanese and Chinese churches in Java."[188] But the teachers wrote precious little about their actual work, making it very difficult gain insight into Bavinck's teaching methods and the development of his missionary talents in this area. Johannes Verkuyl states that one of the main facets of Bavinck's work at the Theological School consisted in the fact that he "gave much more attention than previously had been the case to the cultivation of *theologia in loco*," i.e., the encouragement of indigenous theological expressions of the faith. "Together with his colleague Pos, he gave more substance" to the study of Java's traditional culture by delving deeply into its literature and religion.[189]

In addition to teaching, the instructors were also expected to produce

---

[185]*HZB*, 32 (1934), 110-111.

[186]*HZB*, 33 (1935), 24; cf. also F.L. Bakker, "In memoriam prof. dr. J.H. Bavinck": Bavinck was "one of our best friends with whom we worked for many years."

[187]Cf. F.L. Bakker, "Enkele gegevens over de Opleidingsschool te Djokja," 257-264; J.H. Bavinck, "Het dertigjarig jubileum van de Opleidingsschool te Djokjakarta," 488-491.

[188]F.L. Bakker, "In memoriam prof. dr. J.H. Bavinck."

[189]*Inleiding in de nieuwere zendingswetenschap*, 64; this is corroborated by a short notice in *DM*, 43 (1939), 127-128, detailing the division of teaching and research duties among the three teachers at the Theological School: Bakker was responsible for the subject of Islam, Pos for the study of Hindu influence on Javanese life, and Bavinck for the exploration of the traditional Javanese world view and Javanese mysticism.

textbooks and maintain contacts with former students.[190]   Accordingly, Bavinck teamed up with Bakker to write *De geschiedenis der Godsopenbaring* (The History of Divine Revelation), of which Bakker did the first part on the Old Testament and Bavinck the second part on the New Testament. This book was published in Dutch and Javanese in 1938 and in Indonesian in 1947. It is characterized by both simplicity and quality and therefore could be used profitably by ordinary church members as well as those schooled in theology. The publications that appeared during these years show that Bavinck was not only active in his assigned area of study[191] but that he also often helped think through issues belonging to the area of missionary practice[192] and that he remained throughout essentially a pastor.[193] According to A. Pos, Bavinck termed these years "the finest of his life."[194] And another friend reported that just shortly before he passed away Bavinck termed this period "the most wonderful time of my life."[195] In any case, he gained a veritable treasure of knowledge and experience which was reflected everywhere in his later publications and which qualified him for a professorship in the 'science of mission.'[196] That Bavinck's work was greeted by appreciation not only within but also outside his own circles is demonstrated by the fact that he was named Officer in the Order of Orange Nassau by Queen Wilhelmina in 1938.[197]

---

[190]Cf. *HZB*, 32 (1934), 172.

[191]Publications in this area are: "Is het christendom absoluut?" and "Zijn all godsdiensten gelijk?" *Horizon*, 1 (1934/35) 265-272, 297-302; *Tri-dharma eerste cirkel* (1935); "Drie grote vragen: 1. De vraag van den mensch en zijn plaats," "2. De vraag der openbaring," "3. De vraag van de verlossing," *DM*, 42 (1938), 82-91, 97-104, 178-184; *Tri-dharma tweede cirkel* (1938).

[192]Publications that could be mentioned here are: "Wat kan het christelijk onderwijs aan de bevolking in Indië brengen?" "Het goed recht van het christelijk onderwijs in Indië," "Hoe kunnen wij het recht van het onderwijs der zending bepleiten?" *DM*, 41 (1937), 214-221, 238-246, 341-348, 353-359.

[193]Three important publications in the area of pastoral care that appeared during these years are: *Zielzorg aan eigen ziel* (1935), *Menschen rondom Jezus* (1936), and *Jezus als zielzorger* (1938).

[194]"Leven en werk van Dr. Johan Herman Bavinck," 14.

[195]J.A.C. Rullmann, "Bij het overlijden van prof. dr. J.H. Bavinck."

[196]In the sequel this older term, equivalent to the German *Missionswissenschaft*, will be substituted by the normal English terms: mission studies and missiology, the latter of which is now used universally in Dutch as well.

[197]Cf. *HZB*, 36 (1938), 186.

3. Chapter Summary

The main contours and characteristics of the background and early years of Bavinck's life can be sketched as follows.

1. Growing up in a pious family, his youth was characterized by a close personal relationship with God, which determined his vocation and stamped the entire course of his life: in deep humility he surrendered himself fully to grateful service of Christ.

2. Following in the line of his uncle Herman Bavinck, at university he began to develop a constructively critical stance toward both his own and other Christian ecclesiastical communities of faith.

3. His intellectual capacities and mystical sensibilities combined to lead him to the study of (religious) psychology. When he became involved in mission, his studies missiology.

4. His great love for the worldwide expansion of God's Kingdom coupled with his practical bent and his wisdom and tact made him into a great missionary at the level of both the execution and organization of the work in the field.

CHAPTER TWO

Later Years and Life's End

"Now the missionary nature of the Church is the object of mission studies. And it is obliged to throw light on all aspects of that object from the perspective of the everlasting Word of God." (*IZW*, 13)

1. Life and Work in the Academy

Within the RCN mission there was a growing need for a better training of missionary pastors, doctors, nurses, and teachers. As early as 1900 a missionary pastor named Harmen Dijkstra made a plea for the institution of a "chair of mission studies,"[1] and in 1914 a report containing proposals for such a chair was presented to the General Synod of the RCN by its Mission Deputies. Though the Synod of 1917 took a number of positive decisions respecting the recommendations of this report, they were not put into practice.[2] At the Synod of Groningen in 1927 Rev. Jan Schouten, president of the Board of Trustees of Kampen Theological Seminary, argued anew for the establishment of a chair of mission, but no concrete action was taken until 1930. The Mission Deputies submitted a second report to the Synod of Arnhem in that year, calling for the appointment of a professor of mission, particularly for the training of future mission workers. The Synod responded by setting up a complex procedure for calling and appointing an extraordinary professor of mission studies at Kampen Seminary.[3] It was hoped that a nomination could be made and approved by synod before the end of July 1932, but due to

---

[1] Cf. *HZB*, 37 (1939), 235.

[2] Cf. B.J. Esser, "Ambt en kerkelijke positie der missionair-predikanten in de Gereformeerde Kerken en de Opleiding daartoe," 97.

[3] Cf. *HZB*, 30 (1930), 215 for a description of this procedure: in consultation with the theological faculty of the Free University in Amsterdam, the trustees and professors of Kampen Seminary were to draw up a definitive job description for this new professorship; then the trustees and mission deputies were to search for a suitable candidate in consultation with the professors in Kampen; after that, contact was to be made with the various missionary associations of Central Java and Sumba; and finally, after further consultation with the Free University, the name of a candidate could be submitted to Synod for approval.

44

various problems this was delayed until 1938.

First of all, it turned out to be more difficult than anticipated to draw up a description of the content and parameters of the task of the prospective new professor. Was it fair to expect one man to be well versed in ethnology, indigenous religions and various languages and on top of that to have a thorough command of the theology and history of mission? B.J. Esser wrote that this would be expecting the impossible and that a good, comprehensive course of preparatory mission studies in the Netherlands would require the services of a minimum of three professors. He was more enamored of a period of training in the country of destination, tailored to the candidate missionary's aptitudes and skills and specifically focused on his or her future task. He and others were convinced, however, that a professor of mission should be added to the ordinary theological faculty to teach the history and theory of mission and missionary church polity. Such a professor could also furnish the churches in the Netherlands with solid information and advice on missionary affairs.[4] Though it is impossible to trace the exact details of the discussions that took place on this matter, a missions professorship was finally instituted along these lines.[5]

The next difficulty was finding the right man to take up this position. In 1936 W. Breukelaar wrote:

> We are thinking in the first place of a man equipped with first-rate academic abilities who would give wholehearted and full-time attention to the study and cause of mission here at home. Or to quote Prof. H. Bavinck, "[We need] a man who lives entirely for and devotes all of his powers to mission, who not only busies himself with the history of mission in order to extract lessons for life from it but also reflects on the theory of mission, with all of its pressing problems, in the light of our principles, and who is capable of inspiring a sacred enthusiasm in our future ministers for the Lord's cause."[6]

Breukelaar added that in his view there were people who satisfied this description, among whom "there is one who could be withdrawn from his present duties without causing too much damage to the vital interests of the work in which he is involved." It is not impossible that already at that point he had the erudite nephew of Herman Bavinck in mind.

1.1. Appointment as Professor of Mission Studies (1938-1954)

Johan Bavinck was nominated for the position of professor in mission studies in 1938. On April 5 he was appointed extraordinary professor of mission at Kampen Theological Seminary by the synod of the RCN and at the same time

---

[4]Cf. B.J. Esser, "Ambt en kerkelijke positie der missionair-predikanten in de Gerefor-meerde Kerken en de opleiding daartoe," 106-111.

[5]Cf. a notice by D. Pol in *DM*, 42 (1938), 62-63 in which he describes the task of the future professor of missions as including the study and teaching of the history and theory of mission, as well as elenctics, adding, in the same breath, that the area of mission studies actually comprises too much for one person to handle.

[6]*HBZ*, 34 (1936), 213.

was named to an identical chair in the Faculty of Theology at the Free University in Amsterdam. In addition he was given the task of attending the meetings of the RCN mission deputies in an advisory capacity. Well within the limits of the time given him for consideration of the appointment, Bavinck sent the following telegram on May 5: "Am gladly willing in God's strength to accept appointment."[7] W. Breukelaar articulated the general feeling of satisfaction with respect to this development:

> The name Bavinck has an excellent ring to it in our churches. It will bring joy to many of us that soon there will be a Bavinck teaching at our Theological Seminary once again . . . and that in the disciplines which, as the first Bavinck so emphatically argued, call for full-time professorial attention.[8]

And yet Bavinck's appointment also met with considerable hesitation in some quarters. There exists correspondence, at that time strictly confidential, from which it appears that objections were raised against Bavinck's candidacy by one of the professors at Kampen Seminary, Klaas Schilder, and by one of the members of the seminary's board of trustees, Rev. Geert Diemer.[9] Their criticism was leveled especially at Bavinck's book, *Inleiding in de zielkunde* (Introduction to Psychology).[10] In this work, according to Schilder, Bavinck had ill-advisedly yoked Reformed and un-Reformed thought together. "Association with non-Reformed theories, however unintentional, can, in my view, be detected throughout this work," Schilder wrote,[11] and this was attributable, he argued further, to the method employed by Bavinck, a method whereby "Scriptural principles are mentioned only a posteriori and then related as best as possible to findings arrived at by other means." His conclusion ran as follows.

> In view of so much uncertainty with respect to [his writings] including even the matter of methodology, I'm convinced it would be extremely unwise to appoint a man professor, who, however excellent he may be in many regards, in my opinion should be considered for nomination only if it were to prove

---

[7] *HZB*, 36 (1938), 93.

[8] *Ibid.*; cf. also J. Veenhof, "Honderd jaar theologie aan de Vrije Universiteit," 79, "In [Johan Bavinck] the spirit of his uncle Herman Bavinck lived on: his work was marked by discerning sensitivity and openness, enhanced even further by his experiences in the East."

[9] Two undated letters dealing with this matter, one from Schilder and the other from Diemer, can be found among the personal papers of G.M. den Hartogh (at that time professor of church history), which are located in the archives of Kampen Seminary.

[10] They based themselves on the second edition of this 1926 work, revised by A. Kuypers and republished in 1935.

[11] Letter from K. Schilder, 4, personal papers of G.M. den Hartogh, Kampen Seminary.

impossible to find a better and sharper thinker for this position.[12]
Diemer expressed himself along the same lines in his letter. After having expressed
great appreciation for many of Bavinck's publications, he stated that Bavinck had
not yet achieved "sufficient clarity and consistency of academic insight" and that
it therefore would not "be fair to the churches to nominate him for this position."[13]
Diemer felt that even Bavinck's preaching evinced a lack of clarity. In reaction to
a published sermon by the latter on Ephesians 4:20-24[14] Diemer wrote:

> The point to which I call attention is the relationship between the
> absoluteness of divine grace and human responsibility, both of
> which are duly acknowledged by the writer but not properly
> distinguished from each other, and which he expresses in terms
> that do not fit the Reformed framework but are borrowed from
> other schools of thought.[15]

It was perhaps to counterbalance or forestall negative notes such as these
that Breukelaar, in his later article on Bavinck's nomination, marshaled a number
of positive reviews of Bavinck's earlier publications, written by prominent Dutch
scholars. Such reviews were obviously intended to constitute proof of Bavinck's
formidable academic abilities. And on the 1935 revised edition of *Inleiding in de
zielkunde* (Introduction to Psychology) he cited an RCN leader who was above all
suspicion and who, indeed, had criticized the earlier edition of this publication.

> No less an authority than professor J. Waterink wrote in his
> review of this book: "This is an excellent work; I would like to
> say that I am happy with it. This is a very trustworthy handbook.
> Anyone who has read and understood it may rightly claim that he
> has gained insight into nearly all of the important aspects of
> modern psychology. Moreover, the [way the subject matter is
> dealt with]conforms to [Reformed] principles. Anyone having a
> desire to study will find this work to be a splendid textbook."[16]

One notes a sense of relief in Breukelaar's following words: "It is a source of great
joy that generally speaking his appointment has met with great approval in our
ecclesiastical press."[17]

After acceptance of his appointment, it took Bavinck a year to round off
his work at the Theological School in Jogjakarta. He arrived back home in June

---

[12]*Ibid.*, 5.

[13]Letter from G. Diemer, 1, personal papers of G.M. den Hartogh, Kampen
Seminary.

[14]This sermon appeared in 1936 in *Menigerlei grenade*, a series consisting
of collections of sermons written by leading theologians and ministers.

[15]Letter from G. Diemer, 2, personal papers of G.M. den Hartogh, Kampen
Seminary.

[16]*HZB*, 36 (1938), 93.

[17]*Ibid.*

1939[18] to assume his responsibilities as the first Protestant professor of mission in the Netherlands, [19] delivering his inaugural address entitled, *Christuspfrediking in de volkeren-wereld* (Preaching Christ to the Nations) in Kampen and Amsterdam on respectively October 12 and 13. The central question he dealt with in that address was very dear to his heart and would run like a red thread through the whole of his missiological work, namely: How can Jesus Christ be preached in such a way that the message does not turn into an abstraction but rather becomes tangible and real for people?

Bavinck proceeded cautiously, particularly in Kampen, where, as already indicated, not everyone was equally happy with his appointment. Soon after commencing his work there, he requested a special meeting of the professors "to talk about a few questions in connection with the subjects" he was teaching, matters which he wished to "submit to the judgment of [his] colleagues." Enamored of friendly overture and averse to estrangement, he greatly preferred open dialogue to confrontation. His request was granted and in a meeting on December 14 he gave a paper entitled, "The Phenomenon of Pseudo Religion in Connection with General Revelation." The ensuing discussion went well and built trust in Bavinck to such an extent that the following year he was even asked to teach psychology.[20]

1.1.1. Teaching and Writing Activities

Bavinck was primarily responsible for teaching mission within the standard theological curriculum followed by students preparing for the gospel ministry. This discipline was subdivided into three parts: The history of mission in the Dutch East Indies / Indonesia; The theory of mission according to Reformed principles; and Elenctics or missionary apologetics with specific reference to the non-Christian religions found on the RCN Indonesian mission fields.[21] Making missiology a required subject would not only create the means of inspiring some students to go into active missionary service but would also make those who stayed home aware of the importance of mission, which in turn would lead them, it was hoped, to stimulate love and prayer and giving for mission in their future congregations. That this desired effect was in fact realized is shown by a 1943 report of the Kampen

---

[18]Cf. *HZB*, 37 (1939), 67.

[19]The Catholic University in Nijmegen had already appointed Alphons Mulders as senior lecturer and in 1936 as professor of mission theology; cf. J.A.B. Jongeneel and E. Klootwijk, 15-16.

[20]Cf. the Minutes of the Meetings of Professors (Kampen), October 30, 1939, December 12, 1939, June 24, 1940, and September 21, 1940; according to the latter set of minutes, Bavinck reported that the RCN Mission Deputies had no objection to his teaching psychology and that he therefore was willing to take on this task.

[21]Cf. the Minutes of the Meetings of Professors (Kampen), February 21, 1939.

student union, *Fides Quaerens Intellectum*,[22] in which it is stated: "The stimulating influence of professor J.H. Bavinck continues to make itself be felt."[23] Bavinck's surviving lecture notes betray a great erudition, a broad knowledge, and a worldwide orientation. In the area of the history of mission he dealt not only with Indonesia but also with India and China. In his courses on the theory of mission he did not limit himself to Reformed views but also took into account the development of missionary thinking throughout the centuries, including the modern ecumenical views of mission articulated at the International Missionary Conferences that had been held since 1910. In the area of missionary apologetics he busied himself extensively with the history and phenomenology of religions.[24] In addition to his official lectures he also led well-attended missionary study groups in Kampen and Amsterdam in which he discussed important missiological publications - such as Hendrik Kraemer's *The Christian Message in a non-Christian World* - with interested students. Further, Bavinck was also expected to take part in the two-year certificate training course for prospective missionary pastors.[25]

Bavinck had a generally good relationship with his students. Many who studied under him remember him as an open, warmhearted and wise man. The low-keyed piety which permeated his lectures often made a deep impression on his students, one of whom, B.J. Aalbers, wrote years later:

> We [of the 1948 class of students at Kampen Theological Seminary] were captivated from the very beginning by the figure of Bavinck. . . . It may sound a trifle exaggerated, but when Bavinck was in top form, we sometimes had the feeling that 'our dear Lord Himself' was standing behind the lectern speaking to us. . . . Bavinck also had something prophetic about him: when he spoke, it was with great inner authority. . . . What always struck me, too, was [his] unpretended, thoroughly genuine humility and modesty. . . . When you're sitting in class at around the age of twenty, it is not only the subject matter being taught, but no less the whole attitude and manner of your professor that makes an impression on you.[26]

---

[22]"*Fides quaerens intellectum*: faith in search of understanding, a dictum concerning the relationship of faith and reason from the *proemium* to Anselm's *Proslogion*, which closely follows the Augustinian model of *Crede, ut intelligas*," Richard A. Muller, 117.

[23]*HZB*, 41 (1943), 5.

[24]Cf. the J.H. Bavinck Archives, Appendix 1, in the CHDDP/FIJA.

[25]Cf. *HZB*, 37 (1939), 235, and H. Baas, 7.

[26]Letter from B.J. Aalbers to R. van Woudenberg, July, 25, 1992; that the modesty which commanded such great respect sometimes proved to be something of a hindrance to Bavinck is illustrated by the following anecdote related to me by one of his former students, L.J. Woltius: Once when a student had clearly failed an oral examination, Bavinck couldn't seem to find a way to tell him that. It remained quiet for awhile until the student himself finally said, "Shall I come back later and

And in 1964 A. Pos stated: "[Bavinck] never ceased fascinating large groups of students. It is impossible to say how many have been gripped for life by the vision of God's worldwide work that Bavinck imparted to them."[27] It was often precisely the students who rejected the strongly antithetical atmosphere so evident in the Reformed Churches in the Netherlands in those days who found in Bavinck an example of how theology could be done in a different way, without at the same time doing violence to the truth. As Aalders wrote: "The hard intellectualistic spirit that reigned among the church leadership and that had a determinative effect on the synods, for example, was completely different from the gentle, irenic, cultured and courtly manner that Bavinck radiated."[28]

Bavinck was also commissioned by synod to set up a year-long missionary training course for medical doctors, nurses, and 'missionary sisters,'[29] which commenced on January 25, 1940. The need for a preparatory course directed toward the specific needs of these categories of missionary workers had been felt for a long time - in fact, this had been one of the main arguments adduced for appointing a professor of mission in the first place. During the discussions on Bavinck's teaching responsibilities within the framework of this new training course, it was realized that one person could not do everything and priority was given, in his case, to missiological subjects, while other fields were entrusted to adjunct teachers. Offered once a week in two locations, Amsterdam and Utrecht, the course consisted of one-hour sessions of instruction in four disciplines: the theory of mission; the history of mission, particularly in the Dutch East Indies; Indonesian indigenous religions; and geography and ethnology. Interest in this course, which required students to engage in a great deal of independent study, exceeded all expectations: it attracted a first group of no fewer than 33 participants. The course was not only meant for missionary workers who had already been appointed, however, but was also deliberately aimed at those who had an active interest in mission, with a view to building up a 'missionary potential.'[30] After the initiation of this training course the following synodical rule took effect.

No [missionary candidates] may be sent out unless they are in possession of a certificate issued by the professor of mission attesting to the fact that they have satisfactorily completed the required course of study, along with an additional testimonial certifying that they have made serious work of studying the

---

try again?" Bavinck breathed a sigh of relief and replied: "Yes, why don't you do that."

[27]"Bij het sterven van prof dr. J.H. Bavinck."

[28]Letter to R. van Woudenberg, July 25, 1992.

[29]These 'missionary sisters' were sent out with the special task of proclaiming the gospel to Indonesian women, whose world was virtually inaccessible to men.

[30]Cf. *HZB*, 38 (1940), 28, 75.

language they will need to use in their missionary service.[31]
Only in very exceptional cases could a candidate missionary worker be granted
dispensation from this rule.

After the war Bavinck began to move in broader circles. At the request of
its theological students, a sister denomination (the *Christelijke Gereformeerde
Kerk)* decided to add missiology to the standard curriculum of its seminary located
in the town of Apeldoorn, and Bavinck was asked to teach this subject there, which
he agreed to do in the form of biweekly lectures beginning in November 1945.
Within his own church this guest lectureship was considered to be a *nomen
honoris*.[32] In October and November 1947 he lectured in the United States at
Calvin College and Seminary in Grand Rapids, Michigan, and in the fifties he
traveled to South Africa three times at the request of the Theological Education
Fund of the International Missionary Council. His first trip, which lasted from June
26 to September 9, 1952, consisted of a tour of orientation for purposes of
acquainting himself with pressing South African missionary issues. During the
second visit, from March 2 to October 2, 1953, he lectured on missiology, dogmatics,
psychology, philosophy, and various related subjects as adjunct professor at
Potchefstroom Theological Seminary, where, it was reported, interest in his courses
was "extremely great."[33]   In 1959 he was asked by the South African Committee
on Science and Freedom to assess the proposal set forth in the University Extension
Bill to establish separate faculties for blacks.[34] In September 1960 he delivered a
lecture at Presbyterian Theological Seminary in Louisville, Kentucky,[35] and in
1961/1962 he taught as guest professor at the Federated Theological Faculty of the
University of Chicago. With respect to the latter, Verkuyl writes that the sensitive
"analysis of the morphology of religions" in Bavinck's book, *Religieus besef en
christelijk geloof* (Religious Consciousness and Christian Faith) "was so striking
. . . that the world's greatest scholar of the morphology of religions today, Mircea
Eliade, invited Bavinck . . . to lecture to his students" of comparative religion.[36]
Bavinck's third visit to South Africa, once again under auspices of the Theological
Education Fund, was in 1963 to offer a course for seminary teachers of missiology.
Meanwhile, he also gave countless lectures and speeches throughout the years to
diverse groups in the Netherlands, both within and outside his own ecclesiastical

---

[31]*HZB*, 38 (1940), 3-4.

[32]Cf. D. Pol, *HZB*, 43 (1945), 16.

[33]Cf. *HZB*, 51 (1953), 174.

[34]Bavinck was not against this, but he emphasized the need to aim for
integration; cf. the J.H. Bavinck Archives in the CHDDP/FUA, document no. 50.

[35]This given is based on the dedication written in Bavinck's copy of R.S.
Sanders, *History of Louisville Presbyterian Theological Seminary*: "To Dr. Johan
H. Bavinck, on the occasion of his lecture at Louisville Seminary, September 23,
1960"; this book from Bavinck's library was made available by L.J. Wolthuis.

[36]*Contemporary Missiology: An Introduction*, 40.

and academic circles.[37]

Because Bavinck was such a stimulating teacher he attracted many domestic and foreign graduate students, both at the master's and the doctoral level.[38] He greatly encouraged this kind of academic research and provided his graduate students with intensive, expert supervision. J. Verkuyl, who did his own doctoral work under Bavinck, writes in this regard that Bavinck's exceptional impact as professor can be measured by, among other things, "the stream of dissertations which flowed from the pens" of his students, and further that

> Bavinck never served his students by weighing every line they
> wrote: the secret of his influence lay in things which are harder
> to pinpoint. He was a 'guru' for his students, an Eastern guru.[39]

Because the topics of his students' dissertations were often closely related to his own missiological interests, it can be safely said that he had a significant international following in the field of missiology.

Bavinck wrote prolifically during this period, though he contributed relatively few essays to international missiological journals. In the articles that appeared in various Dutch periodicals he either dealt with missiological issues or gave his views on practical missionary problems faced by his church. With respect to the latter, he wrote a great deal on the question of the decolonization of Indonesia and, in connection with that, the changing relationships between the indigenous churches and the mission, matters which touched a very sore spot at that time and gave rise to no little tension within the church. By means of a number of carefully measured articles in the RCN weekly, *Gereformeerd Weekblad*, he managed to convince the ecclesiastical home front that these developments were irreversible and that it had a vocation to deal with them in a positive manner.[40] In addition, he began to reflect more and more on the task of church and mission in a changing world, calling attention to the danger of rising nihilism amidst all the material progress taking place in East and West and to the difficult task of carrying out the gospel in this spiritual vacuum. He also looked critically inward, continually trying to rouse the church to new expectations. A few years after the war he wrote in this vein:

> If at sometime a strong faith were to be awakened in our

---

[37]Bavinck had a reputation for delivering many of these speeches extemporaneously, often asking shortly before mounting the podium, "What subject am I to speak on?" That his great erudition and formidable reasoning powers made it possible for him to give talks with no specific prior preparation is confirmed by a remark in the "Introduction" to J.H. Bavinck, H. Kraemer, K.H. Miskotte, *Salve Rex*, that Bavinck's chapter in this book "is a stylistically reworked account and expansion of a resumé of a lecture made during the course of its delivery."

[38]Most of his foreign graduate students came from North America and South Africa; cf. the appendix at the end of this book.

[39]*Contemporary Missiology: An Introduction*, 40; for similar testimonial statements by other students of Bavinck's cf. A. Pos, "Leven en werk van Dr. Johan Herman Bavinck," 25-26.

[40]Cf. the bibliography of these writings during the period 1945-1949 in A. Pos, *et al.*, *Christusprediking in de wereld*.

churches that through our word God can do wondrous things in this modern world too, that Christ wishes to use us in His triumphant forward advance, that we have every reason to expect great things, very great things from Him, then our whole attitude toward life could change instantly.[41]

Bavinck's most important missiological works, which appeared almost without exception after his appointment as professor in Kampen and Amsterdam, manifest a gradual deepening of insight, most notably those that evolved from his theological reflection on the relationship of the Christian faith to other religions. Since the content of these books will be dealt with in subsequent chapters, brief mention of them will suffice here.

De boodschap van Christus en de niet-christelijke religies (The Message of Christ and non-Christian Religions, 1940). This book provides a summarizing account of the argumentation in Hendrik Kraemer's *The Christian Message in a non-Christian World*, which Kraemer wrote for the 1938 International Missionary Conference in Tambaram and in which he defended the essential incompatibility of Christian faith and non-Christian religions. Bavinck was deeply impressed by Kraemer's approach and considered his thinking on this question to be so important that he took on the task of producing a résumé of it in Dutch, to which he also added a number of critical notes in respect of Kraemer's radical view of Christianity, his notion of Biblical realism, and his voluntaristic concept of God.

Alzoo wies het Woord (And Thus the Word Grew and Increased, 1941). In this book Bavinck busied himself with the methods of the apostle Paul, with a view to developing a responsible contemporary discharge of the missionary calling. Especially his interpretation of Paul's speech on the Areopagus recorded in Acts 17 shows how intensively Bavinck had become engaged in reflection on the relation between Christianity and the other religions.

Zending in een wereld in nood (Mission in a World in Need, 1946). This work, intended as a basic introduction to the principles of mission for interested church members, deals at some length with the history of mission in general and that in the Dutch East Indies in particular.[42]

The Impact of Christianity on the Non-Christian World (1948). This collection of the lectures Bavinck delivered at Calvin Theological Seminary in Grand Rapids in 1947 is a well thought-out reflection on missionary apologetics. In the Foreword to this publication, C. Bouma wrote: ". . . the present book is a real contribution to contemporary missionary literature. Though not as wide in scope, as to spirit and content it should be classed with Hendrik Kraemer's *The Christian Message in a Non-Christian World.*"

Religieus besef en christelijk geloof (Religious Consciousness and Christian Faith 1949, 1989[2]). In this study, one of his most engrossing works, Bavinck elaborates on the ideas of Kraemer presented in the first book mentioned above, developing them according to his own thinking and insights. Questions having to do with the reality of general revelation, the origin and content of

---

[41]*OKZK*, 34.

[42]Initially this book appeared under the title, *Ons zendingsboek* (Our Mission Book), which Bavinck had written at the request of the Dutch Leagues of Young Women's and Young Men's Associations. In 1946 an amplified edition of it was put out, which is the one used in this study.

religious consciousness, and the relation of these two to the revelation of God in Jesus Christ are answered particularly in light of Romans 1. Characterized by a combination of theological reflection and psychological insight this book sometimes takes surprising turns and according to J. Verkuyl belongs to the category of the "modern classics."[43]

Het woord voor de wereld (Word for the World, 1950), a fine, clear-cut interpretation of the *totaliter aliter* character of the Biblical message as compared with the teachings of the non-Biblical religions, is a practical apologetic work meant to serve as an educational aid for the discerning churchgoer.

Inleiding in de zendingswetenschap (Introduction to the Science of Mission, 1954). This handbook, which consists of an expanded treatment of the main content of the publications mentioned above and which also appeared in English translation in 1960, constituted the first Reformed standard work in the area of missiology to be published in the Netherlands. The way the various missiological themes are developed in this work is of course colored by Bavinck's ecclesiastical background and personal experience, and, in terms of approach, the book clearly bears characteristic traits of the colonial era.

The Church Between Temple and Mosque (1966). This last important work, a posthumous publication of Bavinck's 1962 lectures in Chicago and closely related to his earlier book, *Religieus besef en christelijk geloof*, deals anew, in a detailed and profound way, with the content of religious consciousness in relation to Christian faith.

Bavinck's interests were not limited to missiology, however. He also published two studies that can be reckoned as belonging to the area of biblical theology: *De Bijbel, het boek der ontmoetingen* (The Bible, the Book of Encounters, 1942), and *De mensch en zijn wereld* (Man and His World, 1946). These works witness not only to Bavinck's great erudition but also to his deep pastoral concern. In addition, he also produced an original exegetical study of the last book of the Bible, entitled, *En voort wentelen de eeuwen: Gedachten over het boek der Openbaring van Johannes* (And Age Follows Upon Age: Reflections on John's Book of Revelation, 1952).

As attested by many contemporary observers, all of Bavinck's published works are characterized by a combination of learnedness and lucidity, academic rigor and simplicity, which made them attractive to a broad reading public, ranging from top theologians to ordinary church members. In his review of *RBCG* H. Harrestein writes: "This book deals with a hard subject, but Bavinck builds his argument so evenly and writes so lucidly that anyone used to reading anything beyond novels will be able to follow it with no difficulty." [44] A few years later another commentator, J.C. Gilhuis, also pointed to this gift in Bavinck. After remarking that Bavinck had succeeded in explaining extremely involved problems in a very simple way in his inaugural address, Gilhuis added: "And that this had been done purposely can be seen from what [Bavinck] said at the beginning of the address: 'The struggle on the faraway front requires that the church in the fatherland learns to think and pray along with [those working on the field].' "[45] Further, in his

---

[43]Cf. "Woord vooraf," *RBCG*, ix.

[44]*HZB*, 48 (1950), 78.

[45]*HZB*, 50 (1952), 27.

review of *IZW*, Gilhuis stated: "This book is of a definitely scholarly nature, but because Prof. Bavinck understands the art of writing about complicated things in a simple way, church members not afraid of reading will find a great deal of unusually enriching material in it."[46]

1.1.2. The War Years and the 'Schilder Conflict'

The Second World War broke out soon after Bavinck had taken up his position as professor in Kampen and Amsterdam. True to character, Bavinck published a volume of five sermons together with his clergyman brother, C.B. Bavinck, entitled *Inkeer en uitzicht* (Repentance and Prospects, 1940), with a view to furnishing the congregation of Christ with practical spiritual guidance in the midst of the confusion of those days. At around this same time, he advanced the idea in a newspaper article that the horrors of the war could also have a positive side if they led to a cessation of ecclesiastical debate and to a renewed willingness to listen to the message of God: "It is certainly not unthinkable," he wrote, "that wonderful days lie before us, days of a surprising revival of spiritual life, days in which God will inform our lives with the riches of His gifts of grace."[47] Even as professor he remained before all else a servant of the Word, a shepherd of God's flock.

One of the direct consequences of the war was that the relationship between the Netherlands and the Dutch East Indies was broken. Appointed missionaries could not be sent out; the work of mission in Indonesia would now have to be carried out, and the 'younger churches' there would have to get along, without guidance and support from the Netherlands. There was naturally a great deal of uncertainty about whether this would be possible. After an initial period of stagnation, a hunt began for new ways of giving shape to the missionary task of the church in this changed situation, and Bavinck, along with others, played a prominent role in this search.

One of the most important activities undertaken during this period was the intensive training of missionary ministers, doctors, teachers and nurses to take up the task that awaited after the war. At a meeting of sending churches and mission deputies on October 2, 1941 a missionary doctor, J.S. Wiersema, whose return to Indonesia had been interrupted by the war, proposed the establishment of a special, authorized missionary school for purposes of training a topnotch corps of future missionary workers. Not only would a course of study at such a school greatly benefit the future work of mission, he argued, but it would also help to counteract decreasing missionary awareness in the churches. Moreover, it would constitute a means of implementing the pre-war ruling that only well-prepared people were to be sent out as missionaries. "It is surely clear to all of us," he said, "that a hasty selection and sending out of insufficiently trained workers must become a thing of the past."[48] Wiersema also indicated that in his opinion this missionary training school should be led by Bavinck. For specialized studies use could be made of faculties of Indology and various hospitals. Wiersema's proposal was adopted, and a Committee on Preparatory Training, consisting of one member from each of the

---

[46]*HZB*, 52 (1954), 141.

[47]"Veel vragen en één antwoord."

[48]*HZB*, 39 (1941), 171.

sending churches and two members from the RCN Mission Deputies, was set up to implement this plan.[49]   Once it was launched, Bavinck devoted a great deal of energy to this project, organizing courses and conferences, drawing up study assignments, and hearing examinations.[50]   In a 1991 interview one of the former graduates of this training program, Anton G. Honig, later professor of missiology at Kampen Seminary, stated: "Bavinck prepared us for missionary service in those years in a truly superb way."

Gradually the desire emerged   within the ranks of the Committee on Preparatory Training to establish a center from which the general interests of the mission could be efficiently served.   There was already a Missions Bureau in existence, which had been founded in 1931 to see to matters of missionary propaganda, administration and correspondence.   But now that the concept of a centralized course of training for missionary workers had taken such firm hold, the need for a reorganization of current arrangements became more keenly felt. Bavinck drew up a plan to this end, which, after initial discussion in various mission jurisdictions, was presented by the Denominational Mission Deputies to the RCN Synod of Utrecht in 1943, where it was adopted with great unanimity.   The plan was to institute a Center for Mission under the supervision of the Denominational Mission Deputies, where future missionaries would be trained , where a missionary library would be housed, where the Missions Bureau would be located, and where conferences could be held for various groups of church members with an eye to stimulating a greater degree of missionary awareness among them.

The fact that many church people recoiled from this idea of far-reaching centralization, however, can be inferred from the demulcent words penned by D. Pol, editor of *Het Zendingsblad* and chairman of the Denominational Mission Deputies, in an article dating from that time.

> There is no need to have any fear whatever that the Center for Mission would assume a place of dominance, threatening our [official position] that mission belongs to the *church.* For the guidance of missionary work remains entirely a matter for the local sending churches. . . . There is neither talk nor thought of a Center for Mission that would be in charge of our mission work or missionary organizations.[51]

The principle of the ecclesiastical decentralization of mission established by the Synod of Middelburg in 1896 remained, thus, in force.   Nevertheless, no small amount of misunderstanding continued to exist with respect to the purpose of the Center for Mission.   And that there was also some substantial resistance to these plans may be concluded from the fact that Bavinck later found it necessary to reiterate the goal envisaged for the Center: service of the work of foreign mission and active stimulation of mission awareness at home.   Through these activities, he wrote, "we will become churches that are not only 'vaguely involved in mission' but

---

[49]Cf. H. Baas, 8.

[50]Others involved in this school were the physicians J. Offringa and J.S. Wiersma (for medical missionary candidates), and H.J.W.A. Meyerink, the former director of the Teachers Training College in Solo (for missionary educators), cf. *HZB*, 42 (1944), 44, 47.

[51]*HZB*, 41 (1943), 71.

that truly engage in mission out of the sense of responsibility born from obedience to the commission of Him who has sent us out." Bavinck and others set energetically to work on the realization of the project. Although no suitable accommodation had as yet been found for it, Rev. Barend Richters was appointed future director of the Center on April 12, 1944,[52] with responsibilities in the areas of organization, administration and dissemination of information.[53]

Unfortunately, Bavinck's lectures in Kampen and Amsterdam had to be suspended from 1943 to 1945 by order of the German occupational authorities. That this grieved him deeply can be seen from the following quotation from the diary he kept during the last year of the war: "I have been deprived of my regular work, the contact with students, everything that gave life luster and purpose."[54] He used most of this enforced free time for study. "Yesterday," he wrote in his war diary, "I drew up an outline for a new book, a kind of introduction to the history and phenomenology of religion. It will take a number of years before the book is finished, but the initial spadework has been accomplished in the time of war."[55] In addition to this, he also busied himself, by invitation, with the future of Dutch politics, becoming immersed in discussions on the possibility of forming a people's party with a view to breaking through old political alliances.[56] Further, he was appointed to a number of new positions during these years: in May 1941 he was named chairman of a fund that raised money for the Moravian Mission in Surinam,[57] and elected member of the board of the Council for Mission Study, a broadly based denominational society that occupied itself with a variety of missionary questions.[58] Finally, he was also actively involved in the work of the Dutch Missionary Council.[59]

The war years were filled with a great deal of personal anxiety for Bavinck

---

[52]Richters, at that time pastor of a local church in the province of North Holland, was later described by W.G. Harrenstein as "the right man at the right time," *HZB*, 45 (1947), 54; cf. also H. Baas, 10, who states that Richter's spirituality and businesslike mentality were guarantees for outstanding leadership.

[53]*HZB*, 42 (1944), 37-38.

[54]*Herinneringen aan het laatste oorlogsjaar 1944-1945*, 49; this 162-page diary, which was never published, is in the possession of the Bavinck family.

[55]*Ibid.*, 59; it is not entirely clear what later publication evolved from this wartime outline, but it was most probably *Religieus besef en christelijk geloof,* 1949.

[56]*Ibid.* 55.

[57]Cf. *HZB*, 39 (1941), 95.

[58]Cf. *ibid.,* 94; in 1948 this study group was disbanded when the RCN began participating in the broader consultation forum offered by the Dutch Missionary Council.

[59]Cf. *ibid.,* 152, and *HZB*, 41 (1943), 63-64.

and his wife due to the fact that their two sons and at a certain point also their daughter were actively involved in the Dutch resistance movement. Both sons were arrested within one week in June 1944, the elder of whom was held in German custody until September 1944, while the younger was deported to Germany and imprisoned in the concentration camps Sachsenhausen and Rathenau, from which, to the great joy of his parents and siblings, he eventually returned unhurt in June 1945.[60]

Sadly enough, a serious theological conflict flared up in the RCN during the war years, which in the end led to a church schism, the so-called *Vrijmaking* (Liberation), in 1944. The conflict centered on the views of one of the professors at Kampen Seminary, Klaas Schilder, who contested, *inter alia,* the Kuyperian notion of a baptism of presupposed regeneration. It is not necessary within the parameters of this study to go into this conflict at any length. Of interest to us is the role that Bavinck played in the matter. At the invitation of the Student Union, *Fides quaerens intellectum,* Bavinck gave a lecture in Kampen on November 2, 1942, entitled, *De toekomst van onze kerken* (The Future of Our Churches),[61] in which he addressed the then-current situation of tension within the ranks of the church. He was specifically chosen to talk on this topic, on the one hand because he had only been back in the Netherlands for a relatively short period of time and therefore could stand somewhat aloof from the whole matter, and on the other hand because, being averse to conflict, he was not a party man. In this speech Bavinck sketched the evolution of the spiritual currents that had arisen within the Reformed Churches in the Netherlands, hoping in this way to trigger a fruitful discussion of the 'Schilder controversy.' It is important to look at this speech in greater detail because it not only offers a good profile of general developments in the RCN at that time but also illuminates the framework within which Bavinck's own theological growth unfolded.

The very introduction was vintage Bavinck: he indicated that he wished to enter into discussion "with no pretense whatsoever," that he didn't want to cause anyone pain, and that what he said should not be construed as a reference to anyone personally. He then went on to describe, in four points, the intellectual climate that obtained during his student years. First, there was a growing interest at that time in "spiritual perceptions and experiences," which was linked to the experimental approach and argumentation that characterized the whole of scientific thought. If theology wished to be a 'science,' it would not do for its practitioners "to confine themselves to the enunciation of dogmatic formulas." Instead they would have to "prove, as it were, that Christ is a reality, whose powerful operation continues to make itself demonstrably felt in our modern times." Second, there was a strong tendency toward psychological reflection which also made itself felt within the Reformed Churches in the Netherlands in those years. Starting from the idea that God had disclosed Himself "through the souls of living people," the question arose as to whether a thorough study of the human psyche was not required for a proper understanding of divine revelation. This new inclination "converged with the [existing] current of old Pietism," which placed great emphasis on the inner

---

[60]This information is based on Bavinck's wartime diary referred to above.

[61]This originally stencilled address, a copy of which can be found in the RCN archives at the National Service Center of the Uniting Churches in Utrecht, came out in published form in 1943; cf. J. Kamphuis, 60, note 23.

experience of truth. A third characteristic of those years was the openness toward and appreciation of non-Christian science and culture. The reality of "God's common grace" disallowed the limitation of truth and beauty to one's own circles. Cooperation with non-believers in various and sundry areas would have an enriching effect on those immediately involved and on society as a whole. Fourth, those years were pregnant with the threat of spiritual relativism, a relativism which led some to ask whether

> the whole of Reformed thought was not just a relatively coincidental, historically determined differentiation of the one great, powerful life, the driving force that informs the Church of all ages. . . . Is [Reformed thinking] not sustained by the psychological disposition of the inhabitant of the lowlands by the sea, a disposition characterized by words like sobriety and rationality and grounded in a certain inclination toward amiability and mysticism?

The period after the First World War witnessed a break in this development, according to Bavinck, and a "new spirit" emerged: people no longer had any hesitations or feelings of doubt but felt absolutely certain about things. Bavinck's assessment of this new way of thinking, which also carried through into the church, was very evenhanded. At the very beginning of his analysis he disposed of two possible misunderstandings: although he recognized its links with developments outside the church, he refused to relativize this new spirit as nothing more than a passing phenomenon of the times and thereby deny its objective validity; on the other hand, it was not his intention to identify this "new thinking" with any one group of people, or to launch personal attacks against even its most vigorous advocates in the church.

Bavinck delineated seven characteristics of this new way of thinking. The first of these was its "tendency toward absolutism." Though on the one hand this could be viewed as an "important step forward" in comparison with the "indecisive attitude" of former years, there was a danger that this absolutism would take over even "where a greater degree of reticence and reserve would be more advisable," making dialogue impossible. Moreover, the terseness of formulation employed by the representatives of this new thinking led to an often incomprehensible use of words. A second feature of this school of thought was the negativism of its adherents, their habitual manner of thinking in polemic forms: "they are constantly looking for a fight, constantly on the defensive, constantly beating off enemies." Even their sermons degenerated into polemical exercises. A third distinguishing mark of this new thinking was its objectivism, which expressed itself in terms of a radical aversion to psychology and all inner experience. One-sided emphasis on "the constancy of the Word" gives rise to the danger of failing to recognize "the work that the Spirit effects in our hearts by that Word," which would lead to a spiritual condition of "inner barrenness." The fourth trait of this school was its great interest in the history of salvation. Although this *heilsgeschichtliche* emphasis did have its positive side - Bavinck even averred that the increased attention given to world history had been used by God to awaken the church's interest in the history of salvation - it also led to excesses. Everything was approached from this point of view, theologians were constantly making new finds, ministers were preaching "'I see, I see what you don't see'-type sermons." The fifth thing that typified the new thinking was the fact that everything was lumped together under the notion of God's covenant. Apart from the one-sidedness of this position - Bavinck pointed to other central notions that needed to be taken account of, e.g., the Kingdom of God - it also presupposed the automatic working of the covenant, as a result of which everything became "too flat, too cheap, too external." A sixth characteristic of this way of thinking was the totalitarian emphasis it placed on Christian action within Christian circles, which led believers to the point where they no longer wanted to have anything to do with the surrounding world. The expression 'evangelistic address' was used solely as a term of abuse for a sermon bereft of content. And the final mark of the new thinking was the attitude toward culture. The concept of common grace fell into discredit and the advocates of this way of thought were ever less inclined "to listen appreciatively to what others [outside the church] have thought and said."

According to Bavinck all of this had engendered an inner crisis in people's hearts and lives, which, coupled with the formation of opposing groups, could prove fatal to the future of the church. Without really knowing where the theological fronts lay, people, wanting to "speak strong words and do bold deeds," were contending with each other in a manner that violated "the bounds of circumspection and justice." To Bavinck's mind the disagreements between leading theologians were only differences of accent, and the whole struggle had "something unreal" about it. In his opinion people were fighting against shadows and chimeras, whereas there was in deepest essence only one enemy, namely, "that we sometimes have so little understanding of and so little trust in each other, so little love for one another." Continuing along this way would inevitably lead to "dissension, schism and misery," and would be totally irresponsible, particularly in view of the darkness of the times and the task the church would face after the war.

Bavinck ended his talk with an appeal to end the encouragement of factionalism, to work for the restoration of mutual trust, to seek the inner calm prerequisite to brotherly discourse, to assume a humble listening stance toward the other, and to counter perpetrated injustice with forgiveness. The striking closing sentences of the speech were clearly inspired by Bavinck's mission-mindedness.

> There is one thing that lives as ardent wish and fervent plea in my heart and in the heart of many others in our churches, and that is that you who will soon be called to the ministry will be able to withstand the sucking power of all the controversy going on in our churches at the moment. . . . Be humble and childlike, hold fast to God's Word. Always be ready to learn from the other, provided he stands in the same faith that forms the foundation of your life. May our almighty God and Father, who has called us in Jesus Christ and made us children of His marvelous Kingdom, keep us together by faith and mutual love. May He teach us all, may He teach His Church everywhere not to dissipate her strength by dissension and disagreement but to turn firmly and decisively to the outside world with the message of redemption, with the gospel of salvation.

This talk made a deep impression on the students, one of whom wrote later: "A probing, a warm and emotional appeal was made to us. . . . Was it not indeed so that we within our 'little church' in a 'big world' were getting all worked up about trifling matters, futilities?"[62] And yet the Student Union, after further discussion with Bavinck, was not prepared to back publication of the speech: no one doubted Bavinck's good intentions, but neither was there any willingness to bury

---

[62] J. Kamphuis, 31.

the hatchet without further ado.[63] Schilder, who had been sent a report of the speech at the secret address where he was living at the time, contested Bavinck's argumentation at every point.[64] The tone of Schilder's written reaction to Bavinck was very sharp. He stated, for example, that he considered Bavinck's call for "brotherly dialogue" to be mere eyewash at that stage of the controversy. Moreover, he accused Bavinck of being the one who lacked a sense of *ecclesia*, proven by the fact that he, Bavinck, had co-authored a book with theologians who undermined the Reformed concept of the church.[65] Though one would not wish to call Schilder's sincerity into question, it is quite clear that he misjudged Bavinck's deepest intentions. As far as is known, Bavinck did not reply to Schilder's letter, perhaps in the realization that every word would only deepen the conflict.

On May 5, 1945 the Netherlands was liberated from the Germans by the allied forces. On the following Sunday, May 8, Bavinck officiated at a packed service in one of the largest churches in Utrecht, preaching a sermon on I Timothy 1:17: "Now to the King eternal, immortal, invisible, the only God, be honor and glory forever and ever. Amen." He wrote in his diary concerning this text and church service: "[Those words] lived in our hearts. The congregation was deeply thankful and full of joy. And I found it wonderful that God gave me the opportunity to close off these hard and difficult years in this way."[66]

1.1.3. The Post-War Years

After the capitulation of Japan on August 18, 1945, the RCN sought ways to return to its mission fields in Central Java and Sumba as quickly as possible. During the war years a pool of potential missionary workers had been formed who could now be sent out. Bavinck was very closely involved in this whole matter. On the day the Japanese capitulated he wrote a brochure, entitled, *De zending nu!* (Mission Now!),[67] in which he delineated the expected difficulties and new possibilities for mission in Indonesia. At that point it was not yet clear, he wrote, how the young indigenous churches in that land had weathered the Japanese occupation. Not only had contact with the 'mother church' been broken, but also all the missionaries in

---

[63] *Ibid.*, 32.

[64] Cf. *ibid.*, 39-58, which contains the complete text of Schilder's reaction, accompanied by a few explanatory notes by Kamphuis.

[65] Of the publications Bavinck wrote in collaboration with others (see the rubric 'Co-authored works' in the bibliography), Schilder was no doubt referring to *Salve Rex* (1941).

[66] *Herinneringen aan het laatste oorlogsjaar 1944-1945*, 152.

[67] In this brochure Bavinck avouches the continuing significance of a celebrated speech A. Kuyper gave on mission in 1890, though at the same time stating that "our opinions with respect to some points have changed somewhat." He was referring here particularly to what he viewed as Kuyper's too optimistic assessment and too impersonal approach to Islam. See for a succinct review of this matter H. Mintjes, 153-155.

the field had been interned. Would the 'younger churches' prove to have been up to the situation or would it turn out that they had fallen into ecclesiastical disorder and had succumbed to the temptation of syncretistic dilution of the gospel? Had the unification forced on the Protestant churches by the Japanese occupational authorities had a positive or negative effect on Indonesian church life? Which churches would need the most help and what aid would be required first? Bavinck then concludes: "We would be wise to expect to see a great deal of confusion and disruption in our mission fields. And precisely because of that, it is of the highest importance that we act with great alacrity."[68]

But how were the churches to act? The RCN Synod came to the conclusion, in accordance with the joint advice of the Committee on Preparatory Training and the RCN Mission Deputies, that it was necessary under these unusual circumstances to depart from existing missionary policy. Because it was not clear which area was in the greatest need, it was considered undesirable to have the various sending churches dispatch missionaries separately to the fields for which they bore responsibility. It was decided instead to send the ten trained and waiting missionary pastors out as a group under the temporary supervision of the post-war Commission for the Reconstruction of the Chief Work of Mission.[69] That this deviation from customary procedure did not bother Bavinck can be seen from the following quotation: "I consider it a boon that under the pressure of necessity we were able, in the form of a temporary measure, to make this transition to [a far greater degree of missionary centralization]."[70] In fact, he viewed the development and changes taking place as a blessing from God.

> Let us not forget that the task for which these men and women are girding up their loins is a wondrously beautiful thing. People are only very seldom offered the opportunity to begin over. This has always held for mission, too, right throughout its history: only very seldom has the Church been afforded the chance to begin its work anew. But that is exactly the possibility God is granting us now.... We are being given the chance to avoid the mistakes we have come to recognize in our past work, to determine our method of operation afresh free from the hindrances imposed by tradition.[71]

The latter allusion to tradition bore reference especially to the changing political relationship between the Netherlands and what was shortly to become Indonesia, a shift away from the colonial linkage of the two countries that was to have an effect at the level of the church as well. The strong movement toward independence that

---

[68]"De zending nu!," 2.

[69]This commission was disbanded in 1950, when responsibility for the 'main service' of mission was returned to the various sending churches, while 'auxiliary missionary services,' e.g., education and medical care, were provided for and supervised corporately by a new Council of Cooperation set up for this purpose. Cf. H. Baas, 14.

[70]"De zending nu!," 4.

[71]*Ibid.*, 5.

had been taking shape in the Dutch East Indies implied that mission should consist, "more strongly than was earlier the case," of " teamwork and open-hearted cooperation with our churches in the mission field."[72]

There was also an attempt made at this time to send out ten medical doctors and fifteen nurses in the short term, but in initiatives of this nature the churches were bound by post-war Dutch government policy and therefore were not free to act on their own: missionary doctors and nursing staff could only be sent out via the Dutch Indies Civil Administration, and were also assigned their specific task and place of work by this government authority. The dispatch of teachers to Indonesia was temporarily halted by the Dutch government because it wanted first to effect a reorganization of the whole educational system there.[73] Although Bavinck foresaw many difficulties arising from the new situation, particularly the potential threat to missionary work that would be posed by the overwhelmingly large Islamic presence in the new Indonesian government that was to be formed, he nevertheless laid stress on the positive missionary challenge presented by all of these recent developments:

> It [mission] must conduct its work in such a way that no one will want to see it cease to exist. . . . The independence of Indonesia requires one thing from mission: that everything it undertakes from now on must be of such a nature that the Indonesian world will voluntarily request its services. Anything less than this will not suffice. If our missionary work does not measure up to this criterion, it will become impossible within a few years time.[74]

Bavinck's whole approach to these new post-war and nearly post-colonial circumstances was thoroughly informed by a harmony of realism and conviction of faith.

In 1946 Bavinck and two colleagues, F.L. Bakker and A. Pos, were commissioned by the synod of the Reformed Churches in the Netherlands to make a trip to Indonesia the following year for purposes of deliberation with the churches that had come into existence as a result of RCN missionary activities.[75] In his report on the gathering they organized, the so-called Kwitang Conference,[76] Bavinck wrote that the distrust among the young Javanese churches against new forms of Western domination appeared to be much greater than was at first expected: it was "an

---

[72]*Ibid.*, 7.

[73]*Ibid.*

[74]*Ibid.*

[75]Cf. *HZB*, 44 (1946), 3, and *HZB*, 45 (1947), 11.

[76]This conference, held in Kwitang church in Batavia (Jakarta), took place from May 19-24, 1947. Some of the attending Javanese churches had roots in the mission of the RCN and others in that of the NRC, but they had been officially cooperating with each other since May 1946. Cf. K.J. Brouwer, 56-57. For more detailed information on this gathering see J. Verkuyl, *Gedenken en verwachten*, passim, and J.C. Gilhuis, *Ecclesiocentrische aspecten van het zendingswerk*, passim.

almost painful revelation." Gradually trust was completely restored, however, due to the fact that "we argued emphatically at every turn that our only concern was with the coming of the Kingdom of Jesus Christ."[77] In the prayer meeting before the conference Bavinck had already set this tone by speaking on the second petition of the Lord's Prayer, 'Thy Kingdom Come.'[78] Verkuyl writes: "Without any doubt this conference was stamped particularly by the views of the Central-Javanese pastor B. Probowinoto and those of . . . J.H. Bavinck."[79]

Bavinck's report was deliberated at length at the RCN synod of 1948. After a deep-going, intense discussion,[80] synod unanimously accepted the basic ideas formulated by the Javanese churches that missionary work from now on would rest mainly with the Indonesian churches and that they would carry out this task in close cooperation with other Javanese- and Malaysian-speaking churches.[81] Foreign churches would be allocated 'only' an assisting role in mission. This new relationship would bear the character of 'partnership in obedience,' a term that figured strongly at the 1947 International Missionary Conference held in Whitby, Canada. Practically speaking, this meant that the sending churches in the Netherlands would enter into cooperative agreements with the sending churches in Indonesia. Bavinck demonstrated that the decision that had been taken was completely in line with the thinking of the 1896 RCN Synod of Middelburg, at which one of the principles of missionary work was formulated as follows:

Since every local church, also those in Java, is complete in itself and stands directly under King Jesus, the sending church, as mother church, may support and advise but may never take it upon itself to exercise authority over such a church in Java. The Javanese Church stands in a relation of coordination with us and is not placed in a position of subordination to us.[82]

The 1948 synod of the Javanese Churches in Magelang, which Bavinck also attended, adopted the report of the Kwitang conference. Bavinck wrote later about this: "That such a thing was possible in these difficult and confusing times is something for which we can give God hearty thanks."[83] In Bavinck's case such expressions were more than pious slogans. It was in his nature not to approach

---

[77]*HZB*, 45 (1947), 40-42.

[78]*HZB*, 46 (1948), 26.

[79]*Gedenken en verwachten*, 157.

[80]H.N. Ridderbos reported that Bavinck was very deeply involved in this discussion since he felt that there was so much at stake; cf. "In memoriam prof. dr. J.H. Bavinck," 2.

[81]*HZB*, 46 (1948), 56-58.

[82]*HZB*, 46 (1948), 21-22.

[83]*HZB*, 47 (1949), 24-25.

these developments only objectively but also spiritually.[84] A striking example of this is an article that he wrote in connection with the fact that regular mission work had been at a standstill for ten years.

> Ten years! Sometimes I'm troubled by the question of why God has bound our hands for so long. Did he want to humble us in the presence of His majesty? Did He want to teach us to recognize what a great blessing it is that He still wants to use us despite our personal and ecclesiastical sins? Does He want to teach us to be thankful, grateful in a childlike way for every day that we may continue to work in His service? . . . Does He wish to teach us to pray daily more earnestly than we perhaps have in the past? And is it His purpose to teach us to do our work from now on in the conviction of His miraculous power? . . . In God's presence we can only speak stumblingly about these things. But if it happens, if the bonds that restrained our hands for ten years are broken, what a great thing that would be! That would constitute more than an opportunity for organizing and building as we did in the past. It would be a gracious gift of God, a gift that we forfeited by our sinfulness. . . . How will we be able to resume the work in a worthy manner? This will be possible only if we are willing to receive this great task from His hand in the deep consciousness of our sinfulness and weakness but also with intense gratitude and childlike trust.[85]

The question of the independence of the indigenous churches was closely tied to the conservative views of the Anti-Revolutionary Party (ARP)[86] on Dutch colonial policy. Although Bavinck did not involve himself directly in political affairs, he did consistently offer resistence to this conservative bent of the AR A striking example of Bavinck's progressive views is displayed in a letter he wrote to one of his friends, J. van Baal, who was also in disagreement with the politics of the ARP and had been asked by this party to become a candidate for parliament in 1951. Van Baal asked Bavinck for advice on this matter and the latter wrote in reply: "Do you know who the other candidates are? . . . Are they young fellows who are somewhat progressive? . . . Or are they generally older figures once again?"[87] Meanwhile, he constantly tried to explain that the course the ARP was pursuing was biblically untenable and practically unfeasible. According to J. Verkuyl, Bavinck, both in his period as missionary pastor in Surakarta and as teacher at the Theological Seminary in Jogjakarta as well as later in South Africa, consistently pointed, in his mild manner, to the indefensibility of the notion of colonial guardianship as guide for Western policy with respect to lands in other

---

[84]Cf. J. van den Berg, "Prof. Bavinck 40 jaar in het ambt."

[85]*HZB*, 47 (1949), 131-132.

[86]This was the Christian political party associated with the RCN at that time.

[87]J. van Baal, 278-280.

parts of the world.[88] Bavinck also wrote the introduction to a booklet[89] authored by the missionary pastor H. van den Brink, published with the approval of fourteen of his colleagues, in which Van den Brink raised strong objections to the continuation of Dutch colonialism.[90] By virtue of his calm and wise method of argumentation,[91] whereby he invariably took account of the fact that most people were not personally aware of the sensitive relationships obtaining in Indonesia, he was able to convince many of the correctness of his position, even in this period of sharp differences of opinion on missionary and colonial policy.[92] Nor did his knowledge and insight remain unremarked in broader circles. He was invited to be an advisor at the Round-Table Conference where the question of the independence of Indonesia was discussed at government level.[93]

Bavinck continued to be involved in developments at home as well as in those overseas, viewing them as being closely related to each other. Especially dear to his heart was the establishment of the Center for Mission. He concluded his brochure, *De zending nu!*, with an appeal to church members to contribute loyally to the realization of this center. "For," he wrote, "mission will demand a great deal of our attention in the coming years."[94]

> Our theologians, including those who remain here, will have to reflect more on the large, important questions raised in the mission field. Our doctors, teachers, nurses, in fact, all of the members of our congregations will have to acquire an ever clearer view of missionary activity as a great work in which we are privileged to engage in the name of our Lord Jesus Christ at this precarious juncture of world history. We need to stand as one man behind our missionary enterprise. The gift in the collection plate is not enough; missionary work demands your devoted concern, *which can only be truly informed after the*

---

[88]Cf. "De spanning tussen westers imperialisme en kolonialisme en zending in het tijdperk van de 'ethische koloniale politiek,' " 206.

[89]*Een eisch van recht*, 1947.

[90]Cf. J. Stellingwerf, 353.

[91]Cf. J. Verkuyl, *Gedenken en verwachten*, 142-143, where he relates that once at a pastors' conference where he and Bavinck had shared the platform, the chairman of the meeting, in his closing remarks, likened their differing styles of political and ecclesiastical criticism to the difference between wool(Verkuyl) and silk (Bavinck), a jacket and a jacquet. In a personal conversation Verkuyl indicated to me that this strong side of Bavinck was also his vulnerable side: his modesty and delicacy sometimes led to a weakening of his argument.

[92]Cf. J.A. Boersema, 69.

[93]Cf. "J.H. Bavinck: bekende zendingsman en bij velen geliefd auteur," *Trouw* (June 24, 1964).

[94]"De zending nu!," 8.

Center for Mission has come into existence.[95]
After searching for a long time in vain, Richters and Bavinck finally found a suitable building for the Center for Mission in the town of Baarn, where it was officially opened on February 20, 1946. On that occasion Richters said: "No one could have imagined that professor Bavinck's plans would be realized so quickly. This center is a witness to unswerving faith in the Kingdom of Jesus Christ."[96] Bavinck took up residence in Baarn and became deeply involved in the work of the Center, contributing in particular to the training of missionary pastors[97] and to the missionary conferences organized for church members.[98] On the one hand, the center met a clear need as location for missionary training and source of information, but on the other, it was viewed negatively by many congregations of the Reformed Churches in the Netherlands because it was inexactly identified with the advocates of Indonesian independence, which was opposed by the ARP and therefore the majority of RCN members. It was only after the transfer of sovereignty to Indonesia in 1949 that a change came about in this attitude.[99] From the tenor of the special issue of the missionary magazine, *Het Zendingsblad,* published on the occasion of the tenth anniversary of the founding of the Training Center in Baarn, it is apparent that the new line of thinking, which the Center had helped bring about, had been broadly accepted by the churches. [100]

In the meantime Bavinck's work had taken on such extensive proportions that he needed assistance, which came in the person of H.A. Wiersinga, who had served the RCN mission in Indonesia for years. Wiersinga was appointed by the RCN synod in 1946 to assume all of Bavinck's tasks at the center that did not belong specifically to his academic work, notably, leadership of courses and conferences, provision of advice to the churches, and maintenance of contact with other missionary bodies.[101]

After the war, contacts between the RCN and other churches at both the national and international level were gradually expanded. Bavinck was concerned to stimulate this development, not only because he himself was ecumenically minded but also because he was convinced that the church is ecumenical in its very

---

[95] *Ibid.*; the italics are Bavinck's.

[96] H. Baas, 10.

[97] Beginning in 1956 this educational facility was given the name 'missionary seminary' to emphasize the fact that it offered a professional training program; cf. H. Baas, 16. In 1951 Bavinck also offered a course for interested young ministers, who—though not yet called as missionaries—formed a potential future missionary pool.

[98] In the announcements of these missionary conferences in *Het Zendingsblad* Bavinck is consistently named as keynote speaker.

[99] Cf. H. Baas, 10-11.

[100] Cf. J.H. Bavinck, *HZB*, 54 (1956), 26.

[101] Cf. *HZB*, 44 (1946), 5.

essence.[102] In 1946 the RCN joined the Dutch Missionary Council (DMC) and by virtue of this also became affiliated to the International Missionary Council (IMC).[103] In that same year Richters was instructed by synod to seek direct contact on its behalf with missionary agencies in other countries.[104] In addition, a permanent RCN delegate, in the person of S.C. Graaf van Randwijck, was appointed to the meetings of the IMC, and in 1947 J. Blauw, likewise a member of the RCN, was named general secretary of the DMC.[105] Though Bavinck himself had no official position in the DMC, he was on the editorial board of its missionary journal, *De Heerbaan* (The Highway of the Lord), which commenced publication in 1948 as replacement of two earlier missionary periodicals.[106] Further, Bavinck participated as "consultant member" in a gathering of the IMC in the Dutch town of Oegstgeest in 1948, and he also took active part in the missionary conferences organized by the DMC.[107]

In 1947 the RCN also took part in the inaugural meeting of the Reformed Ecumenical Synod (RES) in Grand Rapids, Michigan, at which various American, South African and West European Reformed churches were represented. Bavinck warmly supported the adoption of a proposal at this gathering to set up an international cooperative committee for purposes of studying the implications of Reformed principles for mission and discovering ways of disseminating these principles through mission. Once back home, he made a passionate plea for this idea and delineated the benefits of such a collective effort: both church and mission would greatly gain from joint reflection on topical missiological questions and from the mutual sharing of services, experiences and strengths.[108] The second assembly of the RES, held in Amsterdam in 1949, instituted the International Reformed Missionary Council, which, again, was very warmly endorsed by Bavinck.[109] Bavinck was appointed delegate to this council,[110] in connection with which he

---

[102]Cf. *IZW*, 207.

[103]The RCN synod of 1946 decided on full membership in the DMC especially with a view to association with the IMC and on the condition that, *inter alia*, it would not be expected to subscribe to any ecumenical confessional statement that ran contrary to it's own confessional symbols; cf. *HZB*, 44 (1946), 3.

[104]Cf. *HZB*, 45 (1947), 67, 121 where Richters reports on his visits to Basel and London and Bavinck's to North America.

[105]Cf. *HZB*, 45 (1947), 29.

[106]Cf. *HZB*, 46 (1948), 45-46.

[107]Cf. *ibid.*, 109.

[108]Cf. *ibid.*, 6-7.

[109]*HZB*, 47 (1949), 147-148.

[110]Cf. *HZB*, 48 (1950), 30.

attended the 1950 synod of the Christian Reformed Church in Grand Rapids for purposes of discussing the takeover of a mission field in Indonesia,[111] and visited South Africa for a few months in 1952 to help a sister Reformed church there in its efforts to build up and expand its missionary work.[112]

In 1948 the World Council of Churches (WCC) was founded in Amsterdam. Various RCN synods from 1930 onwards had rejected participation in the ecumenical movement and, later, membership of the WCC because it was feared that this movement and new council were pursuing unity at the cost of truth.[113] Though Bavinck recognized the right of people to entertain this fear, he very much regretted these synodical vetoes. To him, the Basis formulated and adopted at the first assembly of the WCC in Amsterdam—namely, "The World Council of Churches is a fellowship of churches which confess the Lord Jesus Christ as God and Savior according to the Scriptures"[114]—justified membership in this ecumenical body. Moreover, official participation in the WCC would make it possible for the RCN to render a positive contribution to the understanding of truth at the global-church level. Finally, it would be irresponsible to ignore this ecumenical calling, he argued, because of the strong and long-lasting influence such international gatherings have on the thinking and life of the churches throughout the world.[115]

Despite his position as leading RCN authority in the area of mission, Bavinck remained deeply humble, as strikingly witnessed by the words he penned in 1953 on the occasion of the 50th anniversary of the missionary magazine, *Het Zendingsblad*:

There [in the mission field] there are no 'sirs' and 'madams.' In fact, we all stand there as small children involved in that great, unfathomable work of God, being privileged to serve for a time as the means whereby He accomplishes his miracles of salvation.... There you only have ... feeling[s] of weakness, of extreme smallness and powerlessness, and reverence for the miracles wrought by God—astonishingly through us.[116]

Following a long, wasting illness, Bavinck's wife, Trientje, died on January 12, 1953, which was an unspeakable loss for him and their children. Her close interest in all of Bavinck's work had been a great support to him throughout the years. Her character was stamped by sobriety, openness and warmth, and her living relationship to Christ was the mainspring of her life, providing her with

---

[111]This information appears in an undated report of the General Mission Deputies of the RCN.

[112]Cf. *HZB*, 50 (1952), 110.

[113]Cf. A. Wind, *Zending en oecumene in de twintigste eeuw*, Part I, 208-210.

[114]Cf. M. Kinnamon and B.E. Cope, 4, 469.

[115]Cf. "De vergadering van de Wereldraad van Kerken," 276.

[116]*HZB*, 51 (1953), 3-4.

comfort in her death. After a number of years of loneliness Bavinck married his second wife, Fennechine van der Vegt, on April 11, 1956.

1.2. Appointment as Professor of Practical Theology (1954-1964)

Finally, his praxis-oriented approach and psychological insight made him a natural choice for appointment to the position of professor of Practical Theology at the Free University in Amsterdam in 1954, in which capacity, however, he continued to teach missiology in addition to the various new disciplines for which he had assumed responsibility.

Bavinck was appointed professor of practical theology at the Free University in Amsterdam, beginning on January 1, 1954.[117] This appointment was made on both substantial and practical grounds: Bavinck possessed a high degree of religious-psychological insight and expertise combined with homiletic and pastoral qualities.[118] He accepted this position because, at his age, he was beginning to find the constant travel between Amsterdam, Kampen and Baarn too taxing.[119] Bavinck continued to teach missiology in Amsterdam, however, which was not so surprising seeing that in his handbook on missiology he subsumed this discipline under practical theology.[120] His acceptance of this appointment resulted in the termination of his work in Kampen, although he did not take official leave from the theological seminary there until October 5, 1956, after his successor had been appointed.[121] The subject of his farewell lecture was *Het evangelie en het mystiek levensgevoel* (The Gospel and the Mystical Sense of Life),[122] which thus dealt with the same theme as his inaugural address seventeen years earlier, namely, the confrontation of the Christian faith with non-Christian religions. The words spoken at his farewell pointed to the kind of professor he was. The senior member of the seminary board of trustees said in his speech: "What you taught was never only cerebral but always cordial; you always projected warmth."[123] And the praetor of the student union, *Fides Quaerens Intellectum*, remarked strikingly: "You taught us

---

[117]A. Pos, "Leven en werk van Dr. Johan Herman Bavinck ," 17, incorrectly reports 1955 as the year of Bavinck's appointment.

[118]Cf. J. van den Berg, "The Legacy of Johan Herman Bavinck," 172.

[119]Cf. *HZB*, 54 (1956), 166-167.

[120]Cf. *IZW*, 15-16(cf. *ISM*, xx), where Bavinck argues that the main theme of missiology is the divine calling to service (*diakonia*) of the church in the world and that this field of study therefore must be reckoned as belonging to the diaconal disciplines of theology.

[121]Cf. *HZB*, 52 (1954), 30. H. Bergema and J. Verkuyl had been nominated for this position; of these two the RCN synod of 1955 chose the former by majority vote; cf. *HZB*, 53 (1955), 171-173.

[122]This lecture was published in *DHB*, 9 (1956), 157-165.

[123]Cf. *De Bazuin*, 99 (1956).

not only by a certain way of thinking and studying but also by a certain way of life."[124]

This new phase in Bavinck's life was marked not so much by a change of interest as by the addition of new interests.[125] A. Pos wrote in this regard:

Twice we saw Bavinck switch to a new area of investigation without permanently abandoning the old one. The publication of his *Inleiding in de zielkunde* [Introduction to Psychology] in 1926 constituted the high point and the end point of his direct academic reflection in this field, though the results of this research continued to play an important, perhaps we should even say dominant, role in his practical and academic missionary activities. And the publication of his *Inleiding in de zendingswetenschap* [Introduction to the Science of Mission] in 1954 was the crown of his professorship in mission, but the findings of this study continued to influence his work in practical theology. It was, thus, both psychology and missiology that qualified him for this new task.[126]

In his new position Bavinck taught homiletics, poimenics (pastoral theology and psychology) and evangelism. His lectures, delivered with love and dedication, were well attended and made an unforgettable impression on many of his students. The sermon sketches he offered in class were diligently copied down and were a great inspiration to many a future preacher.[127] The lecture notes of one of his courses were posthumously published in 1967 under the title, *De mens van nu* (Contemporary Man). This volume clearly betrays the psychological and missiological dimensions of his work: in it he attempts to analyze modern man in the context of his time in order to arrive at a more effective preaching of the gospel and exercise of pastoral care. He clearly recognized that also within his own church confessional faith was dwindling; the experience of sin and grace, the practice of leading a Christian life in the world, eschatological orientation, in short, life lived in and according to the Holy Spirit was on the wane. Notably, however, even here he does not conclude in a minor key but broaches a positive challenge: "With regard to all of these things, we have a wonderful calling to rescue people from the various ideas and practices that have grown up in the last century."[128] He urged his students to take up this challenge in the same way he had always tried to do that: "[in seeking to fulfill our calling] we must never lose sight of the Holy Spirit and we must always

---

[124]*Ibid.*

[125]Cf. J. van den Berg, "De wetenschappelijke arbeid van Professor Dr. Johan Herman Bavinck," 40.

[126]A. Pos, "Leven en werk van Dr. Johan Herman Bavinck," 17.

[127]This was corroborated in an interview I had with Bavinck's nephew, H.J. Bavinck, who himself attended his uncle's classes.

[128]*DMN*, 74-75.

speak from the Scriptures. Only then will we be speaking in the name of God."[129] But Bavinck's voice also reached a larger public beyond the classroom by means of the series of radio talks he gave in 1959 and again in 1962.

In the past Bavinck had interpreted missionary issues for the local churches; now he did the same thing in terms of practical theology, publishing several articles during these years in an educational magazine for church elders and deacons. For all that, the 'teacher' remained a 'shepherd' to the very end. For a number of years he published concise meditative articles in *Gereformeerd Weekblad*, a popular Reformed weekly. The following quotation from the Foreword to the bound edition of these articles typifies both writer and content.

> It was often not easy for me to compose these articles. Yet, I am
> thankful that I was able to do this. This exercise constituted a
> learning experience by which God wanted to show me that it is
> possible to read the Bible in such a way that the most ordinary,
> daily things of life are called up at every turn and, conversely,
> that it is possible to live life in such a way that we are continually
> cast back on the Bible.[130]

In the same key he gave regular short talks on the Dutch-language World Service.[131] On the matter of the contemporary chilling of spiritual life, he wrote, in addition to various articles,[132] a discerning book entitled, *Ik geloof in de Heilige Geest* (I Believe in the Holy Spirit, 1963). In this work he prophetically pointed to the cultural reversal whereby God was becoming the great Absent One, which constituted a religious crisis affecting the life of the church as well. Actually, Bavinck recognized this development much earlier, when it was still largely unseen. In a 1948 publication, he stated the following.

> I would like to see the total number of people who in one year
> are won for Jesus and His church by means of the activity of our
> evangelization committees and all the other work of the church.
> And if then, in comparison with that, we could see the number of
> those who in one year are attracted by the temptations of the
> world, who turn their backs on Jesus Christ, I fear that we would
> have reason to be deeply ashamed.[133]

And in 1952 he wrote: "There is such a thing as devotional practice and on that point we are becoming very lax."[134] He wrestled with the emerging a-religious spirit of the times in which science and technology were given the last word.

Do not let God sink completely beneath the horizon of our

---

[129] *Ibid.*, 75.

[130] *FF*, 5.

[131] These collected talks were published in 1986 under the title, *Stille tijd in vrije tijd.*

[132] Cf. *GW*, 11 (1956), 305, 314, 321, 329.

[133] *OKZK*, 37.

[134] "Mystiek dus niet—wat dan wel?" *GW*, 6 (1952), 361.

human knowledge and abilities! Please let us cling to the faith that God is still present, that you can feel him, that his miraculous power can renew and fill our lives! Let us stop living so far 'below our means'. . . . Sensual things, our technological culture, our prosperity and our skills, that whole big powerful block of excessive expertise and capability and at the same time anxiety and madness that we call our modern world, penetrates our entire existence with such overwhelming force, nestles so deeply in all the chambers of our heart, that we become utterly bewildered. Can nothing be done about this? . . . Or is it possible through the Holy Spirit to apprehend what Job perceived many centuries ago when he said: "My ears had heard of you but now my eyes have seen you" [Job 42:5]? Is it still possible, to partake of God, to be, as it were, completely immersed in him?[135]

As a true shepherd, he led God's flock through the dark valley of this crisis with the staff of God's Word. His last book, *Wij worden geroepen* (We Are Called, 1964), consisting of a collection of meditations, illustrates this pastoral concern. This work clearly evinces the passion which filled him throughout his entire life: namely, the deep desire to interpret the message of scripture to his listeners and readers in as intelligible and relevant a way as possible.

Finally, it should be mentioned that he was productive in another area as well. Together with a colleague, he edited a new Dutch-language annotated Bible,[136] which came out in 1957 and in which he himself wrote the explanatory notes to Titus and Philemon and the pastoral letters of Paul to Timothy.

2. Continuing Missionary and Other Activities

In addition to his lectures on missiology, Bavinck remained active in other ways in the area of mission, though the accent had shifted. He became less directly concerned with denominational missionary activities, while increasing his contacts at the international level. Though he continued to be involved in the affairs of the missionary seminary in Baarn in his capacity as president of its board of trustees, he seldom taught there anymore.[137] His intense interest in everyday missionary practice on the field also decreased, and after 1954 he no longer had much contact with missionaries on home leave.[138] On the other hand, he carried on as advisor

---

[135]*OKZK*, 9.

[136]*Bijbel in de nieuwe vertaling met verklarende aantekeningen.*

[137]According to a letter from Richters to Bavinck, dated April 24, 1959, Bavinck's name no longer appeared on the class roster in Baarn.

[138]This was related to me by A.G. Honig, who added that he, and others with him, could not understand this because it was so unlike Bavinck. The following factors may have played a role here: Bavinck's advancing age, the death of his first wife, his increasing international orientation, a withdrawal in favor of others who were officially responsible for maintaining contact with workers on furlough.

to synod on missionary matters and, with a view to that work, saw to it that he was kept informed about important developments on the mission fields of the RCN.[139]

Bavinck's increasing international reputation and invitations from overseas churches and academic institutions were due largely to the publication of some of his works in English. A nice example of this growing transcontinental appreciation for Bavinck can be found in a letter that N.E. Christy of the United Presbyterian Church of the USA wrote to the Secretary of the Commission on Ecumenical Mission and Relations of the IMC concerning Bavinck's translated books, *The Impact of Christianity on the Non-Christian World* and *An Introduction to the Science of Missions.*

> Having read most of the first of these books, I suggest that the Commission consider making it more widely available to its missionaries and fraternal workers. Perhaps it could be used in The Study Fellowship, if it is not already being used there.[140]

In addition to the lectures he gave in America and South Africa referred to earlier, he visited a number of churches in Ceylon and India in 1955,[141] and in that same year took part, at the request of the IMC, in a meeting of Muslim and Christian academicians in Tunis, held with a view to achieving a higher degree of mutual understanding between the two religions they represented. Further, he paid a three-week working visit to Surinam in 1960 - a trip having no specific missionary significance but undertaken as part of a larger review of government policy in the remaining Dutch colonies - on the basis of which he wrote a broadly appreciated popular comparative study of Hindustani and Western European cultural expressions in that land.[142] During his several visits to South Africa in the fifties and early sixties Bavinck made in-depth studies of existing race relations and the system of apartheid, which he rejected both in light of the biblical message and from the perspective of mission. Thanks to his integrity, his upright speech and demeanor, whites in South Africa were far more willing to listen to his criticism than to that of many other contemporary commentators.

In these years, during which, as already mentioned above, he also taught evangelism, Bavinck became closely associated with the evangelization work of his denomination, becoming a trustee of the Center for Evangelism, which was also located in Baarn. He was especially active in this center's Committee on Questions of Human Existence (*Comité Levensvragen*), in which he had already been involved before the war. Many of the lecture series and discussion groups organized by local RCN evangelism committees, in the attempt to reach unchurched intellectuals with

---

[139]Cf., e.g., a letter from Bavinck to Richters, dated September 2, 1960, in which Bavinck requests Richters to keep him posted on missionary developments.

[140]Cited in a letter from Richters to Bavinck, dated June 13, 1961.

[141]Bavinck wrote a report on this visit in the form of nine articles in *GW*, 12 (1956).

[142]This report can be found in the J.H. Bavinck Archives in the CHDDP/FUA.

the gospel, featured Bavinck as the main speaker.[143] For a number of years Bavinck was also chairman of a post-war circle of intellectuals who met on a regular basis to reflect on current social topics. Moreover, he continued his activities in the area of one of his old loves, youth work and Christian education, acting, together with G.C. Berkouwer and others, as advisor to the RCN umbrella organization for work among young people,[144] writing many brief, appealing articles in various youth magazines, and serving in the post-war years as president of the board of a Christian high school in the town of Hilversum.

3. Life's End

A serious kidney ailment had been sapping Bavinck's strength during the last two year's of his life, making it necessary for him to limit his activities more and more. This is apparent, for example, from his reply to a letter from Richter proposing that he, Bavinck, compose missionary annotations on the various Lord's Days of the Heidelberg Catechism: "It would involve a huge amount of rigamarole. . . . Let someone younger do it. . . . It doesn't really seem feasible to me."[145] He spent the spring of 1963 in Italy for health reasons,[146] and the next year, just before the 25th anniversary of his appointment as professor, he was admitted to hospital in Amsterdam, where he fell asleep in Christ on June 23, 1964. On June 26 his body was sowed in the earth of Zorgvlied cemetery in Amsterdam to await the day of God's great harvest. At Bavinck's own request it was a sober funeral without speeches or flowers: even in his death, thus, he magnified the *gloria Dei*, the same honor and glorification of God that, in life, he had set as the ultimate goal of mission. At the end of the funeral service the mourners sang a hymn about Jesus Christ who, in the midst of the vast universe in which we find ourselves, will conquer the kingdom of darkness once and for all, the Savior who lives among us and under whose dominion we are blest and free, the Lord to whom glory and power are eternally due—a hymn that reflected the secret of the life of Johan Herman Bavinck.

4. Chapter Summary

The main events and activities of the later years of Bavinck's career can be recapitulated as follows.

    1. As the first RCN professor of missiology he engaged in careful reflection on the principles of mission from the theological and confessional perspectives of his church, giving this Reformed model of mission studies a place

---

[143]These talks were published in the journal, *Horizon*.

[144]Cf. J. Veenhof, "Geschiedenis van theologie en spiritualiteit in de Gereformeerde Kerken," 61-62. This evangelism-minded and ecumenically oriented youth movement sought to develop an independent interpretation of the Reformed position in opposition to traditionalism and intellectualism.

[145]Letter from Bavinck to Richters, dated February 6, 1963.

[146]Cf. letter from Richters to Bavinck, dated April 10, 1963.

both in the Netherlands and elsewhere.

2. His "fascination with the problem of God and the human soul"[147] not only lent a distinct color to his missiological reflection but also equipped him in an outstanding way for the pursuit of studies in the field of practical theology.

3. He was more a passionate thinker and prophetic seer than a systematic theologian: he was a man "of great vision" who thought along "broad lines" and in terms of "the perspective of eternity"; he "repeated what he had learned to see through reflection and passed on what he had received."[148] He attempted to illuminate the depth dimensions of human life and world history in the light of Scripture, which for him was the source of ultimate truth,[149] and tried to communicate his message in clear language to as broad a public as possible. This is clearly reflected in his publications, in which academic rigor and inner conviction go hand in hand.

4. He possessed a naturally open mentality and developed an ecumenical attitude without compromising the truth.[150] Close friendships beyond denominational boundaries, such as that with Hendrik Kraemer, contributed to his openness.[151] He played a pioneer role in his church by helping it to break out of its isolation and enter into ecumenical relationships.

5. His personality was most notably characterized by a harmonious alliance of feeling, intellect and will,[152] and he was, further, keen of mind, modest (which at times caused him to be somewhat too hesitant), sincere, and warm-hearted, all of which imparted a special authority to his words and actions. His prophetic vision was always accompanied by priestly concern.

6. Militant action was completely foreign to him: neither his disposition nor his faith allowed for such practice; moreover, to his mind, such conduct yielded no practical benefit.

7. His character, his religious belief and his theological work all evidence a clear similarity to that of his ancestry. What J. van den Berg wrote with respect to Herman Bavinck can be applied with equal warrant to J.H. Bavinck: "In the

---

[147]J. van den Berg, "The Legacy of J.H. Bavinck," 173.

[148]J.A.C. Rullmann, "Bij het overlijden van prof. dr. J.H. Bavinck."

[149]Cf. H.N. Ridderbos, "In memoriam prof. dr. J.H. Bavinck," 2.

[150]Cf. *ibid.*, where Ridderbos writes with respect to Bavinck's attitude toward truth that he displayed an aversion to "shallow prophets of certainty" but also refused to have anything to do with the current "exhibitionistic crisis of certainty," while at the same time radiating from his own person "something unassailably positive."

[151]Cf. *ibid.*, where Ridderbos remarks that Bavinck's friendships were characterized by his "immaculate respect for the freedom and individuality of the other," and by the fact that "no one ever got the chance to move him to say or do anything with which he disagreed."

[152]According to J. Verkuyl in a letter to the present author, dated February 2, 1990.

tradition of the Reformed Churches the name 'Bavinck' is associated with the catholic and irenic form of Reformed thought."[153]

---

[153]"The Legacy of J.H. Bavinck," 171.

CHAPTER THREE

Content and Context of Bavinck's Missionary Theology

> "Considering that the Church has been actively en-gaged in mission throughout its entire existence. . . , it is surprising that the academic discipline of mission studies took so long to develop." (*IZW*, 5)

1. Introduction

The present chapter, a bridge between the portrayal of Bavinck's life and career in the preceding chapter and the analysis of his missiology in the following ones, deals with a number of matters of an introductory nature: the composition and internal organization of Bavinck's missionary theology, its name, the place assigned to it within theology as a whole, and, finally, its contextual setting. The sequence in which these prolegomena are treated here corresponds with that found in Bavinck's handbook, *Inleiding in de zendingswetenschap* and its translated version, *An Introduction to the Science of Missions*.

2. Missiology Defined

2.1. The Divisions of Missionary Theology

Bavinck distinguished three main areas of concern for missiology: theory of mission, elenctics, and history of mission.[1]

Theory of Mission. Following Gustav Warneck[2], who had become a leading authority in this area, Bavinck gave pride of place to the study and development of missionary theory, consisting of reflection on the biblical foundation, the essence, the approach and the aim or goal of mission. Bavinck took his departure here from the fundamental presupposition that the Bible contains the

---

[1]*IZW*. 16-17. In *ZWN*, which may be considered to be a forerunner of *IZW*, Bavinck employs only two divisions: theory of mission and history of mission.

[2]Cf. G. Warneck, *Evangelische Missionslehre*, Part I.

"complete revelation of God valid for all times and all peoples."[3] This point of departure, which of course can never be anything other than an article of religious conviction, implies that the development of a proper theology of mission can only be achieved through an attentive listening to what God reveals to us about this matter in His Word.

Elenctics. This division of Bavinck's missionary theology concerns itself with the search for a biblically responsible view of and approach to other religions. Citing Walter Holsten,[4] Bavinck argues that any serious missiology must engage in the development of a *theologia religionum* because the church's assessment of other religions is of decisive importance for its perception of the missionary task.[5] And Bavinck heeded his own counsel. Although *IZW* offers less than might be expected by way of theology of religion, the main lines of thought it does present in terms of this field of study were the fruit of thorough inquiry and reflection on Bavinck's part. Earlier works of his that predated the articulation of his missionary theology, such as *CMO, BCNCR*, and especially *RBCG*, as well as the posthumous publication *CBTM* witness to the fact that *theologia religionum* assumed a consistently prominent place throughout the entire period of Bavinck's missiological development.

Missionary History. In *IZW* Bavinck deals with the history of mission as the great work of God in this world, describing it in the light of Scripturally derived missionary principles and with a view to learning lessons from it for contemporary missionary practice.[6] In giving missionary history a place in his missiology Bavinck departed from Gustav Warneck, who viewed that subject as a sector of general church history.[7] Bavinck thought it "better not to treat the history of missions as a subdivision of the history of the church. It is better to regard it as a separate branch of study," first, because "the history of mission requires its own principle of division" which will yield results different from "the usual divisions of the history of the church," and second, because the theology of mission "cannot do without it."[8] These two disciplines go hand in hand, he argued.

> It is perfectly clear that a theory of mission without history of mission can never be fully satisfying. For it is only in history that

---

[3]*OKZK*, 8-9. Bavinck states in no uncertain terms that if that revelation is denied or its truth is relativized, there is no longer any basis or room for Christian mission.

[4]*Das Kerugma und der Mensch*, 55: "Die Religionswissenschaft ist von hier aus gesehen nicht eine Hilfswissenschaft der Missionswissenschaft, sondern sie bedingt die Missionswissenschaft, wie sie von ihr bedingt ist; beide gehören zusammen als ein Ganzes." This was generally accepted by missionary theologians, cf. e.g. K. Hartenstein, *Die Mission als theologisches Problem*, 23 ff.

[5]*IZW*, 17.

[6]Cf. *ibid.*, 280-281.

[7]Cf. G. Warneck, *Evangelische Missionslehre*, I, 35.

[8]*ISM*, 281.

theoretical questions become actualized. Realized in history they do not remain vague and bloodless, but acquire form and become more sharply defined. The converse is also true. The history of mission cannot get along without the theory of mission, for it is from that theory that the former must derive the norms it needs to judge what has taken place in the past. The history of mission can assess historical givens correctly only if it views them from the perspective of Scripture.[9]

And in dealing with the history of mission subsequent to his discussion of the theory of mission, Bavinck rejected the position taken by an earlier Dutch student of mission, François E. Daubanton, who had argued for the opposite sequence on the grounds that this was the only way to ensure the 'scientific quality' of missionary theology.[10] According to Bavinck, Daubanton was "of the opinion that the theory of mission must derive its material entirely from the history of missions and thus [that the former] must literally be built [on the latter]."[11] Bavinck writes that this is an "incontestably mistaken notion."

In a conceptual framework of this nature the function of the history of mission is definitely overestimated. The history of mission is not capable of determining the foundations of mission, it is not even able to provide proper insight into the missionary method that should be employed according to the demands of God's Word.[12]

Though the history of mission should definitely be pursued within the field of missiology, it does not take priority over the theory of mission. Indeed, it occupies a secondary position relative to the latter.

The theory of mission antecedes the history of mission because such [theoretical reflection] leads us back to the Word of God and thereby determines the theological character of [mission studies]. It is only then and only on that basis that the history of mission can be studied as the science of the history of missionary work, the work that God himself has accomplished by means of His church throughout the ages.[13]

For Bavinck there was no sharply drawn line between 'normative' biblical-theological and 'descriptive' historiographical missiological disciplines. To his mind the history of mission never consisted of a mere registration of empirical facts but, as description of God's deeds, always had a theological dimension as well. Bavinck was the first RCN theologian in the Netherlands to try to construct a complete Protestant missiology. Within that framework it is not surprising that in

---

[9]*IZW*, 280-281.

[10]Cf. F.E. Daubanton, *Prolegomena van protestantse zendingswetenschap*, 202.

[11]*IZW*, 279.

[12]*Ibid.*

[13]*Ibid.*, 282

his missiological writings religious reflection on the biblical missionary mandate takes precedence over the more descriptive study of missionary history.

2.2. Bavinck's Name for Missiology

Bavinck subsumed his three divisions of missiology under the term 'science of mission,' which was in common use at that time among both Protestant and Roman Catholic Dutch and German missionary scholars.[14] In the "Introduction" to *IZW* Bavinck explains his choice of nomenclature, specifically against the background of what Abraham Kuyper had written on this matter.

Kuyper had proposed two terms that he deemed suitable as designations for the study of Christian mission: 'apostolics' and 'prosthetics.' He regarded 'apostolics' to be an acceptable term to denote this academic discipline because the Hebrew and Greek words on which it is etymologically based allow for the inclusion of both the work of Christ and that of the prophets, apostles, evangelists and other servants of the church. Nevertheless, Kuyper did not adopt this term because he thought it too suggestive of the office of apostle which no longer exists as such, and because it places a one-sided emphasis on the missionary mandate, whereas the study of mission covers a far broader area. To Kuyper this breadth of concern was far better expressed in the concept of 'prosthetics.' This term was derived from the New Testament verb *prostithenai*: to add to (the community of believers), which Kuyper understood not only in a quantitative but also a qualitative sense. According to Kuyper 'prosthetics' also implied that it is in the nature of the church to radiate a strong attractive force *toward* and exhibit expansive power *in* the world. An additional advantage of this term, he argued, was that it locates mission squarely within the framework of the church, thereby safeguarding it from all forms of individualistic interpretation and action.[15]

In Bavinck's view, however, there was an important objection that could be raised against the term 'prosthetics,' namely, that in the New Testament the verb *prostithenai* always has God as its subject (cf. Acts 2:41, 47 and 11:24). "The obvious meaning [of *prostithenai* in New Testament usage] is that this 'adding' does not lie within human capability," Bavinck writes, "and that it must be seen exclusively as a holy and inscrutable" divine exercise, whereby God acts freely according to His own "good pleasure."[16] Thus, because the New Testament verb to which it harks back refers explicitly to the work of God, Bavinck considered the term 'prosthetics' to be "unsuitable." The study of mission, he stated, consists of systematic reflection on "*our* (italics added) calling to preach the gospel, to announce the name of Christ down through the ages."[17] Bavinck considered the name 'apostolics' to be more appropriate than 'prosthetics.' Kuyper's objection to the former term is untenable, he contended, because the apostolic calling, contrary

---

[14]E.g., the Protestants F.E. Daubanton, H.W. Schomerus and W. Holsten, and the Roman Catholics A.J.M. Mulders and J. Schmidlin.

[15]Cf. A. Kuyper, *Encyclopaedie der heilige Godgeleerdheid*, III, 519.

[16]*Ibid.*

[17]*Ibid.*, 12-13.

to what Kuyper maintained, was not terminated at the death of the apostles but instead was passed on to the church of all ages, as can be adduced from the missionary mandate found in Matthew 28:19-20.[18]   Understood correctly, he avouched, 'apostolics' could "certainly be used" as a designation for mission studies.[19]

In the end, however, Bavinck did not adopt the term 'apostolics' either but, as already indicated above, opted for the appellation 'science of mission.' In support of this choice he employed both biblical and practical arguments. He wrote:

> The church is and remains a 'sent community,' just as Christ is the Sent One of the Father (cf. John 20:21). This means that the sending forth of the church is the object of the science of mission. And it is incumbent on this science to investigate its object in all of its aspects from the perspective of the eternally enduring Word of God.[20]

Some commentators have objected to the term 'science of mission' because it would seem to leave little or no room for the more theological-biblical branches of the discipline and to put too much emphasis on its more empirical components.[21] In the opinion of the present author, however, it is by no means clear that the concept 'science' is inapplicable to theological and biblical reflection. Can scientific knowledge ever exceed evidentiary boundaries? And is the evidence of what is known by faith less valid than that of knowledge gained by science?[22] In any case, a distinction such as this between science and theology, between knowledge and faith is altogether alien to Bavinck, for whom knowledge of God contains the highest degree of objectivity.[23]

This is also clear from his view of the history of mission: "Missionary history is a subdivision of theology. The immediate implication of this is that the history of mission is concerned with God, with what God wishes, with what God has done in the course of the centuries."[24]   Historical description is complete not merely when the facts have been compiled but only when God's activity has been

---

[18]Cf. *IZW*, 11-12.

[19]*Ibid.*, 12.

[20]*Ibid.*, 13. Bavinck already used the term 'science of mission' in his inaugural address, *Christusprediking in de volkerenwereld*, 5.

[21]Cf., e.g., J.A.B. Jongeneel, *Missiologie*, I, 52-54.

[22]This is a point of ongoing discussion both in philosophy and theology but also among those engaged in the exact sciences. It is interesting to note in this connection that a Dutch physicist has recently argued convincingly that the evidence of scientific knowledge and that of the knowledge of faith are equally valid. Cf. A. van den Beukel, *De dingen hebben hun geheim*, 122-131.

[23]Cf. *RBCG*, 110.

[24]*IZW*, 273.

searched for and discovered in these facts.[25] "The history of mission," wrote Bavinck, "displays a motley mixture of motives which compelled [people to engage in] missionary work. . . . But sometimes through all of this confusion shines *The Motive*, the great motive of God. . . . Such is the interesting panorama of the history of mission."[26] In an earlier book Bavinck had already argued this principle in opposition to Hendrik Kraemer, who drew "empirical Christianity" into "the relative sphere of history." Bavinck stated in reaction to this: "Church history is a theological discipline. It is to be distinguished from profane history. It is a powerful attempt to view the history of the church in a meaningful way as the territory of the wrestling of God with His people."[27] As already indicated earlier, in this present study the contemporary term 'missiology' will be used as a synonym for Bavinck's term 'science of mission.'

2.3. The Place of Missiology

In his 1939 inaugural address Bavinck argued not only that missiology should be granted a rightful independent place within the encyclopedia of theological disciplines, but also assigned it a specific location: it belongs to ecclesiology, he averred, which has as its object reflection on the essence and task of the church.[28] At this point Bavinck did not yet support his argumentation theologically but merely contended that the increasing complexity and importance of missionary work made it "completely natural" to give mission studies a regular place in academic theology.[29]

    In *IZW* Bavinck once again discusses the place of missiology within the corpus of theology. Harking back to what he wrote earlier, he states that the science of mission views the church from the special viewpoint of its missionary obligation, which means that this discipline is concerned with "two realities: first, the divine calling and ordination [of the church], and after that, the actual realization of that calling in the course of history."[30] Consequently, there is a close relation between missiology and the theological subjects of exegesis, dogmatics, ethics, homiletics,

---

[25]Cf. *ibid.*, 273-278.

[26] *Ibid.*, 275-276.

[27]*BCNCR*, 93.

[28]*CPVW*, 6. Bavinck adds here that missiology is also related to dogmatics and elenctics because of its confrontation with pseudo religion.

[29]It is interesting to note here that G. Warneck had already advanced a theological ground for this position in his 1877 publication, *Das Studium der Mission auf der Universität* (11): "Der Missionsgedanke ist ein integrirender Bestandtheil der gesammten Heilsoffen-barung in Christo (The concept of mission is an integral part of the entire revelation of salvation in Christ)...." Though Bavinck would undoubtedly have subscribed to this theological argument in 1939, he employed it explicitly for the first time in *IZW*, 13 ff.

[30]*IZW*, 15.

and church history. Missiology does not stand alone, detached and isolated from the rest of theology. On the other hand, however, it may not be melded with or absorbed by the fields of theological study with which it is linked. Bavinck, like Gustav Warneck and Joseph Schmidlin before him,[31] made a case for the independence of missiology. But Bavinck differed from Warneck and Schmidlin in terms of his understanding of the constitution and encyclopedic place of missiology.

As already indicated, Bavinck agrees that the study of mission has to do with the church, but he also pointed out that its specific object is the *missionary calling* of the church, which means first that this area of inquiry constitutes a distinct discipline consisting of the various elements referred to earlier, grouped together to form a single entity. And this position has additional implications for the question as to where missiology fits in the larger body of theology. In the intervening years since he delivered his inaugural address Bavinck had changed his view on this matter. With the passage of time he had come to the conclusion that the study of mission could no longer simply be considered to be a subdivision of ecclesiology. Following in the line of Kuyper,[32] he argued that missiology, consisting as it does of reflection on an aspect of the *diakonia* (ministry) of the church, deserves a rightful place among the several disciplines of practical theology.[33] He parries the objection that this taxonomy does not do justice to the history of mission as subdivision of missiology with the argument that the chief object of the study of mission is and remains the divine calling of the church.[34]

Bavinck criticizes Kuyper, however, for classifying missiology among the didascalic group of practical-theological sub-disciplines, the group concerned with the ministry of the Word. On one side he recognizes the legitimacy of this because the *didaskalia* - education and proclamation - do indeed constitute "the heart of the missionary task." On the other hand, however, he feels that this classification "limits the scope of the missionary task a bit too much."[35] Referring to Warneck,[36] Bavinck points to the complexity of the missionary task: "Mission is emphatically concerned with the ministry of the Word, but on the mission field that Word operates in intimate union with the ministry of mercy and that of church government." He then concludes that mission studies "cannot be classified

---

[31]Cf. Warneck, *Evangelische Missionslehre*, I, 32-44, and Schmidlin, *Einfürhrung in die Missionswissenschaft*, 8-11.

[32]Cf. *Encyclopaedie der heilige Godgeleerdheid*, III, 487.

[33]Cf. *IZW*, 15.

[34]*Ibid.*, 15-16.

[35]*Ibid.*, 16.

[36]Warneck speaks of the office of missionary as "ein kirchliches Kollektivamt," and states further that it is "seiner Natur nach" a "Gesamtministerium, aus welchem sich natur gemäss alle andern Diakonieen entwickelt haben und fort und fort entwickeln," *Evangelische Missionslehre*, I, 249.

exclusively with the didascalic cluster of disciplines within practical theology."[37]

Bavinck was right to claim an independent place for missiology within the whole of theology, and it is clear that it must retain this status if serious academic reflection on the missionary calling and task of the church is to continue in existence. Moreover, in the opinion of the present author, he was also right to classify missiology under practical theology on the grounds that its object of study consists of an aspect of the diaconal activity of the church. And finally, he was right in insisting that the theological and empirical branches of missiology must be kept together and studied in tandem: the sub-disciplines concerned with the description of the *facts* of mission have a distinctive place within the whole of missiology, but it would be passing strange and even unthinkable if at a certain point the *magnolia Dei* weren't recognized in these facts.

3. Bavinck's Missiology in Context

3.1. Introduction

It is apparent from his many publications and lecture notes[38] that Bavinck was extremely well read in the various areas with which he dealt as a missiologist. He was especially well versed in the field of religious studies. A great deal of the knowledge he acquired through this research was integrated into his missiological reflection, but since this integration, generally speaking, bore a strongly incidental character, in many cases the sources he cited had no essential influence on his own thinking. Moreover, many of his references are of a descriptive nature, meant only to sketch a historical development or theological position. Below follows a delineation of the most important frames of reference within which Bavinck's missionary theology took shape and advanced. His positive and negative reactions to the various sources he used, furnish a clear indication of the position he took on the issues with which he was dealing. It should be mentioned here that because he used relatively few footnotes, it is difficult to obtain a sharply focused image of the context of Bavinck's missiology. In keeping with the presentation of the content of Bavinck's missionary reflection in the following chapters of this present study, a distinction is made here between his theology of religion (*theologia religionum*) in context and his theology of mission in context, though it should be remembered that these two foci are not always strictly divided in Bavinck's work.

3.2. Bavinck's Theology of Religion in Context

Aurelius Augustinus. In *CMO*, his first important publication in the area of the theology of religion, Bavinck wrote that Augustine's thought bore significance for his own reflection in the Indonesian setting "because [Augustine] struggled with the same powers, as it were, that now reign so compellingly in the East."[39] There are three elements of Augustine's thought that were of decisive importance for Bavinck.

---

[37]*IZW.*, 16.

[38]These notes can be found catalogued in the CHDDP.

[39]*CMO*, 9. Bavinck quoted especially from Augustine's *Confessiones, De Trinitate*, and *De Civitate Dei*.

First, over against the concept of abstract Being, into which human beings are reabsorbed at the end of life, Augustine stated that the essence of God finds its expression in the divine attributes or virtues. God is, thus, not only the absolute Being through whom all being comes into existence but also the holy Other with whom the (sinful) human being can never become one. This was an important insight for Bavinck in his struggle against various forms of mystical union.[40]

Second, according to Augustine the being of God and the human soul are inextricably tied together. Although Bavinck espied clear Neoplatonic influences in this notion, he felt free to adopt the idea of the immanence of God, provided it was understood biblically as the sustaining power of our entire existence. In the reality of this inextricable bond between God and man lies the secret that it is impossible for human beings to disengage themselves from God and that in one way or another they are conscious of God. Despite differences in the way Augustine and Bavinck developed this notion, it served as the initial point of departure for Bavinck's theological interpretation of the consciousness of God present in all human beings: namely, that this awareness is initiated by God.[41]

Third, Augustine rejected the cosmological approach, which represented an attempt to apprehend the divine on the basis of an understanding of the cosmic order, in favor of a theological way of thinking, whereby he sought to comprehend created reality in terms of his understanding of the Trinity. Though Bavinck had hesitations with respect to the way in which Augustine elaborated this central idea, the principle involved was of decisive importance for him: the truth of existence can only be grasped on the basis of the revelation of God.[42]

John Calvin. In further developing his theology of religion Bavinck clearly followed the line drawn by Calvin in his *Institutes of the Christian Religion*. Here, too, three points deserve special mention.

First, according to Calvin religion is not a purely human invention but results from the fact that God continues to make himself known in the world. This means that religion is a fundamentally theological phenomenon.[43]

Second, Calvin also speaks about a naturally endowed sense of God in every person, an awareness that can never be destroyed and that is stimulated by the revelation of God in nature and in the ordering of human life.[44]

Finally, it is evident to Calvin that this knowledge of God is always immediately smothered or corrupted. Consequently, his evaluation of all extra-biblical religion is negatively charged.[45]

Though Bavinck's reflections generally led him to a confirmation of these

---

[40]Cf. *CMO*, 112-117.

[41]Cf. *ibid.*, 120 ff.

[42]Cf. *ibid.*, 173 ff.

[43]Cf. J. Calvin, *Institutes of the Christian Religion*, Vol. I, Bk. 1, Ch. III.2.

[44]*Ibid.*, Ch. III.1 and Ch. V.1.

[45]*Ibid.*, Ch. IV.1-2.

Calvinist principles, he became gradually more critical of the Neo-Calvinist interpretation of Calvin's notion of the naturally implanted human perception of God. He came to think that this consciousness is present not so much in an *a priori* as in an *a posteriori* sense: it is not an independent organ of knowledge for the reception of God's revelation but rather a consequence of that revelation. The mode of its existence is more relational than substantial.[46]

Friedrich Schleiermacher. Initially Bavinck was influenced by the religious-philosophical thought of Schleiermacher, but at the same time he also had profound theological reservations about certain aspects of this brilliant theologian's work.[47] There was one point, however, on which Bavinck was in wholehearted agreement with Schleiermacher, namely, his rejection of the rationalistic construct of *religio naturalis*, the concept of an abstract religion of which the miscellaneous empirical religions were considered to be offshoots and corruptions. Schleiermacher was concerned solely with the various historical religions and their phenomenological development through time. Bavinck adopted this basic Schleiermacherian stance as a primary point of departure for his own work.[48]

Rudolf Otto. In the early phase of his missiological studies Bavinck supported many of the views articulated by Otto in his 1922 publication, *Das Heilige*, including the idea that the religious feeling inherent in humans is activated by and simultaneously opens them up to experiences of God. Later on Bavinck rejected this type of religious *a priori* on theological grounds, but he never lost his sympathy for Otto's description of human religious sensitivity.

Abraham Kuyper. It is clear that Bavinck acquainted himself thoroughly with Kuyper's views in the area of the theology of religion. But because Kuyper's ideas are comparable to those of Herman Bavinck and since our Bavinck refers more to the latter than to the former, we will limit ourselves to two matters here. It is striking that, in his discussion of elenctics in one of his important multi-volume works, Kuyper developed his view of the 'non-Christian religions' in the light of Romans 1:18 ff.[49] It is not inconceivable that in using this scriptural passage as point of departure for his own reflection Bavinck was following Kuyper's lead. In any case, there was one view of Kuyper's that made an indelible impression on Bavinck, namely, his perception that the witnessing Christian stands in essentially the same position as his non-Christian auditor because the Christian, too, is naturally drawn to pseudo religion.[50] Bavinck accentuates this insight time and time again in his own work.

---

[46]Cf. *RBCG*, 147, 148.

[47]Cf. P.J. Visser, *Geen andere naam onder de hemel: De missiologie van Johan Herman Bavinck*, masters thesis, Utrecht, 1987, for a treatment of three of Schleiermacher's views with which Bavinck deeply disagreed, *viz.*, the image of God: absolute immanent causality; the Bible: a collection of religious experiences; Christian faith: a step on the way to pure monotheism.

[48]Cf. *RBCG*, 99-102.

[49]Cf. *Encyclopaedie der heilige godgeleerdheid*, III, 446-448.

[50]Cf. *Ibid.*, 449.

Herman Bavinck. Bavinck acquainted himself thoroughly with Herman Bavinck's dogmatic reflection, particularly as this had taken shape in the latter's publication, *Gereformeerde Dogmatiek* (Reformed Dogmatics).[51] In accordance with the classical Reformed theology to which he was heir Bavinck elaborates four main points relative to theology of religion.

First, religion exists because God is God and because God wishes to be served by His rational creatures. God is thus the *principium essendi* of all religion.[52]

Second, because He wishes to be so served, God reveals himself to mankind in nature, history and the human conscience (*principium cognoscendi externum*) and renders human beings subjectively able to receive this revelation (*principium cognoscendi internum*).[53]

Third, the knowledge of God naturally present in human beings is inadequate on the one hand, but on the other hand it keeps the awareness alive in their hearts that they have been created in God's image and gives rise to inclinations and yearnings which aspire to fulfilment in Christ.[54]

Fourth, general revelation is accordingly the foundation upon which the edifice of special revelation is raised, and in the natural knowledge of God lies a point of contact for the gospel.[55]

Initially Bavinck's thinking followed along this path, though it was less philosophically and more psychologically colored than that of his uncle. On the one hand, his increasingly biblical-theological reflection led him to emphasize Herman Bavinck's basic principle that religion is a theological phenomenon. But on the other hand, because he could find no scriptural grounds for it, he disclaimed the logically contrived notion of *principium cognoscendi internum* as a possible point of contact.[56]

Karl Barth. Karl Barth did not really have any direct influence on Bavinck. Barth resolutely rejected any possible connection between general revelation and the origin of religious consciousness. For Barth religion was not a theological phenomenon but rather an "Angelegenheit des gottlosen Menschen."[57] Bavinck's reading of Romans 1:18 ff. led him to disagree fundamentally with this Barthian position. Bavinck was, however, indirectly influenced by Barth via

---

[51]This work appeared in 1901, was revised in 1911 and was reprinted for the last time in 1918.

[52]Cf. H. Bavinck, *Gereformeerde Dogmatiek*, I, 287.

[53]Cf. *Ibid.*, 286-290.

[54]Cf. *Ibid.*, 334-335.

[55]Cf. *Ibid.*, III, 248.

[56]Cf. *RBCG*, 160 ff.

[57]K. Barth, *Die Lehre vom Worte Gottes*, 329.

Hendrik Kraemer, as will become evident in the following chapter.[58] This influence consisted especially of Barth's rigorous insistence on the employment of the revelation of God in His Word as the sole point of departure for theological reflection. Bavinck recognized that Barth had radically shifted the helm in respect of this matter and subscribed wholly to this strict orientation toward Scripture.[59]

Emil Brunner. Bavinck refers only summarily to Brunner, even though there are clear similarities between Brunner's notion of the dialectical relationship of God and man and Bavinck's concept of the vital divine-human "dialogical relationship."[60] Bavinck feels some hesitation, however, with respect to Brunner's intentions: he questions whether Brunner does not adopt certain elements which follow naturally in the line of "the old *theologia naturalis.*"[61] However, it is not inconceivable that in the end Brunner's views on this matter had more influence on Bavinck – perhaps also via Kraemer[62] – than he himself indicates.[63]

Hendrik Kraemer. From the very beginning of his missiological career Bavinck had fairly intensive contact with the Reformed missionary theologian, Hendrik Kraemer. They had known each other since student days, but became better acquainted in Solo, Indonesia, where, in the period between 1930 and 1934, Kraemer introduced Bavinck to the secrets of Javanese literature and mysticism. Later Bavinck wrote that it was a privilege to have had Kraemer as a teacher during this period,[64] and Kraemer wrote subsequently that he had never had a student who had absorbed Javanese mysticism as quickly and thoroughly as Bavinck had.[65]

---

[58]Kraemer also influenced Bavinck in terms of his departures from Barth, e.g., when on the basis of Scripture he argued, contrary to Barth, for a link between religious awareness and general revelation.

[59]Cf. *RBCG*, 156.

[60]For Brunner there is continuity in the divine-human relationship in consequence of the fact that man as *imago Dei* is always orientated toward God and possesses "Wortmächtigkeit" or "Sprachfähigkeit" vis-a-vis God, which makes it possible to speak with people about God. But this relationship also exhibits discontinuity, which lies in the fact that it exists in a loveless or hostile world and that man answers God accordingly. Cf. his *Natur und Gnade* and *Der Mensch im Widerspruch.*

[61]*RBCG*, 159.

[62]Cf. J. van Lin, *Protestantse theologie der godsdiensten: Van Edinburgh naar Tambaram (1910-1938),* p. 357, who cites the influence of Brunner on Kraemer, as does T. Yates, *Christian Mission in the Twentieth Century,* 113.

[63]An indication of this is Bavinck's somewhat offhand but, in view of its context, nevertheless important question *RBCG*, 160: "Or is it...better to speak only of 'Wortmächtigkeit,' but then what do we mean by that?"

[64]"Kraemer als denker en medewerker," 86.

[65]Cf. J. Verkuyl, *Inleiding in de nieuwere zendingswetenschap,* 63.

Bavinck's 1934 publication, *CMO*, may thus be viewed as partly a fruit of Kraemer's tutelage.

At a later stage Kraemer had a decisive influence on Bavinck in terms of the latter's reflection on *theologia religionum*. Kraemer's study, *The Christian Message in a Non-Christian World*, written for the International Missionary Conference held in Tambaram, India, in 1938, led Bavinck to change his views with respect to other religions. The biblical-theological approach put forward by Kraemer in this book became the point of departure for Bavinck's own reflection in this area of study: Kraemer's views led to a radicalization of Bavinck's theological position on the matter of the relation of Christianity to the surrounding world.[66] Conversely, Kraemer had a great deal of appreciation for the way in which Bavinck, making use of his psychological insights, interpreted Romans 1:18 ff. in his book, *RBCG*.[67]

Bavinck's agreement with Kraemer, however, was not without important critical moments. Over against Kraemer's Barthian outlook and views, Bavinck emphatically maintained the Reformed, Neo-Calvinist position. For example, he qualified Kraemer's biting indictment of empirical Christianity, placed more emphasis on dogmatic reflection in contrast to Kraemer's biblical realism, and argued on the basis of scripture that Kraemer's voluntaristic scheme should have been supplied with an ontological basis.[68]

3.3. Bavinck's Theology of Mission in Context

3.3.1. Reformed Missionary Theology

Gisbertus Voetius. Bavinck spoke very appreciatively of Voetius, the first Reformed theologian to elaborate a number of missionary principles.[69] It should be noted here that within the RCN Voetius was recognized as an important authority. This was particularly evident during the Synod of Middelburg in 1896, at which the RCN attempted for the first time to develop a biblical view of mission.[70] Though it appears that Bavinck had only an indirect knowledge of Voetius' writings via a dissertation written many years earlier,[71] Voetius clearly influenced Bavinck,

---

[66]This matter will be dealt with at greater length in the following chapter.

[67]Cf. H. Kraemer, *Religion and Christian Faith*, 79-81.

[68]Cf. *BCNCR*, 89 ff., 94 ff. and 101 ff., as well as *IZW*, 247, and "Kraemer als denker en medewerker."

[69]Cf. *IZW*, 8 and 21, and *ZWN*, 31. For Voetius' writings on the theology of mission see J. Jongeneel, "Voetius' zendingstheologie: De eerste comprehensieve protestantse zendings-theologie," 123.

[70]Cf. J. Jongeneel, "Voetius' zendingstheologie," 142-143.

[71]H.A. van Andel, *De zendingsleer van Gisbertus Voetius*, 1912. Bavinck even failed to refer to a translation by D. Pol of one of Voetius' important missionary works, *Tractaat over de planting en planters van kerken.*

particularly by way of the missionary principles formulated at the Synod of Middelburg, in five distinct areas.

1. Voetius' theocentric point of departure, the *missio Dei*, which he understood to mean that mission is primarily God's work and only secondarily the work of the church, formed the foundation of Bavinck's missionary theology,[72] though it needs to be pointed out immediately that Bavinck's understanding of this concept was less determined by the doctrine of predestination than was that of Voetius.

2. In opposition to the conception of mission as the affair of special societies or sodalities set up for this work, Bavinck advocated the ecclesiocentric conception of mission propounded by Voetius, i.e., the view that the task of mission belongs exclusively to the church.[73]

3. In his discussion of the aim and purpose of missionary activity Bavinck adopted Voetius' idea of the threefold aim of mission: the conversion of unbelievers (*conversio gentilium*), and the establishment of the church *(plantatio ecclesiae),* leading to the glorification of God (*gloria gratiae divinae*).[74]

4. Voetius' understanding of the comprehensive character of mission, whereby a distinction is made between the actual (ecclesiastical, official) missionary work of ordained ministers of the Word and the ancillary services of medical personnel and teachers, is reflected in Bavinck's distinction between the *cardinal* ministry of mission, consisting of the proclamation of the gospel, and *auxiliary* missionary ministries, including medical care, education and social services. Notwithstanding this similarity, however, it should be noted that in Bavinck's thinking these chief and adjunct ministries were more intimately related to one another than they were in Voetius' position: for Bavinck all of them together gave expression to the one missionary mandate.[75]

5. Particularly under the influence of Abraham Kuyper, Bavinck revitalized Voetius' *theologia elenctica,*[76] giving it a prominent place in his handbook on missiology.[77]

The Synod of Middelburg (1896). It was at the Synod of Middelburg that

---

[72]Cf. *ZWN*, 5. Bavinck began this book with the revealing sentence, "Mission is that activity of Jesus Christ by which He makes himself known to all peoples in and through His church, and takes them up into the splendor of His work of deliverance."

[73]Cf. *ZWN*, 32 ff. Bavinck points out here that it wasn't actually Voetius but Adrianus Saravia (1531-1613) who was the first Protestant theologian to argue on the basis of the missionary mandate in Matt. 29:18-20 that mission is a church matter; cf. also *IZW*, .65-70 / *ISM*, 57-62.

[74]Cf. *IZW*, 157-161 / *ISM*, 155-159.

[75]Cf. *ZWN*, 51 ff., and *IZW*, 113-121 / *ISM*, 107-116.

[76]Cf. J.A.B. Jongeneel, "Voetius' zendingstheologie," 121, n. 8.

[77]Cf. *IZW*, 222-272 / *ISM*, 221-272. The subject of elenctics will be dealt with at length in chapter eight.

the RCN drew up the basic guidelines with respect to its missionary task. Bavinck's initial missionary reflection took place within this frame of reference and he continued to relate all of his subsequent work to it as well. His writings contain scores of references to the *Acts* of this synod, particularly in connection to the points just mentioned above. In his foreword to the 1940 republication of the resolutions of the Synod of Middelburg with respect to mission, he expressed his great appreciation for "the depth of insight' reflected in them.[78] At the same time he also recognized that these determinations were a product of their time.

> Fifty years ago the Synod of Middelburg laid down the lines along which the work of mission was to develop. A half century has gone by. Everything in the world, everything in Indonesia has changed. There should be another "Middelburg," that is to say, we should once again apply our best efforts toward an organization of missionary work that will correspond completely with the needs of Indonesia, with the growing independence of the Javanese churches, and with the new relationship which is emerging between us and Indonesia.[79]

In his biblical-theological reflections Bavinck not only further elaborated the views of "Middelburg" but also subjected them to critical discussion. He objected especially to the synod's assumption regarding the possible presence of elements of truth in the 'non-Christian' religions and to its teaching that the so-called auxiliary missionary services should be seen merely as preparation for the gospel. On the other hand, it is striking that Bavinck remains silent with respect to the synod's questionable two-sided interpretation of the doxological motive and end of all missionary activity. Middelburg stated that

> the glorification [of God] is most clearly disclosed when [mission] leads to the salvation of the lost, causing the wondrous riches of the grace and mercy of God to shine forth, but [mission's ultimate] goal may not be understood in these terms. Even when [mission] does not lead to salvation or meets only callosity of heart, the same highest end [the glorification of God] is served and achieved.[80]

Bavinck nowhere denies this latter assertion, but neither does he ever speak about it explicitly.

Developments within the RCN in the area of theology of mission. In his own church Bavinck was the first but not the only one to have engaged in systematic reflection on mission.[81] Through the years several other RCN scholars, notably a

---

[78]Cf. *Historisch Document* (which also contained a reprint of the speech Abraham Kuyper gave at the missionary conference held in Amsterdam in 1890), I-III.

[79]"Nieuw oriëntering in ons zendingswerk," 23-24.

[80]*Historisch Document*, 1

[81]After Middelburg and before Bavinck began writing there had been hardly any systematic reflection in his church on the biblical-theological foundation of mission. Herman Bavinck made a modest attempt in this direction in an article

number of his former doctoral students, including J. Verkuyl, J. Blauw, A.G Honig and J. van den Berg, have made significant contributions to this area of study. It was especially during his period as professor of mission that Bavinck played a leading role in the development of missiology within the RCN, and as is evident from his references to their publications, his relationship with the missiologists he trained was one of fruitful interaction.

3.3.2. Other Protestant and Roman Catholic Missionary Theology

Bavinck thoroughly acquainted himself with the publications of other, particularly Protestant, missionary theologians at home and abroad, using their insights to a greater or lesser degree in the development of his own missiological reflection.

Gustav Warneck. Bavinck acknowledged his scholarly indebtedness to the great German Protestant missiologist, Gustav Warneck, calling the latter's *Evangelische Missionslehre* (1892) "one of the most important sources for the academic study of mission."[82] He wrote that Warneck's treatment of the subject matter of missionary research "has exercised a great influence upon all who have subsequently dedicated themselves to the study of the theory of mission," including himself.[83] One could think here, for example, of Warneck's elementary insistence that all reflection on mission must be biblically grounded. It is particularly with respect to this issue of the biblical foundation of mission that many similarities between Bavinck and Warneck can be observed. Bavinck refers in this connection to the fact that at the beginning of the 20th century Warneck, following Martin Kähler's lead, raised strong objections to Ernst Troeltsch's tendency to conceive of mission "as a sort of *'Verständigung,'* a discussion with other religions"[84] instead of as the church's witness to Christ as taught in Scripture. While it is certain that Bavinck made a careful study of Warneck's publications and it may be concluded, therefore, that he integrated many of Warneck's views into his thinking,[85] he seldom employs direct quotations from Warneck, making it difficult to trace explicit influences of the latter upon the former. It is only in terms of a few incidental areas, e.g., the question of the transmission of culture in mission[86] and the matter of the

---

entitled "De zending in de Heilige Schrift," in: H. Beets, *Triumfen van het kruis,* 7-30. Remarkably, Bavinck nowhere cites this study, though it is inconceivable that he could have been unaware of its existence.

[82]*ZWN,* 31.

[83]*IZW,* 22 / *ISM,* 7.

[84]*ISM,* 299 / *IZW,* 296.

[85]In addition to *Evangelische Missionslehre* Bavinck refers to other books authored by Warneck, e.g., *Die gegenseitigen Beziehungen zwischen der modernen Mission und Kultur,* Gütersloh, 1879 and *Abriss einer Geschichte der protestantischen Missionen,* Berlin, 1905.

[86]*IZW,* 107 / *ISM,* 101.

exercise of discipline within newly established churches on the mission field,[87] that he cites Warneck approvingly.

But Bavinck is also critical of Warneck on two core issues. The first of these concerns the foundation of mission.[88] Warneck spoke not only of the biblical footing but also of a historical and ethnological basis of mission, by the latter of which he meant "the capacity of all people for Christianity, irrespective of their nationality or cultural level."[89] Following in the line of Hans Schärer, who wrote that "there can and may be only one single ground of mission,"[90] Bavinck radically rejected this notion of a multiple foundation of mission. Secondly, Bavinck submits Warneck's view of the agent of mission to serious criticism. Warneck stated that in theory it is the church that is called to mission. But he contended that in practice it is better for the missionary task to be carried out by an active, mission-minded fellowship within the church, an *ecclesiola in ecclesia*, "stimulated and encouraged by prophets and teachers" to support and send out missionaries "under the guidance and inspiration of the Holy Spirit."[91] Though Bavinck felt much appreciation for Warneck's insistence that mission belonged properly to the church rather than to separate sodalities or missionary societies,[92] he flatly rejects the idea of a missionary *ecclesiola in ecclesia*:

> This [notion] militates against the Scriptural way of thinking. The Bible knows nothing of an 'inner circle' within the church having a special calling to assume responsibility for mission.... Scripture makes it clear that it is the Church, the body of Christ, that constitutes the organ through which and in which the glorified Christ wishes to reveal his great work of redemption to the world.[93]

Other missionary theologians. As already indicated earlier, Bavinck had

---

[87]*Ibid.*, 185 / 182.

[88]*Ibid.*, 71 / 63.

[89]*Evangelische Missionslehre*, I, 301: "...die Fähigkeit der Menschen aller Nationalitäten und Kulturstufen für das Christentum."

[90]H. Schärer, *Die Begründung der Mission in der katholischen und evangelischen Missionswissenschaft*, 37.

[91]*Evangelische Missionslehre*, II, 31: the missionary calling should be fulfilled by "die auf Anregung von Propheten und Lehrern unter Antrieb und Leitung des heiligen Geistes handelnde Gemeinde," which has "die Machtsbefügnis zur Sendung."

[92]Cf. Also T. Yates, *Christian Mission in the Twentieth Century*, 19-20, who points to Warneck's reaction, (in "Die moderne Weltevangelismus-Theorie," *Allgemeine Missions-Zeitschrift*, XXIV [1897], 305-325) to the popular, modish Anglo-Saxon understanding of mission as the evangelization of the world by means of faith missions operating independently of the church.

[93]*IZW*, 66 / *ISM*, 58, 59.

first-hand knowledge of the works of leading non-RCN Protestant and Roman Catholic missiologists. In Bavinck's oeuvre one comes across references to Dutch, German, Anglo-Saxon, and Third-World theologians such as J.C. Hoekendijk, Hendrik Kraemer, A. C. Kruyt and B.M. Schuurman; Walter Freytag, Bruno Gutmann, Karl Hartenstein, Walter Holsten, Christian Keysser, Julius Richter, Joseph Schmidlin, and Johannes Thauren; the missionary pioneer William Carey, Roland Allen, G.E. Phillips, Stephen Neill, M. A.C.Warren, and Harry R. Boer; the Indian Vengal Chakkarai and the Japanese Toyohiko Kagawa. But there are also many others who could be mentioned.

Generally speaking it is not always easy to pinpoint the influence these figures had on Bavinck or, conversely, to determine precisely where he distinguished his own perceptions from theirs. On the one hand, he was often in agreement with the views of others and incorporated their insights into his own thinking.[94] On the other, there are instances of objection to the work of fellow authors in the area of mission, disagreement which helped to sharpen his own positions.[95] Moreover, he regularly made objective use of the specialized knowledge of other theologians and missiologists.[96] There is no indication that he had a special preference for one or more of the thinkers listed above, with the single exception of Hendrik Kraemer, as already indicated above.[97]

3.3.3. Ecumenical Missionary Theology

It is clear that Bavinck followed the main developments that were taking place in ecumenical missiological reflection, some parts of which he found to be congenial to his own thinking, whereas various other of its elements met with criticism in his work.

Bavinck's general reaction to ecumenical missionary thought. A steadily increasing awareness of the need for ecumenical cooperation in the area of mission during the last quarter of the 19th century led to the organization of the first international missionary conference in history which was held in Edinburgh in 1910. One of the most important results of this conference was the establishment of the International Missionary Council (IMC), which, delayed by the First World War, finally took place at a meeting of the Edinburgh Continuation Committee in 1921

---

[94]Here the influence of Kraemer and Hoekendijk stands out and to a lesser degree that of Schuurman, Freytag, Hartenstein, Richter, Holsten, Allen, Neill and Phillips.

[95]Bavinck criticizes ideas and arguments of especially Gutmann, Keysser, Schmidlin, Thauren, Chakkarai, and Kagawa and to a lesser degree those of Hoekendijk and Kraemer.

[96]Among the many names that could be cited this connection, those of Hoekendijk, Kraemer, Kruyt, Warren, Chakkarai, and Kagawa require special mention.

[97]Bavinck wrote two highly appreciative articles on Kraemer: "Dr. Hendrik Kraemer als denker en medewerker," *DHB*, XI (1958), 84-96, and "Hendrik Kraemer de zendingsman," *Trouw*, 16 August 1958.

at Lake Mohonk, New York. The IMC organized a series of additional international missionary conferences, including Jerusalem 1928; Tambaram, India 1938; Whitby, Canada 1947; Willingen, Germany 1952; and Achimota, Ghana 1958/59. In 1961 at the Third Assembly of the World Council of Churches (WCC) in New Delhi, the IMC was integrated into the WCC where it assumed a new identity as the Division of World Mission and Evangelism (DWME), which took on responsibility for the organization of subsequent international missionary conferences, only one of which, Mexico City, 1963, was held prior to Bavinck's death in 1964.[98]

Bavinck was in basic agreement with the position that matters of mission should be approached ecumenically with a view to the credibility of the gospel and the advantages to be derived from cooperative efforts in the attempt to fulfill the missionary obligation of the church.[99] He recognized that the tendency of ecumenical conferences to produce disparate views and statements constitutes a basic weakness of such gatherings, but at the same time considered this diversity to be a manifestation of their strength. In a reaction to the founding of the WCC in 1948, he offered the following evaluation of ecumenical meetings.

> The various spiritual and intellectual currents flowing through the church are brought into contact with each other, are forced into the same area of focus at conferences of this nature. [These currents] contend with each other, they are weighed against one another, each becomes infused with the others. In short, a process of fermentation takes place that sometimes continues to work even after many years have passed. Therefore it is very naive, indeed, on the part of those who, with a certain air of condescension, look down upon such international gatherings as something not worth the time and money [they require]. Anyone who talks in this way displays a sore lack of vision with respect to the supranational character of the Church and [a sad dearth of awareness regarding] the tremendous strengths revealed in the

---

[98]The conferences held after Bavinck's death were: Bangkok 1972/73; Melbourne 1980, San Antonio, Texas 1989; Salvador de Bahia, Brazil 1996. Of the huge body of literature dealing with these IMC conferences, we mention just one or two Dutch- and English-language examples: A. Wind, *Zending en oecumene in de twintigste eeuw* I and IIa; J.J.E. van Lin, *Protestantse theologie der godsdiensten: Van Edinburgh naar Tambaram 1910-1938*; J.D. Gort, "Van Edinburgh 1910 naar San Antonio 1989: Een doorlopend verhaal," *Wereld en Zending*, (1989); "Edinburgh to Melbourne," theme issue, *International Review of Mission*, with essays by Harry Sawyerr (Edinburgh), J.D. Gort (Jerusalem), E. Jansen Schoonhoven (Tambaram), F.V. Carino (Whitby), R.C. Bassham (Willingen), R.C. Winter (Ghana), Anastasios Yannoulatos (Mexico City), and John V. Taylor (Bangkok); R.C. Bassham, *Mission Theology 1948-1975: Years of Worldwide Creative Tension, Ecumenical, Evangelical, and Roman Catholic*; and T. Yates, *Christian Mission in the Twentieth Century*, which gives special attention to the thought of leading missiologists.

[99]Cf. *IZW*, 202-207 / *ISM*, 199-204.

life of the various churches.[100]

Even judging by this quotation alone it would seem quite obvious that Bavinck must have been fairly well informed in the area of ecumenical thought. In any case, he regularly refers to themes that were dealt with as part of the ongoing reflection at successive international missionary conferences. At the same time, however, the paucity of attention he gives to the various individual conferences makes it impossible to provide a chronological description of his assimilation of the discussions at these gatherings. On that account, the most important instances of Bavinck's agreement and disagreement with ecumenical missiological insights will be presented thematically and in logical sequence in the following paragraph.

Bavinck's views on major ecumenical missiological themes. Which of the key themes that were developed during the course of the deliberations of the international missionary conferences did Bavinck deal with explicitly in his writings and how did he himself respond to these issues?

1. Missio Dei. The Trinitarian basis for all missionary work had already been firmly laid at the 1910 Edinburgh conference: in carrying out its missionary task, the church is involved in the mission of the Father, the Son, and the Holy Spirit. This Trinitarian starting point, the conviction that God is "a missionary God,"[101] which has figured strongly throughout modern ecumenical history, was highlighted in a particular way at Willingen 1952.

> The missionary movement of which we are a part has its source in the Triune God Himself. Out of the depths of His love for us, the Father has sent forth His own beloved Son to reconcile all things to Himself, that we and all men might, through the Spirit, be made one in Him with the Father in that perfect love which is the very nature of God.[102]

Bavinck subscribed wholeheartedly to this missiological point of departure, though it is perhaps more correct to say that he was in sympathy with rather than specifically influenced by the discussions on this issue at Willingen and earlier conferences,[103] since the Trinitarian foundation of mission had already been posited by Abraham Kuyper in his speech at the missionary conference in Amsterdam in 1890[104] and officially affirmed to by the Synod of Middelburg in 1896. On the other hand, it does seems that Bavinck was prompted by ecumenical missionary

---

[100]"De vergadering van de Wereldraad van Kerken," 276. Cf. also *ZWN*, 200, where Bavinck terms ecumenical reflection and cooperation "a cause for joy."

[101]Norman Goodall, "Towards Willingen," 13.

[102]Norman Goodall (ed.), *Missions Under the Cross*, 189 ff.

[103]Cf. I.P.C. van 't Hof, *Op zoek naar het geheim van de zending: In dialoog met de wereldzendingsconferenties 1910-1963*, who argues that the theme of the Trinitarian basis for mission was either directly discussed at or clearly presupposed by all of the international missionary conferences he studied, beginning with Edinburgh 1910.

[104]Cf. *ibid.*, 17.

theology to view the concept of *missio Dei* less in terms of the doctrine of predestination than did Middelburg.

2. *Missio ecclesiae.* From the very beginning of the ecumenical movement emphasis was placed on the missionary character of the church. Mission, it was argued, not only contributed to the well-being of the church but belonged to its very essence:[105] mission was "accepted as 'a part of the functioning of the Church as a living body'–both in the home base and overseas."[106] Bavinck welcomed this generally accepted notion as backing for the RCN idea of mission as mission of the church.[107] He also reacted positively to Tambaram's understanding of the missionary task as including both evangelism and (diaconal) witness and as having a centripetal as well as centrifugal character.[108]

In post-Willingen missionary theology, which had been highly influenced by the thinking of J.C. Hoekendijk, the church gradually came to be seen as a "function of the apostolate" rather than the other way around, *and missio ecclesiae* was defined more in terms of the coming of God's Kingdom than the planting of the church.[109] Bavinck firmly rejected this view. For him the *raison d'être* of the church was not defined exclusively by the apostolate[110] but also by its doxological calling and nurturing task.[111] And in his view the advent of God's Kingdom will be realized by means of the conversion of people to the Christian faith and the planting of the church.[112]

Although not everyone went as far as Hoekendijk did, after Willingen 1952 many missionary theologians began to explicate the concept of *missio ecclesiae* within the eschatological framework of the Kingdom come and coming. It is striking that from this time onward Bavinck's missiology also bears traces of

---

[105]Cf. *ibid.*, 35.

[106]Harry Sawyerr, "The First World Missionary Conference: Edinburgh 1910," *IRM*, LXVII / 267 (July 1978), 272.

[107]Cf. *IZW*, 67, see also 298 / *ISM*, 59, see also 300.

[108]Cf. *ibid.*, 69 / *ibid.*, 61.

[109]Cf. A. Wind, *Zending en oecumene in de twintigste eeuw*, I, 221 ff.

[110]This idea was rooted in the deliberations of Jerusalem (cf. Van 't Hof, 113) and in the thinking of missionary leaders such as Hendrik Kraemer, who argued in 1936 that "at the same moment the Church was born, mission was born" and that the event of Pentecost shows clearly "that to be church is to be missionary, and to be missionary is to be church," *(Kerk en zending*, 24), and Karl Hartenstein, who stated in 1939, "Wer Kirche sagt, sagt Mission" ("When one says Church, one says mission," cited in Van 't Hof, 114).

[111]Cf. *IZW*, 76-77 / *ISM*, 68-69; it is clear that Bavinck was reacting here to both Kraemer and the discussions that took place at and subsequent to the International Missionary Conference held in Willingen in 1952.

[112]Cf. *ibid.*, 157 ff. / *ibid.*, 155 ff.

this tendency. He not only began to use the term "Kingdom of God' more frequently – in *IZW* (1954) he even included it in his definition of mission – but he also expressed theological appreciation for the fact "that the eschatological moment is being given a place of great importance in more recent thinking on mission."[113] The missionary task of the church must be seen in the light of the imminent return of Christ.

> All mission work is directed toward the end. It is apparent from some of his testimony that Paul felt the end was near in his day. But [precise timing] is not the point. Whether the end is near or far off is unimportant in comparison with the consideration that the work of mission, by virtue of its very essence, inclines toward a final goal, the realization of which will receive visible form only in the coming age beyond the horizon of world history.[114]

3. Church Partnership. At the IMC conference in Jerusalem in 1928 great strides were made with respect to the perception and clarification of the relationship between 'sending churches' and 'mission field.'[115] Not only did Jerusalem replace this traditional nomenclature with the new designations, 'older' and 'younger churches,' it also stressed the fundamental equality of both of these categories of church, and even employed terms such as 'partnership,' to describe their relations.[116] There was even talk of the need to invite younger churches to send missionaries to the West.[117] The theme of partnership was taken up again in a new way at Whitby 1947. In complete harmony the younger and older church delegates agreed upon the phrase "partnership in obedience" to describe the mutual relationship which they believed was necessary in order to carry out the worldwide missionary task. The concept 'partnership' expressed the formal equality of all churches, and the term 'in obedience' referred to the common obligation to obey the gospel. For a number of delegates "the whole world was seen as the mission field, so that churches whether older or younger were in a missionary situation in which each must assist the other in the fulfilment of their common missionary task."[118] Since the RCN had already stated at the Synod of Middelburg in 1896 that the churches in the mission field were equal to the sending churches in the Netherlands and therefore should become independent, it is not surprising that Bavinck adopted

---

[113]*Ibid.*, 58, cf. also 300.

[114]*IZW.*, 58.

[115]Cf. A. Wind, *Zending en oecumene in de twintigste eeuw*, I, 77.

[116]*Ibid.*; cf. also *IZW*, 211, n. 5 / *ISM*, 319, n. 5.

[117]I.P.C. van 't Hof, *op. cit.*, 81.

[118]F.V. Carino, *IRM*, 67, 267 (1978), 318; cf. also A. Wind, *Zending en oecumene in de twintigste eeuw*, I, 168 ff.; as Wind points out, this notion of partnership in obedience constitutes a prelude to the theme of the IMC missionary conference in Mexico City in 1963: 'mission in six continents.'

Whitby's views in this regard without reservation.[119]

Whitby had little awareness of the concept of 'mutual assistance,' nor did Bavinck at this point in time. When this notion was introduced at the IMC conference in Mexico City in 1963 in response to the increasing secularization taking place in the Western world, Bavinck also began to see its importance. This is indirectly illustrated by an affirmation found in one of his publications dating from 1966: "And it is not merely the message of the Western nations to those of other parts of the world. It is God's message to all of us, without distinction of race and people."[120]

4. *Comprehensive approach.* Jerusalem 1928 launched the idea of the 'comprehensive missionary approach,' consisting of proclamation, education, medical care, and social-economic aid. From then on it became customary to speak of mission as having a four-dimensional character embracing the whole of life.[121] Whereas in Jerusalem concern was directed mainly toward change at the level of microstructures, in Tambaram emphasis was placed on the need to transform the macrostructures of human society as well.[122] Immediate criticism was raised against this proposition by a number of observers within the RCN.[123] And Bavinck, too, had his doubts about it. He did not reject the notion of 'comprehensive approach' as such – and in fact made use of it in his writings – but he oppugned the way in which it was conceived in ecumenical missionary theology: he held that the four-dimensional approach could easily lead to an attenuation of the decisive significance and central place of the proclamation of the gospel in mission.[124] At the same time, however, he engaged in serious biblical-theological reflection on the notion of comprehensive missionary witness in word and deed.[125]

---

[119]Cf. *IZW*, 210 ff. / *ISM*, 207; Bavinck recognized that questions could be raised regarding this new relationship but argues that "both [younger and older churches] must try to think in terms of a higher, more ecumenical, more Catholic perspective: [namely, that] they are doing the work [of mission] together in service of the same Lord and King," *ibid.*, 211 / *ibid.*, 208.

[120]*Church Between Temple and Mosque*, 205.

[121]*IZW*, 114 / *ISM*, 108.

[122]Cf. A. Wind, *Zending en oecumene in de twintigste eeuw*, I, 77 and 152.

[123]Cf. e.g., H.A. van Andel, who, in an article entitled, "De conferentie op de Olijfberg," wrote: "Mission as proclamation of the gospel plants the seed in people's hearts from which a Christian social and political life can take its rise, but it does not provide an agenda for social reform or a program of political action," 72.

[124]*IZW*, 113 ff. / *ISM*, 107 ff.

[125]It seems very likely that as an extension of his own reflection on this issue, Bavinck stimulated one of his doctoral students, Anton G. Honig, to devote his dissertation to it; referring to Bavinck, Honig wrote in the introduction to his thesis that the RCN were in a state of 'painful disarray' at this time (1951) with respect to the subject of comprehensive approach.

5. Theologia religionum. The question of the theological evaluation of the so-called 'non-Christian' religions came up for thorough discussion at the very outset of the modern ecumenical movement at the 1910 Edinburgh conference, and the debate on this matter continued through Jerusalem 1928, reaching its provisional climax at Tambaram 1938. In the discussions that took place on 'continuity' and 'discontinuity' between Christianity and other religions, the two main contending parties at Jerusalem and Tambaram were made up of those belonging to the Anglo-Saxon school of theology, on the one hand, and the Continental school, on the other; the Asiatic participants, too, were rather divided in their views on interreligious relationships.[126]

Bavinck was not only keenly interested in the discussions that took place prior to and at Tambaram but also made a modest contribution to them in the form of a booklet entitled, *The Faith by Which the Church Lives*,[127] in which he delineated Christian teaching in regard to man and divine revelation vis-à-vis the cosmic apprehension of life.[128] Two reasons may be adduced for Bavinck's ardent involvement in the debates occasioned by Tambaram. First, there was his personal fascination with expressions of religious consciousness, coupled with his avid missiological urge to plumb the deepest meaning of the 'non-Christian' religions. Second, this interest can also be explained in terms of the close personal contacts he maintained with Hendrik Kraemer, one of the main theological protagonists at Tambaram. As already pointed out previously in this chapter, Bavinck's theology of religion was decisively influenced by Kraemer's basic stand that God's revelation in the cross of Christ constitutes a witness to God's judgment of the religions of a sinful mankind. This led him to a definitive departure from his earlier view, in the line of Abraham Kuyper and Herman Bavinck, that other religions contain points of contact for the gospel.

4. Chapter Summary

Since there was no settled RCN frame of reference that he could use as a guide in the domain of theology of religion, Bavinck developed his thinking fairly independently in this area. Abraham Kuyper and Herman Bavinck had engaged in limited deliberation on matters related to this field, but Bavinck did not feel bound to their views. Initially, because of his psychological predilections, his reflection in this realm of study was oriented toward Rudolf Otto's thought and (with more critical distance) that of Friedrich Schleiermacher. In terms of apologetics he fell back on a number of Augustine's insights. Reacting to criticism from within his own circles, he did integrate some of Herman Bavinck's theological ideas into his work. Acquaintance with Hendrik Kraemer's views led to a breakthrough in

---

[126]Cf. A. Wind, *Zending en oecumene in de twintigste eeuw*, I, 71 ff.; J.D. Gort, "Van Edinburgh 1910 naar San Antonio 1989," 260-263ff.; and T. Yates, *op. cit.*, passim.

[127]This booklet, which can found in the archives of the WCC in Geneva, also appeared in Dutch entitled, "Het geloof waaruit de kerk leeft," in *De Opwekker*, 82 (1937), 520-547, and in slightly revised form under the title, "Drie grote vragen," in *DM*, XLII (1938), 82-91, 97-104, and 178-184.

[128]C. J.J.E. van Lin, *op. cit.*, 286-287.

Bavinck's thinking in this connection. Influenced by Kraemer's interpretation of dialectical theology, directly involved in the discussions that took place at the time of Tambaram, and making more extensive use of the ideas of Calvin than he had before, Bavinck developed an RCN theory respecting the relationship between Christianity and other religions that may justifiably be termed an original contribution to theology of religion.

In the area of theology of mission Bavinck took his departure from Reformed thinking, particularly as that came to expression in the teachings of Gisbertus Voetius and the missionary views that had been developing within the RCN since the Synod of Middelburg in 1896.[129] He subjected the lines set out by Middelburg to further scrutiny and elaboration. At the same time, however, he familiarized himself extensively with existing missiological literature published both at home and abroad, not only by Reformed and other Protestant authors but also by ecumenical and Roman Catholic ones. This is the more remarkable when seen against the background of the voluntary theological isolation of the RCN in those years and is illustrative of Bavinck's capacious ecumenical vision. By integrating the knowledge he gained in this way into his own reflection, he brought Reformed missiology into dialogical encounter with other missiological schools of thought. J. van den Berg described Bavinck's missiological qualities in a very striking way: "He wittingly opened himself to countless influences, displaying an expansive, immensely sensitive receptivity coupled with powerful creative abilities. . . . [And] he transposed those influences into the key of his own life experience."[130]

In summary it can be stated that the Protestant missionary theologian Bavinck developed his missiology not only in a spirit of deep loyalty to and gratitude for the riches and resources of his own tradition but also in a mood of constructive criticism and ecumenical commitment and openness.

---

[129]It should be noted here that Bavinck did very little with the missiological aspects of Calvin's theology, cf. for this W.F. Dankbaar, "Het apostolaat bij Calvijn," in: *Hervormers en humanisten*, 185 ff., and S. van der Linde, *Zending naar gereformeerd beginsel*.

[130]J. van den Berg, "De wetenschappelijke arbeid van Professor Dr. Johan Herman Bavinck," 41.

CHAPTER FOUR

Other Religions and General Revelation

"The subject we are discussing here is a very old one.... It is
certain that this problem has never been so urgent as in our own
day."[1]

1. Introduction

The question of the relationship between "religious experience and God's revelation
in Jesus Christ" is *the* theme that governed the whole of Bavinck's missionary
theology.[2] In the deepest sense, this thematic emphasis of Bavinck's work was
engendered by the ongoing existential joust in his own heart between the general
religious feelings that were part and parcel of his consciousness[3] and the Christian
faith in which he was grounded by the grace of God. Against the background of this
internal spiritual combat one can understand why, in his student days when he
became intrigued with psychology, he attempted with a certain degree of passion
to provide a psychological interpretation of religious life as a general human
phenomenon, but at the same time was acutely concerned to differentiate 'religion'
from the Christian faith. And when he turned to mission, he became even more
deeply engrossed in the articulation and analysis of this whole problem.[4] Later he
himself wrote about this period: "Again and again it was the question of the
relationship between the religions that came to the fore in our work."[5] Thus, it was

---

[1]J.H. Bavinck, *CBTM*, 11-12.

[2]J. van den Berg, "The Legacy of Johan Herman Bavinck," 173; cf. also
ICNCW, 81, where Bavinck refers to this as the "ruling problem" for missiology.

[3]In an interview, W. Balke suggested to the present author that it is not
entirely impossible that the Bavincks, coming as they did from Bentheim, had
internalized something of the old Saxon nature-mysticism of that area; cf. also W.
Balke, 25 ff., where he describes Saxon faith and religion.

[4]It should be noted here that one of the factors playing a role in Bavinck's
great interest in this problem was its prominence as object of Reformed scholarly
investigation in the 1920s.

[5]"Hendrik Kraemer als denker en medewerker," 161.

both personal interest and missionary necessity that drove him to try to fathom Eastern religiosity on the one hand and at the same time to underscore the 'otherness' of the gospel.

But these were not the only factors involved. Between 1930 and 1934 Bavinck was in fairly close contact with Hendrik Kraemer, who had entered the lists against the spiritual relativism found in missionary circles in that day and bore Bavinck along in this struggle, as it were. In Bavinck's own words: "...it was Kraemer who pointed out to me time and again that [the] question [regarding the relationship of the religions] should govern the whole methodology of missionary work."[6]   The publication of Bavinck's book on Christ and Eastern mysticism (*CMO*) in 1934 was a direct fruit of his reflection on these matters. But it was especially Kraemer's seminal 1938 book, *The Christian Message in a Non-Christian World*, along with the reactions to it in international missionary circles, that confirmed Bavinck in his conviction regarding the decisive importance of the issue of the relation between Christianity and the other religions and that led him to reflect ever more deeply and broadly on this subject.

In light of the foregoing it would seem obvious that a discussion of Bavinck's missionary theology should begin with an examination of his views on 'non-Christian' religions.   Formally speaking, this approach is not supported by Bavinck's own arrangement of the material in *IZW*, in which the issue of the relation between Christianity and the other religions is not dealt with in Part One on the Theory of Mission, but rather in Part Two on Elenctics, and then only implicitly. That this approach is warranted in a material sense, however, is shown by the opening pages of *IZW* where Bavinck states that the assessment of 'non-Christian' religions is closely bound up with the *primary* missiological question concerning the foundation of mission[7] and that the issue of the other religions is "so essential and so indispensable" for mission that missiology could not possibly be carried out adequately without dealing with it.[8]

Bavinck's views on the religions evolved gradually. One can distinguish two phases in this development.   Initially, he took his departure from   the conceptual resources of the psychology of religion, which he then tried to substantiate theologically. Later on, the approach was reversed: biblical-theological inquiry came to assume the position of first importance in his work, and he began to elucidate the psychological processes involved in the emergence of religiosity in the light of that inquiry.   Two important concepts with which Bavinck grappled in this connection are general revelation and religious consciousness; Bavinck's

---

[6]*Ibid.*

[7]Cf. *IZW*, 18-19.

[8]*Ibid.* 19; in support of this contention Bavinck cites W. Holsten: "Religionswissen-schaft ist   ...   nicht   eine   Hilfswissenschaft   der Missionswissenschaft, auch nicht ein Kapitel in ihr, genannt Missionsapologetik oder änlich, sondern sie bedingt die Missionswissen-schaft, wie sie von ihr bedingt ist; beide gehören zusammen als ein Ganzes," (The study of religion is ... not an auxiliary discipline belonging to missiology, nor is it a chapter in the latter called missionary apologetics or the like, but rather it presupposes missiology, just as it is presupposed by missiology; the two belong together as one whole), *Das Kergyma und der Mensch*, 55.

apprehension of the first of these will be dealt with later in this chapter and his views on the second will be examined in the following chapter. Before addressing this second, theological line of approach, however, we must first turn our attention to the earlier stage of the development of his understanding of religiosity.

2. Psychological Approach

2.1. Religious Feelings

In his first publication in the area of psychology (*ZKO*, 1925), Bavinck calls religion the ultimate and most fundamental complex of human emotional life.[9] He describes the essence of religious feeling as "the impulse to communion with God."[10] This inner urge, which is always and everywhere present among people, is founded in the fact that the human 'I' is incapable of existence apart from God. God is "the ground in which that 'I' is rooted."[11] Religious sense and feeling, however, are always shot through with a tremendous amount of ambivalence.

> God is experienced as the fearful one, as ineffably terrifying, awesome and repelling and simultaneously as the powerfully, magically enchanting one. On the one hand, people evince intense timidity before God, are overcome with an acute desire to flee from Him; and yet they are also fascinated by God, as it were, and constantly driven toward Him.[12]

This ambivalence is caused by the fact that there are three fundamental complexes of feeling found in the human soul: self-awareness, social awareness (feeling for the other), and religious awareness (feeling for God). The relationships among these three poles—the self, one's fellow man and God—are decisive for the composition and disposition of the human personality. From a logical point of view there is only one right relationship: love of God above all else (inasmuch as God is the ground of our being) and of the neighbor as oneself, and oneself as the neighbor (because man is always both the fruit and the source of community). This relational balance, however, has been thoroughly disrupted by sin. Man has made himself into a god and placed himself above and at the center of everything. Social and religious feeling has become overgrown with feeling for self. Man's personality has become unbalanced and is out of joint.[13] "It is the ascendancy of the feeling for self that keeps causing man to repulse the God whom he is seeking."[14] Bavinck

---

[9]This is in line with the conclusion of his dissertation, *viz.*, that feeling, emotion, and intuition are extremely important factors in mysticism and/or religion; cf. *EGAHS*, 92-95.

[10]*ZKO*, 96.

[11]*Ibid.*, 103.

[12]*Ibid.*, 96.

[13]Cf. *ibid.*, 100-104, *IZK*, 277-280, and *PWB*, 36-41.

[14]*PWB*, 171.

described this process as 'willingness' and yet 'non-willingness,' a 'turning toward' that is at once a 'turning away.'[15] Human beings can never escape this contradiction between dedication and defalcation at the center of their being, no matter how hard they try to overcome it.[16] Even when engaged in the deepest of religious pursuits, mysticism, man's quest for God is profaned by his obsessive bent toward self-deification, and thus the maintenance of self.[17] Reading Scripture through the spectacles of psychology, Bavinck found confirmation for his theory in various biblical passages. For example, he sees the psychological reality of thirst for God and synchronous flight from God illustrated in the narrative of Elijah standing in the presence of the Lord on Mount Horeb: "When Elijah heard [the gentle whisper of God's presence] he pulled his cloak over his face and went out and stood at the mouth of the cave" (I Kings 19:13). Bavinck commented as follows on this text: "God-fearing timidity caused him to cover his face, but the intense allurement he felt nevertheless drove him out to meet the Lord."[18] Bavinck also sees this concept of the inner contradiction at the heart of man's existence confirmed in the words of the Apostle Paul in Romans 7:19: "For what I do is not the good I want to do."[19]

In *IZK* Bavinck details the way in which man's religious life manifests itself. Bavinck locates religious feeling in the diagnostic, evaluative consciousness of the human soul, which is active in three areas: critical observation and assessment of life-events and creation,[20] observance of the law of God written in the human heart and embedded in creation, and mystical experience.[21] Bavinck writes concerning the world ordered by law:

> If you observe the world carefully, you will be moved ever anew
> by the powerful presence of [the principle of] service. The 'law
> of service' supports every creature like an arm, bringing the
> whole of this glorious world into existence. . . . Without that law
> of service, no being could be.[22]

Though these expressions of religious consciousness find their origin in the

---

[15]*Ibid.*

[16]Cf. *ibid.*, 41-42.

[17]Cf. *ibid.*, 145-146, and *CMO*, 222-223.

[18]*ZKO*, 96; cf. also *IZK*, 272-273.

[19]Cf. *ZKO*, 106.

[20]Bavinck does not mention creation in *IZK*, but does deal with it in *LV*, 38-39.

[21]Cf. *IZK*, 265.

[22]In *LV*, 23-28,

creation of man in God's image (*imago Dei*),[23] their activation inevitably bears a subjective character.[24] Bavinck calls this quickening the "great awakening" of the soul as if from a dream:

> It [the soul] has engaged in thought, has desired, hated, loved, sought, hoped, wept, and acted in countless ways. And now suddenly all of that sinks away, and it is as if [the soul] finds itself standing for the first time before that tremendous riddle: the depths of things, the ground of things, the meaning and end of things.[25]

Upon its awakening, "the soul finds itself standing as a beggar, barefoot and attired in shabby tatters of ignorance at the eternal gates of Truth. And it knocks...! Oh God, if Thou dost exist, Oh God...! Tell me what I am and why I am and why everything exists."[26] This awakening can take place in the life of whole peoples as well as in that of individuals, but is by no means certain: "There are many people who barely have an inkling that such questions even exist."[27]

Here, too, Bavinck makes the point that religious life, which is incapable of manifesting itself in anything other than a groping and stumbling manner, constitutes a corruption of true religion. Man's sinful, egoistic concentration upon himself gives rise to a "malevolent apperception of God's providential guidance of life," to manipulation of the divine norm for human life, and to misunderstanding of divine-human relations.[28] Elsewhere, Bavinck writes:

> Every world view is living proof of the strange discord existing in the human soul. No human person can rise above this internal unrest inasmuch as the relationship between man and God is invariably twisted and contorted. The subtle poison of sin creeps into all of man's faculties and appetites. Humans can do nothing other than seek God in view of the fact that they yearn after Him in the very depths of their being, and they can do nothing else than sidestep Him because they fear Him and hate Him with

---

[23]In *LV*, 35-40, Bavinck argues that even after the Fall, man in fact continues—by virtue of his creation in the image of God and consequent endowment with true knowledge, justice and holiness—to be a thinking and moral being who seeks communion with God. And if his religious feeling is awakened, he will begin to yearn after those three highest goods lost subsequent to the Fall.

[24]Cf. "Een woord van verweer tegen prof. Hoekstra en prof. Waterink," 548 ff.

[25]*LV*, 7-8.

[26]*Ibid.*, 8.

[27]*Ibid.*, 9. Nowhere in these reflections does one find the term 'general revelation'; the main point here is clearly the religious instincts or cravings of the human soul itself.

[28]*IZK*, 265-273.

every fiber of their nature.[29]
Religious life can even take on totally secular forms, for example when people try
to slake their thirst for God with money, honor or hedonistic pleasure.[30]

The relation between natural-religious life and Christian faith is one of
discontinuity in continuity: continuity due to the fact that the human heart thirsts
after God, seeks to know Him, enter into communion with Him, and follow His law;
discontinuity because of man's ego complex that prevents him from achieving
clarity of understanding and vision. Religion remains "in many respects untrue"
and must be "broken open from all sides by God's Revelation," which will occur
when "the Eternal Word begins to speak in our heart."[31]   This is the truth that
liberates from the lie.[32] It is on this basis that Bavinck calls the gospel the answer
to man's deep and powerful need: the elimination of the tension between God and
himself. Bavinck describes this tension as follows:

> Confronted with the destiny of human existence, man can do
> nothing other than acknowledge the triple insolvency of his life
> [i.e., bankruptcy with respect to knowledge, righteousness and
> sanctity].... We live with the ideal in view, but we do not achieve
> it. In a higher sense we cannot but feel our life to be a failure.
> No matter how excellent, no matter how brilliant it may seem,
> any deeper assessment leads to the recognition that it has failed
> to realize its essential value. That is why the cry for deliverance
> and the liberation of life has been raised so continuously and so
> earnestly throughout the whole of world history.[33]

In the confrontation with the Holy and with Jesus as the true man of God, people
discover their true sinful nature. "It is in this [encounter] that conversion begins,
here arises the triumphant faith that God is love and takes delight in forgiving the
repentant heart."[34] Bavinck speaks in this connection of "the great turning point in
human life,"[35] or "the great leap" which means nothing less than "the loss of oneself
and the rediscovery of oneself at a higher plane, a dying in order to be raised."[36] He
states clearly that this "is a work of God" that "is beyond all psychological

---

[29]*PWB*, 23.

[30]Cf. *LV*, 47-69; Bavinck even speaks here of the "'tri-unity' of sin," that
attracts and drives human life but that cannot long satisfy the "hunger of the human
heart," 68-69.

[31]*ZKO*, 116.

[32]Cf. *PWB*, 176-177.

[33]*LV*, 82-83.

[34]*Ibid.*, 98.

[35]*Ibid.*

[36]*IZK*, 273.

investigation."[37] In a later work, Bavinck argued that it is precisely at this point that an all-controlling difference between any form of religion and the Christian faith comes to light. "In the gospel, redemption is never only and not even in the first place a psychological process, but before all else, a profound change in the relation of God and man; it consists of reconciliation and justification."[38] Conversion and deliverance can never be fathomed in psychological terms but must always be understood as an inner renewal by the Holy Spirit, as "an essentially new life [wrought] by the strength of God."[39] Rebirth through the operation of the Holy Spirit gives rise to "a different concentration of the personality, a new life-orientation."[40] One ought not to think that Bavinck is talking here about an absolute break with the past, but rather about the maturation and fulfilment of religious life.

From the above it is clear that in the earlier period of the development of his thought Bavinck defined the origin and essence of the religious life of natural man in largely psychological terms, albeit in this, too, he tried to remain within the biblical tradition. Further, it is clear that his theological assessment of religious life, understood as a seeking and feeling after God, was relatively positive. And, finally, it is evident that his psychological approach to religion at this time made it possible for him to speak in a fairly uninhibited way about the similarities between the religious life of natural man and Christian faith.[41]

J. van den Berg points out that Bavinck was influenced in this regard by F.D.E. Schleiermacher.

> The tenor of [Bavinck's] thought is reminiscent of Schleiermacher, who took the notion of religious experience as his starting point. The present writer has in his possession Bavinck's own marked copy of Schleiermacher's *Reden*, in which the underlinings show how much he was preoccupied with Schleiermacher's thought on this subject.[42]

Schleiermacher defined the essence of religion as a sense of the Eternal. It is from the "*schlechthinniges Abhängigkeitsgefühl*" (feeling of sheer dependance) on the Eternal that all religions have grown. The great difference among the religions is explained by the fact that the Eternal is reflected in a variety of ways in human hearts. Religions, thus, are not of equal value. Christianity stands at the apex of all religions due to its utter dependance on the one God, who has been revealed in

---

[37]*Ibid.*

[38]*CMO*, 225.

[39]*IZK*, 271.

[40]*Ibid.*, 275.

[41]Cf. *ibid.* 265-273: in this passage religious experience and Christian experience are allowed to run through each other as if they were basically similar phenomena; here psychology governs exegesis.

[42]"The Legacy of J.H. Bavinck," 171.

Christ. In Schleiermacher's thought, experience and revelation coincide.[43] It is evident that Bavinck was indeed influenced to a certain degree by the fundamental structure of Schleiermacher's approach to religion. But that influence was perhaps less great than Van den Berg indicates. In fact, Bavinck's work gives reason to suppose that he was more directly influenced by the views of Rudolf Otto. Otto proceeded from the assumption that there is a religious a-priori to be found in humans, namely, a sense of the Holy. By virtue of this inner predisposition or impulse, Otto expounded, humans are open to impressions from the Holy and can do no other than react in a religious way to the reality of life and the world. This latently present religious sense can be energized by all sorts of experiences.[44] The similarity between Bavinck's views and those of Otto is clear, and is avouched by Bavinck himself at a later point in time, long after he had abandoned this notion of a religious a priori, when he wrote: "There is something in these arguments of Otto that speaks to us."[45]

2.2. Refutation of Criticism of the Psychological Approach

Bavinck's views were subjected to heavy criticism from within his own circles, particularly by two prominent professors, T. Hoekstra and J. Waterink,[46] who argued that Bavinck interpreted the origin and core of religion too psychologically, i.e., in terms of subjective feeling, and not theologically enough in terms of God's revelation and of objective knowledge. Hoekstra considered it to be in direct conflict with Reformed tradition to place the emotional moment above the epistemological element in religion. Waterink agreed. Following H. Bavinck,[47] he argued that religion always presupposes revelation from God and that therefore, logically speaking, the act of knowledge takes precedence over feeling. Any feeling after God, any desire for God or a life with God absent knowledge of God is simply out of the question.[48]

In his reply to this criticism, Bavinck grants that active religion is indeed

---

[43]Cf. his *Reden über die Religion* and *Der christliche Glaube*; these works are cited by Bavinck in *RBCG* but not employed to any real extent in terms of their content.

[44]Cf. R. Otto, *Das Heilige*, passim.

[45]*RBCG*, 105.

[46]Cf. Hoekstra in his review of *IZW*, in: *GTT*, XXVIII (1927/1928), 233-240, and Waterink, "Iets over de psychologie der religie," *GTT*, XXVIII (1927/1928), 443-517.

[47]Cf. H. Bavinck, *Gereformeerde dogmatiek*, 244: "*Religio subjectiva* is first of all a *habitus*, a certain aptitude or inclination in the human being, which switches over to *actus* through the agency of *religio objectiva*."

[48]Cf. *ibid.*, 277, where H. Bavinck argues that while it is true that religion occupies the whole person and that relationship with God is total and central, there is nevertheless an order in which knowledge leads the way."

impossible without divine revelation and knowledge of God. The fact that his critics came to think that he would deny this, he maintained, is due to a misunderstanding occasioned by his attempt to give religion a place within the realm of feeling. He had no intention in propounding this categorization, he wrote, to suggest that intuition or sense represented anything more than just one side of the origin of religion. The only idea he was trying to get across, he stated, was that subjective religion would be out of the question if divine revelation did not answer to a dormant longing for God in the human heart. At first, this longing is present as a *habitus*, which, according to Bavinck, can be best associated with what Calvin called the *semen religionis*.[49] It remains open to question, however, whether this dispute was only a matter of misunderstanding, as Bavinck averred, or whether—as the present writer tends to think—he initially did in fact position the origin and principle of religion mainly in a God-given, to be sure, but nevertheless *human* aptitude. In any case, it is clear that from this point forward Bavinck emphasized much more explicitly than he had before that religious consciousness is not only a psychological but also a theological phenomenon.[50]

All of this is plainly reflected in the second, revised edition of *IZK* (1935), in which religion is no longer treated within the framework of evaluative feeling but rather in the section that deals with the human ego. And what remained unclear in the first edition of this work is now fully spelled out:

... all human religion rests in and is only possible through the agency of God's continual self-revelation, which has spoken to man from the beginning.... This self-revelation of God is not only to be understood in the sense that both nature and history manifest His virtues to us; it also entails the reality that the human soul is, as it were, moored to God, is created innately oriented toward God.[51]

Furthermore, Bavinck now makes a much clearer distinction between the phenomena of general religious life, on the one hand, and Christian faith, on the other. "When we speak here about the psychological side of religious life," he states emphatically, "we are referring to religious life in the general sense of the word. Hence, it is the religion of the natural man that we wish to discuss [at this

---

[49]The difference between J.H. Bavinck and H. Bavinck with respect to this matter is that the former interpreted the *semen religionis* as an element of the domain of feeling, the emotional life, whereas the latter saw it as an element of the province of thought and knowledge. It is clear that when H. Bavinck identified *religio subjectiva* with the *semen religionis*, he was referring to an inner aptitude for thought: the searchings within the realm of feeling arise from knowledge; cf. *Gereformeerde dogmatiek*, 244-245. Calvin himself did not make distinctions of this kind: the *semen religionis* or *sensus* (!) *Divinitatis* is a reality manifesting both assertive and cognitive sides.

[50]Cf. "Een woord van verweer tegen prof. Hoekstra en prof. Waterink," 544-552.

[51]*IZK²*, 303.

point]."[52] The evaluation of general religious life as compared with Christian faith receives a more negative accent due to the fact that the theological differences between them are emphasized rather than their psychological similarities. The *totaliter aliter* character of a life lived out in the light of God's revelation in Holy Scripture is posited in no uncertain terms: "Where God's Special Revelation spreads its light, everything becomes different."[53]

In his 1934 book, *CMO*, the point of departure for which was his intensive missionary confrontation with Eastern religions, Bavinck provides an impressive phenomenological concretization of the great chasm lying between all forms of religious seeking and feeling after God, on the one hand, and bowing before God's Truth in Jesus Christ, on the other. He has, to be sure, much appreciation for the valuable elements in Eastern religions, which he explains in terms of the metaphysical link between God and man and which he views as points of contact or starting points for the proclamation of the gospel. But in light of the break between God and man in a moral sense, a rupture which cannot be repaired by human effort, Bavinck's core message is that everything is different from the way it is portrayed in human religion: "Life is different and the world is different. God is different and I too am different...."[54] This work clearly demonstrates that for Bavinck the jump from religious consciousness to Christian faith has become longer, though there is still no talk of a radical break between the two. On the contrary, Bavinck continues to descry points of contact for the gospel amid the distortions of the human-divine relationship. Hence, he takes the view that the gospel not only fulfils a critical function as radical corrective to various forms of religious consciousness, but also provides the final answer to all those peoples "who for centuries have sought after and thought about God."[55]

2.3. Summary

Following the trend of the day,[56] Bavinck attempted to couple psychology with official Reformed theology in his earliest systematic reflections on general revelation and religious consciousness. Initially, the origin and essence of religious consciousness were described largely in terms of psychological categories to which he added a theological coloring. Sometimes he used Bible texts to provide subsequent "proof" for his psychological observations.[57] Under the pressure of

---

[52]*Ibid.*

[53]*Ibid.*, 312.

[54]*Ibid.*, 203. Cf. J.J.E. van Lin, 185, note 4 and 187, note 49.

[55]*IZK²*, 232.

[56]Cf. J. Stellingwerf, 107ff. Bavinck himself referred to this trend in *DTK*, 2.

[57]In a letter dating from a later period a well-known Reformed theologian, K. Schilder, expressly states that in Bavinck's early work "Scriptural principles are only mentioned *a posteriori* and are linked as best as possible with results obtained

criticism he began to integrate Reformed views more decisively into his thinking and to define the origin and essence of religious consciousness primarily in theological and only secondarily in psychological terms.[58] Central to this concept was the idea that humans, as creatures inherently oriented toward the Divine, are potentially seekers after God. Religious consciousness, which constitutes the activation of this potentiality by means of general revelation, contains positive elements amidst the adulteration that characterizes it. In this matter Bavinck was basically following in the line of H. Bavinck, without, however, explicitly referring to him. Nonetheless, one significant difference remained between them: Bavinck situated religion primarily in the realm of feeling, whereas H. Bavinck placed it in the capacity for thought and knowledge. The position Bavinck took on this issue at that time would continue to play an essential role in his subsequent thought, as can be illustrated by his later emphasis on the inadequacy of rational argumentation for purposes of convicting people of other faiths regarding the truth of the gospel. At this stage, however, he had yet to engage in an independent biblical-theological examination of this question.

3. Theological Approach

3.1. Introduction

Bavinck's theological evaluation of 'non-Christian' religions gradually took on more negative overtones. This is shown, for example, by a series of three articles he wrote[59] with an eye to the International Missionary Conference held in 1938 in Tambaram, at which the relation between Christian faith and the other religions was to be an important subject for discussion. In these articles he argued that "the witness of the Christian Church" regarding man, revelation and redemption "stands in direct contradiction to the thoughts that live in the hearts of many" in the mission field.[60] This basic shift in thinking seems to have come about as a result of his reflection on the contents of Hendrik Kraemer's 1938 book, *The Christian Message in a Non-Christian World.*

According to Kraemer, who was expressly concerned to approach the question of the relation of Christianity to the other religions in the light of Scripture alone, the origin of religion is to be found solely in the revelation of God's will, which also takes place alongside Scripture in nature, history, and human reason. Religion itself is man's answer to God's revelation, and because man constantly

---

by other means." This confidential letter, carrying no specific date, is found in the archives of Kampen Theological Seminary.

[58]If the concept of *semen religionis* or *religio subjectiva* is viewed as a fruit of common grace, as is true in Bavinck's case, then all religion is in principle a theological phenomenon, however determined it may be subsequently by psychological factors; cf. R.H. Bremmer, *Herman Bavinck als dogmaticus*, 227.

[59]These articles appeared simultaneously under the general title "Drie grote vragen," in a single issue of a contemporary Dutch missionary journal.

[60]"Drie grote vragen: De vraag naar de verlossing," 178.

stands in defiance of God's will, religion as such, even in its most noble forms, can never be or be viewed as anything other than human rebellion against God. Revelation in Christ is not the fulfilment of all religious aspirations, but on the contrary constitutes God's judgment over these endeavors. Execution of this judgment, wherever and whenever it occurs, precipitates radical conversion. In Kraemer's own words:

> [Because] the revelation of God in Christ transcends and contradicts all human wisdom by its divine folly, and all human aspiration and expectation by its entirely unexpected way of fulfilling them, it is wrong to use the term fulfilment. Conversion and regeneration would be truer to reality. At any rate, the term fulfilment in the customary sense of bringing to perfection what had already naturally grown to a more or less successful approximation to the life and truth revealed in Christ, is not applicable to the relation of the non-Christian religions to the revelation of Christ.... God works in man and shines through nature. The religious and moral life of man is man's achievement, but also God's wrestling with him; it manifests at once a receptivity to God and an inexcusable disobedience and blindness to God. The world fails to know God even in its highest wisdom, although it strives to do so. Man seeks God and at the same time flees from him, because his self-assertive self-centeredness of will, his root-sin, always breaks through.... Such was and is the contradictory condition of the world, and of the religious and moral life of the world in its different forms, and the dialectical relation of God to it.[61]

This quotation clearly illustrates Kraemer's two-edged approach to human religion.

In the inaugural address he delivered on the occasion of his appointment as professor of missions at the Free University of Amsterdam, Bavinck termed this publication of Kraemer's an "extremely important and valuable missionary book."[62] The extent to which Bavinck was affected by Kraemer's views is made clear by what he wrote in the introduction to the book-length Dutch summary he produced of Kraemer's work:

> [In Kraemer's book non-Christian religious phenomena] are not only described in a lively and gripping manner, but they are also weighed and, as it were, confronted with the message of Christ, who is beginning to penetrate into the far-away world of the Orient. The important theological problems that are involved in this evaluation are carefully probed and the great significance of these questions is brought clearly to light. [Kraemer] provides a basic vision in respect of all these phenomena, ... a vision through which our understanding of them is greatly deepened.[63]

Eighteen years later Bavinck wrote that in *The Christian Message in a Non-Christian World*

---

[61] *The Christian Message in a Non-Christian World*, 124 and 126-127.

[62] *CPVW*, 22.

[63] *BCNCR*, 6.

the deeply vital question of the proclamation of the gospel in
relation to the other religions is dealt with in such a deep and
honest way that it could not help but make a tremendous
impression not only on countless missionaries but especially on
many younger Christians throughout Asia and Africa.[64]

Inspired by Kraemer, Bavinck began to immerse himself in independent biblical-
theological reflection on the origin and essence of religious consciousness.

In the following discussion, we will deal first with Bavinck's view of
general revelation and thereafter with his concept of religious consciousness. This
sequence speaks for itself since from this time onward these two notions are related
in Bavinck's thought as word and counter-word, summons and response, action and
reaction. It has been necessary to organize the material in the following sections
according to a scheme devised by the present writer, for though he frequently wrote
about these matters, Bavinck himself never dealt with them in a thoroughly
systematic way, not even in *RBCG*, his most important study in this area. The
subdivisions offered below are intended to serve the purpose of providing as
complete and clear an overview as possible of the subject matter in order to
facilitate optimal insight into Bavinck's thinking on the issues involved here. We
will be particularly concerned in our analysis to place Bavinck's views in broader
theological perspective by tracing his intellectual links to John Calvin, Herman
Bavinck, Karl Barth, and Hendrik Kraemer, the four theologians with whom
Bavinck was engaged in dialogue most particularly. But we begin with a
discussion of the elemental point of departure for all of Bavinck's subsequent
reflective endeavors in the field of missiology.

3.2. Basic Point of Departure

There were a number of fundamental questions with which Bavinck was confronted
in his attempt to develop a missionary theology:
Where does religion originate, with man or with God? What is
religion actually? Is it a word, an attitude toward life, a
conviction, a collection of thoughts and sentiments born in the
human heart? Or does it consist in deepest essence of an
answering, a reply to what God said first, a response to what God
did first, a reaction to God's action?[65]

Concepts of the origin and essence of religious consciousness can never be proved
scientifically but can only be posited on the basis of presuppositions and elucidated
accordingly. For when speaking of religious consciousness, we touch on the
deepest foundations of human existence, which human thought is incapable of
fathoming. When reflecting on these matters, Bavinck writes,
we are overcome by that feeling of inexpressible minuteness and
puniness that is so characteristic of our entire human existence.
We stand in this world for a moment, in this utterly enigmatic
world, and we have no inkling as to the great 'whence', the great

---

[64]"Kraemer als denker en medewerker," 88.

[65]*RBCG*, 112.

'wherefore', the great 'whereto,' the great 'how.'[66]
The entire cosmos, our being, our inner life is rooted in mystery. But this is by no means to say that the issues involved here are unworthy of or unfit for academic investigation. On the contrary, "Whoever does not feel that [mystery], whoever has never felt that, is not yet ready for real scientific endeavor."[67]

Bavinck agrees with Kraemer's thesis that, philosophically speaking, the theological approach to religion is just as valid as that of the disciplines of the history and phenomenology of religions. Since the latter do not operate free of 'pre-scientific' opinions, values and choices, the theological approach cannot be disqualified for working with subjective biases of its own.[68] However, Bavinck goes even a step further. From an anthropological point of view, he argues, rejection of a theological approach to and assessment of religion would represent an injustice to human beings, for in the absence of this approach a form of science would come into existence devoid of any existential concern with the most profound questions of life: God, sin, grace, and revelation. He writes that without this concern, this close involvement, "one can dig around in these matters without ever taking a decision, without ever saying 'yes' or 'no.' If one wishes to call that the pinnacle of all of science, then the pinnacle of science would entail the total debasement of our humanity."[69] Moreover, he continues, the 'scientific' approach, involves yet another preconception, namely, that religion is nothing more than an historical phenomenon and that the deepest questions of life are unanswerable.

For a Christian, an important presupposition is that faith in the absolute truth of God's revelation in Scripture is foundational. That is why, before he goes on to an examination of religious consciousness, Bavinck states: "From now on we can only speak theologically. That means that we must listen to God. He alone can tell us what that is, that 'religious consciousness' which we have learned to recognize, [He alone can tell us] where it comes from, where it ends."[70] Elsewhere he adds that a Christian "acknowledges that this view is not based upon reasoning, but is instead a matter of faith."[71] Again he writes in the same vein: "No philosophical reflection can help us here; we will never be able to decipher these things with our human minds; the only thing we can do is listen to what God has to say to us here."[72] And he adds further that "all human speculations are useless; we should only listen to what God himself reveals to us about His work among the

---

[66]*Ibid.*, 110; cf. also *DAC*, 9, 10.

[67]*Ibid.*, 110.

[68]"Religie en het christelijk geloof," 66-67. Cf. H. Kraemer, *Religion and the Christian Faith*, 143.

[69]"Religie en het christelijk geloof," 67.

[70]*RBCG*, 110.

[71]*CBTM*, 19.

[72]"Het evangelie en de andere godsdiensten," 149.

Gentiles."[73]   It is not possible to gain a clear picture of religion through mere reasoning in isolation from what is taught in Scripture. All philosophical and psychological thoughts must be taken captive to make them obedient to the Word (cf. 2 Cor. 10:5).[74] "Only God Himself can judge all this human religion correctly"[75] Thus, here too Bavinck follows Kraemer in his insistence on radical orientation to God's revelation in Christ as the only valid starting point for any discussion of the origin and essence of the 'non-Christian' religions.[76]   Kraemer wrote that the "only possible basis [for this kind of reflection] is the faith that God has revealed *the* Way and *the* Life and *the* Truth in Jesus Christ..., "[77] adding that this belief is more than a subjective choice that could be exchanged at will for another. "The Christian's ultimate ground of faith," he asserts, is to be found in Paul's confession: "'The Spirit bears witness along with our own spirits that we are children of God' (Rom. 8:16); and [the believer] can die for that."[78] "This stance," Bavinck wrote, "may strike some as being scientifically invalid, but they need to come to the realization that in terms of these elemental, decisive questions of human life no one is or can be free from prejudice."[79]   In a later publication Kraemer reiterated his convictions on this matter and defended them against the criticism they had engendered.

> They found [my position] 'unscientific,' prejudiced narrow-mindedness, and required from me a neutral, presumably 'objective' standpoint, as if a Christian has the possibility and the right to have a 'standing-place' whence he may judge Jesus Christ. Moreover they did not see that without any reflection or valid philosophical argument, they took for granted that the revelation in Christ is subsumed under the general Idea of Religion....[80]

Shortly after Kraemer's book appeared, Bavinck wrote that he concurred fully with

---

[73]*ICNCW*, 102.

[74]In *RBCG*, 105-109, Bavinck rejects especially S. Freud's psychological interpretation of religion, but adds: "We stand powerless in one another's presence, we cannot refute each other because we appear to have reached the mysterious limits of our scientific learning and exploration."

[75]*CBTM*, 117.

[76]Cf. *ibid.*

[77]*The Christian Message in a Non-Christian World*, 107.

[78]*Ibid.*, 108.

[79]*BCNCR*, 80-81.

[80]*Religion and the Christian Faith*, 142-143.

these views.[81]

3.3. General Revelation

3.3.1. The Reality of General Revelation

When Bavinck employs the concept 'general revelation,' he rejects the meaning this term was often given during the course of the history of theology. This notion does not signify a disclosure of divine truths that are discovered by reason, but denotes a person-directed, relevant, impinging expression of God's will.

> If we wish to use the expression 'general revelation,' we must not do so in the sense that one can logically conclude God's existence from it. This *may* be possible, but it only leads to a philosophical notion of God as the first cause. But that is not the biblical idea of 'general revelation.' When the Bible speaks of general revelation, it means something quite different. There it has a much more personal nature. It is divine concern for men collectively and individually. God's deity and eternal power are evident; they overwhelm man; they strike him suddenly in moments when he thought they were far away. They creep up on him; they do not let go of him, even though man does his best to escape them.[82]

Bavinck sympathizes with Kraemer's contention, inspired by Karl Barth, that the term 'general revelation' is self-contradictory, since revelation in the sense of God's self-communication can, by its very nature, never be general, i.e., be everywhere and always available in advance. According to Kraemer:

> Revelation is an act of God, an act of divine grace for forlorn man and a forlorn world by which He condescends to reveal His Will and His Heart, and which, [precisely] because it is revelation, remains hidden except to the eye of *faith*, and even then remains an incomprehensible miracle.... Revelation is no object but an action, a divine movement. In this connection 'general revelation,' in the sense of God revealing Himself with compelling lucidity in nature, history and reason, is a contradiction in terms, for what lies on the street has no need to be revealed. By its nature revelation is and must be special. It affirms that God paves the way, not man.[83]

Despite these caveats, however, Bavinck continues to use the term 'general

---

[81]Cf. "Religie en het christelijk geloof," 66-67.

[82]*CBTM*, 124. It should be noted here that earlier on Bavinck spoke in a more static way about general revelation, cf., e.g., *LV*, 38-39.

[83]*The Christian Message in a Non-Christian World*, 118-119. On this matter of divine self-disclosure Kraemer follows Karl Barth, who maintained that it is only from within Christ that one discovers what revelation is, namely, the disclosure "at the human level" of "something which is truly *new*, which was previously unknown because it was veiled and hidden." Cf. also H. Kraemer, *Godsdienst, godsdiensten en het christelijk geloof*, 296-297.

revelation' to denote that self-disclosure of God which takes place alongside the Word.[84]

It is only in *The Church Between the Temple and Mosque* that Bavinck finally accounts for and defends the reality of general revelation theologically by linking it to God's revelation in Christ: "God's self-disclosure in Jesus Christ is the root of His search for man and His ceaseless speaking to him."[85] Thus, it was only later that Bavinck adduced a Christological foundation for general revelation.[86] Earlier, Bavinck connected the notion of God's voice sounding throughout the world with the idea of creation: "The earth is the Lord's and everything in it, the world, and all who live in it; for He founded it upon the seas and established it upon the waters" (Ps. 24:1, 2).[87] On the strength of His status as Creator, God lays claims to the entire world and to full jurisdiction over it: "From heaven the Lord looks down and sees all mankind; from His dwelling place He watches all who live on the earth" (Ps. 33:13).[88] And, Bavinck argues, Paul's word on the Areopagus, too, fits in well with this: "For in Him we live and move and have our being" (Acts 17:28).[89] It is clear that God busies Himself and wishes to busy Himself with each and every member of the human family.[90] Here Bavinck follows John Calvin:

> [God] not only sowed in men's minds that seed of religion of which we have spoken but revealed himself and daily discloses himself in the whole workmanship of the universe. As a consequence, men cannot open their eyes without being compelled to see him.[91]

God does not abandon fallen human beings, but on the contrary visits them with His grace and reveals Himself to them. "In the first place," Bavinck wrote in 1954, "it should be noted that all human persons, no matter how deeply they have fallen or how far they have gone astray, remain within the reach of God's general

---

[84]Kraemer, too, held on to this term: "It is extremely difficult," he wrote, "to find new, generally accepted terms. The most fruitful [way to deal with this problem], it seems to us, [would be to join in] a stubborn struggle to purify the old ones"; *Godsdienst, godsdiensten en het christelijk geloof*, 298.

[85]*CBTM*, 19.

[86]This insight, which, as indicated, came to him via Kraemer (cf. also *The Christian Message in a Non-Christian World*, 103-104), was, however, never subjected by Bavinck to thoroughgoing theological scrutiny.

[87]Cf. *IZW*, 25 (*ISM*, 12).

[88]Cf. *ibid.*

[89]Cf.. *RBCG*, 113; earlier on, Bavinck used this text in reference to the presence of religious yearning in the human heart; cf. *ZKO*, 103.

[90]Cf. *RWBOT*, 136.

[91]*Institutes*, Vol. I, Book 1, Chap. V.1, 51-52.

revelation."[92] A few years later he speaks of the "continual and living presence of God which is almost tangible and visible in everything that happens,"[93] and in his important posthumous publication he states:

> From age to age [God] addressed man and called him to repentance and conversion. The history of mankind is more than just a long account of what man has done, created and invented; its deepest mystery is the story of God's concern with man and man's response to God's revelation.[94]

This idea, Bavinck contends, is evident in Scripture.

> It may appear that during the centuries of Israel's separation God abandoned the other nations to their fate, but this is by no means the case. The other peoples were also the continuous object of God's dealings; over them, too, God raised Himself up as righteous Judge. It is striking how many times the other nations are called upon in the Psalms to recognize and honor God and how often the prophets witnessed against the peoples surrounding Israel. God does not relinquish His jurisdiction over the peoples but demands *their* worship as well and holds them responsible for their apostasy and degeneracy.[95]

In various publications Bavinck cites a total of five Bible passages which, he argues, clearly point to the reality of general revelation as he understands it.[96] (Job 33:14-18) *"For God does speak—now one way, now another—though man may not perceive it. In a dream, in a vision of the night, when deep sleep falls on men as they slumber in their beds, he may speak in their ears and terrify them with warnings, to turn man from wrongdoing and keep him from pride, to preserve his soul from the pit, his life from perishing by the sword."* This text makes it clear that God converses with every human person right throughout his or her life, and that at certain moments God stands very near to that person and whispers something in his or her ear.[97]

(John 1:4, 5, 9) *"In Him [the Word] was life, and that life was the light of men. The light shines in the darkness, but the darkness has not understood it.... The true light that gives light to every man was coming into the world."* From these words we gain some insight into the universal extent and intent of the activity of the Word. All sense of values, all philosophy and religion and all the other things that make up life are subject to the Word of light that shines in the darkness and is not

---

[92] *IZW*, 228 (cf. *ISM*, 227).

[93] *RBCG*, 117.

[94] *CBTM*, 19.

[95] *IZW*, 25-26 (cf. *ISM*, 12-13).

[96] In his publications Bavinck refers repeatedly to these texts, which for him are the most important scriptural passages with respect to the issue of general revelation. This choice of texts is in keeping with a long theological tradition.

[97] Cf. *RWBOT*, 136.

swallowed up by that darkness. It is therein that human life is anchored. In verse 9 this is made even more concrete and individual: *that gives light to every man*. This indicates "that in the life of every human person a conversation takes place, whether noticed or heard or not, between that person and the Word which is present everywhere around him, which always accompanies him, which embraces his entire life."[98]

(Acts 14:15b-17) *"We are bringing you good news, telling you to turn from these worthless things to the living God, who made heaven and earth and sea and everything in them. In the past He let all nations go their own way. Yet He has not left himself without testimony: He has shown kindness by giving you rain from heaven and crops in their seasons; He provides you with plenty of food and fills your hearts with joy."* The works of God's hands speak of His forbearance and goodness. Amongst all the twisted deeds invented by human minds and wrought by human hands shine God's great deeds of benevolence, "a never-ending proclamation of God's mercy."[99]

(Acts 17:26, 27) *"From one man He made every nation of men, that they should inhabit the whole earth; and He determined the times set for them and the exact places where they should live. God did this so that men would seek him and perhaps reach out for him and find him, though He is not far from each one of us."* Man is destined by God to seek and to find Him. Insofar as one can speak of a seeking after God by the nations, that searching is purely and simply the fruit of God's dealings with them and His care over them. He keeps tugging at them, as it were, in the midst of all the darkness, in order that they might perchance reach out to Him. God seeks in one way or another to elicit an answer from man.[100]

(Romans 1:19, 20) *"Since what may be known about God is plain to them, because God has made it plain to them. For since the creation of the world God's invisible qualities—his eternal power and divine nature—have been clearly seen, being understood from what has been made, so that men are without excuse."* For Bavinck Romans 1:19-32 constitutes the most important testimony regarding general revelation (and thus also religious consciousness),[101] which explains why he treats it at such length. In the following paragraph special attention will be devoted to his interpretation verses 19 and 20.

The phrase "what may be known about God" defines the truth referred to in verse 18, but simultaneously implies a limitation: it is not the full riches of the

---

[98]*Ibid.*, 37; cf. also *RBCG*, 128-129. This interpretation of the Prologue to John's gospel, which Bavinck borrowed from H. Bavinck (cf. *Gereformeerde dogmatiek*, 282), was later opposed by various observers, who saw in this passage something quite different, *viz.*, a confirmation of the position that God reveals Himself exclusively in Christ (cf. G.C. Berkouwer, 199 ff.).

[99]*AWW*, 135; cf. *ZWN*, 70.

[100]Cf. *AWW*, 179; *RBCG*, 121; *ZWN*, 70. In an earlier publication, *GGNT*, Bavinck sees in this passage a description of "the nobility of man," 601. This illustrates the progress from a more anthropocentric to a theocentric emphasis in his thinking.

[101]Cf. *RBCG*, 122.

wisdom and knowledge of God that is made plain or revealed, but that which is possible for man to know. The term "is plain" is a translation of the Greek adjective φανερόν (evident, transparent or visible), and the word that is translated by the expression "has made it plain" is not derived from the usual αποκαλύπτω (unveil, reveal), which appears, for example, at the beginning of verse 18 in conjunction with God's wrath, but rather an aorist form of φανερόω (show, make visible or clear). According to Bavinck, the meaning of the clause "because God has made it plain to them" is that God's truth urges itself upon people and that God's voice is so powerful that no one can struggle free from it. And the term "to them" underscores the fact that this truth does not run off people like water off a duck's back, but instead penetrates their consciousness, demonstrating itself to their hearts and minds. "God's invisible qualities" refers to God's virtues, to that which is inaccessible to human eyes. His "eternal power" and "divine nature" denote the two virtues which determine the essential relationship of man to God. The term 'eternal power' points to the fact that God is the bearer of all things, that man lives by the might of God, and thus that man's relationship to God is one of totally dependency. The concept 'divine nature' signifies the 'wholly otherness' of God, which always entails an I-Thou relationship, a relationship of responsibility between man and God. The phrase "since the creation of the world" carries the connotation of 'always and everywhere.' Paul's use of the words "from what has been made" shows that it is not only in nature but also in God's actions in history, in His guidance of life and governance of the world, and in the human conscience that what may be known about God is made plain.[102] Bavinck raised objections to existing translations of the term νοούμενα, such as that in the most popular version of the Dutch Bible, "apprehended by reason,"[103] or that in the New English Bible, "have been visible to the eye of reason." These renderings lead to misunderstanding because of their use of the word 'reason.' Literally translated, this passive participle of the verb νοέω means "becoming understood," and the relevant part of the text should then read: "His invisible qualities—His eternal power and divine nature—are clearly seen, *becoming understood* from what has been made." It would be incorrect to take this participle as having a conditional connotation: '*if* the invisible qualities are understood, they will be apprehended.' As is evident from the whole context in which this passage occurs, Paul is not speaking here of a possibility but of a factual reality. It is important to recognize that there is no reference in this text to anything like a process of reasoning leading to apprehension of what may be known about God.

> The Greek word *nooumen*a, literally, "being intelligently observed," does not refer to seeing with the eyes in this case, but neither does it mean that "seeing God's everlasting power and godhead" is attained by a process of reasoning. It is not a logical conclusion, but a flash that comes in a moment of vision. It comes suddenly to man, it overwhelms him.[104]

The phrase with which these verses end, "so that men are without excuse," expresses the logical consequence of what has gone before. Bavinck comments that

---

[102]Cf. *CBTM*, 125.

[103]Dutch: "met het verstand doorzien."

[104]*CBTM*, 120.

the words 'made it plain to them' in verse 19 "cannot mean that man really sees and understands" what can be known about God. "Whether man indeed comes as far as seeing [this] is another matter. It is possible that man does not see it because it is automatically repressed, as a rule."[105] What has been made plain to man about God "does not lead to knowledge. . . . Man represses the truth. Therefore he is 'without excuse.'"[106] To sum up, it is clear, according to Bavinck, that the central message this passage wishes to convey is that God's wondrous dealings in the world have been heard as a steady knocking throughout history and in every human life.[107]

That this biblical teaching regarding the nearness of God is confirmed by actual practice is shown by two things, according to Bavinck. First, "even the mere fact that all peoples of the world have reflected on God, gods or spirits, and have believed in them, seems to provide cogent demonstration of the fact that man has always been touched in some measure by God's revelation."[108] And secondly, he refers to the fact that deep in their hearts humans always have a vague awareness that they are playing games with the Almighty and that in the final analysis they are constantly attempting to flee from Him, always trying to escape His grasp[109] Bavinck gives a striking illustration of this in a story he tells of a talk he once had with someone in the Far East. At the end of the dialogue, during which Bavinck had tried unsuccessfully to convince this man of the truth of God, the latter, who had spent the whole evening disputing Bavinck, finally said, "Perhaps I have only been opposing you to reassure my heart."[110] Bavinck wrote that he could explain "this [second] phenomenon in no other way than on the basis of the understanding that God's general revelation reaches every person."[111]

Bavinck comes to the conclusion that a human life is never solely two-dimensional, but always includes a third dimension in one form or another as well. In addition to togetherness with fellow humans and the cosmos, there is a permanent togetherness with God, however lost that can become in the whirl of everyday things. Human life consists of a continual dialogue with God, a conversation which

---

[105]*CBTM*, 119. It should be noted here that though there is no basic difference between what Bavinck says in *RBCG*, 123 and 127, and *CBTM*, 119-120) with respect to the concept ἐφανέρωσεν, in *CBTM* his treatment of it is more precise in terms of formulation.

[106]*CBTM*, 120.

[107]Cf. *RBCG*, 123, 124, 127, 163, 167, 168, and *CBTM*, 119-120.

[108]"General Revelation and the Non-Christian Religions," 53.

[109]Cf. *IZW*, 229 (*ISM*, 227-228), and *CBTM*, 124. It would be well to point out here that since these two observable facts can also be explained in other ways, they do not 'prove' anything. They can, however, be said to confirm biblical teaching in the sense that they are in harmony with it.

[110]*PPRAO*, 19.

[111]*IZW*, 229 (cf. *ISM*, 228), see also *AWW*, 148.

God keeps initiating over and over again. This I-Thou relation between us and God comprises the core of our existence.[112] With respect to the effectuation of general revelation Bavinck followed Kraemer, who emphasized the voluntaristic, personal character of God's revelation along with biblical realism as opposed to all philosophical views. Kraemer expressed the view that general revelation

> can henceforth only mean that God shines revealingly through the works of His creation, through the thirst and quest for truth and beauty, through the conscience and the thirst and quest for goodness, which throbs in man even in his condition of forlorn sinfulness, because God is continuously occupying Himself and wrestling with man, in all ages and with all people.[113]

Bavinck summarizes Kraemer's position as follows: "This revelation is not a disclosure of wise ideas, but is an expression of the living, prevailing Will of God, which contravenes our will at every juncture and thus is engaged in a life-and-death struggle with our will."[114] Though Bavinck has some reservations in respect of Kraemer's notion of biblical realism, he sees "something extraordinarily surprising and fascinating" in it.[115] And he follows Kraemer's lead in interpreting general revelation as vibrant event, a dynamic divine activity that stands in direct relation to the full reality of human life. Clearly, Bavinck has bade farewell here to the ideas of Schleiermacher and Otto, for whom the human-divine I-Thou relationship takes its rise from an a priori feeling of sheer dependance (*schlechthinniges Abhängigkeitsgefühl*) on the Eternal or sense of the Holy.

To recapitulate, it can be said that with regard to the substantiation of the reality of general revelation Bavinck followed in the footsteps of Calvin and H. Bavinck,[116] both of whom, each in his own way, engaged in theology from the aspect of creation. But, following Kraemer, Bavinck conceived of the actualization of general revelation in more dynamic terms than either of them did, and later he also indirectly provided general revelation with a Christological foundation.

3.3.2. The Material and Instrumental Modes of General Revelation

Starting from the reality of general revelation, Bavinck also indicates the manner in which God effects this self-disclosure.

In the first place, God reveals himself in the universe, in nature. The overwhelming grandeur of creation compels us, as it were, to come to a recognition of God. And we do not reach that awareness by means of logic, by means of

---

[112]Cf. *RWBOT*, 137; "De onbekende God," 11; *CBTM*, 123-124; *RBCG*, 124.

[113]*The Christian Message in a Non-Christian World*, 125.

[114]*BCNCR*, 27.

[115]*Ibid.*, 96.

[116]"It is remarkable ... that sin ... does not alter the factuality of revelation. God keeps disclosing himself; He does not withdraw himself." H. Bavinck, *Gereformeerde dogmatiek*, 321.

carefully constructed argumentation, but instead arrive at it directly and spontaneously.[117] "The heavens declare the glory of God; the skies proclaim the work of His hands. Day after day they pour forth speech; night after night they display knowledge" (Psalm 19:2, 3). This proclamation bears a paradoxical character: "There is no speech, nor are there words; their voice is not heard; yet their voice goes out through all the earth, and their words to the end of the world." (RSV, vv. 4, 5). This revelation consists, thus, of speech without words, of wordless witness. It is a power that enfolds man on all sides in quiet majesty.[118] It takes place through the medium of the vast star-studded firmament (Psalm 8:3, 4) and the ranges of awesome mountain spires (Psalm 65:6), the mysterious instinct of animals (Jer. 8:7). God meets man in the order of creation, of nature, of the times and seasons, of social and economic life (Psalm 104), the wind, thunder and lightning, in the "radiant beauty of a glorious summer morning."[119] These are just a few examples, for "who can trace the hidden ways by which God proves His existence to man?"[120] God in His totality stands constantly before us.

Second, God reveals himself in the human conscience. "God occupies Himself with man's ... innermost being. God reminds him again and again that responsibility and guilt do exist."[121] Even though 'conscience' does not figure terminologically in the Old Testament, it plainly does in substance. To see this, one need only think of a few examples, such as the passage from Job already cited above (33:14-18); Amos 4:13: "He who ... declares to man what is his thought...." (RSV); and Psalm 139 which clearly witnesses to "the presence of God in the depths of our inner life, in [our] conscience."[122] In the New Testament this notion comes to new expression in the writings of Paul, for example in Romans 2:14, 15:

> Indeed, when Gentiles, who do not have the law, do by nature things required by the law, they are a law for themselves, even though they do not have the law, since they show that the requirements of the law are written on their hearts, their consciences also bearing witness, and their thoughts now accusing, now even defending them.

This passage, too, clearly witnesses to a hidden action of God in the human heart.[123]

---

[117]Cf. "De onbekende God," 8 and *CBTM*, 124.

[118]Cf. *RBCG*, 114 and "General Revelation and the Non-Christian Religions," 53.

[119]*CBTM*, 124; cf. *RBCG*, 114, *CBTM*, 123-124. In an earlier publication Bavinck refers in this connection to the "law of service" that permeates the whole of creation and proclaims something of God's grace, justice and righteousness.

[120]*CBTM*, 124

[121]*Ibid.*

[122]*RBCG*, 115-116.

[123]Cf. *PPRAO*, 10-11. Strangely, Bavinck did not employ this text in *RBCG*.

In that divine action lies the origin of human self-consciousness, the observing and simultaneously critical inner eye. "Man is always at once actor, observer, and judge. He acts but knows that he acts, too, and also judges what he does."[124] Humans both contemplate and appraise their deeds, they see themselves but also view themselves critically. "In that great mystery of the doubleness in our consciousness there is something of God"[125]

Finally, God also reveals himself in the history of peoples and individuals. "There are good and bad days, there are all sorts of vicissitudes and fortunes, and in all of them the great Ruler of our lives speaks to us."[126] The Old Testament in particular teaches clearly that God is present in world affairs, and shows that in human life fortune is sometimes tethered to deeds. In this connection, Bavinck mentions a number of texts from the book of Proverbs (1:31, 5:22, 14:34) which he says may seem to have a 'karma-like' ring to them, but which "in reality always bear a theological significance" and teach individuals and peoples something about God's righteous judgment of the sin which becomes visible and tangible in personal and public life.[127] "In all punishment," Bavinck contended, "something of God is present; God himself is involved in it. Even when sin seems to bring its own punishment, God still has a hand in it."[128]

It is striking that Bavinck also emphasizes the pneumatological aspect of general revelation, that is to say, the Holy Spirit as its instrumental means. According to 1 Corinthians 2:14, 15 it is the Holy Spirit who makes the revelation in Christ known to people. But people are not reached by *general* revelation either apart from the working of the Spirit: "There is ... always the silent activity of the Holy Spirit inside [natural] man, even if he resists Him constantly."[129] Bavinck doesn't mention the Holy Spirit often. In one of the other rare references he makes to the Spirit, he writes: "... I do not wish to deny that the Spirit of God has worked among the heathen more than we often suspect."[130] Despite this lack of specific mention, however, he alludes to the work of the Spirit time after time in his writings. An example of this can be seen in what he writes about the general

---

[124]*RBCG*, 115.

[125]*Ibid.*

[126]"De onbekende God." 8.

[127]*RBCG*, 116-117.

[128]*CMO*, 186. It remains a question whether texts from Proverbs, with their setting in the notion of '*the fear of the Lord*,' are optimally suited to serve as a biblical demonstration that God reveals the link between guilt and punishment to the *nations*. It would be better to adduce other passages for this purpose, for example, I Sam. 5, which relates the story of how God caused the Philistines to experience this link directly and drastically when they seized the ark of the covenant as a war trophy.

[129]*CBTM*, 125.

[130]*AWW*, 186.

revelation of the splendor of God: "It is true that ... the majesty of God ... is universally revealed throughout the entire world, yet every time a person begins to see that majesty, every time his eyes are opened to it, every time it overwhelms him, that general revelation takes on the character of a highly individual intervention."[131]

Bavinck remains wholly within the Reformed tradition with his view that God reveals himself through the universe, the human conscience, and His providential care. Calvin speaks in a similar way of these modes of general revelation,[132] as did H. Bavinck[133] and Kraemer,[134] though the thought of the first two regarding this subject lacks a pneumatological element. Bavinck employed many of the Bible passages that these three commentators used, but also other ones. However, not all the texts he marshals are equally adequate to the task for which he cites them. In any case, discovering a reference to God's revelation via the human conscience in Amos 4:13[135] and Psalm 129[136] seems to be somewhat forced from an

---

[131]*RBCG*, 117.

[132]In the *Institutes*, Vol. I, Book 1, Chap. V.1, 52, Calvin—referring to Ps.104:2, Ps. 19:1 and Rom. 1:19—writes concerning revelation via creation: "You cannot in one glance survey this most vast and beautiful system of the universe, in its wide expanse, without being completely overwhelmed by the boundless force of its brightness"; and in Chap. V.7, 59-60, referring to Ps. 107 and Acts 17:27, he writes about revelation through divine providence: "In the second kind of works, which are outside the ordinary course of nature also, proofs of his powers just as clear are set forth"; Calvin does not explicitly deal with God's self-disclosure through the human conscience; this is treated only implicitly in connection with his discussion of the *sensus Divinitatis* in Chap. III, 43-47, where remarkably no Bible texts are adduced in its support.

[133] H. Bavinck states: "He reveals Himself in nature ... (Job 36 and 37; Ps. 29, 33:, 65, 67:7, 90, 104, 107, 145; Is. 59:17-19; Matt. 5:45; Acts 14:16; Rom. 1:18); He reveals Himself in the history of peoples and persons ... (Deut. 32:8; Ps. 33:10, 67:5, 115:16; Prov. 8:15, 16; Acts 17:26); He also reveals Himself in the heart and conscience of every human being (Job 32:8, 33:4; Prov. 20:27; John 1:3-5, 9, 10; Rom. 2:14 and 15, 8:16)," *Gereformeerde dogmatiek*, 321.

[134]Kraemer writes: "Even in this fallen world God shines through in a broken, troubled way: in reason, in nature and in history" (he mentions no Bible texts here), *The Christian Message in a Non-Christian World*, 120.

[135]This verse has to do with God's judgment over the people of Israel, in which He will make their thoughts known and confront them with what lives in their hearts.

[136]In *IZW*, 262 Bavinck uninhibitedly links Ps. 139 to general revelation: "... [God] is immediately near.... He is present in every event of your life, every day He issues His call to you, He makes claims upon you and surrounds you: 'Where can I go from your Spirit? Where can I flee from your presence? (v. 7)'" This Psalm, however, should be read against the backdrop of the covenant of grace, by virtue of which a person knows, as child of God, that God walks closely with

exegetical point of view.

3.3.3. The Character of General Revelation

It has already been pointed out above[137] that Bavinck considers general revelation to be a dynamic reality. With a view to the great importance he attaches to that quality, it would be useful to examine it more closely.

Bavinck points to the fact that after Descartes, theology tended more and more to separate man and the world from each other along philosophical lines: man came to be viewed as scrutinizing, thinking subject vis-à-vis the world as object. It is incumbent upon theology, however, to rid itself of all such "abstract philosophical additives."[138] In calling for this purge Bavinck was indirectly criticizing his own tradition, and in particular H. Bavinck, whose work was not entirely free of such 'additives.'[139] General revelation is always very concrete and real: "It often pounces on man, as it were, suddenly confronting him with the reality that God exists and that, despite all our efforts at resistance, we can never radically push Him away."[140] Added to this is the fact that general revelation can only take place within the living intimate union, the symbiosis, of man and world. This infrangible association gives rise to a two-pronged experience among humans: on one side they apprehend their hitherto unknown glory, on the other they run up against their desperate misery. This ambivalence, the result of the "fallen state of the human race," constitutes the life-struggle of men and women everywhere. And it is there, in that struggle, of all places, that God appears before them, there lies the point of their encounter with God's revelation. This makes it plain that general revelation has a very existential character, i.e., is less "an entity appealing to human philosophical instincts" and more "a power that man encounters in the [various] relationships of his life."[141] That does not mean that the elements of scrutiny and reflection are entirely absent in the encounter with this form of divine self-disclosure. Nevertheless, general revelation always occurs within an existential setting and the significance of the elements of observation and deliberation in the

---

him or her as a deeply concerned and caring father.

[137]In paragraph 3.3.1.

[138]Cf. *RBCG*, 117-164.

[139]Cf. H. Bavinck, *Gereformeerde dogmatiek*, 320-321. R.H. Bremmer summarized H. Bavinck's position on the matter of general revelation as follows: "Bavinck wished to limit *revelatio naturalis* strictly to creation. It comprises the thoughts of God, which He 'implanted in [His] creatures in a creaturely way so that man, by thinking, could understand them.' H. Bavinck considered history and the heart and conscience of every person to be creatures as well." *Herman Bavinck als dogmaticus*, 163-164.

[140]*RWBOT*, 138.

[141]*RBCG*, 165.

response to it should definitely not be overrated.[142]

And this existential nature of general revelation has an even deeper dimension. Sometimes God appears to capitalize, as it were, on the religious conceptions and representations found among the nations, where such things as dreams and the movement of the stars were often perceived as divine manifestations. Despite the overwhelming biblical rejection of such notions, it is also evident that at certain moments God employed dreams (e.g., in the case of Pharaoh and Nebuchadnezzar) and a star (cf. Matt. 2) to reveal himself.[143]

As already mentioned earlier, it was Kraemer who pioneered the notion that the nature of (general) revelation is thoroughly existential, a concept to which his book, *The Christian Message in a Non-Christian World*, is one continuous witness and from which Bavinck learned a great deal. But while Bavinck was deeply influenced by Kraemer's position on this issue, he was also critical of it. Whereas for Kraemer the existential character of revelation absolutely precluded any consideration of ontology in connection with it, Bavinck argued from Scripture that there is a strong ontological aspect to God's self-disclosure. The first thing to note is that the Bible speaks not only of *existence* but also of *being*; there is no antithesis in Scripture between voluntaristic and ontological concepts of God and revelation. Revelation is not only voluntaristic, i.e., does not originate solely in or consist only of the disclosure of God's will, as Kraemer maintains, for behind God's active will lies His being and essence. In other words, divine will is not the only or dominant factor in revelation: revelation could not be voluntaristic if it were not also ontological. The very first story in the Bible, that of creation, draws a sharp picture of the ontological relationship between God and man, and it is only on the foundation of this relationship that we come to know the divine will.[144] Moreover, if it is true that man is confronted by means of revelation with the reality of God in the *totality* of his existence,[145] ontological considerations with respect to God's self-disclosure cannot be excluded, for this totality "also includes [man's] intellect, his need to view things in logical order."[146]

3.3.4. The Content of General Revelation

Because of the different characters and circumstances of those who are encountered by general revelation, its content varies greatly. This does not mean, however, that nothing can be said about its substance. General revelation consists of "the great self-manifestation of God"; the *Logos* "who gives light to every man" (John 1:9) is none other than the *Logos* who "became flesh and made His dwelling among us" (v.

---

[142]Cf. *ibid.*, 164-166.

[143]Cf. *WW*, 56.

[144]Cf. *BCNCR*, 101-107.

[145]Cf. H. Kraemer, *The Christian Message in a Non-Christian World*, 64-65: "The intense religious realism of the Bible proclaims and asserts realities. It ... challenges man in his *total* being to confront himself with these realities."

[146]*BCNCR*, 97.

14),[147] which relates to God's unicity. He is not a God with two faces; He is One.
We must understand that the Ground of the world, out of Whom
the overwhelming multitude of suns and stars has been born, is
the same as the Regent of our lives who holds us by the hand and
leads us forward step by ste And we must learn to see that this
Director of our lives, who holds all that ebbing and flowing of
our fortunes in His hands, is the same as the God who turned His
Face to us in Jesus Christ. We need to learn to understand that
the Unknown God is the same as the Known God, Whose holy
salvific will we behold in Jesus Christ.[148]

Bavinck finds a further specification of the content of general revelation in the
concepts of "eternal power" (to indicate that God is the bearer of all things) and
"divine nature" (to designate the 'wholly Other,' the 'Holy') in Romans 1:20,
concepts which manifest themselves in manifold ways and place man "in a moral
relationship" with God.[149]

Bavinck feels a tremendous tension rising from this Christological
approach. It is often by no means easy to hear the same word in general revelation
as that which is spoken in special revelation. The former comes to us in a very
hidden way: "Every step I take," wrote Bavinck against the background of WW II,
"it becomes more difficult for me to understand that [the] Unknown God is the same
as [the] God who has spoken to me in Jesus Christ."[150] Here, once again, Bavinck
follows the track laid down by Kraemer, who speaks of the "broken and troubled
way" in which revelation breaks through "in this fallen world."[151] By adopting this
view, Bavinck distanced himself from various extant forms of (neo-Calvinist)
optimism regarding the possibility of gaining saving knowledge from general
revelation.[152]

3.3.5. The Goal of General Revelation

Behind God's dealings with every human life there lies a purpose or aim, Bavinck

---

[147]*RBCG*, 188.

[148]"De onbekende God," 8.

[149]*RBCG*, 124; *PPRAO*, 12.

[150]"De onbekende God," 9.

[151]*The Christian Message in a Non-Christian World*, 120.

[152]Here Bavinck's thinking demonstrates an affinity with Calvin himself,
who on the one hand wrote in a positive light about the *potential* possibility of
achieving (saving) knowledge offered by God through the medium of general
revelation, but on the other hand expressed pessimism regarding the possibility of
gaining *actual* knowledge. Calvin used the image of concentric circles in this
connection: the believer in the innermost circle discovers the *vestigia Dei* in
creation, whereas the unbeliever in the outermost circle neither can nor wishes to
see these vestiges of God. Cf. *Institutes* Vol. I, Book 1, Chap. V.7-10, 59-63.

writes, referring, in this connection, repeatedly to Acts 17:27: "God did this so that men would seek Him and perhaps reach out for Him and find Him...." General revelation, thus, is apparently meant to coax a response from man, is intended to make humans become religiously active. The question respecting the degree to which this end is achieved and whether the nations really seek and find God remains open. Whether it is reached or not, the fact remains that this goal constitutes God's purpose for man.[153]

Remarkably, Bavinck does not really deal with the final clause from Romans 1:20, "so that men are without excuse" (εἰς τὸ εἶναι αὐτοὺς ἀναπολογήτους). This is no doubt explained by the fact that he translates the preposition εἰς in a *consecutive* and *predicative* sense ('so' or 'so that), which makes the phrase it introduces a *result* clause.[154] The meaning is then that man is without excuse as an immanent consequence of his conduct: though having eyes to see and ears to hear, people fail to see and hear, therefore they are without excuse. The alternative would be to take εἰς as *final* ('in order that' or 'to the end that'), which would make the phrase a *purpose* clause.[155] The sense would then be that God reveals himself in order that man would not be able to plead ignorance, that He discloses himself with the aim of making it impossible for people to have an excuse for failing to recognize what can be known about Him. He wants those who do not acknowledge Him to be bereft of any alibi for their behavior.

It is often very difficult to determine whether clauses of this kind denote result or purpose, particularly those introduced by εἰς.[156] This matter can almost never be resolved grammatically but usually only theologically. John Calvin, for whom *gloria Dei* was the final goal of all God's actions, takes this phrase from the end of verse 20 to be a final clause. He speaks of both of the above-mentioned aims or goals of general revelation. He emphasizes that God reveals himself on the one hand because He has ordained the perception and service of Himself as the highest purpose of man: general revelation takes place inasmuch as the "final goal of the blessed life ... rests in the knowledge of God" and 'lest anyone ... be excluded from access to happiness."[157] On the other hand, God discloses himself in order "to prevent anyone from taking refuge in the pretense of ignorance," and so that people who "have failed to honor him and to consecrate their lives to his will" might "be condemned by their own testimony."[158] H. Bavinck, too, argues along these lines: general revelation takes place "to the end that people will turn to God and keep his

---

[153]Cf. *RBCG*, 121, *AWW*, 179, and *ZWN*, 70.

[154]A result clause "states that which is consequent upon or issues from the action of the main verb," Dana and Mantey, 285.

[155]A purpose clause expresses "the aim of the action denoted by the main verb," Dana and Mantey, 282.

[156]Cf. Dana and Mantey, 285, and A. Oepke, "εἰς ," in Kittel, especially 429.

[157]*Institutes*,Vol. I, Book 1, Chap. V.1, 51.

[158]*Ibid.*, Chap. III.1, 43-44.

law or, failing that, be without excuse."[159]   These distinctions fell beyond the purview of Bavinck's attention, which means that we can only guess at why he chose to interpret the last phrase of verse 20 as a consecutive or result clause. It is not unlikely that his deep trust in God's searching love made it impossible for him to entertain the kind of premeditated aim of God's self-disclosure that is implied by the interpretation of this phrase as a final or purpose clause.[160]

3.3.6. The Relation of General and Special Revelation

From what has been written above, it is already clear that for Bavinck general and special revelation are intimately connected, for both consist of the self-manifestation of God.[161]
      Due to the fact that God is One, there exists both a material and an essential unity between the two forms of revelation: both are Christologically qualified.[162]   And yet they also differ substantially. General revelation does not have the capacity for bringing people to a true knowledge of God, does not possess the δύναμις (power) for salvation (Romans 1:16), which is exclusively reserved to the gospel of Jesus Christ.
      Although God has not left himself without witness outside of the gospel, it is only through the medium of special revelation that He makes himself known in the "most intimate way possible."[163]   Special revelation consists of the disclosure of "the mystery of Christ which was not made known to men in other generations,"

---

[159]*Gereformeerde dogmatiek,* 365.

[160]Meanwhile, the intriguing question as to the preferable interpretation of this occurrence of εἰς remains. Many authorities—such as Dana and Mantey; Arndt and Gingrich, who follow Walter Bauer; and A. Oepke, "εἰς," in Kittel: "εἰς τὸ εἶναι αὐτοὺς ἀναπολογήτους [in Rom. 1:20] cannot possibly be final" (431)—argue that we are dealing with a consecutive causal or result clause here. The present writer, however, thinks there is much to recommend the position taken by A.F.N. Lekkerkerker, who, following Otto Michel and Adolf Zahn, states: "We would much prefer to hold to *in order that* [as the meaning for εἰς], basing ourselves on, among other things, evidence provided by Schlatter: 'Ein Ergebnis des göttlichen Wirkens, das nicht von Gott gewollt ist, gibt es bei Paulus nicht, und daran dass er mit *eis* das nenne, wohin das Handeln zielt, ist von seiner Sprache aus kein Zweifel möglich ([The idea of] an outcome of divine activity that is not willed by God is alien to Paul, and there can be no doubt, on the basis of his linguistic usage, that he employs εἰς to designate that to which [God's] activity aims).'"

[161]Cf. *RBCG,* 180-188.

[162]One finds a striking example of this in *LV,* 23-28, where Bavinck argues that the principle of service present in the creation order is revealed fully in Christ.

[163]Bavinck refers here to Ps. 147:19, 20: "He has revealed His word to Jacob, His laws and decrees to Israel. He has done this for no other nation; they do not know His laws."

but "has now been revealed by the Spirit" (Eph. 3:5).[164] God's revelation finds "its heart and its climax in Christ,"[165] a truth to which John 1 also witnesses, according to Bavinck.[166] Despite this difference between them, however, special revelation also has something in common with general revelation, namely, that it does not provide a full, adequate disclosure of the being and essence of God: "Now we see but a poor reflection as in a mirror.... Now I Know in part...." (1 Cor. 13:12). Special revelation, too, has its limits: we shall know fully only when we "see face to face" (*idem*).[167] Bavinck termed special revelation "an analogical representation of what God wishes to be for people"; special revelation, the divine will, "is rendered in such a way that all peoples and generations can find in it" what is possible and necessary for them to know of God's essence: "His love that seeks and saves the lost."[168]

Without subtracting anything from the basal difference between general and special revelation, Bavinck points to the fact that there are "numerous moments in which it is difficult to tell whether one is dealing with 'general' or 'special' revelation."[169] In the Bible we find accounts of situations in which "God bends himself low, down to the level of heathendom ... to reveal his judgment" to people via dreams," or to make known through the stars "that a great King has been born in Israel."[170] And "in the mission field," he adds, "we are even today continually confronted by the surprising fact that God leads people to the gospel by means of dreams and visions, and in such cases we constantly ask ourselves whether we are dealing with 'general revelation' or something very special."[171] He leaves the answer to this question open.

In Bavinck's view there is also a point of agreement between general and special revelation in terms of instrumental mode: it is the Holy Spirit who is active in both forms of divine self-disclosure. This means that general revelation, too, is an act of God in the fullest possible sense, and that the distinction made by H.

---

[164]"Drie grote vragen: De vraag der openbaring," 101.

[165]*Ibid.*, 102; cf. *CBTM*, 180.

[166]In the first chapter of this gospel, Bavinck contends, general revelation is very directly linked to the *Logos*, to the Word that was from the beginning and became flesh in Jesus Christ. It is possible that Bavinck was influenced here by F.W.A. Korff, who held that "The same Logos who comes to man via *revelatio* also came to man earlier via *manifestatio*. In this we find the unity of general and special revelation," 75-76.

[167]Cf. *DAC*, 11

[168]*Ibid.*

[169]*RBCG*, 180.

[170]*WW*, 55-56.

[171]*RBCG*, 180-181.

Bavinck between *revelatio naturalis* and *revelatio supranaturalis*[172] no longer holds for Bavinck. To him, both the revelation that takes place *per naturam* as well as that which occurs *praeter hanc naturam*[173] are profoundly supernatural.

Finally, general and special revelation show similarity in character. As indicated above, the character of general revelation is clearly defined by Bavinck as God's personal involvement in the lives of all humans, whereby the point of encounter is the fallen existence of these lives. And he speaks in a similar way about special revelation: it does not take place apart from or beyond but in the very midst of life.

> If it is true that the Word became flesh, this means that it encounters us in our fleshliness, in our humanity. We never find ourselves nearer the Word than when we are flesh, when life fizzes and boils with energy within us, when we seethe with wrath or longing desire.... There, at that level, [the Word] wishes to encounter us, there it presses in upon us, there it overwhelms us. The point of encounter between man and the Word is found, thus, wherever man really and truly lives and seeks and reaches out from the depths of his heart.[174]

It is plain that Bavinck deems general and special revelation to be firmly bonded by virtue of the fact that they both involve essentially the same thing, namely, the self-disclosure of *God*, which means, among other things, that general revelation, too, contains a Christological and pneumatological element. Nevertheless, Bavinck also sees a decisive difference between the two: The Holy Spirit reveals the hidden things of God exclusively in Christ or, as the case may be, the Word, i.e., solely in the mode of special revelation.

3.3.7. Summary

Making grateful and critical use of both his own tradition and the thought of Hendrik Kraemer, Bavinck developed an original, biblically-theologically anchored view of general revelation. The most important point of his approach lies in the fact that he placed general revelation in a *Trinitarian* perspective, emphasizing in this way the fundamental unity of general and special revelation. Through the force of this position, he essentially filled a mediating role in the controversy between Neo-Calvinists, who pursued theology from the perspective of creation, and the Barthians, whose theology was exclusively Christocentric.[175] Further, it is typical of his position that he conceives of general revelation in an extremely existential way, defining it as a category of personal encounter. Sometimes he exercises less exegetical care than he might have, thereby weakening his argumentation at certain

---

[172]Cf. *Gereformeerde dogmatiek*, 320.

[173]Cf. *ibid.*

[174]*BBO*, 8-9.

[175]Cf. M.E. Brinkman, *De theologie van Karl Barth: Dynamiet of dynamo voor christelijk handelen?*, who provides an historical account of this controversy, without, though, referring to Bavinck.

points. Moreover, Bavinck's interpretation of the last words of Romans 1:20 as a consecutive causal clause and especially the assimilation of this interpretation into his one-sided conception of the goal or purpose of general revelation may, at the very least, be termed remarkable in the light of Reformed tradition.

4. Chapter Summary

Initially, Bavinck developed his view of religiosity on the basis of his insights in the area of psychology of religion and in keeping with Herman Bavinck's theological-philosophical presuppositions. The human person, as divinely oriented creature, is potentially a seeker after God. This potentiality is activated by means of general revelation, through which religious consciousness comes into existence, a consciousness which, though corrupted, also contains positive elements.

Later on, influenced by Kraemer's book, *The Christian Message in a Non-Christian World*, along with the discussions that took place at the 1938 International Missionary Conference in Tambaram, India, and in line with Reformed tradition, Bavinck put his mind to the articulation of a biblical-theological interpretation of the origin, nature and existence of non-Christian religions. His original position, with its central focus on the human longing and quest for God, underwent a fundamental change, gaining, in the process, considerably greater depth. In the elaboration of his ideas on general revelation and its effects—chiefly in his book on religious consciousness and Christian faith—his exegesis of Romans 1:18 ff., which was deeply informed by his knowledge of psychological processes, took on a place of central importance.

It is striking that Bavinck gradually distanced himself from an important idea that had taken hold in the Dutch Reformed theology of his day, namely, that man possesses a substantial or inbuilt capacity (*principium internum*) to pick up the signals of God's revelation. Abandoning this position, he began increasingly to take his departure from the reality of general revelation, which, though initially viewing it solely in terms of the doctrine of creation, in the end he grounded in Christology. He conceived of general revelation as a wordless but ineluctable divine speech directed toward every living soul by way of the cosmos, human conscience and both general and personal history. The Holy Spirit is actively present in this revelation, providing it with a dynamic character. Owing to the unity of God, the content of general revelation is formally identical to that of special revelation in Christ, though materially it differs from the latter.

CHAPTER FIVE

Christian Faith and Religious Consciousness

"We may say that by the grace of God repression and substitution do not always succeed. Time and again we notice things in the history of religion which show that God has really concerned Himself with these people." (*CBTM*, 203)

1. Introduction

As already suggested at the beginning of the previous chapter, the question of the relationship between religious consciousness and Christian faith pervades Bavinck's entire missiological oeuvre, evidence for which is provided by, among other things, the fact that even before writing his missiological handbook (*IZW*, 1954), he had analyzed this problem both historically and theologically in an extensive, separate publication (*RBCG*, 1949). Moreover, his last theological work, *The Church Between the Temple and Mosque* (*CBTM*, 1966), deals with these questions afresh.

2. The Problem of the Inner Religious Principle

God initiates a dialogue with every human person by means of general revelation. But the necessary precondition for a real encounter, for a genuine I-Thou relation between man and God, is a human capacity for hearing what God is saying, for receiving the sound He projects and perceiving the light He emits. Speaking in terms of systematic theology, the *principium externum* requires a *principium internum*.[1] The crucial question here is whether the latter exists and, if so, what it is. And the answer given to this twofold question regarding man's ability to pick up the revelatory signals transmitted by God will be of decisive importance for determining the content and value of religious consciousness and hence for the entire corpus of missionary theology.[2] Bavinck rightly concludes, therefore, that

---

[1] These terms are borrowed from H. Bavinck; they are not always used in this paragraph in the sense that he understood them but as a designation for general revelation and the human capacity for receiving that revelation. Bavinck employed this terminology in a similarly free way, cf. *RBCG*, 168.

[2] Cf. "General Revelation and the Non-Christian Religions," 49, where Bavinck writes that these questions were of preeminent importance to mission: "To the missionary all depends on the ... [question] of how to consider and estimate the

"this is where it becomes prickly, here lies the core of the whole problem."[3]

The first question is whether there is indeed a *principium internum*. Historically, this was never really in doubt; the existence of a human faculty for receiving divine revelation was simply assumed as a more or less philosophical certainty. In Bavinck's time, however, this question had become a key issue in theological discourse because of the stand taken by Barth, and it was against the backdrop of the discussion of that period that Bavinck developed his own viewpoint.

Barth held the view that though it is possible to speak of divine revelation apart from the Word, it is clear from God's revelation in Christ that man has never been able to hear the voice of God by that means. Barth writes:

[Man] will admit that the same eternal Word of God that became flesh can also be heard in nature, in history, in his own heart, conscience and mind. But he will then go further and, to his own shame, will acknowledge that in fact he has never heard it there and never can or will. And he will say that ... because of [his] knowledge of Jesus Christ as the Incarnate Word; because of [his] knowledge of the fact that it has pleased God to use this totally other way of revealing His Word; because he knows that he has received grace [to understand God's revelation] and thus that he needs grace. By means of this intelligence he will know himself to be distinctly incapable of hearing God's Word in creation.[4]

Barth adds that what man hears are merely the voices of the elements of creation, which man then wrongly goes on to clothe with divine dignity. General revelation does not lead to genuine encounter with God,[5] even though it does lead to religion: "God's revelation is in fact God's presence and thus God's concealment in the world of human religion."[6] Barth's categorical refusal to allow any room whatever for an encounter of God and man outside the Word stemmed from his fear that this

---

religion of the people he is working among."

[3] *RBCG*, 168.

[4] Het christelijk openbaringsbegrip, 21-22.

[5] J. Witte summarizes Barth's standpoint here as follows: "Gott hat sich wohl in der Schöpfung und im Gewissen offenbart. Aber die Menschen waren infolge ihrer Sünde ausserstande Gott in dieser Offenbarung zu erkennen." (God did reveal himself in creation and in the conscience. But as a result of their sin, people were not in a position to recognize God in this revelation), *Die Christusbotschaft und die Religionen*, 40.

[6] "Gottes Offenbarung ist tatsächlich Gottes Gegenwart und also Gottes Verborgenheit in der Welt menschlicher Religion," *Kirchliche Dogmatik*, I, 2, 307 (cf. *Church Dogmatics*, I, 2, 282); With respect to Barth's view on this matter, H. de Vos writes: "On the other hand, revelation and religion are tethered to each other. Revelation must lead to religion.... [And] God is present though hidden in religion," 44.

would detract from the exclusive significance of the revelation in Christ and the absolute meaning of faith.[7] Moreover, as Kraemer points out, by maintaining that "revelation is solely God's act and that it is exclusively His grace that creates the new situation for man and the world," Barth "rejects radically any shadow of synergism in the realm of faith, and on the same grounds also anything like natural theology."[8]

Though Kraemer supports Barth in his struggle against all forms of spiritual relativism, he disagrees with Barth's denial of the material reality of general revelation.[9] The question of how God works in the world and human religions cannot be ignored: "Biblical realism requires us to wrestle with it, for the world is still the creation of God, 'who does not abandon the work of His hands,' but continues working in it."[10] Kraemer states that Barth rightly emphasizes the sovereignty of God's grace in Jesus Christ but that he applies this insight too simplistically, using it to block access "to the reality of the living religions as precipitate of the drama that takes place between God and man."[11] Bavinck voices the same criticism of Barth.

> I am prepared to go along with Barth's negative assessment of man, but on this one point I am definitely opposed to him. Barth does not understand that man, also fallen man, sinful man, can and may never be conceptualized separately from the revelation of God.[12]

And Bavinck means revelation, here, in the sense of genuine encounter, adding that in denying any possibility of the recognition of God through the medium of general revelation, Barth faces "no little difficulty when it comes to the interpretation of Romans 1:18 and following."[13] According to Barth's labored exegesis of this passage, Paul is not speaking here about a relation between God and the unbeliever which is based on divine self-disclosure in creation and within which God reveals His wrath. In Barth's view, Paul only meant to say that God's wrath, as His verdict on all religion, is revealed when the gospel of the cross of Christ is proclaimed.[14]

---

[7]Cf. G.C. Van Niftrik, 238, and Kraemer, *The Christian Message in a Non-Christian World*, 120.

[8]*The Christian Message in a Non-Christian World*, 119-120.

[9]Cf. *ibid.*

[10]*Ibid.*, 120; cf. also *Godsdienst, godsdiensten en het christelijk geloof*, 161 ff.

[11]*Godsdienst, godsdiensten en het christelijk geloof*, 161. Oddly, on this point the thinking of the 'father' of modern dialectical theology is decidedly un-dialectic and rationalistic. Cf. Bavinck, "Religie en christelijk geloof," 67-69.

[12]*RBCG*, 176.

[13]*Ibid.*, 159.

[14]Cf. F.W.A. Korff, 113; and also E.J. Beker and J.M. Hasselaar, 26-28.

Following Kraemer, Bavinck points out that it is particularly in Romans 1:18 ff. that Paul repeatedly states in no uncertain terms that revelation does not just slide off people's backs but actually reaches them: "In fact," he writes, "somehow this revelation acts upon man."[15] Bavinck concludes from this that there must be something in man "that makes it possible for him to receive general revelation,"[16] thus providing an affirmative answer to the first question posed above: Does the so-called *principium internum* actually exist?

The next question is: How are we to understand this internal principle? In his book on religious consciousness, *RBCG*, Bavinck demonstrates that historically this issue has been considered in various ways, and since he articulates his own view against this historical background, it would be well to provide a short survey here of the theological voices he cites from the past.

From the time of the Early Church until well into the Middle Ages, theologians (e.g., Justin Martyr, Clement of Alexandria and Thomas Aquinas) situated the *principium internum* in reason, which was usually considered to be a seed or embryo of the *Logos*. According to this view the *principium internum* was primary and the *principium externum* secondary. During the Reformation, leaders (for example, Calvin) spoke of a *sensus divinitatis* (sense of divinity) or *semen religionis* (seed of religion), which was embedded in fallen man by God himself and which was the medium through which general revelation acts upon man on a daily basis. Here *principium internum* and *principium externum* stand alongside each other. Under the influence of the Enlightenment, theologians sometimes identified the *principium internum* with 'pure reason'[17] (Spinoza and Leibnitz) or 'practical reason'[18] (Kant), to which the *principium externum* was totally subordinated. In the 19th century, reason was replaced by the concept of the feeling of sheer dependence on the Eternal (Schleiermacher) or the sense of the Holy (Otto), and here, too, the *principium externum* was subordinated to the *principium internum*. In his treatment of this subject, H. Bavinck reached back to Calvin, positing a *principium internum* as *habitus* that is animated by means of the *actus* of the *principium externum*. Finally, in Kraemer's thought the *principium internum* is more or less absorbed by the *principium externum* due to the emphasis he lays on the reality of God's revelation, which, because of the powerful working of the Holy Spirit, cannot be withstood by man.

Investigation of Bavinck's understanding of the *principium internum* reveals a lengthy, gradual development in his thought. In the period that he interpreted religious consciousness from a largely psychological point of view, he places strong emphasis—following in the line of Schleiermacher and especially Otto—on the *principium internum* as a yearning after God. Later, influenced by Reformed critics such as Hoekstra and Waterink, he moves more in the direction of H. Bavinck: though the *principium internum* remains intact in his thinking, he

---

[15]"General Revelation and the Non-Christian Religions," 53; cf. also *CBTM*, 120 and *RBCG*, 125.

[16]*RBCG*, 170.

[17]*Reine Vernunft*.

[18]*Praktische Vernunft*.

now no longer views it as primary and independent with respect to the *principium externum* but rather as being subject to general revelation.[19] After coming into contact with Kraemer's radically biblical approach, however, particularly his thinking regarding the anthropological consequences of the Fall of man, Bavinck abandons this entire, psychologically inspired concept of the *principium internum*. He now argues that, theologically seen, there is no thirst for God originating in man. In a 1941 publication, he himself gave voice to this reversal of thought by explicitly rejecting what he had written earlier in 1928:[20]

> Earlier I referred now and again to the concept of *Suchen im Fliehen* [a searching for God while simultaneously fleeing from Him]. Now I would like to express the matter differently. No one seeks God on his or her own, not even one (Rom. 1:11). If there is any kind of seeking anywhere, it exists by reason of the *horismos*, the divine purpose and guidance which does not relinquish its hold on [even] a deeply sunken humankind.[21]

Bavinck now places full accent on revelation and speaks extremely cautiously about the *principium internum*. At this point he argues that the reality of an internal epistemic instrument of this nature, an 'organ' for the acquisition of knowledge of God, is taught by Scripture.[22] He infers the existence of such an 'organ' from Romans 1:20, where, in his view, its presence is connoted by the Greek passive participle νοούμενα (being understood or apprehended).[23] Though the specific designation of this vehicle of knowledge in man was in Bavinck's opinion a side issue, he voiced preference for Calvin's nomenclature[24] and abandoned that of H. Bavinck. The most probable reason for this choice, which he himself does not explain, is that he found the latter's approach to be too philosophical and considered Calvin's to be more dynamic.

In his book on religious consciousness Bavinck once again subjects the concept of *principium internum* to scrutiny, asking the question of how it should be conceived. He insists emphatically that this principle may not be sought in human reason, arguing that the term νοούμενα in Romans 1:20—which would constitute the only possible basis for making such an assumption—cannot be construed in that sense. This word does not so much allude to "the various machinations of the intellect," but signifies much more the ideas of "becoming aware, sensing, observing, noticing." Paul is not referring here to "the intellect as a superior, noble organ by means of which man can conquer the truth." The combination of

---

[19]Cf. paragraph 2 above.

[20]In *PWB*, 165 ff.

[21]*PPRAO*, 18.

[22]Cf. *PPRAO*, 15.

[23]Cf. *PPRAO*, 7. Later, as we shall see in the sequel, he speaks much more guardedly about the existence of this kind of organic cognitive medium.

[24]Cf. *ibid.*, 15; "Het problem der '*Anknüpfung*' bij de evangelieverkondiging, 65-66; and *ICNCW*, 104.

νοούμενα with the word καθορᾶται (are clearly seen) suggests "an almost visionary happening, ... suddenly man catches sight of things."[25] This seeing is more than a rational process; it pertains to man in the depths of his being. Bavinck states that on further consideration there are no biblical grounds for Calvin's concepts of *semen religionis* and *sensus divinitatis* and that, in contrast to earlier claims, also the "*principium internum* is in no wise mentioned in Scripture," adding, however, that this does not preclude the existence of just such a principle, just such a "subjective foothold for general revelation."[26] At this point his argumentation takes on a somewhat artificial flavor. Scripture does not speak of this receptor for general revelation in man, he says, because the biblical emphasis lies so strongly on the objective manifestation of God that the subjective "human organ which responds to [this manifestation] is simply overlooked."[27] A little further on he writes:

> It seems as if the Bible is so hesitant to deal with this inner principle because it fears that we would immediately direct all of our attention to it, thereby forgetting the reality of God. The eye cannot see itself; that [would contradict] the meaning of its existence. Likewise, that inner principle does not see itself either; it may only see God. And I am convinced that not even the keenest reflection will ever succeed in discovering it.[28]

The only thing that can be said about the *principium internum* is that "it cannot be added to the credit side of the human ledger, cannot be chalked up to human merit, for it exists only because God has called it into being."[29] It seems that on one side Bavinck wishes to maintain the notion of an "internal principle" in line with Reformed tradition. But on the other side he greatly accentuates the I-Thou relation between man and God:

> Personally, I am inclined to view this one thing as an extremely important matter, namely, that man can assume life solely in the form of communicative interchange. Man is always engaged in converse: he speaks with his cow and with his horse, with his grain seed and with the rain clouds, with the sun and with the earth. It is only in this way that he can exist as a living person. I do not know what this harks back to, what lies behind it, but I am deeply mindful of the fact that man ... can do no other than speak continually with that Someone who stands before him everyday anew.[30]

Thus, Bavinck questions the idea of an inner principle existing separately and

---

[25] *RBCG*, 168-169; cf. also *CBTM*, 120.

[26] *RBCG*, 168-169.

[27] *Ibid.*, 168.

[28] *Ibid.*, 170.

[29] *Ibid.*, 171. This is reminiscent of the matter of the decisive operation of the Holy Spirit in general revelation discussed earlier in this chapter.

[30] *Ibid.*, 170.

independently in man. He is, in any case, of the opinion that Calvin creates an unacceptable rift between general revelation and the *semen religionis* by beginning his discourse on the knowledge of God the Creator in the *Institutes* with a treatment of the seed of religion divorced from, and prior to his discussion of, revelation. "Is that *semen religionis* ... something separate," he asks, "can it really be conceived as an isolated entity? Should it not rather be seen more as a reaction to God's radiant splendor in the surrounding world?"[31] It seems evident from this that Bavinck, following Kraemer's lead, in essence no longer ascribes substantial but rather relational weight to the *principium internum*. At any rate, the term *principium internum* no longer appears in Bavinck's last publication in this area, *CBTM*. In that work his manner of expression had become purely relational: man understands God's revelation owing to that revelation itself, revelation consisting of "the silent activity of the Holy Spirit inside man."[32] And as reactive being whose "whole way of life is a response," man can do nothing else than answer God's wordless speech "either in a positive or in a negative sense."[33]

It can be concluded without any doubt that Bavinck's thinking with respect to the *principium internum* changed considerably through the years, shifting from a perception of it as a noble characteristic in man to an understanding of it as a reality inherent to divine revelation. Every stride Bavinck took on this road removed him a step further from psychological speculation and philosophical considerations, resulting in a deeper biblical-theological rooting of his missiology. This means that when he finally abandoned the *principium internum* in the old sense, he did not harm Reformed theology but helped it along substantially.

3. Human Rebellion

If general revelation does not simply slide off man ineffectually "like a raindrop glides off a waxy tree leaf" but actually reaches him, it turns him into a 'knower': "The juridical position of man is that of one who knows."[34] At the same time, however, the Bible paints a picture of the actual position of man as that of one who does *not* know: "What you worship as unknown...." (Acts 17:23). This implies that the position of man is paradoxical[35] and that the reason for this must be sought in man himself. The question, then, is: Who is man?[36]

---

[31]*Ibid.*, 146-147.

[32]*Ibid.*, 125.

[33]*Ibid.*, 32 and 19.

[34]*RBCG*, 171.

[35]Cf. *ibid.*

[36]In this section attention will be directed to the attitude of man to God, or put in the language of dogmatics, the *imago Dei* in the narrower sense. In other contexts Bavinck also points to the continuing *grandeur* of man as God's creation despite his *misère*, or, put once more in terms of systematic theology, the *imago Dei* in the broader sense. Cf. "De zegen van den arbeid: Het raadsel van ons leven,"

In dealing with this query Bavinck once again chooses Scripture as his point of departure. It is not psychology—valuable though it may be—but only theology that can supply the decisive answer to this interrogative.[37]

> If man is to cultivate right judgment, he will have to free himself
> from the spell of self-speculation and assume a listening stance
> vis-à-vis God. How does God view us? How does God judge
> our lives? It is only through faith in God's Word that the motifs
> of the embroidery work of our lives can be satisfactorily and
> finally explained.[38]

Genesis 3 speaks of a pervasively decisive act by which man became what he now is—the act of doubting God's word, of greedily heeding the slanderous talk of the Evil One, of exiting the safe confines of the knowledge that God is love, of viewing Him as the great besieger against whom man must protect himself by means of ruse, of desiring to be like God.[39] Ever since then man has been in rebellion against God with every fiber of his being and right through to the deepest layers of his existence.[40] Nowhere can there be found "an unsullied piece of ground" of which man can say "here is the inner sanctum." The Bible speaks nowhere of a "foothold" in humans as point of access for "the renewal of life," for from his created condition as "son of God," man has degenerated into a "slave of demonic powers."[41] Man, in his state of alienation from God, is not a "foundling" who is the victim of an unfortunate fate and who keeps searching after his origin, but rather an "exile" who, by his own doing, is and remains far removed from communion with God.[42] Bavinck refers in this connection to Romans 3:9-20, where that reality is trenchantly portrayed in all of its dreadfulness, and also to Matthew 15:19, where Jesus draws a graphic picture of the heart of man. Concerning the latter he writes:

> When Jesus speaks about that heart and the things that proceed
> from it, he lays his finger on 'evil thoughts, murder' and many
> other appalling things, but He does not refer to one single
> unblemished spot, not one solid feature which we could grasp

---

passim; and "Het raadsel mensch," 55-64.

[37]Cf. "Het raadsel mensch," 65. Regarding the role of psychology Bavinck writes here that it "can unravel a few threads from a tangled skein, it can open our eyes to the knots, but it can never disclose the deepest grounds" of man's condition or behavior.

[38]*Ibid.*

[39]Cf. *WW*, 181.

[40]Strangely enough, nowhere in his biblical argumentation does Bavinck refer to Rom. 5:12-21, where Paul forges an explicit link between the "trespass of the one man" and the sin of all.

[41]*WW*, 161, 163.

[42]Cf. *ibid.*, 161, 165-166.

hold of.[43]

He concludes that a biblical anthropology can do nothing else than recognize the fact that in the integral core of his being, man is a sinner, a rebel, who in his deepest nature is frightened of God, avoids God, pushes God away, resists God.[44]

It is clear that Bavinck's assessment of man as sinner became radicalized after his reflection grew less controlled by psychology and more by theology. In his missiological handbook he maintained that the psychology of religion must take careful account of the biblical teaching regarding the deepest underlying psychological given and motive of the life of peoples, namely, "the unwillingness to recognize God, which is rooted in the passionate desire to be 'as God.'"[45] Any idea of a natural seed of desire for God in man, such as that which he proposed in earlier works,[46] is now totally rejected. It would seem obvious that he had been led to turn in this direction by Kraemer's argumentation and, thus, indirectly by that of Barth. Further, it is striking that he makes an oblique reference to the Second World War in this connection, a war which, in the minds of most people, destroyed all idealistic thinking with respect to man and resulted in the emergence of renewed reflection in the area of anthropology: "When, as is now the case, all anchors break loose in the storms of world events which sweep everything away before them ... we are faced with the inescapable problem of the riddle of man."[47]

4. Repression and Substitution

In Bavinck's view, when God manifests himself to man through general revelation, man becomes knowledgeable in a *de jure* (juridical) sense but proves, in that revelatory encounter with God, to be so profoundly sinful that *de facto* (actual) attainment of knowledge does not occur. Man "is a 'knower' who does not know, a 'perceiver' who does not perceive."[48] Bavinck finds support for this notion and his further enlargement upon it in Romans 1:18 ff., placing particular emphasis on two phrases: "men who suppress the truth by their wickedness" (v. 18), and "they exchanged the truth of God for a lie" (25). He attempts not only to exegete these words missiologically but also to analyze them from a psychological perspective.

Whenever God's truth grasps man, man grasps that truth and subjects it to a process of suppression (κατεχόντων). This term bears a connotation of violence, the idea of 'pushing something down' or 'holding something under' as a

---

[43]"Het raadsel mensch," 66-67.

[44]Cf. *IZW*, 126 (*ISM*, 122).

[45]*IZW*, 238 (cf. *ISM*, 237).

[46]For example in *ZKO*, 99-100.

[47]"Het raadsel mensch,". 60. The matter of the war does not figure anywhere else in Bavinck's works and thus apparently exercised only a modest influence on his theological thought.

[48]*RBCG*, 172.

fighter might hold the head of his opponent under water.[49] "I am inclined to take [κατεχόντων] in the sense of 'repression' as this latter concept is understood in modern psychology,"[50] where it points to the reality that man's "cognitive functions operate throughout the whole of the human personality: they do not exist on their own but are inherently connected to emotional and voluntative forces."[51] In other words, "our perceptive life," being "closely connected in diverse ways to our emotional and volitive life," is a very complicated affair. A person never sees anything completely objectively: "we perceive what interests us, we discern what we want to discern,"[52] or, obversely, do not see what we do not wish to see. Bavinck cites Webster's *New Collegiate Dictionary* definition of 'repression' as "the process by which unacceptable desires or impulses are excluded from consciousness and thus being denied direct satisfaction are left to operate in the unconscious,"[53] adding that post-Freudian psychology shows that "impulses or desires which are repressed may be very valuable. Anything that goes contrary to the accepted patterns of life or to ... predominant popular ideas may be repressed."[54] As a rule, this repression takes place "unconsciously; a person does not even know that he is doing it."[55] But this "does not make it any less real."[56] Furthermore, "this repression occurs so immediately, so spontaneously, so simultaneously with 'understanding' and 'perception' that at the very same moment man sees, he no longer sees, at the very moment he knows, he no longer knows."[57] By his use of the term ἐν ἀδικίᾳ Paul indicates that "moral, or rather immoral factors are at play" in the repression of God's truth. The preposition ἐν means here "within the sphere of,"[58] and the concept ἀδικίᾳ signifies the immoral stance that fallen man continually assumes vis-à-vis God.[59] Repression, thus, originates from man's "hidden, invariably unvoiced, often also totally unconscious motive [to stand in]"

---

[49]Cf. *PPRAO*, 8.

[50]*Ibid.*

[51] *Ibid.*, 15.

[52]*RBCG*, 172; Bavinck refers here to *IZK*, 78 ff.

[53]*CBTM*, 118.

[54]*Ibid.*, 119.

[55]*Ibid.*

[56]*RBCG*, 122; cf. also 172.

[57]*Ibid.*, 172.

[58]*Ibid.*, 173.

[59]Cf. *ibid.*, 122-123.

moral opposition to God."[60]

Immediately connected to this repression is the act of substitution, the Greek terms for which, ἤλλαξαν (ἀλλασσω) and μετήλλαξαν (μεταλλάσσω), occur three times in Romans 1 (vv. 23, 25, 26).[61] Bavinck observes that substitution is also a well-known principle in psychology and that, in using this word, Paul "once again touches upon one of those very remarkable phenomena to which current psychology points."[62] Psychology has shown that stifled impressions and repressed experiences continue to operate in a person's unconscious life: though "they play no part in man's conscious life" they nevertheless "remain strong, and try to reassert themselves again and again," succeeding in "showing every now and again that they still exist."[63] In Bavinck's opinion these insights can also be applied to man's response to the revelation of God: "It seems to me that Paul touches upon these things."[64] Though God's truth may be suppressed, this does not mean that it has been destroyed or is dead.[65] On the contrary, it keeps on pressing itself upon the conscious mind in fragmentary ways. General revelation impinges upon man but is immediately muffled, "and the sparse, totally decontextualized elements deriving from it that do manage to stick in the conscious mind form nuclei around which conceptual complexes of a totally deviant nature crystalize."[66]

In an attempt to clarify this process somewhat, Bavinck employs the analogy of the dream. In the dreaming state, too, all sorts of objective and real phenomena, such as the sound of running water in an eaves trough, the flash of the headlights of a car going by, the rumble of a train passing in the distance, or the monotonous ticking of an alarm clock, are registered but immediately torn out of context, endlessly magnified, and turned into fulcrums for chains of thought which differ radically from the reality of the phenomena which occasioned them. In the world of dreams we see the processes of 'repression' and 'substitution' in intimate association. Reality is smothered and at one and the same time this muted reality manifests creative power. The result is one huge fantasy, a colorful collection of confused images from which the objective elements on which they are built can be disentangled with only the very greatest of difficulty.[67]

Because this is an extremely important matter for the whole of missionary theology, it would be useful to quote an extensive passage from Bavinck's posthumous book in which his views on the suppression of God's revealed truth and

---

[60]*Ibid.*, 173.

[61]Cf. *ibid.*, 177.

[62]*CBTM*, 121.

[63]*Ibid.*

[64]*Ibid.*, 122.

[65]Cf. *RBCG*, 175, and *CBTM*, 121.

[66]*RBCG*, 179.

[67]Cf. *ibid.*, 178-179.

the human fabrication of substitutes for it are succinctly outlined.

Man has repressed the truth of the everlasting power of the divinity of God. It has been exiled to his unconscious, to the crypts of his existence. That does not mean, however, that it has vanished forever. Still active, it reveals itself again and again. But it cannot become openly conscious; it appears in disguise, and it is exchanged for something different. Thus all kinds of ideas of God are formed; the human mind as the *fabrica idolorum* (Calvin) makes its own ideas of God and its own myths. This is not intentional deceit—it happens without man knowing it. He cannot get rid of [these ideas and myths]. So he has religion; he is busy with a god; he serves his god—but he does not see that the god he serves is not God Himself. An exchange has taken place—a perilous exchange. An essential quality of God has been blurred because it did not fit in with the human pattern of life, and the image man has of God is no longer true. Divine revelation indeed lies at the root of [this image], but man's thoughts and aspirations cannot receive it and adapt themselves to it. In the image man has of God we can recognize the image of man himself.[68]

Bavinck maintained that in principle all religions must be judged in light of this perspective, but that there are nevertheless differences of degree among them in terms of repression and substitution: "The history of religion as well as missionary experience teach us that it would be nonsensical to make blanket generalizations" about all religions and their adherents.[69] There are those

among whom the process of repression appears to have succeeded so perfectly that they are, one could say, not even aware that it has taken place. They are the those for whom it is totally impossible to form an idea of what is meant with the little word 'god,' for whom 'God' is so unreal that they have never devoted a thought to Him.[70]

In other cases this process moves along with much greater difficulty or even breaks down completely. "Sometimes it appears that God's presence obtrudes so self-evidently in a person's life that he or she is totally incapable of escaping it, is given

---

[68]*CBTM*, 122. For Calvin's discussion of *fabrica idolorum* see *Institutes*, Vol. I, Book 1, Chap. XI.8, 107-109.

[69]*RBCG*, 174.

[70]*Ibid*. Bavinck cites Calvin here, who, albeit from within a slightly different context, proffers this same interpretation of the repression of truth: "Experience teaches that the seed of religion [the *semen religionis*] has been divinely planted in all men. But barely one man in a hundred can be found who nourishes in his own heart what he has conceived; and not even one in whom it matures, much less bears fruit in its season (cf. Ps. 1:3)," *Institutes*, Vol. I, Book 1, Chap. IV.1, 47.

no chance to repress it, is simply overwhelmed by it."[71]   Because repression and substitution fit together like two cogwheels, or actually constitute the two faces of one and the same process, they evince a certain congruity. Bavinck calls express attention to the fact that both suppression and substitution of divine truth are characterized by gradations of intensity and degree.

> We always encounter the powers of repression and exchange, but that does not mean that they were always of the same nature and strength. We meet figures in the history of the non-Christian religions of whom we feel that God wrestled with them in a very particular way. We still notice traces of that process of suppression and substitution in the way they responded, but occasionally we observe a far greater influence of God there than in many other human religions. The history of religion is not always and everywhere the same; it does not present a monotonous picture of only folly and degeneration. There are culminating points in it, [for example, in Buddhism and Islam][72]

In the event suppression and substitution of God's truth turn out to be less disastrously severe than they could have, that cannot be attributed to human merit of any kind. This moderation of the process of repression and exchange occurs "not because certain human beings are much better than others, but because every now and then divine compassion interferes, compassion which keeps man from suppressing and substituting the truth completely."[73]

According to Bavinck, Romans 1 reveals that there is "something thoroughly tragic"[74] about the process of suppression and substitution. The passive expressions in verse 21, ἐματαιώθησαν ἐν τοῖς διαλογισμοῖς αὐτῶν (their thinking became futile)[75] and ἐσκοτίσθη ἡ ἀσύνετος αὐτῶν καρδία (their foolish hearts were darkened), indicate that this is a process which quite simply escapes man at a given

---

[71]*RBCG*, 174.

[72]*CBTM*, 126; for the references to Buddhism and Islam see 125.

[73]*Ibid.*, 126; cf. *RBCG*, 174.

[74]*RBCG*, 128.

[75]In *RBCG*, 126, Bavinck, though explicitly referring to the "extremely passive" nature of this phrase, interprets it in more of an active sense: they immersed themselves in their thinking and thereby begot their own lostness; in *CBTM*, 120, Bavinck follows the New English Bible: "All their thinking has ended in futility," whereby the passive sense of the Greek text has virtually disappeared. Arndt and Gingrich, following W. Bauer, translate the verb ἐματαιώθην: "be given over to worthlessness," and the phrase in question: "Their thoughts became directed to worthless things," 496. Rienecker suggests: 'eitel machen' (make idle) or 'betören' (befool, delude, beguile) for the verb ματαιόω, 317. And Liddel and Scott render the passive verb: "become foolish," 1084. These latter translations are preferable because they more clearly evince the interwovenness of the active and passive elements of the process of suppression and substitution.

moment, a mechanism "over which he no longer has control."[76]
Man is the offender, who in the service of immorality , in order
to wriggle out of [the obligation to conform to God's] norm,
suppresses and exchanges the truth; but he is simultaneously a
victim, who at a certain moment is no longer capable of calling
a halt [to what he is doing], who has nothing more to hold on to,
who "loses himself." He is the one who does it and at the same
time it washes over and through him, it drags him along, he can
no longer resist [it].[77]

In other words, the continuous process of rejection and replacement of God's truth
makes man less and less receptive to general revelation: "The aerial of man's heart
can no longer receive the wave length of God's voice, even though it surrounds him
on all sides. But in his innermost heart man has turned away from God and now
God has vanished out of sight."[78] This dramatic aspect of man's defiance of God
is clearly reflected in the thrice repeated statement παρέδωκεν αὐτοὺς ὁ θεὸς (God
gave them over) in verses 24, 26 and 28, which harks back to the revelation of the
ὀργὴ θεοῦ (the wrath of God) in verse 18. Bavinck interprets the phrase "God gave
them over" to mean: "they could no longer resist the powers within, which carried
them along."[79] All of this fits together in a mysterious way.

Bavinck sees the reality of the process of repression and substitution
confirmed in missionary experience as well.

[This experience] teaches us that sometimes when a person
begins to be illuminated by the light of the gospel, he suddenly
becomes aware of the terribleness of the process of suppression
and comes to the realization: I have always known but never
wanted to know. It seems to me that much of the unrest, the
primal anxiety, the tension which characterize so many moments
in man's life are related to this elemental phenomenon lying at
the root of his existence. The stance he assumes in the world is
not an honest one.[80]

There are times, in fact, when a person has a vague awareness that he or she is
playing games with God. At the end of a long dialogue, after hearing the final
confessional remark an Indonesian interlocutor made to the effect that perhaps he
had only been opposing Bavinck all night in order to fortify his soul with fresh

---

[76]*RBCG*, 128.

[77]*Ibid.*

[78]*CBTM*, 120-121.

[79]*Ibid.*, 122. Bavinck bestows more attention on this matter in *CBTM* than
in *RBCG*, in which one finds only a brief reference to it on 127; moreover, in
CBTM, 118, he exhibits a greater awareness of the fact that this section of Romans
1 is situated in the context of the revelation of God's wrath (v. 18) rather than in
that of the revelation of God's righteousness (v. 17).

[80]*RBCG*, 173.

assurance,[81] Bavinck relates that his eyes were opened to the reality "that [the] inscrutable power of repression and exchange ... manifests itself spontaneously and continually, but that this process apparently does not proceed so noiselessly that man is unable to pick up something of its sound now and again."[82]

J. Van den Berg rightly calls Bavinck's exegesis of Romans 1:18 ff. "a masterly analysis,"[83] and J. Verkuyl is also correct in saying that in his book on religious consciousness Bavinck "provided a profound analysis of [the] process of enlightenment, repression, and substitution."[84] Kraemer gave the initial impetus to this explication of the pericope in question when he wrote: "God works in man and shines through nature. The religious and moral life of man is man's achievement, but also [the result of] God's wrestling with him; it manifests a receptivity to God, but at the same time an inexcusable disobedience and blindness to God."[85] But it was Bavinck who elaborated this interpretation exegetically and psychologically. With respect to content there is clearly a great deal of agreement between Bavinck's commentary and thought on these matters and that of Calvin, who wrote in conclusion to his discussion of religious consciousness, general revelation, and suppression and exchange of the truth:[86]

> It is therefore in vain that so many burning lamps shine for us in
> the workmanship of the universe to show forth the glory of its
> Author.... Surely they strike some sparks, but before their fuller
> light shines forth, these are smothered.... Therefore, although the
> Lord does not want for testimony while he sweetly attracts men
> to the knowledge of himself with many and varied kindnesses,
> they do not cease on this account to follow their own ways, that
> is, their fatal errors.[87]

Nevertheless, Bavinck's approach is both theologically and anthropologically better founded than is Calvin's.

Despite the great appreciation one feels for Bavinck's exegesis here, the question could be put as to whether his interpretation is not too colored by psychological categories and considerations. In the opinion of the present writer there is reason to answer this question negatively and to suppose that, in using the

---

[81] Reported toward the end of section 3.3.1. above.

[82] *PPRAO*, 19; cf. also Calvin, who expresses himself in a similar way in *Institutes*, Vol. I, Book 1, Chap. III.2 and 3, 44-47.

[83] "The Legacy of J.H. Bavinck," 174.

[84] *De kern van het christelijk geloof*, 17. B. van den Toren also cites Bavinck's interpretation of Rom. 1 approvingly in his recent study, 314, note 82.

[85] *The Christian Message in a Non-Christian World*, 126.

[86] In the *Institutes*, Vol. I, Book 1, Chap. III-V, 43-69. In his commentary on these chapters in Calvin, Bavinck states that Calvin "tried to do justice to all the elements" of Rom. 1:18 ff., *RBCG*, 146.

[87] *Institutes*, Vol. I, Book 1, Chap. V.14, 68.

concepts of repression and substitution, Paul himself was tapping into the psychologizing trend that had taken hold in the philosophy of his day.[88] Various philosophical schools of the ancient world had adopted a critical stance vis-à-vis folk religion, particularly the worship of idols. The religion of the masses was analyzed through the lens of a philosophically purified concept of the divine. Epicurus, for example, repudiated folk religion—which for the most part was ruled by anxiety and intense fear of the gods—on the grounds that it constituted a falsification of the true nature of the deities, i.e., their immortality and absolute bliss.

> For gods there are, since the knowledge of them is by clear vision. But they are not such as the many believe them to be: for indeed they do not consistently represent them as they believe them to be. And the impious man is not he who denies the gods of the many, but he who attaches to the gods the beliefs of the many.... For men being accustomed always to their own virtues welcome those [i.e., gods] like themselves, but regard all that is not of their nature as alien.[89]

It has been shown that Paul's tactful criticism of the deep anxiety people have for the gods in Acts 17:23 ties in with Epicurean thought.[90]

But of even greater importance for Paul's approach was the religious criticism of the Stoics. Seneca, an influential representative of this philosophical current and a contemporary of Paul, wrote concerning the worship of idols: "To beings who are sacred, immortal and inviolable they consecrate images of the cheapest inert material. They give them the shapes of men or beasts or fishes; some, in fact, make them double creatures of both sexes combined or unlike bodies united."[91] It is obvious from Acts 17:18 that Paul was acquainted with these Hellenistic philosophies, which shared a more or less psychological interpretation of the popular religion of the day. And that being the case, it is not improbable that he drew upon them. In any event, the formal similarity in wording between Romans 1:20-23 and Epicurus and Seneca is striking.[92] Seen in this light, Bavinck's approach to Romans 1 is less alien to Paul's intentions than it might appear at first

---

[88]Bavinck does not mention this explicitly in his treatment of Rom. 1, but in *AWW*, 172-174, he does point out in his discussion of Acts 17 that Paul drew from this burgeoning development within Greek philosophy.

[89]C. Bailey, *Epicurus, the Extant Remains*, 83-84. Cf. also Bailey's commentary on Lucretius' text *De rerum natura*, in *Titi Lucreti Cari*, 66-72: "In the first place, traditional religion is an abomination to him. The gods are not such as popular belief supposes them to be, and to accept popular views is in reality an act of impiety."

[90]Cf. e.g., J. van Eck, 132.

[91]Cited in St. Augustine, *De Civitate Dei*, VI, 10. The translation used here is taken from George I. McCracken, 351.

[92]Also remarkable is Paul's use of the prevailing philosophical expression Θεός ἄφθαρτος (immortal God).

blush. And if one also takes into consideration that Paul's argument itself in fact exhibits a psychologizing tendency, Bavinck's interpretation would seem to be even more legitimate. The concepts κατέχειν (to suppress) and ἀλλάσσειν (to exchange) are linked in such a way in Paul's usage here that it would by no means be exegetically irresponsible to construe them psychologically.[93] Moreover, the element of the unconscious that figures so significantly in psychology is certainly also present in this pericope, particularly in verse 22. It may be fairly concluded, therefore, that Bavinck's psychological approach in no way represents a violation of the text.

Another question that could be posed, however, is whether Bavinck does full justice to the passage in question, since he hardly mentions the tension it presents between, on the one hand, the revelation of God's mercy in constantly seeking after man and, on the other, the disclosure of His wrath in giving man over to his own sinful thoughts and desires as well as in the negative verdict passed on all religion.[94] Perhaps Bavinck failed to take sufficient account of the element of God's wrath not only because as missiologist he was particularly interested in the origin of religion, but especially also because it was in his character to be rather one-sidedly focused on the seeking God at the expense of the wrathful God. The concept of divine judgment is of course not completely absent from Bavinck's thinking. But one does discover a certain one-sidedness in his missiological approach, which means that he himself was also somewhat affected by the psychological phenomenon he emphasized so strongly, namely, that human observation is subjectively colored. Though this omission is in itself of little material consequence for Bavinck's total approach to religious consciousness, his negative assessment of human religiosity would certainly have been better grounded biblically if he had taken ampler notice of the element of divine wrath in Romans 1.[95]

5. Origin and Essence of Religious Consciousness

From the foregoing it is clear that for Bavinck the origin of religious consciousness does not lie primarily in man, i.e., religious sensibility is not "part of our human structure."[96] The real origin of religious awareness is God himself,[97] who does not leave himself without witness but reveals himself to every human person (Acts

---

[93]Cf. A.F.N. Lekkerkerker, 60.

[94]Bavinck does bring this tension up in *PPRAO*, 8, where he writes: "God answers [the] cardinal sin of heathendom with the punishment of 'abandonment to sinful desires of the heart'.... With trenchant gravity Paul exposes this consequence three times by means of his thrice repeated 'God gave them over' (vv. 24, 26, 28)."

[95]It may be noted here that Kraemer does take account of the point of God's wrath, be it in a Barthian dialectical way; cf. *The Christian Message in a Non-Christian World*, 126.

[96]*CBTM*, 18.

[97]Cf. *ibid.*, 18-19.

14:17 and John 1:9). This revelation is "so real, so concrete, so ineluctable, so urgent that no one can escape it," no one can do anything other than respond to it.[98] Religious consciousness is thus, before all else, a theological phenomenon, the fruit of God's perduring dealings with humankind.[99] This origin in God is also determinative of the essence of religion: "Religion is never a soliloquy, a dialogue of a man with himself," in which he articulates only his own thoughts on the world, himself and God,[100] but is rather "a human response" to the self-disclosure of God.[101] To this must be immediately added that "all the great religions in history," as man's response to God's revelation, embody the "mysterious" processes of both repression and substitution.[102] That is the gist of the origin and essence of religious consciousness. However, it may not be forgotten, according to Bavinck, that there are a number of ancillary factors which also play a role in the formation and nature of religious life. Though he nowhere provides a systematic synopsis of these determinants, he does mention them separately in various of his publications.

First, Bavinck spoke in a number of places of what he called *proto-word revelation* or primeval divine self-disclosure, by which he meant the revelation of God that took place in the time before humankind became defiled and tainted.[103] Basing himself on findings in the area of religious studies, Bavinck came to the conclusion that all peoples retain garbled recollections of this early revelation and primal state, remembrances which more or less determine their religious life. For this reason it is necessary to take into account

> that all peoples have kept some recognizable memory of what happened in Paradise, be it ever so distorted. In particular those peoples that we usually call primitive have numerous myths telling of the glorious primeval age.... And according to the myths, this blessed period was finished by some blunder or accident.... It is plain that something of the common memory of the things that are related in the first few chapters of Genesis is kept alive by all peoples.... So, considering non-Christian religions, we are not only confronted with general revelation but also with memories of God's revelation in the remotest history of

---

[98]*RBCG*, 187.

[99]Cf. *PPRAO*, 5, and *AWW*, 179.

[100]*CBTM*, 18.

[101]*Ibid.*, 19; cf. also *RWBOT*, 139.

[102]*CBTM*, 125 and *RBCG*, 187-188.

[103]Cf. *CMO*, 23; "Het problem der '*Anknüpfung*,'" 65; "Phaenomenologische classificatie der religieuze structuren," 32; *ZWN*, 70; *PPRAO*, 13; "General Revelation and the Non-Christian Religions," 51; and *IZW*, 235-236 (*ISM*, 234-236).

man.[104]

Next, Bavinck points to the possibility of the *radiation* or *inflow of special revelation* in the religions of the peoples.[105] Although it cannot be determined with any certainty in regard to the past, since "we know precious little about the history of the various religions,"[106] it is not entirely implausible that such an influx did indeed occur. It is possible, for example, that the strong emphasis Hinduism places on grace and surrender to God has its origin in the proclamation of the ancient Christian church in India, and Chinese Buddhism could have been influenced by Nestorian Christianity, which had established itself very early on in the Far East.[107] Bavinck concludes that examples such as this point to "the interesting datum that the non-Christian religions are not truly religions that bloomed fully outside the sphere of special revelation, but that a certain measure of influx has to be regarded as a probability in several cases."[108] With respect to the modern period Bavinck thinks this kind of possibility definitely exists.

Third, he calls attention to the role played by *demonism* in all (non-Christian) religion: "An endless multitude of men and women all over the world are daily oppressed by the powers of ... darkness," as is often witnessed by the frequency with which newly converted Christians themselves mention the devil.[109] According to 1 Corinthians 8:4 and 10:19, 20 sacrifices to idols are offerings to devils. Apparently a demonic power induces people to engage in the lie of idolatry and keeps leading them astray in this manner.[110] Paul's words in Ephesians 2:2, 3: "you were dead in your transgressions and sins, in which you used to live when you followed the ways of this world and of the ruler of the kingdom of the air, the spirit who is now at work in those who are disobedient," also show the frightening power of Satan.[111] The presence and activities of "demonic powers that play games with the human heart" constitute "the dark shadow that lies over all the religions of the peoples."[112]

Finally, Bavinck refers to the fact that the answer man gives in his religion

---

[104]"General Revelation and the Non-Christian Religions," 51; cf. also *ICNCW*, 103.

[105]Cf. "General Revelation and the Non-Christian Religions," 51-52.

[106]*IZW*, p. 235 (cf. *ISM*, 234).

[107]Cf. "General Revelation and the Non-Christian Religions," 51-52.

[108]*Ibid.*, 52; cf. also *ICNCW*, 105-106.

[109]*ICNCW*, 151

[110]Cf. *ZWN*, 70, *IBD*, 28, and *ICNCW*, 98.

[111]Cf. *IZW*, 62 (*ISM*, 53), and "General Revelation and the Non-Christian Religions," 54.

[112]*ZWN*, 70.

to God's revelation never stands alone but is always given within an *existing religious context*: people obtain their view of God from their parents; they grow up within the religion to which they adhere;[113] they are not individuals but members of a group, a religious community,[114] all of which naturally exercises great influence upon their response to God's revelatory call.

In Bavinck's missiological thought the origin and essence of religious consciousness are very complex matters, but the accent lies on God's self-manifestation, of whatever kind, and the response of human beings to that revelation, despite whatever demonic manipulation might be involved in that answer. For Bavinck, thus, religious consciousness is primarily a theological phenomenon and only secondarily a human one. In this respect his view is in line with that of Calvin and is also intimately allied with that of Kraemer, which means that it stands in contrast to that of Barth, who considers religion, as to origin, to be "the affair of godless man"[115] and, in close connection with this, conceives its essence to be "the endeavor of man to forestall that which God wills to do and does in His revelation, the attempt to replace the work of God with a human fabrication."[116] To Barth's mind religion is primarily a monologue, whereas to Bavinck it is more of a dialogue. In light of Romans 1 Bavinck's position is convincing and Barth's is questionable.[117]

6. The Content of Religious Consciousness

The religions of the world differ so greatly and are so complicated and rich in thought that it is utterly impossible, according to Bavinck, to lump them together under one umbrella or reduce them to one common denominator.[118] In itself this contention was nothing remarkable since Schleiermacher had already argued that there could never have been anything like a *religio naturalis* which functioned as a trunk from which the various religions grew as branches. What is new in Bavinck's position is that, in contrast to Kraemer[119] and others, he became increasingly cautious about attempts, made with the aid of the phenomenology of

---

[113]Cf. *CBTM*, 124.

[114]Cf. *ibid.*, 19.

[115]"Die Angelegenheit des gottlosen Menschen," *Kirchliche Dogmatik*, I, 2, 327 (cf. *Church Dogmatics*, I, 2, 300).

[116]"Das Unternehmen des Menschen, dem, was Gott in seiner Offenbarung tun will und tut, vorzugreifen, an die Stelle des göttlichen Werkes ein menschliches Gemächte zu schieben," *ibid.*, 329 (cf. *Church Dogmatics*, I, 2, 302).

[117]Korff demonstrated that Barth's exegesis of Rom. 1:18 ff. is dogmatically biased and distorted.

[118]Cf. *RBCG*, 11.

[119]Cf. *The Christian Message in a Non-Christian World*, 142-228.

religion, to devise classifications of the various historical religions.[120] "Every classification," he wrote, "is to a certain extent justifiable, but it runs the risk of becoming a distortion, or at least an overemphasis, of aspects which are not as central as they seem to be. For that reason I prefer not to make a classification."[121] This does not mean, however, that in Bavinck's opinion no general tendencies can be identified within the broad diversity of religious belief and practice. Bavinck developed an original morphology of religious consciousness, which evidences a thoroughgoing knowledge of particularly the great world religions.[122]

Bavinck indicated that he proceeds from the concept of universal religious consciousness posited by Kraemer,[123] a sensibility "which continues to exist indestructibly amidst all disturbances and confusing evolutions" and "which we encounter in all [the] various religions as the power lying behind them."[124] He provides no explicit argumentation for this contention, but it may be that the inner consistency of what he had said about the origin and essence of religious consciousness was so evident to him that he felt the present assertion needed no further buttressing. "This universal religious consciousness is something

---

[120]It should be pointed out that at an earlier stage Bavinck considered a classification of the non-Christian religions to be feasible, and he himself grouped them into three types: dynamic, animistic, and animistic-dynamic; cf., e.g., "Phaenomenologische classificatie der religieuze structuren." However, h e contended that Christianity was so different from other religions that it could never be included in any classification, which set him in clear opposition to Kraemer, who stated that "the most pertinent division is that into prophetic religions of revelation and naturalist religions of trans-empirical realization" and then classed Christianity among the prophetic religions; cf. *The Christian Message in a Non-Christian World*, 142. In *IZW*, 241 (cf. *ISM*, 240), Bavinck questioned whether one didn't run the risk of "a certain relativism, which in the long run could be fatal," by including Christianity "alongside Judaism and Islam in the category of prophetic religions."

[121]*CBTM*, 29; in *RBCG* he does not voice this rejection quite so explicitly, but nevertheless refrains from engaging in any kind of categorization of the religions.

[122]Cf. J. Verkuyl, "Woord vooraf," *RBCG*, XIII, who suggested the term 'morphology' in this connection, and A.C. Bouquet, 385, who called Bavinck's phenomenological approach "a classification of his own."

[123]Kraemer wrote that as "scientific research and critical thinking both teach, there is no 'natural' religion," but "only a universal religious consciousness in man, which produces many similarities" in terms of the "aspirations, ideas, institutions, symbols and intuitions in all the religions ... of mankind, ... similar data ... of religious and ethical insight." *The Christian Message in a Non-Christian World*, 112-111.

[124]*RBCG*, 11-12; cf. *CBTM*, 29-30.

mysterious," he writes.[125]

> It is not something concrete, something we can grasp and lay hold of. It does not show itself, and we never meet it in its original form. It is vague and nebulous, and we can find it only indirectly, by scrutinizing the various religions in which it has taken shape. Therefore it is not possible to describe this religious consciousness in one word. If we can make any statement about its qualities at all, it is that it is a complicated thing, full of tensions and contrast. On the other hand, it strikes us that this consciousness, notwithstanding the fact that it displays so many varieties, has nevertheless a certain continuity. This continuity is ... comprehensible when we take into account that [people], in spite of the innumerable differences between [them], were forced to follow similar trails.[126]

A deep study of the religions reveals the existence of "a sort of framework within which the religious thought of humankind must move.... There appear to be certain intersections around which all sorts of ideas crystalize ... [or] magnetic points [in the form of primal questions] to which the religious thinking of mankind is irresistibly attracted."[127]

Bavinck delineates five main elements making up the map of religious consciousness: a sense of belonging to the whole, a sense of transcendent norms, a sense of relatedness to a higher or supreme power, a sense of the need for redemption, and a sense of the governance of existence by a providential or destining power.[128] These aspects of religious consciousness cohere with the existential relationships in which people are involved in this world and through which God reveals himself to them, relationships which bear similarities everywhere throughout time due to the "unity of mankind." As a being with limitations, "always restricted by his anthropological structure," man can never "outgrow his own qualities and dispositions," cannot escape the existential links by which he is bound, cannot—"by virtue of his place in the world"—avoid the necessity of struggling "with the basic problems which his existence itself entails."[129] Humans are limited by their human beingness.

If only man could shed his self-being, his individuality, his sense

---

[125]*CBTM*, 30.

[126]*Ibid.*, 30.

[127]*RBCG*, 103.

[128]Cf. *RBCG*, 12-69. These five aspects are also dealt with in *CBTM*, 32-33 and 37-113, albeit in a different sequence: in this later publication the 'sense of relatedness to a higher power' no longer stands in the center but at the end of the list, for which no reason is given. Perhaps Bavinck came to the conclusion that this was a more logical sequence; however that may be, the order in which these elements are discussed makes no *essential* difference since they all form part of a whole.

[129]*CBTM*, 31.

of royalty, if only he could let himself sink down in this world to
the level of a plant or an animal without norms or morals! But he
cannot do that. He is man, bearer of a name at once unutterably
noble and desperately pathetic.[130]

In terms of religious consciousness humans can go in all directions save one: they
cannot avoid the five fundamental problems of their existence, they cannot position
themselves outside "that mysterious framework within which the great questions of
all religious reflection" are urgently posed.[131] Even if a person "never takes the time
and the trouble deliberately to ponder" these questions, his or her "whole way of
living already implies an answer, and *is* an answer."[132] Bavinck submits these five
facets of religious consciousness to a careful and extensive analysis, using many
concrete illustrations to clarify them. We will limit ourselves here to a brief survey
of his discussion in *RBCG* and *CBTM*, following the sequence presented in the
latter, it being the more recent of these two publications.

1. *A sense of belonging to the whole; an awareness of cosmic relationship.*
Human beings have always felt a mysterious affinity with the totality of things
which permanently encompasses their lives, bringing both positive and negative
powers to bear on them. Man feels deeply that this cosmic whole has a divine
origin and character. On the one hand he recognizes that his existence is nothing
more than a brief moment in that totality and therefore that his individual
significance is minimal: he is but an infinitesimal fragment of the vast cosmic
family, "a tiny cell in the colossal body of the universe";[133] on the other hand he
realizes he is part of a divine world, which gives meaning to his life. This sense of
cosmic oneness engenders not so much a feeling of responsibility as of communality
and collectivity. As a result of this erasure of the line of division between God and
man, man becomes a being at once unfathomably insignificant and incomparably
grand. All of this is reflected in the idea of the macrocosm (the universe) and the
microcosm (human life) which are inextricably bound up with each other, implying
the close linkage of theology, cosmology and sociology, and yielding an ethic of
harmony: human behavior requires to be brought into conformity with the cosmic
laws.

2. *A sense of transcendent norms.* Everywhere people realize that what is,
is "not the way it's supposed to be,"[134] that "things are not right as they are" and
should be changed.[135] In everything they think and do or fail to do humans come
face to face with the mysterious phenomenon of the awareness that they could have
entertained other thoughts and acted differently, that they have a choice in these

---

[130]*RBCG*, 166.

[131]*Ibid.*, 104.

[132]*CBTM*, 34.

[133]*CBTM*, 54.

[134]Cf. the title of C. Plantinga, Jr.'s book, *Not the Way It's Supposed to
Be: A Breviary of Sin*, Grand Rapids: Eerdmans / Leicester: Apollos, 1995.

[135]*CBTM*, 112.

matters. Everywhere in the world, humans have known themselves to be wholly subjected in both thought and deed to moral norms and values not of their own making, rules and standards which they feel "have a divine origin" and hence constitute "a divine institution."[136] We humans are very much aware "that the borderline that divides what is permissible from what is impermissible has been drawn by a power that transcends us mightily."[137] Within this sector of religious consciousness, too, the divine and the human are closely interlaced in people's experience, and the sense of norm is often closely identified with the cosmic order. Adherence to or disregard of the norm bears far-reaching positive or negative consequences for humankind and the cosmos, which bespeaks human responsibility: "We are responsible—that is to say, we will have to give an account of our actions."[138] Clearly, there exists a certain degree of friction between this perception of responsibility and the sense of submersion in the cosmic whole, owing to which the 'I' is actually nothing but an illusion. Human freedom is at stake here: to what extent can man resist the divine order in which his own existence is essentially comprehended?

3. *A sense of the governance of existence by a providential or destining power.* At all times and in all places, people have experienced a tension between deed and destiny: they *lead* but also *undergo* their lives, they are struck by the fact that life "seems to have two sides, an active and a passive [one]."[139] Man is continually confronted with powers that are far greater than he and that control the workings and course of his life, a confrontation in which he has always perceived a religious reality. On one side there is the idea that even one's deeds are determined by fate, and on the other, the view that fortune is at least partially dependent on one's deeds. In the deepest sense, there exists a rational and moral link between deed and fate or fortune. If their standpoint is that of the all-embracing cosmic whole, people will always tend to place passivity above activity.

4. *A recognition of the need for redemption.* Man has always been aware that his life in the deepest sense is not what it was meant to be and therefore has unremittingly sought ways to rectify this deficiency, to elevate his life to a higher plane in order that he might live it in true fullness and abundance. There is a sense of 'paradise lost,' a deeply rooted and widespread feeling among people that the earth lies under a curse owing to the fact that the ties between heaven and earth were broken long ago in the primeval age. In "the time before all times, something must have happened that caused man's struggle with numberless insurmountable difficulties, and especially death."[140] On that account, continual attempts have been made throughout human history to redeem everyday reality from this curse through the agency of sacralization, i.e., to endow life with "an additional dimension, the

---

[136] *Ibid.*, 54.

[137] *RBCG*, 27.

[138] *CBTM*, 55.

[139] *CBTM*, 67.

[140] *CBTM*, 83.

dimension of sacredness," which it needs "to be worth living and beneficial."[141] Man hopes to free his life from misery and death and restore the original paradisaical state by means of his religious rituals and endeavors. Man's religion is a clear manifestation of his sense of human sinfulness and his hunger for redemption and salvation.

In many religious traditions redemption is closely related to the minor place man occupies in the cosmic whole and consists, in the final analysis, of nothing other than the loss of the 'I,' the forfeiture of all human passion to the divine order. In most religions redemption has both a personal and collective focus: it has to do with both the salvation of the individual and the deliverance of society or the community as a whole. Moreover, this concept generally bears both an autosoteric and a heterosoteric character. But even when it is understood in the latter sense, that is to say, as a divine gift, it is almost never wholly divested of autosoteriological tendencies, *viz.*, man's attempt to cooperate with the deity in an effort to achieve salvation. And when this synergism "is strongly emphasized, redemption is soon regarded as a fruit of man's labor."[142]

5. *A sense of relatedness to a Superior or Supreme Power.* In all the facets of religious consciousness mentioned above, man experiences a Higher Power to which his life is subject. The history of religion demonstrates that people have always tried to gain knowledge and lay hold of that Power, which often does not bear a personal character. Sometimes it is a He or She, but mostly at the same time an It, the great Unknown behind and under everything, "the deepest being of all being, the hidden, impersonal background of all things."[143] Man perceives the forbidding elusiveness of this divine Power dwelling "in the unapproachable distance."[144] And yet he simultaneously identifies it with the surrounding celestial and natural world: the sun, the moon, the stars, chthonian or benign forces, various phenomena and events. In like manner, it is also often equated or closely associated with man himself, seen as the microcosmic cell in which "all the powers of the cosmos [are] concentrated."[145] In many religions and religious currents God is not viewed as an entity outside of man but as "the innermost being of man ... the hidden secret inside."[146] To sum up: good and evil are joined together in this Higher Power, which has been conceived not so much as one massive transcendent entity but rather as a congeries of hidden powers in the cosmos, the world and man, meaning that the borderline between the natural and the supernatural is often not much more than an indefinite dotted line.

Bavinck emphasizes that, though they can be distinguished, these five features of religious consciousness never exist separately but are always "totally

---

[141]*Ibid.*, 84.

[142]*Ibid.*, 90.

[143]*Ibid.*, 101.

[144]*Ibid.*, 97.

[145]*Ibid.*, 101.

[146]*Ibid.*, 102.

intertwined, the one being subject to conditioning by the other."[147] Taken as a whole, one can say that religious consciousness has two main dimensions. The first of these consists of the feeling of an overpowering *du bist*: the fatalistic sense that the destiny of one's entire life is determined by the fact that he or she is but a microscopic atom in the measureless expanse of the universe, a minute ripple in the boundless ocean of total reality, a tiny spark in the vast fire of cosmic existence. The second dimension consists of the cognizance of a compelling *du sollst*: the galvanizing perception of culpability and accountability in the face of an existing moral norm, and hence of the need for redemption—a cognizance, therefore, that is characterized by a sense of individuality, responsibility, freedom and possibility.[148] If these two dimensions are taken figuratively as a pair of intersecting lines, then the point at which they meet and cross may be viewed as the human feeling of relatedness to a Higher Power, which constitutes the heart of religious consciousness, the very core of all religion. Indeed, it may be said that it is only by virtue of this sense of relatedness to a Higher Power that all the other facets of religious consciousness take on the character of religion: "It is on the strength of this one facet that religion first becomes religion in the true sense of the word."[149]

The oft repeated ways in which the various elements of religious consciousness have been understood and elaborated throughout the ages among the historic religions are myriad in number and recurrently characterized by inner contradiction.

We see that the history of religion depicts a great variety of divine forms and myths.... Again and again the same ideas crop up. Also, this history repeats itself many times. When examining its searching and groping, we encounter so many different ideas. . . . They are sometimes bizarre, unbelievably childlike and foolish; yet sometimes they strike us as being sublime and imposing. At times these ideas led to inhuman, cruel deeds and dreadful wars, but also to self-denial and neighborly love.[150]

For Bavinck the five aspects of religious consciousness discussed above make up the substantive content of humankind's age-long wrestling with the Other, Who—as is taught in Romans 1:18 ff.—encounters man through general revelation. And this whole discourse bears crucial significance for Bavinck's understanding of religion: all the questions involved in religious consciousness "concern man's existential relationships."[151] It is possible for man to be occupied with himself only, he writes, and to look no further.

But as soon as he becomes aware of his relationships, he becomes stupefied and asks: What am I in this great cosmos?

---

[147]*RBCG*, 72.

[148]Cf. *Ibid*., 72-74.

[149]*Ibid*., 75.

[150]*CBTM*, 111.

[151]*Ibid*., 112.

What am I over against the norm, that strange phenomenon in my
life that has authority over me? What am I in my life that speeds
on and on ... ? What am I in the face of that remarkable feeling
that overwhelms me sometimes, the feeling that everything must
be changed ... ? What am I over against that very mysterious
background of existence, the divine powers? It is in the area of
[these] existential relations that man is confronted with the
crucial matters of life—and ... religion is the way in which man
experiences the deepest existential relations and gives expression
to this experience.[152]

In order to preclude any misunderstanding, it should be remarked at this point that
in Bavinck's thought this definition of religion applies to Christianity as well,
except that the latter embodies an answer to God's special revelation in Scripture.[153]

7. Religious Consciousness and Modern Culture

A recurring theme in Bavinck's publications is his awareness that he was standing
on the boundary between two worlds. "The Western Church," he wrote,
which at this point is serving as the apostle to Asia, is itself in a
state of crisis, the likes of which we can hardly imagine. The life
of countless people is infinitely more secularized, hollowed out
and eroded than they themselves realize. Among a multitude of
Westerners faith in science, technology, human thought and
ability, social and nationalist movements has pushed trust in God
far into the background.... [And at the same time, we] find
ourselves in an era in which the old religions, which for long
ages had bound human life up in tight shackles, are wasting
away, as it were, before the onslaught of the new ideals that are
knocking at Asia's gates.[154]

Bavinck once said of Kraemer, who was also very conscious of the problem of the
secularization of modern society: "This matter intrigues him and distresses him.
He, with his pronounced spiritual lifeway, has a difficult time understanding this
religious atrophy of modern man."[155] But this observation is equally applicable to
Bavinck himself and may well furnish an important clue as to why, even though
mentioning this issue regularly, he devotes relatively little space to its discussion.
Despite his summary treatment of this phenomenon, however, Bavinck did clearly
recognize its prevalence and seriousness, attempting to accord it a place in his view

---

[152]*Ibid.*

[153]Bavinck elaborates this question at length in *CBTM*, 129-193, showing
how the five facets of religious consciousness are experienced and interpreted in
terms of God's revelation in Christ; cf. also *RBCG*, 184-186. Since this matter is
not germane to the present discussion, however, it will not be dealt with here, but
only later in the section on elenctics.

[154]"Christus en de wereld van het Oosten," 210-211.

[155]"Dr. H. Kraemer as denker en medewerker," 169-170.

of religious consciousness. He asks himself whether religious consciousness is a thing of the past, something that is dying off in the face of the worldwide secularization of culture, or, conversely, whether it remains alive and well in the present and will continue to figure strongly in the future, albeit in different forms.[156] He offers a twofold answer to this question.

Bavinck acknowledges the massive, pervading loss of a sense of transcendence that has been brought about by the advancement of positivist science and technology.[157] "The process of *Entgötterung*[158] of the [Western] worldview and the secularization of life in general continues apace."[159] Hence, Bavinck avers, the American-British poet T.S. Eliot (1888-1965) was right in a certain sense when he wrote: "Men have left God not for other gods, they say, but for no God: and this has never happened before."[160] From a religious viewpoint the development of modern culture is disastrous: "Something in our thinking has been irreparably broken."[161] The sense of relatedness to a Higher Power has lost its compelling force, the core of religious consciousness is fading away. Any answers that are still given to existential questions of life and death are losing their religious tone and becoming businesslike, sterile, paltry, meager and bitter.[162]

It is especially in the West that this process has left deep traces. Everywhere in this part of the world, people are turning away from the church and setting themselves in opposition to its message. "God is dead, we have murdered Him. A generation is growing up for whom God is in fact not much more than a long forgotten word found in ancient writings, a generation that doesn't feel the slightest twinge of sorrow that it has lost Him."[163] Positivistic natural sciences have made such headway that people have lost complete sight of God, feel that they no longer encounter Him anywhere. An atheistic materialism that manifests itself in many different forms has entered the picture.[164] The altar has been replaced by the

---

[156]Cf. *RBCG*, 76.

[157]Cf. *RBCG*, 5.

[158]Literally 'de-god-ing,' 'un-god-ing,' hence: alienation of, estrangement from, disposal of the gods.

[159]*RBCG*, 6.

[160]"Choruses From the Rock," *The Penguin Poets*, p. 118. Cf. "General Revelation and the Non-Christian Religions," 53.

[161]*RBCG*, 83.

[162]Cf. *ibid.*, 83-91.

[163]*Ibid.*, 91.

[164]Cf. *PWB*, 163.

mirror in which man sees nothing but himself.[165] Nevertheless, one should not forget that even after the disappearance of religion itself, all sorts of religious feelings continue to make themselves felt for a long time, "like the lingering twilight after the sun has already set," retaining their compelling "power throughout many generations."[166] This post-Christian religious consciousness is of a peculiar nature in that it is influenced by Christianity on the one hand but is in strong opposition to it on the other.[167] And at any moment these residual religious feelings can become embodied in all manner of movements, such as nationalism, National-Socialism and Communism, and in so doing, cause them to evince a wondrous religious glow.[168] At a later stage, Bavinck observed that these forms of religiously tinted idealism were also disappearing. An impersonal pattern of mass living was coming into existence, he pointed out. Existentialism and nihilism were burgeoning. A life characterized by hedonism and the incessant search for sensation, a life bereft of spiritual and moral values, was spreading swiftly.[169]

If this were the lone earmark of contemporary life, it would mean that modern culture was witnessing the final death spasms of a few attenuated religious feelings that in principle were doomed to pass away. In short, modern man would be turning into an a-religious being. Bavinck refuses to draw this conclusion, however, since he never considered secularization to be the sole reality of current existence. As was pointed out earlier, he was fundamentally convinced that no human being can peremptorily back out of the existential relationships through which God reveals himself to him or her. "Whether we know it or not, we remain caught in the clasp of the religious questions of humankind,"[170] and our lives constitute an answer to those questions. Everyone responds in some way to the elemental riddles of his or her existence.[171] Thus, every human life, also that of a secularized person, "is essentially a choice and a decision."[172] The five questions involved in religious consciousness remain key to the existence of even nonreligious modern people, and they "must respond to them in some way or other."[173]

This need not be done philosophically—the answer to these basic problems can be given in the course of everyday life. Everyday

---

[165]Cf. "De onbekende God," 20.

[166]*RBCG*, 9.

[167]Cf. *ibid.*, 77.

[168]Cf. ibid., 7-9.

[169]Cf. *DMN*, 38-47.

[170]*Ibid.*, 84.

[171]CF. *CBTM*, 112.

[172]*Ibid.*

[173]*Ibid.*, 111.

actions, one's sense of responsibility or the lack of it, one's ambitions, the things one yearns for, all these are the concrete answer man gives to the basic problems of his existence.[174] As a result of radical suppression of God's wordless speech, this answer can also assume the nature of a denial of God and thereby take on a totally secular cast.[175] Nevertheless, even then it remains a *religious* response, a response given within the framework of the mysterious, veiled dialogue between God and man, for "it touches the deepest religious realities with which man is confronted."[176] What is more, the religious nature of this response holds not only in a formal but also an emotional sense: modern man understands that his entire life unfolds "in the midst of an utterly mysterious reality," which engenders in him "emotions laden with religious urgency."[177] And even when "he renounces the ideas and religious doctrines of earlier generations, the very intensity and rancorous bitterness" with which he does this "resonate religiously in his breast.... Everywhere, one runs up against this peculiar reality of religious sentiment that fills and vibrates in everything."[178]

Moreover, reflection on the course the development of civilization has taken demonstrates that "modern culture, too, is a religious phenomenon, either in the positive or in the negative sense,"[179] which means that the bearers of this culture are not and can never be a-religious in the full sense of the word. Indeed, atheism itself, the denial of God, remains a relative phenomenon, according to Bavinck, who goes even a step further by contending that the sense of a Higher Power keeps haunting the atheist. Even when a man is inclined to abandon belief in "the reality behind reality ... and to become an atheist in the full sense of the word, he is often still overwhelmed by it, as it were. The idea that there is a *Supreme Power* to which he himself is related is apparently something that he can never get rid of."[180] All in all, religious consciousness proves to be a tough force which can by no means be abrogated or ignored by twentieth-century man, for despite all change that takes place, the deeper layers of human existence remain constant.[181] Indeed, the existential questions with which people are trying to deal 'autonomously,' i.e., without having recourse to God, can at any moment become "intensified to such a

---

[174]*Ibid.*

[175]Cf. *CWS*, in which Bavinck deals with the questions and answers of contemporary secularized man under four rubrics: man and community (8), instinct and reason (14), hesitation regarding moral norms (21) and the riddle of history (26). See also "Christus nu," 7-35.

[176]*CBTM*, 111.

[177]*RBCG*, 7.

[178]*Ibid.*

[179]*CBTM*, 23.

[180]*Ibid.*, 33.

[181]Cf. *RBCG*, 76.

degree that they regain the religious pitch they have always had throughout the ages."[182] It is possible, for example, that despair and hopelessness will be the price modern culture has to pay for its godlessness. Shortly after the Second World War, Bavinck wrote:

> The dramatic events of recent decades ... have brought about some change, in the sense that contemporary man has lost something of his inner certitude. He continues to experience the irresistible drive toward the impersonal pragmatism and godless way of life that propels our culture forward, but [now] he is inclined to view this driving force as a tragic process, something he cannot withstand but the precariousness and painfulness of which he feels to the full.[183]

In the midst of this bleakness, something of nostalgia for lost religious values can arise and repressed religious feelings can well up from the inscrutable depths of the heart.[184] This, combined with the fact that God's wordless speech continues unabated despite man's 'no,'[185] means that the revival of religious consciousness is always a realistic possibility, according to Bavinck. But he also observes, with reference to Revelation 13, that "in the last days," the religious dimension in human life can take on extremely dramatic forms. This passage in Revelation paints a vivid picture of a symbiosis between religious experience and religious degeneracy, an unadulterated process of repression and substitution in connection with the beast that rose out of the earth.[186]

Without detracting anything from the grave danger and influence of secularization, Bavinck holds firmly to the conviction that, no matter what, all human life always includes a religious dimension which can never be extirpated. And even if this dimension lies deeply hidden in that life, it is capable of resurfacing at various and sundry moments. This line of reasoning—which derives its authority from Scripture and is broadly supported by many other observers and confirmed by recent developments in the area of spirituality[187]—fits well in the whole realm of

---

[182]*Ibid.*, 84.

[183]*Ibid.*, 7.

[184]Cf. *ibid.*, 7, 92. See also "Worden wij weer primitieve menschen?," in which Bavinck, following G. van der Leeuw (*De primitieve mensch en zijn religie*), argues that modern abstract thought does not satisfy because it clashes with the reality of life, resulting in the rise of a new primitiveness with religious tendencies.

[185]See section 3.3.1. above.

[186]Cf. *EVWE*, 169-196, esp. 188-196; here Bavinck deals at length with the demonic aspect of religion.

[187]Cf. the following: "The modern world is in fact producing more new religions, cults, pseudo religions and idolatries than there ever were before, demonstrating that man possesses an ineradicable religious inclination," H. Kraemer, *Communicatie*, 116; "Many thought that the role of religious

Bavinck's thought. The question does arise here, however, to what extent a post-Christian situation differs both practically and theologically from a pre-Christian one in terms of the reception of general revelation and its assimilation into religious consciousness. Bavinck devotes very little attention to this issue, stating only that "in modern culture religious consciousness has...been more or less bent in a certain direction by Christianity," while the converse is equally true, namely, that religious consciousness "stands in strong opposition to that same Christianity." But whatever the case, religious consciousness "betrays at every moment the significance that...Christianity has had for our culture."[188]

8. The Value of Religious Consciousness

Bavinck's theological assessment of religious consciousness underwent a clear development, an evolution which ran parallel to the change in his view of the essence of that consciousness. His earlier, largely negative appraisal of the content of religion became radicalized at the expense of the positive element it had once contained. In the middle of the 1930s he wrote: "There are in fact many beautiful and true thoughts of deep wisdom in pagan [holy] books.... We need not look upon the prophets of paganism as imposters; indeed, we may freely acknowledge that they, too, may well have heard something of God's voice."[189] Initially, he had spoken of man's search for God *in* his flight from God.[190] In his later reflection, particularly in light of Romans 1:18 ff., this seeking and fleeing coincide: every search for God is in essence a flight from God.[191]

This concurrence of quest and evasion owes its existence to the process of repression and substitution which is activated as soon and as often as God speaks. The first word in the dialogue between God and man is true to precisely the same degree as the second word is false (Romans 1:25), and conversely, man's response is exactly as false as God's initial utterance is true. The divine-human dialogical

---

consciousness and that of religions was played out and that we should gear ourselves to agnosticism and atheism, to an a-religious 'third man' and a 'non-religious Christianity.' However, that time is past. Religiosity is 'in' again ... and many new forms of religiosity are manifesting themselves," H. Berkhof, 169; "For the modern man personally, religious questions remain in effect.... We note a blossoming of religion which is being pursued in all directions.... Everyone is busy with God again," H. Jonker, 13, 111; in this connection specific mention should be made of New Age, which is even being introduced and integrated into the corporate life of high-tech companies: "The rise of New Age in the West and the renaissance of the non Christian religions elsewhere in the world point to a direction different from agnosticism and atheism as the final destination of human history" J.A.B. Jongeneel,"Missie en zending," 582.

[188]*RBCG*, 77.

[189]"Het christendom als absolute religie," 330.

[190]Cf. *PWB*, 165 ff.

[191]Cf. *PPRAO*, 18.

relationship can be likened to a person "standing before a carnival looking glass: the curved mirror reflects the form in front of it, but the image it displays is misshapen in every detail, it is altogether false."[192] This metaphor could give the impression that what emerges from man's warped response to general revelation is simply an *erroneous concept* of God and not a *different* God. But that impression would be mistaken, for this human falsehood bespeaks the kind of unremitting estrangement from the Living God referred to in Ephesians 2:12. There Paul reminds believers that formerly they were "without hope and without God in the world," a condition resulting from the fact that it is most essentially the eternal power and divinity "of Him who sits on the throne of the Universe" that is repudiated in the process of suppression and exchange of the truth.[193] Anyone who views God differently from the way He has revealed himself in Jesus Christ, does not merely have a divergent notion of God but most profoundly another god.[194] Bavinck writes that he could not "express this better and more deeply than Calvin did"[195] in the *Institutes*:

> Indeed, vanity joined with pride can be detected in the fact that, in seeking after God, ... men ... fly off into empty speculations. They do not therefore apprehend God as he offers himself, but imagine him as they have fashioned him in their own presumption.[196]
>
> For at the same time as we have enjoyed a slight taste of the divine from contemplation of the universe, having neglected the true God, we raise up in his stead dreams and specters of our own brains, and attribute to anything else than the true source the praise of righteousness, wisdom, goodness, and power.[197]

Bavinck also adopts Calvin's biblical depiction of true religion[198] and contends that when empirical religions are measured against this yardstick, they are revealed to be forms of spiritual degeneracy and apostasy.[199] That is why in Scripture, terms such as vanity, profligacy, darkness, and ignorance are employed

---

[192]"Het evangelie en de andere godsdiensten," 166.

[193]Cf. *ZWN*, 69; *IZW*, 62 (*ISM*, 53); "General Revelation and the non-Christian Religions," 54; "Het eerste gebod: 'Gij zult geen andere goden voor Mijn aangezicht hebben,'" 88 ff.; and *ICNCW*, 98-101.

[194]Cf. "Het eerste gebod," 91.

[195]*Ibid.*

[196]Vol. I, Book 1, Chap. IV.1, 47.

[197]Vol. I, Book 1, Chap. V.15, 69.

[198]Cf. *Institutes*, Vol. I, Book 1, Chap. II.2, 41-43.

[199]Cf. *PPRAO*, 10. Bavinck also shares Calvin's negative verdict respecting any form of *theologia naturalis* or 'natural religion' as opposed to religion that takes its rise from and is inspired by God's Word, cf. *RBCG*, 148.

to describe them.[200] The "most telling characterization of paganism," Bavinck wrote in a work published in 1941, is found in Acts 14:16, where Paul employs the concept "going their own way" to describe the essential nature of non-Christian religions.[201] Non-scriptural religions are all the product of "the foolish, excited behavior of humans and their musings," whereby they themselves "map out the route [they] wish to follow."[202]

In this latter publication, Bavinck deals at length with Paul's speech on the Areopagus (Acts 17:22 ff.) because of the important role this address has played in the history of the Christian evaluation of the other religions. In the Early Church, leaders such as Justin Martyr and Clement of Alexandria viewed this Pauline discourse as the justification for their attempts to build a bridge between Christian faith and Greek philosophy.[203] Later on, Roman Catholic theologians held that the speech proved that Paul did not consider the religions other than his own "to be totally the work of the Devil."[204] And the Protestant missiologist Gustav Warneck called Paul's oration "a typical example of the art of establishing missionary contact or linkage."[205] The speech on the Areopagus continued to intrigue Christian thinkers in the 20th century as well. Eduard Norden, Martin Debelius and Albert Schweitzer cast light, each in his own way, on the Greek philosophical character of Paul's address, arguing that by reason of the implicit appreciation it evinces for Hellenistic philosophy, it could not possibly have been delivered by Paul himself, because the real Paul, whom we encounter in Romans 1:18 ff. and 3:11, opposed any attempt to palliate or whitewash pagan thought and practice.[206]

Bavinck finds none of these interpretations of Paul's speech satisfactory, preferring instead that of Johannes Witte, a student of Barth's, who upholds the Pauline origin of the Areopagus address and demonstrates that what Paul said to the philosophers in Athens does not differ from what he argued in Romans 1:18.[207] According to Witte, the whole speech should be read through the lens of the term *repentance* ($\mu\epsilon\tau\acute{\alpha}\nu\omicron\iota\alpha$) in v.30. In linking his argument to the altar inscription, "To an Unknown God," Paul was in no way suggesting that the Athenians had already taken a step in the right direction, but rather was expressing the implicit accusation that they did not know God (v. 23) despite the fact that "He is not far

---

[200]In this connection Bavinck refers in *IZW*, 62 (cf. *ISM*, 54), to Eph. 2:18, 19, 4:17, 5:8, Rom. 1:24, 31, and in *RBCG*, 129, to 1 Cor. 2:8.

[201]*AWW*, 134.

[202]*Ibid.*

[203]Cf. *ibid.*, 154-156.

[204]*AWW*, 157; cf. J. Thauren, 12.

[205]*AWW*, 157; cf. Warneck, *Evangelische Missionslehre*, II, 2, 95.

[206]Cf. *AWW*, 157-164; the relevant publications of these three theologians are listed in the bibliography.

[207]Cf. J. Witte, 40 ff.

from each one of us" (v. 27). Paul is speaking here of a *failure* to know, a *culpable* nescience.[208] His pronouncement that "in the past God overlooked such ignorance" (v. 30) by no means implies that he considered this ignorance to be excusable, but points rather to the immensity of God's grace. By adopting this interpretation of Paul's speech, Bavinck highlighted its elenctic character,[209] arguing that the indisputably empathetic tone of the address, which can lead to misunderstanding, serves as a device of missionary communication. In support of this interpretation, Bavinck adduces the term δεισιδαιμονεστέρους in v. 22, which can have both a positive connotation (unusually religious) and a negative one (exceedingly superstitious).[210] Paul's listeners could have taken this term positively, while Paul meant it negatively.[211] Bavinck emphasizes that this speech should not be read as a theological treatise; it was delivered within the context of missionary practice and should be interpreted it that light.

> I repeat that Paul's speech would have been judged differently if it had been examined on the mission field rather than in the study.... The principal standard that holds for any missionary address is that it must be captivating: it must grip people in their innermost being, it must be spoken in the language which is dear to the hearts of the listeners.[212]

When Paul borrowed terms from Greek philosophy, it was not his intention to tie in materially with that realm of thought, but only to make critical use of its terminology with a view to making himself understood.[213] Bavinck adds, here, that Paul had all the more reason to employ Greek philosophical expressions "because

---

[208]Cf. *AWW*, 168; Bavinck refers here to the fact that A. Harnack also speaks of a guilty ignorance in this connection, cf. *Mission und Ausbreitung des Christentums in den ersten drei Jahrhunderten*, 392; see also *RBCG*, 129, for the concept of blameworthy obliviousness.

[209]For an elaboration of this character cf. *AWW*, 174-187.

[210]Cf. G. Bertram, 123: "δεισιδαιμονεστέρους is often used in a critical or even a condemnatory sense. It can even denote superstition."

[211]Cf. *AWW*, 166; a later commentator, D.K. Wielinga, maintains that it was not without reason that Paul refrained from using the positive Hellenistic concepts θεοσεβής or θεοσέβεια, denoting true piety, true religion; herein lies an implicit judgment on the part of Paul, which accords with what he reports in v. 16 about the way he felt while walking around Athens among all its idols, namely, that he was greatly distressed, provoked, irritated, stirred to anger (παρωξύνετο τὸ πνεῦμα αὐτοῦ ἐν αὐτῷ), 11-12; cf. also Bertram, 123-126, and Seesemann, 857.

[212]*AWW*, 170-172; cf. also *RBCG*, 120. Wielinga makes the same point: "It appears to us that, if the attention of the pagan listeners is to be won, it would not be particularly wise to commence with a strong condemnation of their religion," 11.

[213]Cf. *AWW*, 172-173.

that philosophy was in fact used by God as a preparation for what would come."[214] The fact that Greek thinkers had come to the conclusion that the old polytheism was foolishness and had adopted a more monotheistic view was the fruit "of God's merciful dealings with that deeply sunken world."[215] But everything considered, the judgment of all non-Christian religion is, in Bavinck's opinion, not weakened by Paul's speech on the Areopagus.

Does the radical judgment of non-Christian religion mean that the latter has no positive significance whatever? Bavinck answers this question negatively. Following J. Witte's line of thinking, he makes a distinction between the 'thatness' and the 'whatness' of religion.[216] He understands the 'thatness' to be the basal consciousness that there must be a Higher Power, a transcendent norm, and something like redemption, and the 'whatness' to be the manner in which people interpret and give substantive form to this consciousness.[217] In the 'thatness' of every religion the "hidden ways" and "silent activity" of God are unmistakably present.[218] Bavinck wishes to give full weight to the significance of this work of God, calling it "that in which we see something of the compelling power of God's plan for fallen man."[219] Because there are differences of degree in the effect of general revelation due to the sovereign freedom of God's activity among people and their relative openness to His wordless speech, the 'thatness' of religion also manifests shades of depth and breadth.

> Deeper acquaintance with the religious literature which has been passed down to us through other faith traditions often inspires amazement and genuine admiration. Truly, God has not left himself without witness: His presence has been experienced and His Light has clearly shone again and again in the midst of more than one people.[220]

Sometimes people cannot resist God's approach and are overwhelmed by it: "We may say that by the grace of God repression and substitution does not always succeed. Time and again we notice things in the history of religion which show that God has really concerned Himself with" people of other faiths,[221] and "we may

---

[214]*Ibid.*

[215]*Ibid.*

[216]Cf. Witte, 37 ff.

[217]Cf. "Het probleem der '*Anknüpfung*,'" 64-65; "Het evangelie en de andere godsdiensten," 67-58; *IZW*, 229 (*ISM*, 228); *CBTM*, 13-14.

[218]Cf. *CBTM*, 124-125.

[219]"Het problem der '*Anknüpfung*' bij de evangelieverkondiging," 68.

[220]*DAC*, 11.

[221]*CBTM*, 203.

thankfully state *that* they believe in God."[222]   Why is this a matter of gratitude? Because without this 'thatness,' this objective fact of religious consciousness , this *fides qua creditur*, missionary communication would be "utterly impossible"[223]

Bavinck goes on to argue that sometimes this belief contains elements which, after conversion to the gospel, can lead to a better understanding of and deeper encounter with the biblical message. The Oriental way of thinking, e.g., can

> help us to place the wealth of ideas offered to us in the gospel of Christ in an even purer and fuller light.... The Oriental is more strongly convinced of the omnipresence of the divine in all things,... is not so far removed as we are from [the world of] miracle,... is capable of waiting more quietly for the voice of God and can submit to Him with a greater degree of passivity,... is more aware that the form of this world is passing away.[224]

At the same time, however, he consistently refuses to attribute intrinsic theological value to the 'thatness' of religion, i.e., to view primary religious feelings as 'elements of truth'—this, on the grounds that these primary feelings are always enveloped by the fallacious 'whatness,' the subjective matter, the mistaken *fides quae creditur* and erroneous praxis of religion. If the notion 'elements of truth' is used in terms of religious consciousness, it must be done judiciously, according to Bavinck. Everything depends on

> what we mean by an 'element of truth.' If taken in a vague and general sense, it must be admitted that such elements are found in the non-Christian religions. If taken in a more special and defined meaning, then it will be hardly tenable. All central ideas involved in Christian belief, like God, creation, man, sin, salvation, law of life, the conclusion of the world, are found in most religions, but they are all understood in a fundamentally different sense, and applied in a quite different connection.[225]

The residues of revelation never lie hidden as petrified fossils in the soil of pseudo religion. False religion always presents itself as, and in actual fact invariably constitutes, a monolithic aggregate. Consequently, all ideas it absorbs become amalgamated with and deformed by the whole. In other words, it is not possible for isolated elements of verity, sparks of divine truth to exist in the midst of falsehood and error—in fact, if such sparks were present, they would lead to friction in and destruction of the very essence of pseudo religion.[226]   The caution with which Bavinck operates here is shown by the fact that he takes care to point out that while such things as religious confessions of guilt and expressions of praise found in false contexts cannot be extricated from these settings, they may not in themselves be

---

[222]"General Revelation and the Non-Christian Religions," 54.

[223]*CBTM*, 14.

[224]*CMO,* 9, 232. This thought can also be found in Kraemer's later publication, *Religion and the Christian Faith*, 365.

[225]"General Revelation and the Non-Christian Religions," 54.

[226]Cf. *PPRAO*, 14.

viewed as pure "hypocrisy" or be considered "untrue."[227] Thanks to the overwhelming power of God's revelation, certain components of pseudo religion can contain elements of veracity.

Bavinck also makes exceptions for the sincerity and truthfulness of the faith and practice of many individual member of other religions. The negative judgment of these religions does not imply that one "can never find anyone among their adherents who manifests a thought or manner of living that is in evident agreement with the truth of Christ."[228] And elsewhere, he wrote: "Nobody can tell what is happening in the heart of an individual man, nobody can form an idea of what the long-suffering and goodness of God will work in such a heart through His Spirit."[229] Biblical examples of the effect of such divine activity can be cited: "Out of the pagan peoples of the Eastern world, we see Melchizedek and Job emerge like stars in the night."[230] In connection with this, Bavinck poses the rhetorical question: "Does [God] sometimes stop the hidden machinery of unbelief and rebellion by the unconquerable power of His holy Word, even if that Word reaches the heart in disguised form? Here we suddenly feel ourselves confronted with the deepest of all mysteries, the mystery of the power of God."[231] On that account, it is not permissible to judge individuals. Judgments, Bavinck maintains, can only be made about religious systems, which in his view, as already indicated, can contain elements consistent with the truth of Christ. But logically speaking, he argues, such Christ-like religious thought or belief would represent "a *Fremdkörper*" within the non-Christian religion involved taken as a whole, *viz.*, it would remain a foreign substance which could not possibly be truly fit into the aggregate system in which it is found.[232]

A negative theological judgment of this kind does not rule out the possibility of another mode of evaluation of other religions that is positive in many respects, namely, one formulated from a *cultural* point of view. Personally, Bavinck always remained deeply impressed by the religio-cultural expressions he observed in the life of other peoples. For example, he wrote: "The Eastern world of thought is rich in beauty and depth. Deeper penetration into that world brings us into contact with a myriad of exalted conceptions and enriches our inner life."[233] And he points, in this connection, to a number of concrete things: one often sees in

---

[227]*ICNCW*, 97; *CBTM*, 203.

[228]"Het problem der '*Anknüpfung*' bij de evangelieverkondiging," 62; see also *ICNCW*, 96, where Bavinck provides a concrete example of this possibility.

[229]"General Revelation and the Non-Christian Religions," 52, cf. also *BCNCR*, 79-80.

[230]*ICNCW*, 101.

[231]*Ibid.*, 106-107.

[232]Cf. "Het problem der '*Anknüpfung*' bij de evangelieverkondiging," 61-62.

[233]*CMO, 9.*

non-Western cultures a strong social drive that engenders community and creates a sense of mutual responsibility and security; life in its entirety is experienced as religious, with the result that no duality arises between the sacred and the profane; and religious devotion is often very fervent.[234] More broadly, he states that general revelation has had a felicitous, salvific effect on the life of peoples everywhere: "There is some effect on human conscience, something causing Paul to say that gentiles having no law 'do by nature the things of the law' (Romans 2:14)."[235]

It is clear, in other words, that "in the pagan world, too, there are strong moral forces at work, exerting a restraining influence on the general tendency to lawlessness and depravity, forces which are the fruit of what has been divinely written in [people's] hearts."[236] It is precisely within the context of the contemporary secular world, Bavinck contends, that one can better appreciate the value of the protective function religion has had and continues to have in life. In this sense he also speaks very positively about more modern 'religions,' such as the Humanist philosophy of life, which in its "struggle against nihilism ... has contributed not a little to the continuation of our culture."[237] His appreciation for the cultural value of non-Christian religions is also evinced by the fact that he was sharply critical of the fact that people everywhere were becoming religiously and culturally uprooted by the onrushing tsunami of secularized Western influences.[238]

This later position represents a clear departure from H. Bavinck, who clearly assigned *theological* value to religious consciousness and whom Bavinck had cited approvingly earlier on.[239] H. Bavinck distinguished between "sound development and impure adulteration," between "true and false" in the various religions and was of the opinion that the reality of general revelation provides one

---

[234]Cf. "Het evangelie en de andere godsdiensten," 3-4 and *IBD*, 24-26; Bavinck also calls attention, in these same publications, to the theological, less attractive reverse side of these characteristics, cf. respectively 35-37 and 26-29.

[235]"General Revelation and the Non-Christian Religions," 53.

[236]*IZW*, 63 (cf. *ISM*, 54).

[237]"Protestantisme," 44; in this article Bavinck expresses great appreciation and deep respect for Humanism, without, however, doing violence to his theological standpoint. He closes his argument with the words: "As soon as we descend more deeply toward the zone of the core of our existence, we come upon unbridgeable discrepancies [between this view of life and Christianity]. It is extremely painful and even onerous to have to state this, but it is a reality which simply cannot be camouflaged," 48.

[238]Cf. ZWN, 202; along these lines it is interesting that in a 1960 report Bavinck made a plea for the protection and renewal of Hindustani culture in Surinam; cf. *Verslag van prof. dr. J.H. Bavinck betreffende zijn reis naar Suriname in opdracht van de Sticusa*

[239]Cf. "Het christendom als absolute religie," 332; in this article Bavinck, following H. Bavinck, speaks of Christianity as the absolute fulfilment of the idea of religion.

with sufficient grounds for recognizing "elements of truth" in other religious traditions,[240] though he did not go so far as to elevate this *natural* knowledge of God to the status of first stage on the way to *adequate* knowledge of God.[241] He does state, however, that general revelation tethers man to the supersensory world and perpetuates and nourishes his awareness that he can find rest only in God. "*Revelatio generalis* preserves humans," he wrote, " in order that and until they are found and restored by Christ. In that sense *theologia naturalis* was earlier rightly termed a *praeambula fidei*, a divine preparation and pedagogy for Christianity."[242] This line of reasoning led him at a given point to speak of an "*unbewusst Weissagendes*," a certain unconscious prophetic quality possessed by the non-Christian religions.[243] In their finest and most noble expressions, the other religions point to Jesus Christ, who, according to Haggai 2:7, is "the desired of all nations."[244] H. Bavinck, in other words, prized the 'thatness' out of the 'whatness' of religion and ascribed an independent value to it. Bavinck rejected this line of thought[245] decisively: the thirst after salvation, the quest for a Savior in the other religions is never a longing for the Thorn-Crowned One.[246]

> The deliverers and saviors about whom paganism dreams are not types of what Christ is and would be, but are savior-figures thought up by man.... Christ is different, radically different from the deliverers conjured up by the religions of mankind. His gospel is not the answer to the searching and groping of humans but, in a much deeper and poignant sense, constitutes a judgment of all human [religious] whimsy and musing.[247]

Bavinck's position both differs from and demonstrates affinity with that

---

[240]Cf. *Gereformeerde dogmatiek*, Vol. I, 330.

[241]Cf. *ibid.*, 325: "But even though some thinkers attained to a certain level of true and pure knowledge, it was always mixed with all sorts of error."

[242]*Ibid.*, 335.

[243]Cf. *Gereformeerde Dogmatiek*, Vol. III, 248.

[244]Though the Hebrew term translated by "the desired" can refer both to an individual, and thus have Messianic significance, and to articles of value, i.e., "the riches of the nations," H. Bavinck considered the thought expressed by the first interpretation—even though to his mind this rendering was less valid than the second one—to be of a thoroughly Scriptural nature; cf. *ibid.*

[245]Beker and Hasselaar rightly call attention to the inner contradiction of H. Bavinck's position: "If natural knowledge of God does not issue in the shattering of man's heart and the humbling of his pride, how can the sense of 'Erlösungsbedürftigkeit' [the need for deliverance] called up by natural theology be authentic and even provisionally pure?" 16-17.

[246]Cf. *IZW*, 72 (*ISM*, p. 64).

[247]*IZW*, 140-141 (cf. *ISM*, 136).

of Kraemer. Following in Barth's line, Kraemer, taking God's revelation in Christ as radical point of departure, assesses religion negatively.

> Christ, as the ultimate standard of reference, is the crisis of all religions, of the non-Christian religions and of empirical Christianity too.... The Cross and its real meaning—reconciliation as God's initiative and act—is antagonistic to all human religious aspirations and ends, for the tendency of all human religious striving is to possess or conquer God, to realize our divine nature.[248]

Bavinck based his judgment of the religions, in line with Calvin, primarily on the negative witness of Scripture regarding non-biblical forms of religiosity. He worked with the category of true religion and was concerned to measure empirical religions against that norm, which makes it clear that he never identified himself with dialectical theology. On the matter of the *distinction between* but *inseparability of* the essential nature ('thatness') and material content ('whatness') of religious consciousness, as well as the further appraisal of these two elements, Bavinck and Kraemer are in agreement. This is attested to by various of their publications. In his missiological handbook, Bavinck states that Kraemer rightly pointed to the fact that if the various components of a religion are viewed separately, they take on a different meaning than they had before they were extracted from the whole, and that when taken in terms of the whole "concepts such as sin, grace, deliverance, prayer, sacrifice all have a different charge, a different content than [they do] in the Bible."[249] And in his *magnum opus* Kraemer writes that

> every religion is an indivisible and not to be divided unity of existential apprehension. It is not a series of tenets ... [and] practices that can be taken one by one as independent items of religious life ... and that can arbitrarily be compared with, and somehow related to, and grafted upon the similar item of another religion.... [The] point is that one does not know what the real force, value and function of the idea of God or of redemption or of faith or of the soul or of anything else is, if one does not primarily take into account what is the fundamental existential apprehension of the totality of life, which dominates [the] whole religion [involved].[250]

In other words, for Bavinck and Kraemer, every religion is a *sum total*, to which all of its parts are vitally and essentially related. And together they differ from Barth, who declined to recognize the presence of any direct divine activity in non-Christian religions. Kraemer, like Bavinck, kept the door open for individual exceptions, i.e., for the possibility that the Spirit of God has worked and works in the hearts of various adherents of non-Christian religions. And at a later stage he acknowledged that, owing to the light of Christ, footmarks of God can be detected amidst the error

---

[248] *The Christian Message in a Non-Christian World*, 110, 123.

[249] *IZW*, 229 (cf. *ISM*, 228).

[250] *The Christian Message in a Non-Christian World*, 135 and 136; cf. 130-141.

of human religiosity.[251] Finally, he had no less an appreciation than did Bavinck for the cultural value of extra-biblical religions.[252]

9. The Relation Between Religious Consciousness and Christian Faith

For Bavinck the relation between Christianity and the extra-biblical religions is the life-and-death problem with which the church has had to deal throughout all the centuries of its existence.[253] To him this issue of the relationship of religious consciousness and Christian faith is the polar question of all theological reflection on the other religions, a question which can only be answered on the basis of the outcome of that reflection.[254] This means that he rejects all the relativizing answers and analyses forged by historians of religion on the basis of psychological and moral considerations.[255] He expresses his disapproval of such approaches in acerbic tones: "We must wrest ourselves free from the curse of these schools of thought, which aim, with their ethos of scepticism, to deprive us of everything."[256] They constitute a fundamental misunderstanding of "the reality of the Eternal One," and even if they do accept God, "they still fail to take account of [His] revelation."[257] Despite his disapproval of them, he states that in the end these schools have indirectly yielded a significant benefit: the leveling, generalizing results of research in the area of religious studies have forced the Christian church to reflect anew upon the meaning and significance of the revelation of God in Christ and to develop a *theologia religionum* on the foundation of faith in that revelation.[258]

Examination of Bavinck's view of the relation of religious consciousness and Christian faith reveals that to his mind there was a formal similarity between the two. Both the 'whatness' of religious consciousness and that of the Christian faith

---

[251]Cf. *Waarom nu juist het christendom?*, 93-94.

[252]Cf. *The Christian Message in a Non-Christian World*, 106.

[253]Cf. "Uitkomsten der studie van buitenbijbelse religies," 337.

[254]Cf. *ibid.*

[255]Cf. *DAC*, 2-10; see also "Uitkomsten der studie van buitenbijbelse religies," 368-377, and *CBTM*, 15-18. In *DAC*, an undated work published in Bandung and thus predating 1939, Bavinck still places exclusive emphasis on personal conviction as 'proof' of the absolute truth of the Christian faith, building his argument on philosophical rather than exegetical grounds.

[256]*DAC*, 10.

[257]*Ibid.*

[258]Cf. "Uitkomsten der studie van buitenbijbelse religies," 377.

constitute subjective answers to the self-manifestation of God,[259] and in this regard, all religions are alike, for "religion by its very nature is a response ... a communion, in which man answers and reacts to God's revelation."[260] And also the structural grid within which the various answers are given remains the same for each and every religion: all of these responses circle around the same five 'magnetic points,' *the* great life-and-death questions that concern every single human being.[261]

But Bavinck clearly also stresses the substantial difference that exists between religious consciousness and Christian faith. They are separated by a wide rift, they are related to each other as falsehood and truth, they are entirely incompatible, they "live in one house, but are ... dogged enemies."[262] For Christian faith comes into existence where the truth of God's revelation in Christ breaks through the process of suppression and substitution and the Spirit leads people into the truth.[263] The difference between the two is also evident from experience.[264]

> It is remarkable that so many people who have experienced the struggle [of being torn between the old and the new] in their own soul, report straightforwardly that Christianity is totally different from that with which they were formerly acquainted.... Everything has become new! That is surely one of the strongest proofs that all armchair postulates regarding the putative similitude of all religions are in deepest essence unrealistic and incorrect.[265]

The discrepancy between religious consciousness and Christian faith is not only apparent subjectively for believers but is also objectively seen in the crucifixion of Christ by the "rulers of this age" (1 Corinthians 2:8). "The crucifixion of Christ is the concentration point of that continual turning away from the truth, which is the tragic secret of every person's life."[266]

Even a comparison of non-Christian mystical experience with the indwelling of God's Spirit in Christian faith—at which level one would expect to

---

[259]Cf. *RBCG*, 188-189.

[260]*CBTM*, 18-19.

[261]The five questions of religious consciousness are dealt with in section 3.4.5. above. Bavinck describes Christian faith in terms of these five points in *CBTM*, 117-193 and *RBCG*, 180-186.

[262]*RBCG*, 190.

[263]Cf. *ibid.*, 188.

[264]Bavinck was fond of supporting his theological positions with arguments from practice; interestingly, for Calvin an argument from practice constituted a theological argument: God also teaches by means of experience (*experientia docet*).

[265]"Zijn alle godsdiensten gelijk?," 302.

[266]*RBCG*, 129.

encounter the greatest number of similarities—reveals a wide gap between Christianity and the other religions. "The God of Pentecost," Bavinck avers in an article on Pentecostal yearning among the nations, "is different from the gods with whom pagan peoples have sought such intimate communion." The indwelling of God by the Spirit is possible only "if a person has been reconciled to God," for in the absence of such conversion there exists nothing more or less than "an immeasurable distance between God the Holy One and man who is bound in guilt and sin." With respect to non-Christian religions, one can ultimately speak only of "psychological change," i.e., change in the sense of disengagement "from the illusion of individuality, from the dream of being something," whereby people would automatically experience "unification with god." This proves "that their god is not the same as the God of Abraham, Isaac and Jacob."[267]

Bavinck emphasizes that this fundamental difference by no means signifies that Christianity may assume an air of superiority vis-à-vis religious consciousness and the other religions. The Christian church must never lose sight of the fact that it, too, has been guilty of suppressing and replacing the truth and "that its guilt in this respect is much greater than that of the other religions, because it has so often obscured the revealed and clear gospel of Jesus Christ behind all kinds of cunning human reasonings," which have been overcome solely by God's grace.[268] Nor is this process of repression and substitution within Christianity in any way a thing of the past alone: "in the Christian, too, the pagan continues to live and breathe."[269] And this holds not only for the individual believer but also for the church as a whole, which has turned its entire history into a drama of "formation, deformation and never ending reformation."[270] Because Christian faith continues to be infiltrated by religious consciousness, it is always subject to the criticism of the gospel.[271] This makes it impossible to speak of the absolute truth of Christian faith; it never constitutes an adequate reflection of the content of the gospel. Absolute truth—which can never be proven but only discovered and affirmed through faith—holds only for objective religion, *viz.*, God's revelation in the gospel of Christ.[272]

Comparative analysis shows that in respect of this matter, too, Bavinck's position differs from that of H. Bavinck and Barth and is closely allied to that of Kraemer. On the one hand, H. Bavinck speaks of a gulf between *religio naturalis* defined as "tainted religion" and Christian faith defined as "pure religion,"[273] but on

---

[267]"Pinksterverlangen in de volkerenwereld," 16-17.

[268]*CBTM,* 200.

[269]*RBCG,* 189.

[270]*Ibid.,* 190.

[271]Cf. *Ibid.,* 189; Bavinck refers in this connection to 2 Cor. 10:5.

[272]Cf. *DAC,* 10-15, and *RBCG,* 189.

[273]Cf. *Gereformeerde dogmatiek,* Vol. I, 244-245.

the other, he links the two together as, respectively, preparation and fulfillment.[274] For Barth there is no connection whatsoever between religious consciousness and Christian faith, except that as soon as people embrace the latter it degenerates into the former, i.e., into human religion. Barth's thinking on this issue is clearly illustrated by the following three citations.

> Religion is *unbelief*; religion is an affair, one must plainly say: *the* affair, of *godless* man.[275]

> That there is a true religion is a reality resting on God's act of grace in Jesus Christ, more precisely: in the outpouring of the Holy Spirit, even more precisely: in the existence of the Church and the children of God.[276]

> If we would wish to speak of the Christian religion independently of the name of Jesus Christ, there would in reality be only two things left to us: first, the universally human religious possibility, which is of course as open to the so-called Christian as it is to all other people.... [And] second, the swiftly and totally crumbling ruin of a religion-like entity that once was called and perhaps also actually was Christianity but now, after being severed from its taproot, does not even have the viability of a non-Christian religion.[277]

Kraemer discusses the relationship between religious consciousness and Christian faith explicitly in a publication dating from 1960, a number of passages in which make it clear that he and Bavinck are fundamentally of the same mind on this matter. With respect to the point of departure for the study of religion, Kraemer states:

> Briefly put, ... I propose to expose the religions, including Christianity, to the light of the Person of Jesus Christ, who is *the* Revelation of God and the only lawful critic (i.e., discerning,

---

[274]Cf. *Gereformeerde dogmatiek*, Vol. III, 246-248.

[275]"Religion ist *Unglaube*; Religion ist eine Angelegenheit, man muss geradezu sagen: die Angelegenheit des gottlosen Menschen." *Kirchliche Dogmatik*, I, 2, 327 (cf. *Church Dogmatics*, I, 2, 299-300).

[276]"Dass es eine wahre Religion gibt, das ist Ereignis im Akt der Gnade Gottes in Jesus Christus, genauer: in der Ausgiessung des Heiligen Geistes, noch genauer: in der Existenz der Kirche und der Kinder Gottes." *Kirchliche Dogmatik*, I, 2, 377 (cf. *Church Dogmatics*, I, 2, 344).

[277]"Wollten wir von der christlichen Religion abgesehen von dem Namen Jesus Christus reden, dann würden wir tatsächlich nur zweierlei in der Hand behalten: 1. Die allgemein-menschliche religiöse Möglichkeit, die allerdings den sog. Christen ebenso zu eigen ist wie allen anderen Menschen.... Und 2. Die in rascher und völliger Auflösung begriffener Trümmer eines religionsähnlichen Gebildes, das einmal Christentum hiess und vielleicht auch war, das aber nun, nachdem ihm die Lebenswurzel abgeschnitten ist, nicht einmal mehr die Lebensfähigkeit einer nicht-christlichen Religion hat." *Kirchliche Dogmatik*, I, 2, 380-381 (cf. *Church Dogmatics*, I, 2, 346-347).

incisive judge) of all religions and of everything that takes place in and proceeds from man.[278]

This criterion of God's self-revelation in Christ is not subject to human choice—*it chooses us*. The affirmation 'God manifests himself in Christ' is not a rationally demonstrable proposition, but rather a verity that engenders "living communion with a world of spiritual reality in which God—who is known and thus loved with the heart alone, with all the strength of soul, spirit and mind—is the central figure."[279] When measured against this criterion, Kraemer contends, the other religions—despite all the goodness that can be descried in them, up to and including 'footmarks of God'—are "in terms of their deepest and most essential intention and meaning *miscarriages of truth*."[280] Although nothing human is foreign to the Christian faith, it distinguishes itself from other religions "in one *cardinal* respect, namely, that it stems from the Revelation of God in the Person of Jesus Christ."[281] But he also very strongly emphasizes the fact that the Christian faith as empirical religion is indistinguishable from other religious traditions in that it continually falls into error and is therefore subject, along with the other religions, to the critical judgment of God's revelation.[282] In short, "it is not Christian faith that is absolute, but rather the source and object of this faith, *viz.*, God's self-announcement in Jesus Christ."[283]

Notwithstanding all the similarity between Bavinck and Kraemer, however, there is one point in the latter's thought with which Bavinck found himself in disagreement. He felt that Kraemer went too far in assigning empirical Christianity or Christendom and the other religions an equal position with respect to the judgement of God's revelation in Christ. He agreed that Christendom requires to be clearly distinguished from the gospel. But, he argued, great care needs to be exercised in the application of this distinction, because Christendom also entails Christianity and Christian faith, which means that Kraemer's radically critical construction of things, if carried to its logical conclusion, would lead to highly unacceptable consequences. First of all, if Christianity is too sharply distinguished from the gospel and too closely aligned with the other religious traditions, that is to say, is simply placed alongside the other religions "in the relative sphere of history,"[284] the legitimacy, indeed, the very possibility of theology would be ruled out. "We ... would no longer be able to speak about God's revelation in Christ," for, if Kraemer's position were granted, it would mean that "anything I say about

---

[278] *Waarom nu juist het christendom?*, 11.

[279] *Ibid.*, 67.

[280] *Ibid.*, 85, 93.

[281] *Ibid.*, 103; cf. also H. Kraemer, *Godsdienst, godsdiensten en het christelijk geloof*, 286.

[282] Cf. *Waarom nu juist het christendom?*, 104.

[283] *Ibid.*, 15.

[284] *BCNCR*, 93.

that Revelation," would "at that selfsame moment become 'Christendom,'"[285] and thus would have no theological but, at most, merely historical and possibly sociological significance and value. And second, he contended that Kraemer's position implied that the Church as manifestation of the Christian faith could never at any moment be considered to be 'true," which would be tantamount to a misapprehension of the work of the Holy Spirit in church and theology. However true it may be that Christian faith (and certainly Christianity in general) does not coincide with the gospel, it is not right, Bavinck asserted, to set them over against each other in this way.[286]

10. Chapter Summary

As pointed out in the previous chapter, Bavinck maintains that God's general revelation in directed toward all people without exception. The outcome of this ubiquitous and continuous divine self-manifestation, he argues, is the existence of a divine-human relational reality: all humans stand in an I-Thou relationship with God. All religious consciousness—including Christian faith and even atheism—develops within the realm of that relationship and represents the human response to God's self-manifestation, and in this sense all religion may be seen primarily as a *theological* phenomenon.

That response, however, is always characterized by a process of displacement and substitution in consequence of universal human rebellion, which means that in a secondary sense religion is to be viewed as a psychological or *anthropological* phenomenon. Bavinck's sense of the reality of this human rebellion led to a radicalization of his theologically negative view of religion.

In developing his standpoint Bavinck was influenced by Kraemer's views,[287] but his elaboration of them was original in two respects: first, he formulated a psychological interpretation of the process of suppression and substitution, and second, he worked out a morphological scheme of universal religious consciousness. Notwithstanding all the manifestly different ways in which humans respond to the divine, there is a universal religious consciousness which, according to Bavinck, encompasses five perdurable life-and-death matters: the place of humankind in the totality of reality; the quest for normative truth; the relation between human action and fate; the longing for redemption; and the sense of relatedness to a higher power.

---

[285] *Ibid.*, 91.

[286] Cf. *BCNCR*, 89-93; Bavinck notes here that though Kraemer himself also felt this was wrong, he did not express this plainly enough.

[287] It should be emphasized once again that Bavinck never simply 'copied' Kraemer but rather enlarged upon the latter's ideas, working them out in a distinctly independent and original way. Bavinck himself alludes to this in his review article, "Religie en het christelijk geloof," dealing with Kraemer's later publication, *Religion and the Christian Faith*: "What Kraemer says about general revelation still does not appeal to me.... A few years ago I summed up my own views in [my book on religious consciousness and Christian faith]. After reading this new book by Kraemer, I came to the conclusion that I prefer to stick with the position I developed in my book," 70.

On one side, Bavinck acknowledged the truth of the objective 'thatness' of religious consciousness. At the same time, he emphasized that 'thatness' always lies enclosed in subjective 'whatness.' In keeping with this, he argued—more sharply than did H. Bavinck and more subtly than did Barth—that according to the biblical witness all religious consciousness comprises falsification: an unbridgeable chasm yawns between all existing religion, on the one hand, and the Christian faith engendered by the Word and the Spirit, on the other. Howbeit, the manner in which Bavinck dealt with these issues manifested a deferential caution inspired by his firm conviction that God himself is actively present among people right throughout the world, and was characterized by a deep respect for everything of value that religions, as cultural phenomena, have to offer. "God's way with the Gentile nations," he wrote, "is a very mysterious one."[288]

As one recent commentator has rightly observed, Bavinck's approach entailed an important departure from prevailing Reformed ecclesiastical thinking: reflection on man and his religion was no longer determined by epistemology but rather by the concept of existential dialogue between God and man: "In Bavinck's view man comes into the picture. In his [missiology] man is not faceless, is not one of the many specimens of the genus mankind, whose nature and being have been completely and adequately charted by theology.... Bavinck was concerned with the concrete person standing in the light of God's revelation."[289]

In general, it can be concluded, on the one hand, that Bavinck divested the Reformed concepts of *revelatio generalis* and *religio naturalis* of H. Bavinck's philosophical interpretations and, on the other, that, as opposed to Barth, he clung firmly to the notion of the unbreakable bond between God's revelation and human religion as word and counter-word, summons and response.[290] Further, it is apparent that, despite the great influence Kraemer had on him, Bavinck did not become an exponent of dialectical theology[291] but instead clearly continued to be a representative of Reformed theology.

---

[288]*ICNCW*, 106.

[289]P.N. Holtrop, 166-168.

[290]R. van Woudenberg characterizes Bavinck as a "theologian of Word and counter-word," in "Dr. Johan Herman Bavinck (1895-1964), 7.

[291]This is shown most clearly by the fact that Bavinck never went along with Kraemer's Barthian view of grace. In *The Christian Message in a Non-Christian World*, 126, Kraemer wrote: "Above the dialectical unity of yes and no ... there rises triumphantly an ultimate divine yes in God's saving Will towards mankind and the world." Remarkably, Bavinck never brought this crucial point up in an explicit way; this may be explained by the fact that he found polemics very distasteful, certainly if their use involved the thought of someone to whom he owed so much.

CHAPTER SIX

Foundation and Essence of Mission

It goes without saying that one's concept of mission is of essential importance for the actual work of mission. ("Zendingsbegrip en zendings-werkelijkheid," 1)

1. Introduction

Although, as indicated earlier, there were various missiological handbooks already in existence, Bavinck was the first to attempt to frame a solidly Reformed theology of mission that was at the same time topical. His concern with relevance is illustrated by the fact that he commenced his reflection on the theory of mission in *Inleiding in de Zendingswetenschap* (*IZW*) with a large number of questions, some of which had been dealt with by missiologists in the past—such as the foundation of mission, the object of mission, the place of the church in mission, the relationship between community and individual—and others of which derived from the missionary discussions of his own day—for example, the relation of mission and evangelism, the missionary calling with respect to Israel, the relation between word and deed, the matter of point of contact, the inculturation of indigenous churches, the relation between 'mother' church and 'younger' church. Bavinck stated that in attempting to answer these questions, he looked to the witness of Scripture as essential guide.

> Missionary theory must seek to discover answers [to these questions] in Holy Scripture. For the work of mission is so much a work of God, [so much a work] which takes place in his service, that it is not permissible for us to engage in independent improvisation. At every step we will have to ask ourselves what God requires of us.[1]

At the same time, however, Bavinck realized that the Bible does not furnish a direct answer to all current problems and questions: "It will not always be easy to find the right course in the midst of stubborn workaday practice...."[2]

After this survey of urgent questions, Bavinck discusses the divisions of

---

[1] *IZW*, 21 (cf. *ISM*, 5).

[2] *Ibid.*

184

missionary theology suggested by a number of his predecessors,[3] before going on to provide his own classification of that discipline. Bavinck's own arrangement of the subject matter of missionary theology, which draws upon these previous systems of categorization, allows full room for extensive treatment of the topics and themes he considers to be of primary importance. Following Bavinck's lead, with one important exception,[4] we will deal with these matters in the present chapter under two main headings, and in the following chapter under three titles.

From 1930 onward Bavinck began to reflect ever more intensively on matters of missionary theology, which was reflected in several of his publications, including a large number of articles and various books.[5] The most extensive and systematic of the latter is *IZW* (1954). In this standard work Bavinck brings together much of what appeared in earlier writings, thus providing a clear survey of his cumulative missiological thought. It is this publication, thus, that constitutes the chief source of our analysis of his missionary theology. Earlier publications are used for purposes of comparison, to point up a progression or shift in his thinking on a particular matter. In cases in which there is no disparity between the *Inleiding* and these earlier works, the latter will only receive mention in the footnotes.

2. The Foundation of Mission

Bavinck declared his intention to search the Scriptures with a view to tracing the biblical principles on which the missionary task is grounded, but in this area of biblical-theological accountability it is evident that he worked less independently than his stated aim would seem to imply. In an earlier publication he makes a general reference to the arguments put forward and the positions taken on this matter by other missiologists, such as Gustav Warneck, Johannes Richter, Karl Hartenstein and Godfroy E. Phillips.[6] He also makes mention of a number of important studies on Paul's missionary views and activities, such as Roland Allen's seminal work, *Missionary Methods: St. Paul's or Ours?*.[7] Unfortunately, he refers to these publications only sporadically, even in his missiological hand-book, *Inleiding*. However, his conception of the biblical foundation of mission would seem to indicate that he borrowed heavily from his fellow missiologists in this area

---

[3]*Ibid.*, 21-23 (*ISM*, 6-7.)

[4]The sequence of our treatment deviates from that of Bavinck in that we deal with missionary aims (see the following chapter) rather than missionary approaches immediately subsequent to the matter of the foundation and essence of mission because, in our view, the questions 'why?' and 'to what end?' fit logically together.

[5]Among the most important of these books are: *AWW*, 1941; *ZWN*, 1946; and *ICNCW*, 1948.

[6]Cf. *ZWN*, 227.

[7]The other books on Paul he names are those by Paul Wernle, Martin Schlunk, and Johannes Warneck, (see bibliography for titles and publication details).

and that he engaged less extensively in independent biblical-exegetical research than one might have expected.

In any case, thorough exegesis is often lacking and Bible texts are frequently merely cited. It is evident that he sometimes employed the Bible as norm rather than as source. Although it can be argued that this use of Scripture was responsible for the relatively limited contribution Bavinck made to missiological reflection in the specific area of the biblical foundations of mission, I would nonetheless maintain that it in no way diminished the overall results of his stated intention to develop a Reformed biblical theology of mission.

In *IZW* (1954) Bavinck successively discusses the Old Testament, the inter-testamentary period, and the New Testament. This same order will be observed in the following sections, which contain both a systematic overview of his argumen-tation as well as a number of critical questions and comments. In connection with the latter, particular use is made of the seminal contribution Johannes Blauw, one of Bavinck's students and kindred spirits, made to the biblical theology of mission, *Gottes Werk in dieser Welt: Grundzüge einer biblischen Theologie der Mission* (1961, Eng. Tr.:*The Missionary Nature of the Church*, 1962), in which Blauw not only elaborates his own views but also recapitulates the thinking of biblical theologians and missiologists on the topic of mission in the Bible up until that time.

2.1. Mission in the Old Testament

2.1.1. The missionary thrust of the Old Testament witness

For Bavinck it is quite obvious that "from the first page to the last the Bible is a book which has the whole world in view and which unfolds the divine plan of salvation with respect to that world."[8] It is therefore inevitable, according to Bavinck, that the OT witness should also furnish building materials for a biblical foundation of the missionary calling. He then delineates nine elements in the OT that have potential missionary content. Comparison shows that these points are largely borrowed from Gustav Warneck.[9]

1. Beginning with Genesis 1:1 the Bible makes it clear that the God of Israel is the Creator of the world and of all the nations who dwell in it. He is no tribal God, like the gods of the nations, but Lord of all the earth. Genesis 1-3 and the table of the nations of Genesis 10 show that all peoples share in the same glory and the same misery and are in principle equal before God. Bavinck, in keeping with the general view of the day,[10] calls this "one of the most far-reaching foundational principles of the doctrine of mission" and asserts that this is the basis for the missionary mandate of Matthew 28:19. "Without that basis the great

---

[8]*IZW*, 24 (cf. *ISM*, 11). Cf. *ICNCW*, 139-40: 'In the Bible God is wrestling with the world, persuading, reproving, admonishing, beseeching the various people of the world to accept the truth and be reconciled to God."

[9]G. Warneck, *Evangelische Missionslehre*, 1, 136ff. Direct references are lacking.

[10]In addition to G. Warneck, cf., e.g., K. Hartenstein, "Heidentum und Kirche," 5.

commission could not exist."[11]

2. On the basis of this reality, God concerns himself with the other nations, also in the period of Israel's separation (Pss. 24 and 33). They are the objects of his care; he judges them and calls them to worship.[12]

3. In the OT the idea that YHWH is the only God continually leads to the unconditional condemnation of all idolatry (Deut. 4:39; Jer. 10:10). Implied here, at the same time, is the possibility of the missionary mandate and the missionary promise.[13]

4. It is precisely Israel's isolation, the isolation that starts with the call of Abraham, that proves to have a missionary thrust. On the one hand, Israel be-longs to God in a special sense: "You only have I chosen of all the families of the earth" (Amos 3:2). The covenant, with its embedded legislation, served as the framework for the utterly unique place of Israel in the midst of the nations. On the other hand, from the very beginning this isolation is presented as temporary, as a phase in God's plan of salvation for this world. Three times Abraham was assured that in his descendants all the nations of the earth would be blessed (Gen. 12:3; 18:18; 22:18). Guided by the context, Bavinck brings out all the more sharply the missionary thrust of this thrice-repeated promise. On Gen. 12:3 he writes: "Implied in God's promise was that Abraham's descendants would one day have to make their way back . . . to proclaim the blessing they themselves had received." On Genesis 18:18 he writes, "...when Abraham in priestly fashion invoked God's mercy upon Sodom, God assured him that it was his sacred intent to one day make him a blessing for all the nations of the earth." And on Genesis 22:18: "At the very moment when Abraham so clearly portrayed the work of the Messiah, God himself already indicated at this place that that blessing would come to all the nations by way of sacrifice."[14]

5. The covenant structure contains room for mission. In the covenant relation between God and Israel there was no identification such as the nations experienced with their gods. YHWH is no tribal God who rises and falls with Israel. The bond between YHWH and Israel is rooted solely in God's electing love. "Israel does not have any special claim on God" and it is therefore entirely conceivable "that other nations too will one day share in the blessing of that covenant and be included in it."[15]

---

[11] *IZW*, 25 (cf. *ISM*, 12). Cf. *ZWN*, 10: "By thus emphatically stressing the unity of the human race [in the grandeur of creation and the misery of the fall], very strong foundations are laid for the coming call to missions." H. Bavinck emphatically points out that in that period the covenant of grace was universal, cf. "De zending in de Heilige Schrift," 8.

[12] *IZW*, 25-26 (cf. *ISM*, 12-14).

[13] Cf. *IZW*, 26 (*ISM*, 12-13).

[14] *ZWN*, 11-12. Cf. *IZW*, 26 (*ISM*, 13), where only Gen. 12:3 and 22:18 are cited.

[15] *IZW*, 27 (cf. *ISM*, 14). Cf. H. Bavinck, "De zending in de Heilige Schrift," 8-9.

6. Israel continually viewed its history as enacted on the stage of the world, "before the eyes of the surrounding nations." Repeatedly we hear the prayer that God may intervene so that the nations will acknowledge his Name (e.g., Exod. 32:12; Num. 14:16; Josh. 7:9; Isa. 37:20). Israel realized "that its history was not a private affair which was of no concern to anyone else; [it knew] that God pleaded His case with the other nations through its history and hence that in the ups and downs of that history God extended the concerns of his heart to the whole world."[16]

7. In close connection with the preceding point, Bavinck points out that in all this we do not so much witness a missionary passion for the salvation of the nations as a theocentric yearning that the whole world might see that only YHWH is God. In this light we must also view the numerous cries of exhortation to the nations which summon them to honor YHWH (Psalm 47 and 99).[17]

8. Israel's deep awareness of separation excluded official missionary activity toward the surrounding world. At certain moments, however, it is evident that "missionary fire was not lacking in Israel." From time to time there were people who bore witness to YHWH in foreign lands (2 Kings 5:1-3; Daniel).[18] This awareness remains an incidental phenomenon, however. According to Bavinck, Jonah's journey to Nineveh does not belong to this category: in the book of Jonah there is no mission in the true sense, because the purpose of Jonah's mission is not "to found a congregation of God in Nineveh."[19] But in light of the examples mentioned earlier, this argument is inconsistent. It seems that Bavinck here has simply followed Gustav Warneck, who nowhere refers to the missionary import of Jonah.[20] This is, to say the least, remarkable, given the fact that Hendrik A. Wiersinga, who was also Reformed (RCN), articulated an opposing view in the same period.[21] Furthermore, the meaning of the book of Jonah—namely, that God's

---

[16] *IZW*, 28 (cf. *ISM*, 15).

[17] Cf. *IZW*, 29 (*ISM*, 16).

[18] *IZW*, 29-30 (cf. *ISM*, 16-17).

[19] *ZWN*, 13. In *IZW* the book of Jonah is no longer even mentioned.

[20] G. Warneck was not alone in this respect. Cf. J. Blauw, *Gottes Werk*, 54, who comments that the missionary significance of Jonah is denied in various quarters.

[21] *Zendingsperspectief in het Oude Testament*, 60: "The God of Israel does not let go of the world …. For Israel too there is a calling with respect to the pagan world. The history of Jonah exists in Israel as a sign and prophecy of God's universal plan of salvation. Thus in this book the early dawn of the gospel already shines brightly: Christ, the Savior of the world." See also H. Bavinck, "De zending in de Heilige Schrift," 11-12. On this point Bavinck had no following, even among like-minded Reformed scholars. J. Blauw, *Gottes Werk*, 34, is certain of the universal thrust but cautious with respect to the missionary view of the book of Jonah. This latter point "can at most be inferred" (lässt sich höchstens daraus ableiten). J. Verkuyl, *Inleiding in de nieuwere zendingswetenschap*, 131ff, goes much further—too far perhaps?—when he calls the book of Jonah profoundly

mercy extends beyond the borders of Israel—would have fit very well in the overall perspective of Bavinck's thinking.

9. The fire of missionary zeal did become more intense mainly as a result of the Exile and subsequent life in the Diaspora.[22] Bavinck's reasoning on this point, however, is not entirely clear. On the one hand, he justifies Israel's antithetical attitude; on the other, he criticizes that attitude when he says that the hard realities of the exile were necessary for them to break through it. There is no further explication of what he means, a fact that leaves his view of things rather debatable.[23] It may be, however, that he meant to reiterate H. Bavinck's thinking on this matter, namely, that the judgment of the exile was especially aimed at the opinionated self-elevation of Israel, "which, lacking the fear of the Lord, living according to a form without content, and lapsing in practice into paganism," was no longer able to fulfill its calling among the nations. As a result of divine chastening in the form of the exile and the ensuing direct confrontation with other nations, it became possible for Israel to give shape to that calling once again.[24]

In the above nine points Bavinck sought to build a bridge between the OT witness and the NT missionary mandate.

> As we survey all of this, it becomes clear to us that contained in the revelation of God in the OT there are fundamental principles capable of sustaining the idea of mission. The latter is not an alien element in the whole of Scriptural preaching but is, rather, integral to it and must, accordingly, come to full development in God's own time.[25]

While the data he advances are valuable from a missionary perspective, it is unfortunate that he did not connect them by means of a few main biblical-theological lines, e.g., the universal character of the OT as the basis for the later missionary calling;[26] OT traces of a centripetal missionary awareness as the antecedent of the

---

meaningful for the biblical foundation of the missionary task and then discusses it as a "book concerning the education of a missionary."

[22]Cf. *IZW*, 29-30 (*ISM*, 15-16) and *ZWN*, 13.

[23]Bavinck (*IZW*, 28 [cf. *ISM*,16]) speaks on the one hand of a "holy apprehension" with respect to paganism, while stating on the other hand (p. 29) that Israel's isolation rendered it powerless in terms of mission. In this way he turns its religious strength into its missionary weakness. In light of the OT witness, however, this is a false contrast. J. Blauw (*Gottes Werk*, 25, 45) shows that it was precisely in the fulfillment of its sanctified position that Israel's missionary power lay, and vice versa.

[24]H. Bavinck, "De zending in de Heilige Schrift, 10. Later Bavinck pointed in this same direction, stating that Israel was "too strongly inclined toward pagan practices to be a robust witness in the world of its day," *IZW*, 30 (cf. *ISM*, 17).

[25]*IZW*, 30 (cf. *ISM*, 17).

[26]Cf. J. Blauw, *Gottes Werk*, 27.

centrifugal[27] mission mandate in the NT; and the antagonistic and doxological motifs implied in the OT yearning for the worldwide recognition of YHWH.[28] This would have clarified the connections with his discussion of the prophetic part of the OT.

2.1.2. The Universal Promises of Salvation in the Prophets

In his missiological handbook Bavinck gives separate attention to the missionary perspective in the prophetic writings. After establishing that the prophets carried out their public ministry in a time when Israel—as a result of the paganizing influence and expansionist drive of the superpowers surrounding it—fell into a spiritual and political crisis, Bavinck arrives at eight considerations, which, due to overlap, can be summarized in six points.[29]

1. On one hand, the prophets see a spiritual and an accompanying political collapse taking place. On the other, "the bright sunlight of the universal promise of salvation" breaks through in their prophecy.[30]

2. The condition for the fulfillment of this promise is Israel's conversion. The prophets expect this as "a fruit of God's gracious expressions of concern." Bavinck here refers to Ezekiel 36:26 and Jeremiah 31:31, where we read of a new beginning and a new covenant.[31]

3. This renewal is consistently centered around the figure of the Messiah. In him the old era, in which Israel experiences defeat in the world, will end and a new era will dawn "in which God will ascend to his royal throne in the world." This is an eschatological event and is linked to the outpouring of the Holy Spirit upon all flesh (Joel 2:28). At the same time this redemptive process is described from a theocentric viewpoint: at issue here is the global sanctification of God's name, the name that had been desecrated among the nations by Israel (Ezek. 36:22, 23).[32]

4. The coming of the Messiah—and the day of the Lord associated with it—not only brings salvation to the world but also means judgment on the nations.

---

[27]The concepts "centripetal" and "centrifugal," which will be used regularly in this study, do not yet occur in Bavinck, but the concepts they imply do.

[28]Cf. J. Verkuyl, *Inleiding in de nieuwere zendingswetenschap,* 130-131.

[29]*IZW*, 30-36 (*ISM*, 17-24) It is not entirely possible to determine whether Bavinck borrowed this view of a separate place for the prophets from others. G. Warneck, *Evangelische Missionslehre*, 1, 141ff, in any case does not make this distinction. In this connection Bavinck does refer to J. Blauw's dissertation, *Goden en mensen: plaats en betekenis van de heidenen in de Heilige Schrift*, completed in 1950 under Bavinck's supervision, cf. *IZW,* 31 (*ISM,* 18). The reference is only general, but it is plain that Bavinck made rather extensive use of the results of Blauw's study.

[30]*IZW*, 32 (cf. *ISM,* 19).

[31]*IZW*, 32-33 (cf. *ISM,* 19-20).

[32]*IZW*, 33, 35-36 (cf. *ISM,* 20, 22-23).

As is clear from texts like Joel 1:15 and Malachi 3:2, Israel itself will also have to reckon with this dark side of his coming.[33]

5. In the prophecy of the OT all emphasis falls on the spontaneous coming of the nations to the salvation revealed in Israel. Bavinck refers to Isaiah 2:2ff.; 19:23-25; 55:5; 66:18-19; and Zechariah 8:23. Only in Isaiah 55:5 is there any mention of a mandate to engage in 'missionary activity': "under the blessed rule of David's great Son, the ruler and commander of the peoples, Israel will summon nations it does not know."[34]

6. The salvation that will be extended to Israel and the nations is an all-embracing, comprehensive occurrence that will encompass the whole of life (Isa. 11:5-9; 25:6-9; Ezek. 36:30 and Hos. 2:20, 21). "The full implications of the concept of *Shalom* will then manifest themselves in visible form."[35]

Bavinck sees in this prophetic declaration a fruitful basis for the development of later missionary ideas. It shows the universal salvific event that is simultaneously theocentric and Israel-centric in character: through his salvific action in Israel God makes a worldwide name for himself.[36] At the same time Bavinck does not view the OT witness as such as being missionary in nature, since it contains barely any missionary commands.[37] This view is, of course, connected with the fact that Bavinck essentially construes mission as a centrifugal activity. He does recognize in the existence of the centripetal notion in the prophecies of universal salvation (the "spontaneous coming" of the nations),[38] however, which he sees as an OT expression of, and first step toward, the centrifugal mission activity of the NT. The Israel-centric character present in the revelation of universal salvation will achieve its fulfillment in the "missionary activity" of the coming Messiah. "The Messiah will reveal himself as the great 'Witness to the nations.' He will participate in God's great lawsuit with the world and by his witness lead the

---

[33]*IZW*, 33 (cf. *ISM*, 20).

[34]*IZW*, 34 (cf. *ISM*, 22). Bavinck immediately relativizes this by adding: "But the conclusion of the very same verse again points in the direction of a spontaneous coming.... That which will make the missionary calling powerful and effective is not so much the force of the call itself but the fact that God will have glorified Israel."

[35]*IZW*, 35 (cf. *ISM*, 25).

[36]*IZW*, 36 (cf. *ISM*, 24).

[37]*IZW*, 34 (cf. *ISM*, 22). It is strange, for that matter, that Bavinck, in search of centrifugal mission ideas in the OT, does refer to Isa. 55:5 but not to Isa. 42:4 and Isa. 49:6; cf. C. Graafland, "De bijbelse fundering van het zendingswerk," 25.

[38]Bavinck, *IZW*, 36 (cf. *ISM*, 23) sums up the prophetic perspective strikingly as follows: "Israel . . . will lie radiant in the midst of the world and like a magnet draw the nations to itself."

nations to an understanding of their rebellion."[39] One is struck by the fact that, in contrast to Gustav Warneck, Bavinck does not refer to the prophetic idea that the calling of the Servant of the Lord must in the first place be related to Israel.[40]

Bavinck had a clear eye for the *universal* thrust of the OT but did not fully recognize its *missionary* significance, because he did not view the centripetal thoughts in the OT as a true missionary reality but rather interpreted them as a provisional expression of the centrifugal activity present in the NT.[41] It seems to me that this constricted understanding of the missionary significance of the OT is a result of the fact that he examined and evaluated the missionary content of the OT witness too much from the perspective of the centrifugal missionary mandate of the NT. Fortunately he was not consistent in this: in his discussion of the missionary mandate of the NT church he views its centripetal element as a fulfillment of OT prophecy, thus attributing missionary significance to the latter in light of the NT.[42]

2.2. Missionary Motifs in the Intertestamentary Period

Bavinck discusses in passing the missionary development in Israel during the intertestamentary period. In *ZWN* (1947) he incorporates it in his discussion of the

---

[39]*IZW*, 36 (cf. *ISM*, 23).

[40]G. Warneck, *Evangelische Missionslehre*, 1, 141.

[41]J. Versteeg, 25-27, provides an excellent description of the missionary character and significance of the OT: "In the relationship between the centripetal and centrifugal the emphasis clearly falls on the centripetal, without, however, the centrifugal being thereby excluded. Likewise, in OT prophecy the emphasis falls clearly on the bringing of the message of salvation to the nations in the future, but this emphasis does not preclude a bringing of that message in [Israel's] present." He points out that this is related to the "specific situation of Israel in the OT dispensation." Israel's election precluded full equality of Israel and the nations, but it implied at the same time that the (missionary) task of the Servant of the Lord (Isa. 42:4 and Isa. 49:6) was already a task for Israel as a whole. Blauw, *Gottes Werk*, 44-46, concludes that the OT provides little by way of foundation for mission, but he also recognizes that what Bavinck calls *theocentric* and *Israel-centric* constitutes an extremely important missionary point for the church of the NT. He quotes R. Martin Achard, "The evangelization of the world is not so much a matter of words or activities, but rather of presence: the presence of God's people in the midst of humanity, the presence of God among his people. It is not without benefit that the OT reminds the church of this." (Die Evangelisation der Welt ist weniger eine Sache von Worten oder Aktivitäten, sondern von Gegenwärtigkeit: Gegenwärtigkeit des Gottesvolkes inmitten der Menschheit, Gegenwärtigkeit Gottes unter Seinem Volk. Es ist nicht ohne Nutzen, daß das AT dies der Kirche in Erinnerung bringt.)

[42]*IZW*, 51 (cf. *ISM*, 40). "What the prophets had so clearly foreseen—that in the last days people from all manner of nations, speaking all manner of tongues, would join Israel, because they had heard that 'God is with you'—began to be realized in the early Christian church in all manner of forms."

OT data, and in *IZW* (1954) he begins his discussion of the NT data with it.[43] In view of the preparatory significance of this period for the missionary activity in the NT, this shift is correct. However, it would have been more appropriate in this context had he treated the description of the historical development between OT and NT as an 'intermezzo,' since in the nature of the case biblical theology of mission concerns itself with a synthesis of OT and NT theology of mission.[44] But in light of Bavinck's way of thinking, which interprets history in frankly theological terms, his method is understandable.

Bavinck states that in principle nothing changed during the period in question: theologically Israel continued to think in terms of separation and the "wall that separated" Jew and Gentile was still intact.[45] But due to changing political and cultural factors, breaches developed in that wall.[46] Politically, Israel had been incorporated in the Roman Empire, which led naturally to closer contact with the surrounding nations and internally to confrontation with (interested) Romans.[47] Culturally the most important factor for this development was the emergence of the Jewish diaspora in the East (a result of the fact that the majority of Jews did not return from captivity) and in the West (a result of the establishment of trade colonies in the Hellenistic world). Bavinck then lists six points, all relating to the western Diaspora.[48]

1. The Jews were initially confronted with contempt and misunderstanding on the part of the Greek world.

2. Gradually they found much appreciation, due to their monotheistic faith and high moral standards, which caused many to join the Jewish religion; thus groups of proselytes came into being.

3. Slowly a strong missionary zeal developed in some Jewish circles (cf. Matt. 23:15).

4. Jews, with their spiritual concept of God, resonated with the Greek intellectual world, which had distanced itself from the ancient religious myths. Greek philosophy came to be seen as a derivation from the OT. Conversely, the OT world of ideas was identified with Greek philosophical ideas.

5. The translation of the OT into Greek (the Septuagint) and its distribution played an important role in the nascent interest in the Jewish religion.

6. The Jewish communities were also politically and socially attractive because they had come to occupy an important place within the social order of those days.

---

[43] *ZWN*, 13-14; *IZW*, 36-40 (cf. *ISM*, 25-29).

[44] J.A.B. Jongeneel, *Missiologie* 1, 68.

[45] *IZW*, 36, 40 (cf. *ISM*, 25, 29).

[46] *IZW*, 40; cf. *ZWN*, 14.

[47] *ZWN*, 13-14. In *IZW* this aspect is barely mentioned.

[48] Bavinck, *IZW*, 37-39 (cf. *ISM*, 26-29), lists seven points, but because of an overlap between points four and five there are actually six.

Following Gustav Warneck,[49] Bavinck assigned theological significance to these historical developments: "When we survey this entire period, it is immediately clear that it occupies a large place in God's providential order." Viewed in retrospect it is clear that in this way "God himself was introducing a new period, namely, the period in which his church, starting from Jerusalem, would preach the message of salvation in Christ to the world of that day."[50]

Bavinck's rather unabashedly theological interpretation of the intertestamentary stage stands in contrast to the view that although from a *historical* perspective this period cannot be left out of any biblical-theological discussion, no *theological* conclusions may be attached to it.[51] Nevertheless, Bavinck's theological interpretation of it is not entirely without basis, considering what the book of Acts has to say about the place of the so-called *God-fearers* from a missionary perspective. Furthermore, such a treatment of the intertestamentary period makes clear that Bavinck was a biblical, but not a biblicistic theologian.

2.3. Mission in the New Testament

2.3.1. Development of the Missionary Mandate in the Gospels

OT prophecy views Messianic salvation as one comprehensive whole that is realized in the last days, and that encompasses both the spiritual renewal of Israel and the spontaneous coming of the nations and radical transformation of the world order. But the development as described in the Gospels, however, faces us initially with an enigma, because it does not at all follow the prophesied pattern.[52] Further reflection, however, shows that the *manner* of the fulfillment differed from that what was expected on the basis of the OT, but that the fulfillment did not fall short of the *content* of the expectation created by the OT. In other words, the nuances and concretization given by Jesus are in principle already present in OT prophecy. Already in Jesus' day many people were unable to square this unexpected interpretation with the OT witness, which Bavinck explains from the fact that the theological movements of that day had "distorted to a not insignificant degree the

---

[49]G. Warneck, *Evangelische Missionslehre*, 1, 145, speaks of the "pedagogical wisdom" (erzieherische Weisheit) of the universal divine plan of salvation in the intertesta-mentary period.

[50]*IZW*, 40 (cf. *ISM*, 29). H. Bavinck, *De zending in de Heilige Schrift*, 12-14, only draws a historical line from the intertestamentary period to NT mission when he writes, "...in general the Jewish Diaspora paved the way for Christian mission."

[51]Cf. J. Blauw, *Gottes Werk*, 69-70. Blauw is of the opinion that also historically and genetically the lines from proselytism to NT missionary activity can be drawn only with great caution.

[52]Bavinck, *IZW*, 40-41 (cf. *ISM*, 29-30), even chose as heading "The Enigma of the Gospels" ("Het raadsel van de Evangeliën").

over-all picture that the OT presents to us."[53]

After these introductory comments, in which he establishes the unity of the OT and NT over against the seeming contrast between the two, Bavinck traces step by step how in the gospels the missionary mandate comes to the fore. Although referring to it only indirectly in a formal sense,[54] with respect to content he links up here with a theological discussion which had been going on since the nineteenth century and in which the central question was the extent to which Jesus' outlook was particularist or universalist in nature.[55] Bavinck followed Warneck, who, in contradistinction to J. Weiss and others, rejected an evolution in Jesus' stance from particularism to universalism.[56] It is unclear to what extent he was familiar with the landmark study of Bengt Sundkler and A. Fridrichsen,[57] who resolved the dilemma by pointing to the eschatological significance of Zion.[58]

According to Bavinck the Gospels have a *universal* tenor. This is already apparent in Simeon's hymn of praise, in which Jesus is called "a light for revelation to the Gentiles" (Luke 2:32), and from the narrative of the wise men who come spontaneously to the King of the Jews (Matt. 2:1-12). A variety of words of Jesus also have this universal scope: "You are the salt of the earth" and "You are the light of the world" (Matt. 5:13-14); "For God so loved the world" (John 3:16); "many will come from the east and the west, and will take their places at the feast with Abraham, Isaac and Jacob in the kingdom of heaven" (Matt. 8:11); "The hour has come for the Son of Man to be glorified" (John 12:23). Bavinck then concludes: "Thus we see throughout the gospel that the Savior always saw his life in the broad context of the ancient prophecy of salvation...."[59]

This universal tenor does not alter the fact that Jesus' early ministry was characterized by *particularism*. This found expression, for example, in the fact that

---

[53]*Ibid.* Bavinck points specifically to the neglect of the prophecy concerning "the suffering Messiah figure" (e.g., Isa. 53).

[54]*IZW*, 43 (cf. *ISM*, 32). Bavinck here rejects the position of A. von Harnack, who, in *Mission und Ausbreitung des Christentums in den ersten drei Jahrhunderten,* 1, 39, had stated that Jesus "had addressed his message exclusively to his fellow Jews" (seine Botschaft ausschliesslich an seine Volksgenossen, die Juden, gerichtet hatte) and that "a formal mission to the Gentiles cannot have been within Jesus' purview" (eine förmliche Heidenmission nicht im Horizonte Jesu gelegen kann haben).

[55]Cf. J. Blauw, *Gottes Werk,* 167-168. This brief but clear survey of the discussion is cited by J.A.B. Jongeneel, *Missiologie,* 1, 78-79.

[56]Cf. G. Warneck, *Evangelische Missionskunde,* 1, 162ff. Warneck's influence is clearly noticeable in the argument and in the use of biblical references.

[57]*Contributions à l'étude de la pensée missionaire dans le Nouveau Testament,* 1937.

[58]Cf. J. Blauw, *Gottes Werk,* 168.

[59]*IZW*, 43-44 (cf. *ISM*, 32-33).

He sent out his disciples initially with the emphatic instruction *not* to go among the Gentiles or to enter any town of the Samaritans (Matt. 10:5), and later, when he answered a non-Jewish woman that he had been sent only "to the lost sheep of Israel" (Matt. 15:24). The period of separation did not suddenly come to a close. The great unfolding of salvation throughout the whole world did not dawn immediately.[60]

Bavinck then points out that it gradually becomes clearer in the words of Jesus that the way of the ultimate *parousia* of redemption runs via the detour of the Cross and Resurrection—which Israel did not expect.[61] This detour has two sides. On the one hand, it brings the "great delay" in the manifestation of the fullness of God's kingdom. This delay is the result of the official rejection of Jesus by the spiritual representatives of Israel. Jesus makes this clear by means of several parables, such as the Parable of the Great Feast (Luke 14:15-24) and the Parable of the Wicked Tenants (Matt. 22:33-46). The kingdom now will be given to a different nation. Thus the reality of the *interim period* comes into being. The events are now extended in time.[62]

On the other hand, the Cross and Resurrection have universal significance and form the foundation for the worldwide missionary task that was to begin in Jerusalem (Matt. 28:19; Luke 24:47; John 20:21; and Acts 1:6-8). The interim now becomes the period of the fulfillment of the Scriptures: the coming of the nations to the salvation that is realized through the missionary activity of the church.[63] Bavinck sees this expressed in the Parable of the Ten Pounds (Luke 19:11-27) and in Jesus' rejection of the misconception that the kingdom of God will be established in Israel and that salvation will be realized in an Israel-centric manner (Acts 1:6-8). He concludes that "in the teaching of Jesus the idea of mission very slowly and cautiously emerges from the totality of the Messianic expectations."[64] And in line

---

[60]Cf. *IZW*, 44 (cf. *ISM*, 33) and *ZWN*, 15.

[61]Bavinck, *IZW*, 41 (cf. *ISM*, 30) speaks here, following H.N. Ridderbos, *De Komst van het Koninkrijk*, 389-390, of "two lines" in the prophecies of Jesus: one that ends in Jesus' death and resurrection, and one that ends in his parousia, two lines that ultimately join in the one line of the coming Kingdom by way of the suffering Servant.

[62]*IZW*, 42-43 (cf. *ISM*, 34-36). In *ZWN*, 16, Bavinck sees this thought confirmed in Rom. 11:11ff., where Paul writes that Israel's rejection of the Messiah has turned into salvation for the Gentiles. In *EVWE*, 142-151, Bavinck discusses in great detail the "enigma of the delay," which he detects throughout the entire NT witness.

[63]*IZW*, 45-46 (cf. *ISM*, 35-36). In *ZWN*, 15-16, Bavinck finds this notion confirmed again later in the NT, when Paul writes in Eph. 2:13-16 that in the cross of Jesus the wall of separation between Israel and the nations has been breached.

[64]*IZW*, 43 (cf. *ISM*, 35).

with Hendrik Kraemer's position on this matter,[65] he states that mission is the element that characterizes the interim period.[66] He also cites J C. Hoekendijk in this connection: "The walls of history are held apart by mission."[67]

Bavinck asks himself whether this course of events does not mean that there is a contradiction between the OT promises and the NT realization of salvation. For according to Genesis 12:3 the nations would be blessed *in* the seed of Abraham, but it actually happens *in spite of* Israel, through its apostasy. He finds the answer to this question in Galatians 3:8-16, where Paul via a linguistic argument states that the singular 'seed' does not apply to the nation (which consists of many), but to the Messiah (as the one true son of Israel). The promise has thus assuredly been fulfilled, albeit in a different manner "than the Israelites had dreamed of." In fact, argues Bavinck, Israel plays a decisive role in the entire event, not in a positive sense (because of its faith) but rather in a negative sense (by means of its unbelief). Concurring with Paul, Bavinck sees in this tension between promise and fulfillment a cause for worship (Rom. 11:33).[68]

Finally, Bavinck sees three important motifs in the various missionary mandates that Jesus gave after his resurrection.

In John 20:21 ("As the Father has sent me, I am sending you") the missionary task appears to be the immediate continuation of the sending of the Son by the Father. Both instances of sending involve "the one continuous work of God's mercy that reaches out to the world, in the Son and then also in the apostles." The missionary task is therefore anchored in the *missio Dei*.[69]

In Matthew 28:18-19 ("All authority in heaven and on earth has been given to me. Therefore go...") the word "therefore" links the acquired authority of Christ with the mandate given to church to claim the whole world for him. Thus mission stands in the service of the rule of Christ or Christocracy.[70]

In Luke 24:45-47 ("This is what is written...") it is affirmed that Cross, Resurrection, and the worldwide missionary calling of the church that flows from these are a fulfillment of the Scriptures. The missionary mandate of the church rests

---

[65]Cf. H. Kraemer, *Kerk en zending*, 25: "The church is an interim, an intermediate phenomenon between the time of Christ in the flesh and the time of Christ's appearing in imperishableness and glory.... The position of the church is that it connects these two points in time and must live out of the consciousness of this interim. And mission in its entirety is included in this interim."

[66]Bavinck, *IZW*, 46 (cf. *ISM*, 34), speaks in this connection of a mysterious *and* necessary shift from Israel to the world, from the few to the many, from already to not yet.

[67]Hoekendijk, 223.

[68]*ZWN*, 17-18. Cf. also *IZW*, 59 (*ISM*, 50).

[69]*ZWN*, 18. Though Bavinck must have been familiar with this term, he never uses but always paraphrases it. Cf. also *IZW*, 45 (*ISM*, 34).

[70]*Ibid.*, 19. It is not clear why Bavinck does not also refer here to Mark 16:15f., where Christocracy is manifested in concrete signs.

on the foundation of "God's promises, which have been communicated to us in the OT."[71]

Bavinck's missiological thinking concerning the gospels, yield the following important elements: the salvation-historical interpretation of the transition from a particularistic to a universalistic vision; the crucial boundary-shattering significance of the Cross; the centrifugal realization of centripetal conceptions; the interim period leading to the coming of God's kingdom; and the continuity between the OT and NT. Yet Bavinck's argument also seems somewhat forced at times, as when he takes "the enigma" of Israel's rejection of the Messiah as a significant point of departure for the development of the concept of mission. In light of the OT he interprets the phenomenon of the interim period primarily as a practical necessity. A careful exegesis of the message of the gospels, however, leads to the conclusion that the realization of salvation proceeds not from necessity, but in a fundamental sense takes place initially in a provisional manner.[72]

In this light the interim loses that forced character and only illustrates the eschatological tension that dominates the coming of the kingdom of God in Jesus. This has been formulated succinctly by Johannes Blauw: "This [the coming of the kingdom] is no longer an end*point* on the time line of history; rather, this endpoint has itself become a *line* leading toward a later, definitive endpoint."[73] In all of this, Israel's rejection of the Messiah is an incident—albeit terrible—matter, rather than a central datum in the course of God's redemptive involvement with this world.[74]

2.3.2. The Implementation of the Missionary Mandate in Acts.

Bavinck clearly views the book of Acts as an important source for missiological reflection.[75] His discussion of the spontaneous missionary activity of the NT church

---

[71]*Ibid.*, 19.

[72]Cf. J. Blauw, *Gottes Werk*, 75-79; on p.78 he states that continuity between old and new, past and future involves both identity and distinction: identity in the sense that the Kingdom of God spreads worldwide, from Israel via the Cross, and distinction in the sense that its realization has a provisional character, that the Kingdom always stands in the tension of the "already" and the "not yet." Cf. also J.P. Versteeg, 28-36.

[73]*Gottes Werk*, 84 ("Dies ist nicht mehr ein End*punkt* auf die Linie der Geschichte, sondern dieser Endpunkt ist selber zu einer *Linie* geworden, die auf einen späteren, und dann definitiven Endpunkt weist"); on page 82 Blauw points out that God's redemption comes as a seed, which presupposes time and space to grow and ripen for the harvest (cf. Matt. 3).

[74]Israel's rejection of the Messiah only accelerates the coming of the gospel to the nations. (cf. A.F.N. Lekkerkerker on Rom. 11:11).

[75]Remarkably, in *ZWN*, 20-31, after discussing the gospels, he narrows the focus of his biblical-theological reflections to the person of Paul and then deals in one breath with foundation, goal, and method of mission.

is closely related to Roland Allen's *The Spontaneous Expansion of the Church.*[76] Bavinck distinguishes six elements with respect to the foundation of mission.[77]

1. The idea that mission is a concern of the exalted Christ, that what He began in Israel he continues in the world (Acts 1:1-2), runs like a red thread through the entire book of Acts.[78] On the Feast of Pentecost it is Christ who pours out the Holy Spirit (Acts 2:33). The signs and wonders always happen through the Name of Christ, who implicitly makes his living presence known (Acts 3:16; 4:10, 30). Remarkable are also, according to Bavinck, the instances of guidance "with which Christ prompts his church to take to heart the work of mission" in, for example, Acts 6, 10 and 13. This guidance is very clear in Paul's life (Acts 9; 16:6-7, 9-10): "It is evident on every page that Paul experiences his entire work as something in which Christ always maintains the initiative, in which Christ is always the real Author and in which he (Paul) is merely the one who implements (Acts 18:9-10)."[79]

2. Mission is not only a direct fruit of the outpouring of the Holy Spirit, but is also viewed—in direct continuity with OT prophecy (Acts 2:17: "'In the last days,' God says, I will pour out my spirit on all people'")—as an eschatological event, a sign of the end time, a phenomenon of the Last Days. The promised messianic redemption is realized in this way until the day of Christ's return.[80]

3. In the course of Acts it becomes increasingly clear that mission as God's work is at the same time both a task and a responsibility of the church. This begins in Acts 13, where the church in Antioch sends Paul and Barnabas, and it continues in Acts 15 and 21, which relate the bringing of a report to and instructions by the church of Jerusalem with respect to the missionary task.[81]

---

[76]In his treatment of Acts in *IZW*, 47-51, Bavinck does not mention this book, but he does refer to *AWW* , in which he speaks of Allen's study with great appreciation (p. 33).

[77]Cf. *IZW*, 47-51 (*ISM,* 36-40); *AWW*, 60-63.

[78]Bavinck, *IZW*, 47 (cf. *ISM,* 36), states, following F.W. Grosheide (*De Handelingen der apostelen,* 7-8), that Luke's opening sentence already presupposes this continuation. When Luke writes that the gospel is about all that Jesus *began* to do and teach, it implies that the second book deals with all that Jesus *continued* to do and teach.

[79]*IZW*, 48 (cf. *ISM,* 38). Cf. also *AWW*, 59-60. In *ZWN*, 20-21, Bavinck points to the permanent and temporary aspects of this guidance. What is permanent is that all missionary work has its origin in Christ, what is temporary is that the words and actions of the apostles have a place in God's revelation as recorded in the Bible.

[80]*IZW*, 48-49 (cf. *ISM,* 38). Cf. also *AWW*, 13, where Bavinck writes that mission involves an eschatological orientation that stimulates to the highest degree of diligence.

[81]*IZW*, 49 (cf. *ISM,* 38-39). In *AWW*, 51-55, Bavinck points out that in Acts 13 a change in missionary work takes place. The spontaneous dissemination of the gospel now becomes in principle structured, under the guidance of the Holy

4. The church itself is missionary in its essence.[82] The spread of the gospel happens initially spontaneously through church members in their daily contacts with others and through lay preachers from among persecuted church members (Acts 8:4; 11:19-20). Paul, the one to whom God had given a special mission, continues to avail himself gratefully of their services. He did fight against excesses by increasingly advocating a measure of order and imposing that order with apostolic authority.[83] In *AWW* (1941) Bavinck points out that on his second and third missionary journeys Paul increasingly focuses his work on strengthening already established churches, so that these could develop into strategic points for missionary activity.[84]

5. While the centrifugal movement is dominant, centripetal movement also clearly continues: more than once mention is made of "the spontaneous coming of outsiders, who are simply attracted to the new life that finds embodiment in the church" (Acts 2:47; 5:13). OT prophecy (e.g., Zech. 8:23) is realized in the NT church.[85]

6. The course followed by Paul (as well as the church) in his missionary work aimed toward both the circumcised and the uncircumcised is stated in principle when Paul says to the Jews in Antioch, "We had to speak the word of God to you first. Since you reject it and do not consider yourselves worthy of eternal life, we now turn to the Gentiles" (Acts 13:46). The apostle always remained true to this principle, he

> understood that in each locale the Jews first had to determine their position vis-à-vis their Messiah, who was crucified in Jerusalem. When they made themselves guilty of the same sin as their leaders, the rejection that came over the leaders also applied to them.[86]

Bavinck comes to the conclusion that in the preceding points concerning the foundation of mission nothing new is added to what is found in the gospels. In the Acts of the Apostles he sees a fulfillment, affirmation, and elaboration of the directions outlined in the gospels. We should think here of the "indescribably great significance of the miracle of the outpouring of the Holy Spirit, in whom Christ

---

Spirit, into an essential mandate of the church.

[82] In *ZWN*, 6, Bavinck points out that this has an objective and a subjective side. The church's missionary orientation stems primarily from obedience to Christ's command and secondarily from compassion for this world.

[83] *IZW*, 49-50 (cf. *ISM*, 39-40). In *AWW*, 32-51, Bavinck gives a rather extensive description of this spontaneous spread of the gospel, of which Paul finally becomes the "focal point." In close connection with this he discusses, in *AWW*, 65-77, the mobilization and equipping of new laborers in the service of the gospel, such as Silas, Timothy, Aquila and Priscilla, and Titus.

[84] *AWW*, 56-60.

[85] *IZW*, 50-51 (cf. *ISM*, 40).

[86] *AWW*, 60-63.

himself remains present in his church"; of the expanding rule of Christ; of the decisive function of the church in the implementation of the missionary mandate (also indirectly, via the apostles); of the theological place of Israel and the nations; and of the eschatological perspective within which the missionary task stands.[87] Bavinck provides good insight into the significance of the book of Acts for missiology, but it is curious that he does not pay any attention to what is perhaps the most important message of the book—which even determined its structure—that the message of the gospel goes from Jerusalem, the center of Israel, to Rome, the center of the world.[88] The particularist view had been replaced by the universalist vision, and this change of perspective is theologically undergirded in the NT letters, particularly those written by Paul.

2.3.3. The Elaboration of the Missionary Mandate in the NT Letters

Bavinck states that the letters of the apostles stand in a missionary context and therefore contain many data concerning the essence and functioning of the missionary calling.[89] He views what the epistles provide as a later development and further elaboration of the missionary mandate in the gospels, without taking into account that the letters were written earlier than the gospels. He writes that Paul rarely reaches back to the missionary mandate of Christ, adding that "The missionary mandate had been given so recently that it seemed almost superfluous to remind his readers of it."[90]

Bavinck begins his discussion of the epistles in *IZW* by listing a number of missionary perspectives, which are in part related to elements mentioned earlier.[91] Next he traces the theological position of Israel and of the nations in the epistles. And he concludes with some comments on the all-encompassing character of salvation. This structure will be followed in the discussion below. As already stated above, Bavinck occasionally made use of important studies of others, but he does not include specific references, regardless of whether he agrees or disagrees with the author in question.

Bavinck distinguishes six important missionary perspectives in the NT epistles.

---

[87]*IZW*, 51 (cf. *ISM*, 40-41).

[88]Cf. J. Blauw, *Gottes Werk*, 104.

[89]Bavinck, *IZW*, 51 (cf. *ISM*, 42), also mentions the book of Revelation but ignores it in what follows.

[90]*IZW*, 52 (cf. *ISM*, 42).

[91]*IZW*, 51-58 (cf. *ISM*, 42-49). Formally Bavinck distinguishes four perspectives, subsuming the eschatological aspect under the missionary function of the church. But it would seem preferable to view the former as a separate point. In *ZWN*, 20-31, Bavinck deals only with Paul's missionary activity, discussing first its unique, time-specific and local nature and then mentioning three facets of its permanent significance: the character of Paul's call, and the goal and plan of his work.

1. The mystery of missionary work "is implicit in God's miraculous work of making every object a subject." Bavinck sees this articulated most clearly in 2 Cor. 5:18-20:

> All this is from God, who reconciled us to himself through Christ, and gave us the ministry (*diakonia*) of reconciliation: that God was reconciling the world to himself in Christ, not counting men's sins against them. And he has committed to us the message (*logos*) of reconciliation.

When people become the object of reconciliation, they immediately also become subjects of the worldwide ministry of reconciliation. God's personal turning toward people always involves missionary intent; reconciliation to God always serves a worldwide goal.[92]

2. The place of the one who is sent is automatically determined by this act of reconciliation. He or she is God's envoy. This implies nobility, because the one sent is no less than a representative of Christ. It also implies humility, because those sent are never more than Christ's mouthpiece.[93] To Bavinck these aspects are especially evident in the way in which Paul "uses the dangerous word 'I.' " The apostle maneuvers between the Scylla of delusions of grandeur and the Charybdis of a sense of powerlessness when he says, "I worked harder than all of them—yet not I, but the grace of God that was with me" (1 Cor. 15:10). Bavinck states, "That marvelous, profound confessional statement 'I—yet not I, but grace' is the foundation that makes missionary work possible."[94]

3. The above implies that missionary work always "takes place on the edge of the miraculous." By virtue of its nature it is dependent on "the gracious working of the blessed nearness of God." Paul articulates this repeatedly, specifically when he speaks about the necessity of an open door (1 Cor. 16:9; 2 Cor. 2:12; Col. 4:3). "It is striking that Paul always sees this opening of the 'door' as something that God has reserved as his prerogative."[95] And when Paul takes stock of the missionary work that had taken place, he comes to the conclusion that "neither he who plants nor he who waters is anything,, but only God, who makes things grow" (1 Cor. 3:7).

4. As they grow qualitatively, the churches in the NT epistles are increasingly shown what the missionary calling is that they are to fulfill. This must find concrete expression in three ways.

In the first place, the church has the important task of intercession, "that the message of the Lord may spread rapidly and be honored" (2 Thess. 3:1; cf. also 1 Thess. 5:25; Eph. 6:19 and Col. 4:3).[96]

Next, the church has the centripetal task of behaving as children of light,

---

[92]*IZW*, 53 (cf. *ISM*, 43). Bavinck calls this "the mysterious character of all God's work" from the beginning of the creation of the earth.

[93]Cf. *IZW*, 53 (*ISM*, 44) and *ZWN*, 26.

[94]*IZW*, 53 (cf. *ISM*, 44). Bavinck also refers here to Gal. 2:20: "I no longer live, but Christ lives in me."

[95]*IZW*, 54 (cf. *ISM*, 45).

[96]Cf. *IZW*, 55 (*ISM*, 45-46).

so that unbelievers may be drawn to it and Christ like bees to flowers (cf. Phil. 2:14-15). Furthermore, the church's witness can only truly bear fruit when it lives as a "glorified" *ecclesia* (cf. Isa. 55:5). The church must be conscious of the fact that it "lives before the eyes of the world," elicits contradiction, and therefore must not give offence (cf. 1 Cor. 10:32-33), but rather, "by doing good ... should silence the ignorant talk of foolish men" (1 Peter 2:15). The church must behave properly and be wise in the way it acts toward "outsiders" (cf. 1 Thess. 4:12, Col. 4:5), and overseers must maintain "a good reputation with outsiders" (1 Tim. 3:7). The proper functioning of the offices is also, in the final analysis, aimed at the spread of the gospel as is shown by Eph. 4:11-16: when the offices function in the interest of equipping believers for service and edifying the church (v. 12), it becomes a body "joined and held together," growing and building itself up (v. 16).[97]

Finally, the church is called to continual witness. It must with one mind strive for the faith of the gospel (cf. Phil. 1:27), it must make "the most of every opportunity [to speak a good word on behalf of Christ]" (Eph. 5:16), and do this in such a way that its speech is "always full of grace, seasoned with salt" (Col. 4:6). The church is "involved in a permanent discussion with the world around it." This is the work of the Lord, in which the church must abound and which is not in vain in the Lord (cf. 1 Cor. 15:58). Part of the church's spiritual armor are "feet fitted with the readiness that comes from the gospel of peace" (Eph.6:15).[98] Bavinck sees the calling of the church described most clearly in 1 Peter 2:9. It is called out of the world to be "a chosen people, a royal priesthood, a holy nation, a people belonging to God." But its calling is at the same time a call to service in and to the world: "that you may declare the praises of him who called you out of darkness into his wonderful light."[99]

5.   Following Anton G. Honig,[100] Bavinck emphasizes the all-encompassing character of salvation: proceeding from the central given of reconciliation, the apostolic letters teach that salvation encompasses all of life. "Everything changes where Christ has placed his hand upon humankind," in Christ people become "a new creation" (2 Cor. 5:17; Gal. 6:15). There is therefore no "human relationship and no human condition" that remains untouched in the parenesis of the epistles. They speak "about marriage and about child rearing, about the relationship to government and the relationship between master and slave,... about greed and ambition." There is not a single neutral area in our life,

---

[97]Cf. *IZW*, 55-57 (*ISM*, 46-47). Bavinck's exegesis of Eph. 4:11-16 is dubious. As A. van Roon, 109-10, has shown, this text refers to qualitative rather than quantitative growth of the church and is thus directly relevant for ecclesiology but only indirectly for missiology.

[98]*IZW*, 57 (cf. *ISM*, 48). Bavinck notes here Paul's link with Isa. 52:7, which speaks of "the feet of him who brings good news" and concludes that "the whole church is characterized as a bringer of good news."

[99]Cf. *IZW*, 57-58 (*ISM*, 48-49). Cf. also "De kerk, zendingskerk," 20.

[100]Cf. A.G. Honig, *Bijdrage tot het onderzoek naar de fundering van de zendings-methode der 'comprehensive approach' in het Nieuwe Testament*, 41-71. This 1951 dissertation was written under the supervision of J. H. Bavinck.

nothing falls outside the power of sin and nothing is excluded from God's redemption. As a result of faith, "the whole of society is reborn."[101]

6. The whole of the missionary task stands in eschatological perspective. Through mission God is at work, in preparation for the fullness of time, "to bring all things in heaven and on earth together under one head, even Christ." (Eph. 1:10). Where once there were unbridgeable chasms—for example, between Jews and Gentiles (cf. Eph. 2:11-22)—nations are now brought together into one. All missionary work reaches toward this final goal, "the realization of which will take visible shape only in the age to come, beyond the horizon of world history."[102]

All of the above-mentioned missionary perspectives are valuable. But, it is strange that here too, as in his discussion of Acts, Bavinck bypasses the most important point: the universal reach of redemption as expressed particularly in the Pauline epistles (especially Romans, Galatians, and Ephesians), where it is rooted in the concept of the justification of the godless by faith. The NT understanding of redemption as offered and available to all people must inform any treatment of biblical foundations in a *Reformed* theology of mission. Bavinck's omission is all the more surprising when we remember that this point is found in all accepted NT theologies of mission.[103] It appears furthermore that Bavinck has paid little, if any, attention to the missionary motifs appearing in letters other than those by Paul. Finally, the first three points of the preceding summary are less relevant in the context of a biblical theology of mission than Bavinck makes it appear.

2.3.4. The Theological Position of Israel and the *Goyim*

Continuing the thought of point six in the preceding section, Bavinck discusses the question of how the *theological position of Israel* in the realization of God's promises is viewed in the epistles. After all, since the rejection of Jesus as Messiah by official Israel the trustworthiness of the OT promises, which bear witness to an Israel-centric dissemination of redemption, is at stake.

First he points again to Galatians 3:16, where Paul shows that in Christ the promises made to Abraham are realized. "All that is said of Israel has become fully true in that true Son of Israel, who has ascended the throne of David."[104]

Next, Bavinck discusses the main argument of Rom. 9-11.

Central to Paul's thinking is the immovable certainty that it is not possible "that God's word had failed" (9:6). The promises God gave in the OT to his covenant people have been fulfilled in

---

[101]*IZW*, 63-64 (cf. *ISM*, 55).

[102]*IZW*, 58 (cf. *ISM*, 49).

[103]Cf. G. Warneck, *Evangelische Missionslehre*, 1, 194ff., and J. Blauw, (*Gottes Werk*, 109), who writes that Paul teaches what is unbelievable to Jewish ears: "the line of descent from Abraham runs via Christ to the world of the gentiles, and Abraham himself is the prototype of the gentile Christians" (die Linie der Abstammnung von Abraham verläuft über Christus zur Heidenwelt, und Abraham selbst ist der Prototyp der Heidenchristen).

[104]*IZW*, 59 (cf. *ISM*, 50).

one way or another, or they will yet be fulfilled.[105]
Paul then describes the actual situation, in which Israel has lost its privileged position, so that Jews and Gentiles are now called to salvation without distinction: "For there is no difference between Jew and Gentile—the same Lord is Lord of all and richly blesses all who call on him, for, 'Everyone who calls on the name of the Lord will be saved.' " (Rom. 10:12-13).[106] After that Paul speaks of the concrete fulfillment of the promises that were made. There is "a remnant chosen by grace" (11:5). Around this core, which has confessed Jesus as Messiah, many from the nations have gathered. This new people of God can now, conversely, provoke the vast unbelieving majority of Israel to jealousy (cf. 11:11). In summary Paul concludes that "Israel has experienced a hardening in part until the full number of the Gentiles has come in. And so all Israel will be saved" (11:25-26).

Bavinck rejects John Calvin's notion that Israel here refers to the church of all ages.[107] This is a promise for the nation of Israel.[108] The word *so* ("*so* all Israel will be saved") should, according to Bavinck, be understood to mean "that the coming in of the full number of the Gentiles will have an effect on Israel. Israel will be stimulated to jealousy by this, and *so*, i.e., in this way, out of jealousy all Israel will be saved."[109] The fact that Rev. 7:1-8 speaks of the 144,000 sealed ones from all tribes of Israel has for him no special significance. He follows what he considers to be the most widely accepted exegesis of this phrase, namely that it refers to the entire NT church.[110]

Bavinck points out in passing that this is unrelated to the political restoration of Israel (1948): "In Romans 11 Paul certainly does not speak of Israel as a political entity; rather, he speaks of Israel as the people of the covenant."[111] No theological significance can therefore be attached to the establishment of the State

---

[105] *IZW*, 60 (cf. *ISM*, 51).

[106] Cf. *IZW*, 60 (*ISM*, 51).

[107] John Calvin writes in his commentary on Rom. 11:26, "Many understand this of the Jewish people, as though Paul had said, that religion would again be restored among them as before: but I extend the word Israel to all the people of God...." Bavinck errs, however, in holding that Calvin did not see a future promise for Israel, for Calvin immediately continues, "...according to this meaning: 'When the Gentiles shall come in, the Jews also shall return from their defection to the obedience of faith; and thus shall be completed the salvation of the whole Israel of God, which must be gathered from both....' " He even adds emphatically, "...and yet in such a way that the Jews shall obtain the first place, being as it were the first-born in God's family" (transl. John Owen).

[108] Cf. *IZW*, 61 (*ISM*, 52). Bavinck interprets "all Israel" to mean "those in Israel who are elected to eternal life."

[109] *IZW*, 61 (cf. *ISM*, 52).

[110] Cf. *IZW*, 62 (*ISM*, 53).

[111] *IZW*, 61-62 (cf. *ISM*, 53).

of Israel.[112]

On the basis of the Pauline testimony, Bavinck contends, Israel has lost the unique position it had in the OT, but the promise of redemption for Israel remains in force. Though this replacement theology[113] is to an extent defensible, it is at the same time disputable because it fails to take into account the continuing mystery between God and his people. Further, Jongeneel rightly argues that a theological positioning of Israel, if it is to be in accord with the NT, must also incorporate Jesus' view of the Jews.[114]

Next Bavinck traces the *theological position of the nations*, as described in the epistles. On the one hand the demonic character of their existence is fully emphasized. They follow "the ways of this world and of the ruler of the kingdom of the air" (Eph. 2:2). They are "without hope and without God in the world" (Eph. 2:12) and "darkened in their understanding" (Eph. 4:18). They have given themselves over to "licentiousness" (Eph. 4:19 NRSV) and are entangled in dread and hubris (in the power of "the elemental spirits of the universe," Col. 2:20 NRSV). On the other hand it appears that "the requirements of the law are written on their hearts" (Rom. 2:15), which, states Bavinck, is "striking proof that these Gentiles also stand within the reach of God's mercy." But this never leads to a spontaneous asking after Christ among the nations. And thus the character of the missionary task is determined: "mission is not a going out by invitation" but rather "by command."[115]

2.4. Summary

In his efforts to provide a biblical foundation for mission, Bavinck on the one hand described in detail various OT and NT missionary motifs, while on the other he sometimes remained too fragmentary in his reflection with regard to basic biblical patterns. Moreover, he failed to engage in a thorough investigation of the central OT and NT terms *shalach* and *apostellō*.[116] This, however, does not alter the fact that his treatment of the biblical foundation of mission incorporates a number of important structural elements.

In the first place, there is a *Trinitarian* scheme, whereby in the OT the accent falls on the *theocentric* aspect, and in the NT successively on the *Christocentric* and the *pneuma-centric* aspect. Although in the whole of his

---

[112] According to G.J. van Klinken, 532, Bavinck intended this as a warning against an overly great (theological) optimism with respect to the State of Israel.

[113] In 1978 RCN theologian J. Versteeg articulated this concept as follows: "Israel has lost its unique OT position. Israel now can only be redeemed together with the nations. But in this way—together with the nations—there is salvation for all Israel," 38.

[114] Jongeneel, *Missiologie*, 1, 80.

[115] *IZW*, 62-63 (cf. *ISM*, 54-55). For an extensive discussion of these ideas, see *IZW*, 70-74 (*ISM*, 62-65).

[116] Cf. Jongeneel *Missiologie*, 1, 73, 78.

missiological reflection Bavinck devoted much attention to "those who are sent," in his biblical theology of mission all emphasis falls on the "Sender": there is no *anthropocentric* accent at all.[117]

Second, Bavinck's biblical theology of mission has a *salvation-historical* orientation; he makes use of the prevailing distinction that the focus of the OT is especially particularistic and centripetal and that of the NT particularly universalistic and centrifugal. The universal thrust of the OT finds fulfillment at God's time through the cross and resurrection of Christ and the outpouring of the Spirit. Because of its rejection of the Messiah, Israel's special calling is transferred to the church. Bavinck, however, fails to develop the most important salvation-historical aspect, namely, that the covenant with Abraham finds its universal fulfillment in Christ.

Third, Bavinck sees an *ecclesiocentric* tendency in mission as carried out in the NT. There mission is about the church: it is both the object of reconciliation and the subject of the ministry of reconciliation. This ecclesiocentrism does have a certain *basileia-centric* focus because of the meaning of redemption that encompasses all of life and the eschatological expectation of the Kingdom of God. Discussion of the comprehensive nature of salvation on the basis of the epistles alone, however, does not do justice to biblical teaching regarding the meaning of the Kingdom.

3. The Essence of Mission

After dealing with the four basic motifs or aspects that, according to Bavinck, define the essence of mission, the focus in this section will shift to his definition of mission. Because we want to trace whether there was a development in his thinking on this score, our discussion will not be limited to an analysis of the final definition given in *IZW* but will also include a treatment of his earlier attempts at delineation. Finally, in this context we will address the question to what extent Bavinck sees agreements and differences between mission in general, on the one hand, and mission among the Jews and evangelism, on the other.

3.1. The Salient Elements of Mission

3.1.1. Mission as God's Work

Bavinck considers it important to view mission first and foremost "as a work of God" that has its origin in divine compassion and is realized in the sending of the Son (John 3:16).[118] He further defines mission as "The great work of Jesus Christ through which he, after his finished work as Mediator, draws all nations to his salvation and makes them partakers of the gifts which he has acquired for them."[119] Bavinck sees this Christocentric character of all missionary endeavor expressed

---

[117]This anthropocentric accent is found in *ZWN*, 20-31, where the missionary significance of Acts and the epistles is discussed entirely on the basis of the experience of "Paul, as one sent to the Gentiles."

[118]*ZWN*, 7.

[119]*IZW*, 65 (cf. *ISM*, 57-58).

especially in Matt. 28:18-20. He writes:
"Go therefore!—I am with you." The implicit meaning is: 'In
you I send Myself, in you I go. I send you, but all that you
actually do and accomplish is my doing.' Understood in the
deepest sense, Christ is the only *apostolos* (Heb. 3:1).[120]
He also refers to Matthew 16:18: Christ himself will build the church on the *petra*
of confession, and to Eph. 2:21, which speaks of the growth of the church as a
growing up in the Lord that "is, as it were, a soundless, mysterious process.[121] Thus,
missionary work is fundamentally and exclusively grounded in "the gracious
pleasure of God in Christ Jesus."[122]

In this connection Bavinck refers to the concept of 'double missionary
foundation' espoused in the work of the Protestant missiologist Gustav Warneck
and that of the Roman Catholic missiologist Joseph Schmidlin.[123] According to this
notion the reason for mission lies not only in God's pleasure but also in human
desire.[124] Following Hans Schärer, Bavinck forcefully rejects this idea,[125] since
there is no biblical basis for it whatsoever. The traditional appeal to Haggai 2:7

---

[120]"Zendingsbegrip en zendingwerkelijkheid," 1. In this article Bavinck
comments on Matt. 28:18-20, "because [these verses] cast, with incomparable
power and depth, light on the missionary task of the church."

[121]*Ibid.*, 2. Cf. also *IZW*, 65 (*ISM*, 57), where Bavinck points out that the
Heidelberg Catechism (Answer 54) rightfully says that "the Son of God gathers to
himself a church out of the human race."

[122]*IZW*, 70 (cf. *ISM*, 62).

[123]Cf. *IZW*, 71-73 (*ISM*, 62-65).

[124]G. Warneck, *Evangelische Missionslehre*, 1, 240-304, speaks of an
"ecclesiastical, historical, and ethnological foundation of mission" (kirchliche,
geschichtliche, ethnolo-gische Begründung der Sendung). Concerning the latter he
says that "the people of all nationalities and cultural levels have a faculty for
Christianity" (Fähigkeit der Menschen aller Nationalitäten und Kulturstufen für das
Christentum, 301). J. Schmidlin, *Katholische Missionslehre im Grundriss,* 96,
states that "the nations are each and all qualified for Christianity" (die Völker samt
und sonders für das Christentum qualfiziert sind"). In this context Bavinck, *IZW*,
72, n. 13; *ISM*, 64, n. 13, also mentions the Roman Catholic author Otto Karrer,
who calls the gospel "God's answer to the misery of the world," 125.

[125]H. Schärer, *Die Begründing der Mission in der katholischen und
evangelischen Missionswissenschaft,* 37-38, states, "The foundation of mission in
evangelical missiology can and should only be singular ... [its elaboration] can and
should only take place on the basis of the revelation of God in Jesus Christ, which
cancels and rules out every other 'revelation,' any other knowledge concerning
God" (Die Begründung der Mission in der evangelischen Missionswissenschaft
kann und darf nur eine einfache sein ... kann und darf nur geschehen auf Grund der
Offenbarung Gottes in Jesus Christus, die jede andere 'Offen-barung,' jedes andere
Wissen um Gott, aufhebt und ausschliesst).

was based on a faulty interpretation of this text. It was often understood as God saying, "I will shake all nations, and the Desire of all nations [i.e., Christ] shall come," whereas it is better rendered: "I will shake all nations, so that the treasure of all nations shall come" (NRSV)[126] Other texts that might point in this direction, such as Isa. 11:10 (cited in Rom. 15:12), 42:4, 51:5 and 60:9, appear exegetically not to refer to a continual "unconscious longing" for God among "the heathen" but rather to "a very specific redemptive event" that will be revealed "in the last days . . . at the time of the Lord's pleasure." Bavinck then concludes:

> Viewed objectively it is true that the nations without Christ cannot find peace and that they need him, but that does not mean that they long for him and seek him on their own initiative. The gospel of Christ is 'not something that man made up' (Gal. 1:11), nor is it the message of redemption to which the nations have eagerly looked forward.[127]

This exclusive foundation of mission in God's revelation in Christ does not affect the necessity of a religious a priori (see chapter three above), "without which all speaking of God hangs suspended in a hopeless void."[128]

3.1.2. Mission as Task of the Church

Mission as God's work includes rather than excludes human work. God was in Christ reconciling the world with himself, but the administration of this reconciliation has been entrusted to us.[129] Viewed thus, missionary work is nothing other "than the human side of a great, divine seeking and speaking that continues through all ages of history."[130] It is for Bavinck unquestionably clear that this task has been reserved for the church of all ages: "The Scriptures make it absolutely clear that it is the church, the body of Christ, that constitutes the organ through and in which the glorified Christ wants to reveal his great redemptive work to the world."[131] And he concludes, "We will have to apply this principle to our own

---

[126]Cf. *IZW*, 71 (*ISM*, 63), where Bavinck states that the older rendering of this text is directly based on the Vulgate translation: "*et movebo omnes gentes; et veniet Desideratus cunctis gentibus.*"

[127]*IZW*, 72 (cf. *ISM*, 64). Cf. *AWW*, 120, where Bavinck states, "The [gospel] contradicted the searching on the part of the people of those days just as much as it contradicts the desire of the nations where it is being preached today.... It may at times spread more easily than in other times, but despite everything, it remains madness and foolishness to every human heart."

[128]*IZW*, 74 (cf. *ISM*, 65).

[129]Cf. *IZW*, 65-66 (*ISM*, 57-58).

[130]*OKZK*, 10. Bavinck points out that the word *mission* always encompasses these two sides: there can be no mission without both a Sender and those who are sent.

[131]*IZW*, 66 (cf. *ISM*, 59).

situations in our own way."[132]

In developing this principle he closely followed the lead of the discussions and findings of the earlier-mentioned 1896 Synod of Middelburg, which is not surprising in view of the fact that the RCN had played a pioneering role in the area of church-based mission work. The synod's concluding statement was, "The question who, after the ascension of Christ, has the authority for mission should therefore be answered thus, that according to Matt. 28:19 and Acts 13:1ff this authority has been placed by Christ in the church."[133]

In line with the argument presented there, Bavinck first points out that the promise made in Matt. 28:19 is addressed to the church of all ages, which is built on the foundation of apostles and prophets and is therefore also heir to the calling of proclamation to all creatures.[134] Second, he rejects a fulfillment of this task by "societies" or "sodalities," because they lack the authority to administer the sacraments, whereas Matt. 28:19 specifically mentions the administration of baptism as an essential part of the missionary task. "It is the church to which the sacraments have been entrusted. It is therefore also the church from which the missionary work must emanate."[135] At a later stage Bavinck no longer mentions this argument. Perhaps he came to realize the anachronism of applying Reformed ecclesiology to Matt. 28:19 in this line of reasoning. Nevertheless, he maintains the fundamental rejection of mission carried out through missionary societies. His reason now is that there are no biblical arguments for a missionary *ecclesiola in ecclesia*.[136] Third, he points to Acts 13:1ff, where it appears that the Holy Spirit involves the church in the sending out of Paul and Barnabas. "All this is the more remarkable," he writes, "because Paul, as apostle of Jesus Christ, in fact did not need to be sent out by the Church of Antioch. He had been called directly by his Master to be 'apostle to the Gentiles.' "[137]

Bavinck does not limit himself to these few, significant verses but, referring to Hendrik Kraemer, also points continually to the fact that in light of the NT witness, mission—as living witness in word and deed, nearby and worldwide—is an essential characteristic of the Christian church and of each

---

[132]"Kerk en zending," 100.

[133]Extract from the *Acta der generale synode* (Middleburg 1896), 24; cf. *IZW*, 67-68 (*ISM*, 59-60).

[134]Cf. *ZWN*, 34; "Zendingsbegrip en zendingswerkelijkheid," 6; *IZW*, 67 (*ISM*, 59).

[135]*ZWN*, 38. Cf. J.C. Gilhuis, *De zendingstaak der kerk*, 8, who also employs this argument.

[136]In *IZW*, 66-67 (cf. *ISM*, 58-59), he emphatically rejects the position of Gustav Warneck, *Evangelische Missionslehre*, 2, 31, where the latter argues that mission is in principle a responsibility of the church, but that it is best carried out in practice by an *ecclesiola in ecclesia* driven by missionary motivation.

[137]*ZWN*, 35-36; cf. *IZW*, 66 (*ISM*, 59).

believer.[138]

It is the church as heir of the promises God had given to Israel, the true Israel in Christ Jesus, that on the one hand may call people to salvation in Christ and that on the other hand, through its life in continuous association with the Lord, arouses the nations to envy, so that they come spontaneously, because they have heard that God is with the church.[139]

The power to attract others is part of the essence of the church.[140] In a brief but significant article in *HZB* he gives a fivefold biblical interpretation of this concept: the church has the power to attract by being a community (John 13:35), by being clear in its liturgy (1 Cor. 14:23), by manifesting the embodiment of Christ in its attitude toward life (Matt. 5:13-16), by its spiritual joy (Acts 13:52), and by its openness to the world in order to pass on the secret of salvation without any reservations (Col. 4:5).[141] This plainly shows that the missionary calling of the church has a double focus: centrifugal and centripetal, concerning the relationship of which he writes:

the life of the church of Christ in the midst of a desperate world is such a clear witness that it cannot but make an impression. That is, as it were, the sounding board that gives the content of the proclamation its penetrating power.[142]

However much he kept emphasizing this essential characteristic of the church,[143] Bavinck, in contrast to Kraemer and Hoekendijk, consistently refused to define the nature of the church exclusively in terms of its missionary calling, Kraemer had stated his position as follows:

In my view the raison d'être, the reason for the existence of the church is that it is present *because of* and *in* the distress of the

---

[138]Cf. *AWW*, 219-221: "The main point is, however, that every living member of the church militant should be aware of" his or her task; and *IZW*, 75-76 (cf. *ISM*, 67): "The Bible thus sees the missionary mandate as a calling that not a single church member may turn away from." Cf. *BCNCR*, 15-16, and *IZW*, 67 (*ISM*, 59), where Bavinck quotes Kraemer with approval: "mission, i.e., the apostolic going out to the world near and far, belongs under all circumstances to the nature of the Christian Church," *Blijvende Opdracht*, 8.

[139]*IZW*, 69 (cf. *ISM*, 61).

[140]Cf. "Nieuwe uitzichten in het zendingswerk," 12, where Bavinck terms the mis-sionary character of the church, which he views as comprising missionary and evangelistic work, the "normal mode of existence of the church."

[141]*HZB*, 49 (1951), 131-32.

[142]"Wat is zendingsarbeid?" *HZB*, 50 (1952), 36.

[143]Cf. *IGHG*, 103: "As the Bible clearly indicates, the Spirit makes the church aware of the world; through the Spirit the church will come to understand that it is an instrument in the hands of Him to whom is given all power in heaven and on earth."

world.... The reason for the existence of the church of Christ is
that in it, as in His body, the divine movement of mercy toward
the world progresses.[144]

But Bavinck was not prepared to turn the church into a function of the apostolate.
On the contrary, he argued that the church's significance is threefold. Above all it
has a doxological function: "the Church does not exist in the first place because of
the world, nor because of the distress of the world, but it exists in the first place
because of God and to the glory of God"; next it has a "motherly" task: "The
Church works continually on itself, it makes the Word of God known to the
generations to come"; and only then does it have a missionary calling: "The same
God who preserves his church also gives it increase."[145]

In this context Bavinck further points to four things. First, he maintains the
view, held since 1896 Synod of Middelburg, that the primary responsibility for
mission lies with the local church: "It is not the church as a whole that baptizes, but
only the locally instituted church."[146] Second, referring to the 1947 conferences
held in Makassar and Kwitang, he emphasizes the ecumenical character of this
mandate: the church, which reveals itself everywhere in the world, has a collective
missionary responsibility.[147] Third, the church is called to fulfill its missionary
mandate not only in obedience, but in trusting expectation[148] and loving concern:

If for us [mission] is a matter of duty, of acting on the basis of
[divine] command, that would appear to be scripturally sound,
but [such motivation by itself] lacks precisely that which gives
mission its powerful appeal: the holy power of love, which is
ultimately nothing but the love of Christ himself, which in us and
through us reaches out to this broken world.[149]

And fourth, the official missionary mandate of the church is complemented by the

---

[144]*Kerk en Zending,* 15, Cf. *The Christian Message in a Non-Christian
World,* 30, where Kraemer states that the church is meant to be "a fellowship of
believers, rooted in God and his redemptive order, and therefore committed to the
service and the salvation of the world."

[145]*IZW,* 76-77 (cf. *ISM,* 68-69).

[146]Cf. *IZW,* 68 (*ISM,* 59-60), and *Acta der generale synode van
Middelburg,* 67.

[147]Cf. "Zendingsbegrip en zendingswerkelijkheid," 6; Bavinck insists here
that the older churches must abandon their colonial sense of superiority in favor of
a biblical concept of ecumenicity.

[148]Cf. *OKZK,* 32-34, where Bavinck points to the necessity of faith in the
work of the risen and glorified Christ; the strength for mission emerges in the
presence of a deep faith "that God can still do amazing things in this modern world
through our words," a faith "that Christ will advance triumphantly..."

[149]*OKZK,* 30; cf. also *ZWN,* 5-7, where Bavinck points to charity of heart
as that which gives rise to spontaneous proclamation of the gospel. Obedience to
God's command is foundational, but ideally this obedience incorporates charity.

individual missionary activities of believers in the social, medical, and economic realms.[150]

3.1.3. Mission as Proclamation of the Rule of Christ

From the very beginning of his missiological reflection Bavinck pointed to the twofold nature of the missionary mandate. As early as 1934 he described mission not only as "an attempt to lead human souls to the Light of Jesus Christ, so that they surrender to Him and rest in him in life and in death," but also as a "wrestling with other cultures."[151] In his 1939 inaugural address he begins by adopting the same position: in confrontation with traditional and modern currents of thought, mission is called to the difficult task of giving voice to its message that Jesus is the Christ.[152] In a 1947 publication he applied to mission the Kuyperian concept of the implementation of the Christian principle in all areas of life.[153] In a book published in 1948 he speaks of the "comprehensive reach of our Reformed way of thinking," which he says is fundamental to the provision of basic principles for the solution of practical and technical problems on the mission field.[154]

Bavinck calls this the theocratic or, by preference, the Christocentric idea and sees this already expressed in the Great Commission in Matt. 28:18-29. The missionary mandate begins with a proclamation of the kingly rule of Christ: "All authority in heaven and on earth has been given to me." And it ends with a call to obedience: "Go and make disciples of all nations, . . . teaching them to obey everything I have commanded you." From this Bavinck concludes that Christ

> wants to be Lord of the whole of life. . . . It is impossible to make someone a partial disciple of Jesus Christ. If one is a disciple, he has to become a disciple wholly, he must follow Christ in his personal life as well as in his social, economic, and

---

[150]Cf. *IZW*, 68-69 (*ISM*, 60-61). It should be pointed out here that Bavinck was not advocating assigning these tasks to private initiative without further consideration; he argued that the church also has an (official) diaconal task to fulfill in this area, namely, that of the "priestly extension of charity" alongside that of "prophetic witness." But practically speaking, private initiative is also needed because it is impossible for the church to fulfill all of its tasks as it should, 76.

[151]*CMO*, 5.

[152]*CPVW*, 5-6. Bavinck emphatically rejects a romantic view of the missionary mandate—"proclaiming the gospel to cannibals."

[153]*ZWN*, 8-9. It is remarkable how easily Bavinck links this Kuyperian principle with the Barthian principle that the preaching of the Kingdom of heaven permeates critically all of existence. Cf. *BCNCR*, 20-23, where Bavinck approvingly summarizes Kraemer, even though the latter, following Barth, did not want to have anything to do with "Christian principles." Apparently the practical similarity—the renewing effect of the gospel *and* its provisional character—outweighs for Bavinck the fundamental distinction.

[154]*OKZK*, 23-25.

political relationships.[155]
He also described how this principle was applied in the NT church. It was not possible for the church to renew society immediately and comprehensively; the gospel did not lead to revolutionary action. But the church did proceed in a radical way in the sense that it sought "to reveal a new way of life for all manner of relationships, a way of life that would ultimately burst through the old forms" and "give shape to a new society."[156] Bavinck stresses in this connection that the struggle of the gospel with culture always presupposes pluriformity. One may not "force one's own culture on . . . other nations"; rather those working in mission must always seek to establish and give form to the rule of Christ in "living relationship to that which is central in the culture" of a given people.[157]

Though it is true that according to Scriptural teaching redemption is all-encompassing in nature and scope and that this constitutes the foundation for a comprehensive approach to missionary,[158] Bavinck remains convinced that, within this broad understanding, proclamation of the gospel and reconciliation with God through faith remain the primary spearhead of mission. "Essentially and centrally, the issue is restoring relationship with God, reconciliation through Christ. But from the starting point of reconciliation all of life will be renewed and elevated to a higher plane."[159] To Bavinck the central character of proclamation is plainly reflected in the OT and NT terms that are used to denote the missionary calling of the church: the Hebrew verbs *basar* (to bring a joyful message) and *qara* (to call), and the Greek verbs *euaggelizesthai* (to bring good news), *kērussein* (to proclaim), and *marturein* (to bear witness).[160]

Gradually Bavinck began to make use of the concept of the Kingdom of God in a more consciously theological way in his approach this essential aspect of mission. Thus he writes in 1961: "The idea of the coming Kingdom of the Lord, with its immense blessing of *shalom* (peace) is by far the most dominant factor" in both the OT and NT. Mission takes place in the service of the coming of God's Kingdom: "in that immense work of God we are his hands."[161] The more consistent use of this concept, however, did not mean a change in principle but rather a

---

[155]"Zendingsbegrip en zendingswerkelijkheid," 4-5.

[156]*AWW*, 205. Cf. also *IZW*, 64 (*ISM*, 55-56), where Bavinck writes that the letters of the apostles touch all of existence radically, i.e., down to its very roots.

[157]"Zendingsbegrip en zendingswerkelijkheid," 5-6.

[158]Cf. *IZW*, 64 (*ISM*, 55) and "Zendingsbegrip en zendingswerkelijkheid," 4-5. Bavinck is willing to adopt this concept only if it is interpreted in a critically Reformed manner.

[159]*IZW*, 64 (cf. *ISM*, 55). Cf. also *ZWN*, 7-8, and *CMO*, 5.

[160]Cf. *IZW*, 74-75 (*ISM*, 65-66).

[161]"Theology and Mission," 64-65; earlier, on page 63, he speaks of the Kingdom as "that almost always forgotten chapter of doctrinal theology, that is one of the most dominant ideas when we are dealing with missions."

deepening from a biblical-theological perspective. We will return to this central biblical notion of the Kingdom in more detail in section 3 of Chap. 5.

3.1.4. Mission in Eschatological Perspective

Mission has its own place in redemptive history. It is part of "the sequence of the last things."[162] Bavinck emphasizes the eschatological nature of mission not only on the grounds of biblical-exegetical considerations, but also on the basis of various developments taking place in missiology at that time. He refers explicitly to what the German missiologists Walter Freytag and Johannes Reinhard had written on this matter.[163]

Already in the OT the coming of the nations to Mount Zion is viewed as a sign of a new age, in which "the all-encompassing and all-permeating salvation of the Messiah will dominate all of life."[164] Again Bavinck refers to the missionary mandate as found in Matt. 28:18-20, where the church is called to mission on the basis of the reality of the Cross and Resurrection and with a view to "the end of the age."[165] The missionary mandate, thus, is implemented between initial fulfillment and final culmination, in the period during which salvation always takes the provisional form of a balance between "already" and "not yet." With that in mind, Bavinck warns against too great an optimism concerning the realization of redemption in the here and now, pointing to 1 Cor. 7:29-31, where Paul places strong emphasis on the tentative aspect of redemption due to the fact that the form (*schema*) of this world is passing away.[166] Hence Paul, standing within "the great present of the new age," states that now God "commands all people everywhere to repent" (Acts 17:30), adding that such repentance serves the purpose of the mystery of God's will—which he will "put into effect when the times will have reached their fulfillment—to bring all things in heaven and on earth together under one head, even Christ" (Eph. 1:10).[167]

---

[162]*IZW*, 69 (cf. *ISM*, 62).

[163]Cf. "Zendingsbegrip en zendingswerkelijkeid," 3; W. Freytag, "Mission im Blick aufs Ende," 321ff.; J. Reinhard, 175ff.

[164]*IZW*, 69-70 (cf. *ISM*, 61).

[165]"Zendingsbegrip en zendingswerkelijkeid," 2.

[166]Cf. *Ibid.*, 3 and also "Theology and Mission," 66: "The history of missions has shown, that we are always in danger either [of] overemphasiz[ing] the 'already' or [of] lay[ing] too much stress [on] the 'not yet.' [In] doing the first, we forget that. . .'all things,' are to be united 'in Him. . . .' On the other hand, [if] we overemphasize the 'not yet,' we are in danger [of being in too much of an] eschatological hurry."

[167]Cf. *IZW*, 70 (*ISM*, 62).

3.2. The Definition of Mission

Through the years, Bavinck provided four definitions of mission that incorporate the aspects discussed above. These definitions are presented seriatim in this section with a view to ascertaining whether and, if so, to what extent they show development and shifts in accent. On one point, in any case, there is a clear correspondence among them: they are all ecclesiocentric in nature.

OZB (1941) opens with the sentence: "Mission is that activity of the Church by which it preaches the gospel of God's grace to all nations in joyful and humble obedience to the command of Christ."[168] The emphasis here falls entirely on the grace of God provided for sinners and thus on personal conversion and reconciliation, which makes this definition both *theocentric* and *soteriocentric*. The adjectives "joyful" and "humble" point to the *spirituality of faith* as an essential element for all missionary activity.

In *ZWN* (1947) Bavinck modified the above formulation as follows: "Mission is that activity of Jesus Christ by which he, in his church and through his church, makes himself known to all nations and incorporates them into the abundance and splendor of His redemptive work."[169]   This definition is *Christocentrically* focused. It is clearly a fruit of continuing reflection on the biblical-theological aspects of mission. The missionary task of the church is primarily anchored in the *missio Dei*. The phrase "in his church and through his church" point to the *centripetal* and *centrifugal* aspects of the missionary calling. Moreover, the term "the abundance and splendor of His redemptive work," which cautiously allows room for a broader conception of salvation and its ultimate fulfilment, shows that this definition is less soteriocentric in nature than the earlier one.

In his article "Zendingsbegrip en zendingswerkelijkheid" (1949) Bavinck gave the following definition:

> Mission is that activity of the church throughout the whole world—which in deepest essence is an activity of Christ himself—through which it calls the nations in their diversity to faith in and obedience to Jesus Christ, demonstrates to them by the signs of [its] service and ministry how the salvation of Christ encompasses all of life, and at the same time teaches them to look forward to the perfection of the Kingdom, in which God will be all and in all.[170]

This is the most detailed definition given by Bavinck in that it incorporates, in a carefully balanced way, the above-mentioned four elements that constitute the essence of the missionary task: it points emphatically to the *Christocentric, ecclesiocentric, comprehensive* and *eschatological* nature of mission. In addition, two further important aspects are included in this definition: the *ecumenical* ("the church throughout the whole world") and *pluriform* ("the nations in their diversity") character of missionary work.

We find the fourth definition in *IZW*:

---

[168]*OZB*, 5.

[169]*ZWN*, 5.

[170]"Zendingsbegrip en zendingswerkelijkheid," 7-8.

Mission is that activity of the church—which is in essence nothing other than the great activity of Christ himself, exercised through his church—by which the church, in the period of the postponement of the end, calls the nations to conversion and faith in Christ, in order that they may be made into His disciples and be incorporated by baptism in the community of those who expect the coming of the Kingdom.[171]

In principle this definition does not differ from the preceding one, although the ecumenical and pluriform aspects have been omitted. The formulation "the postponement of the end"—quite understandable from Bavinck's perspective—is exegetically open to question, but it does safeguard the *heilsgeschichtliche* place of mission. Incorporation by baptism is introduced as a new element, which makes this definition even more strongly ecclesiocentric than the earlier ones. Another difference between the previous definition and this one is that in the latter the comprehensive character of mission, though implicitly present in the concept of discipleship, is not explicitly referred to. This could have potentially led to a narrower understanding of the essence of the missionary task, which is something Bavinck himself in his reflection on the approach to mission expressly warns against.[172]

3.3. Summary

If the first, limited definition above is left out of consideration, one discovers no fundamental shifts in Bavinck's thinking regarding the nature of mission. This conclusion is supported by the fact that Bavinck himself never makes critical references to earlier definitions. Apparently he saw himself moving along a consistent trajectory. What *is* evident is that he engaged in ongoing reflection and further refinement of his thought in this regard. This led him to lay increasing emphasis on the eschatological focus and the comprehensive character of mission.

A second observation that can be made is that the doxological element seems at first blush to be somewhat underdeveloped in Bavincks's definitions of mission. This would be inconsistent with Bavinck's view on the purpose of mission, which he formulated, following Gisbertus Voetius, as *conversio gentilium* (conversion of the nations), *plantatio ecclesiae* (planting of the church), and *gloria et manifestatio gratiae divinae* (the glorification and revelation of divine grace). There is, however, good reason to assume that Bavinck did indeed take the doxological element into account, for when he speaks of "the glorification of God" as the ultimate, single objective of mission, he describes this as "the coming and the extension of God's kingdom" in which the main thing at stake is "God, his glory, his greatness, and his grace."[173] And this element is stated explicitly in the last two definitions.

Finally it is striking that Bavinck did not explicitly link mission and the doctrine of election, as did Middelburg (1896) following Voetius, who defended the thesis that mission takes place with an eye to the *conversio electorum* (conversion

---

[171]*IZW*, 70 (cf. *ISM*, 62).

[172]Cf. *IZW*, 118 (*ISM*, 113-14).

[173]*IZW*, 157 (cf. *ISM*, 155).

of the elect).[174] In Bavinck's view mission must be viewed as standing squarely within the framework of God's eternal plan for the redemption of this world, whereby the church, as the object of election, is called to serve the counsel of God. In this respect Bavinck's thinking was more in line with that of Walter Holsten[175] and other Protestant missiologists and with the concept of *missio Dei* that emerged from the International Missionary Conference in Willingen (1952) than with the resolutions of the Synod of Middelburg.

4. Chapter Summary

In contrast to what G. Warneck taught on the matter, Bavinck grounded mission exclusively in the biblical witness. The missionary burden of the Old Testament lies especially in the fact that the God of Israel is the creator of all peoples; in the covenant with Abraham; and in the prophetic universal promise of salvation. Old Testament centripetal expectation is brought to centrifugal fruition in the New Testament—particularly owing to the Jewish rejection of Jesus as the Christ—in the calling to proclaim the crucified and risen Christ to all nations (including Israel). This mandate, which is carried out in the so-called time between the times, is charged with Trinitarian dynamics and construed in ecclesiocentric terms.

With respect to the nature of mission Bavinck set down five fundamental premises.

1. Mission is God's work. It is above all *theologically* determined: it is from God and turns back to God. Its foundation is the *missio Dei*. And the ultimate purpose of mission is doxology and *gloria Dei*.

2. Mission is a task of the church. It takes place *ecclesiocentrically*. The triune God acts in the world, including Israel, in principle by means of the church. Although mission does not exhaust the meaning of the church and the church is not a function of the apostolate, the church loses its significance in the world when it does not exercise this missionary function.

3. Mission is the proclamation of Christocracy or the rule of Christ. It is always *christological* in nature, for Christ is preeminently the Sent One from the Father, the true Israel in whom God provides salvation for this world. In him the Kingdom of God is realized. He is therefore also the axis around which the content of mission coalesces. Extrapolating from this fundamental orientation toward Christ, mission can only be understood as a prophetic proclamation of the Kingdom of God, in which the priestly aspect of reconciliation with God and the kingly aspect of the renewal of existence go hand in hand.

4. Mission takes place in *eschatological* perspective: it is fulfilled in expectation of the breakthrough of the Kingdom that has come, that is to say, in the field of tension between the "already" and "not yet."

5. Missionary praxis is *pneumatologically* determined. The work that God accomplishes in Christ is realized through the Spirit who has been poured out. This applies to the missionary subject as well as to the missionary object.

It is on these principles that Bavinck predicated his definition of mission as that activity of the community of believers—which endeavor in reality is nothing

---

[174]Cf. H.A. van Andel, *De zendingsleer van Gisbertus Voetius*, 62ff, and Extract from the *Acta der generale Synode* (Middelburg, 1896), 31

[175]Cf. W. Holsten, *Das Evangelium und die Völker*, 156.

more or less than the great work of Christ himself operating through his church—whereby it calls the peoples of the earth, during the period of the delay of the *eschaton*, to repentance and faith in Christ with a view to their discipleship of Him and their membership through baptism in the *koinonia* of those who are in expectation of the coming of the Kingdom.

CHAPTER SEVEN

Missionary Aims and Approaches

> God takes us and [those to whom the message is addressed]
> seriously and we as servants of God must do that too. . . . I must
> bring the message of God's grace in Jesus Christ to . . . real
> people immersed in the actual circumstances of their lives. But
> then it is obvious that I would make a grave mistake if I did not
> take their culture and history seriously. *(IZW,* 87)

1. The Addressees of Mission

In the context of his definition of the essence of mission, Bavinck refers in *IZW* to
a threefold division of missionary activity that had long prevailed: (1) Mission
among unbelievers ("heathen") and Muslims; (2) mission among the Jews; and (3)
evangelism.[1] For Bavinck it is so self-evident that the first point, "mission among
unbelievers and Muslims," belongs to the essence of the missionary task that he
does not pursue it further. Reflection on the distinction between "unbelievers" and
"Muslims" therefore is also absent from *IZW.* In what follows the question will be
posed whether he elaborates on this question in other publications. In *IZW* he does
discuss the other two points: "Mission among the Jews" and "Evangelism." Thus,
from a systematic perspective he did strive for comprehensiveness, but in terms of
content his reflection remained rather limited.[2] Dialogue with people of other faiths
as such is in any case completely absent.

1.1. Mission among Unbelievers and Muslims

As stated above, Bavinck formally adopts the term "mission among unbelievers and
Muslims" without further substantive discussion. It looks as if the distinction, once

---

[1]*IZW*, 78 (cf. *ISM,* 69)

[2]Bavinck devotes only five pages to mission among the Jews (*IZW,* 78-82;
cf. *ISM,* 69-74) and a mere two pages to evangelism (*IZW,* 82-84; cf. *ISM,* 74-76).
However, he did write, a series of articles on the latter topic under the title "Zending
en evangelisatie" in *HZB*, 42 (1944): 3, 12, 19, 35, 42. One has the impression that
in *IZW* he merely gives a summary of these articles.

made, has no further significance.[3] This conclusion is justified by the fact that nowhere in his other publications does Bavinck appear to make an essential distinction between the missionary mandate as it relates to Islam on the one hand and other non-Christian religions on the other. Both in his first missionary-elenctic publication *CMO* (1934) and in the posthumously published *CBTM* (1966) he discusses and approaches Islam as one of the world religions alongside Buddhism and Hinduism.[4] It is not unthinkable that this equal treatment is related in part to the fact that Bavinck dealt with the religions, including Islam, especially from a morphological perspective.

1.2. Mission among the Jews

In his biblical-theological reflections Bavinck already discussed the position of the Jewish people in the NT.[5] From this flows the question to what extent and how the missionary mandate of the church also applies to Israel. His discussion is more groping and searching than certain and sure. He sees two lines that intersect.

The first line is that there is no essential difference between mission among the nations and mission among Israel. In both Luke 24:47 and Acts 1:8, Jerusalem and the nations are mentioned in one breath as the aim of the missionary mandate. In Matt. 28:19 Israel is not even mentioned separately. Israel apparently is simply part of the world, distinguished only by chronological priority. This priority is fully honored in the apostolic missionary practices. The question here was "to what extent the Jews, both in and outside the land of Israel, affirmed and approved of the official sentence of their Supreme Court. If they did not, and did accept Christ as their Redeemer, then they belonged in Him to that true Israel around which God wanted to build his Church of all ages."[6] This temporal priority did not bring with it, however, a more prominent place in the church for the Christians of Jewish origin. Paul's argument in Rom. 1-3 is clear on this point. The chronological priority has long since become inoperative, and Israel is now simply one of the nations of the world to whom the gospel must be preached.[7]

The second line is that Israel remains the nation of God's redemptive promises. On the one hand Bavinck sees these promises fulfilled in Christ and in that portion of Israel that has accepted Jesus as the Christ, from Pentecost up to the present time.

> We see that the NT views the outpouring of the Holy Spirit on the Day of Pentecost, and the conversion of numerous children

---

[3] This is apparent also from the fact that as early as 1945 Bavinck criticized the distinction derived from Voetius and adopted by A. Kuyper. Cf. *De zending nu!*

[4] We find the same approach in *IZW*, 248ff (cf. *ISM*, 264ff), where Bavinck discusses the "outline of elenctics."

[5] See also section 2.3.4 in the previous chapter; some overlap with that section is unavoidable here.

[6] *IZW*, 79 (cf. *ISM*, 71)

[7] *IZM*, 78-79 (cf. *ISM*, 71).

of Israel that followed, as a fulfillment of the promises of that conversion given in the OT. On the day of Pentecost Peter openheartedly quotes the well-known words of Joel. The conversion of Israel, predicted by Isaiah and Jeremiah and by all the prophets, *has* taken place, has become a reality centered in the Christ.[8]

On the other hand he realizes, especially in light of Rom. 11:25-26, that it is possible "that God still has remarkable plans for this nation."[9] At the intersection of these two lines the necessity of mission among Israel is intensified because of the promise that is as yet unfulfilled. Bavinck states it in these words: "From all this, then, it appears that beside mission among the other nations, mission among Israel also calls for our complete attention. Israel has no priority, no precedence, but neither must it be forgotten."[10]

Bavinck remains extremely cautious in interpreting the founding of the State of Israel in 1948.

> Although there are in the return of numerous children of Israel from various countries to the present State of Israel many elements that are strikingly similar to what the ancient prophets said, it is nevertheless possible that, viewed spiritually, [this return] is in essence something completely different, something that lies entirely outside the horizon of prophecy.[11]

Earlier he had even written rather negatively about it and had called the founding of the state an extra obstacle to fruitful missionary work.[12] On the other hand there are, according to him, so many indications in prophecy that a return to the land from the Diaspora and true conversion will go hand in hand that we "can put forward the possibility that God will use this new gathering of the nation of Israel in the ancient land as a means to a new, spiritual flowering."[13] His conclusion is, "Therefore Mission among the people of Israel remains ... an extremely important event, and we await with reverence what God will do with it."[14]

---

[8] *IZM,* 81 (cf. *ISM,* 73).

[9] *IZM,* 82 (cf. *ISM,* 74).

[10] *Ibid.*

[11] *IZM,* 81 (cf. *ISM,* 72-73).

[12] "Overal, behalve in Israel." Bavinck approached this matter not only theologically but also sociologically: mission would have a difficult time of it in the face of "interpretation of prophecies in a purely worldly form," and "religious patriotism"; see G.J. van Klinken, 532.

[13] *IZW,* 81 (cf. *ISM,* 73).

[14] *Ibid.* The RCN became actively engaged in mission to the Jews in Israel in 1916 when Rev. J. Nes was sent out. In 1957, when Bavinck wrote this, the number involved in mission among Jewish people had grown to four. (Cf. H. Bergema, 46.)

Unfortunately Bavinck says nothing about how this missionary task of the church vis-à-vis Israel should be understood. Did this perhaps lie too far outside his purview? He seems to make very little, if any, substantial distinction between the task of the church among the Jewish people and the missionary mandate as it relates to the nations. It is, however, difficult to imagine that a sensitive person like Bavinck would fail to make such a distinction. There is in any case a brief but significant indication that points in a different direction. In a footnote Bavinck refers, without comment, to a publication by J.J. Grolle, then secretary of the NRC Council on Church and Israel, which argues that with respect to the Jewish people the missionary task should take the form of witnessing dialogue.[15] And in light of this one may assume that he followed with approval the postwar development in the RCN, whereby the term "mission to the Jews" was replaced by "proclamation of the Gospel among the people of Israel," to indicate that the relationship of the church to Israel must be dialogical in nature, but also that the term "dialogue with Israel" includes communication of the gospel of Jesus the Messiah.[16]

1.3. The Work of Evangelism

Bavinck begins with a definition: "As a rule we understand *evangelism* to mean work among the members of the covenant who have strayed, to bring them back to the Lord Christ and to his church,"adding, though, that

> It is difficult to say where the line should be drawn, because we
> do not know who belongs to the covenant. Yet there always
> remains a certain difference between the work that is carried out
> in a land where the gospel has never been preached before and
> that which is done in a land that has already lived for many
> centuries under the influence of the gospel.[17]

Thus, he makes a clear distinction between mission and evangelism, which he summarizes as follows: mission has to do with the "not yet," evangelism with the "no longer."[18]

However, this definition of terms cannot be derived from biblical linguistic usage, according to Bavinck. The verb *euaggelizesthai* (proclaiming the gospel), which is found frequently in the NT and from which the word *evangelism* is

---

[15]See *IZW,* 81 n.20 (cf. *ISM,* 73 n.20). In support of the drafting of art. VIII of the NRC Church Order of 1951 Grolle wrote: "As a community of faith that confesses Christ and is placed in the world, the church fulfills her apostolic mandate especially through her dialogue with Israel. In this dialogue the church addresses the synagogue and all who belong to the chosen people to declare to them from the Holy Scriptures that Jesus is the Christ."

[16]Cf. J. Verkuyl, *Inleiding in de nieuwere zendingswetenschap,* 189.

[17]*IZW,* 82 (cf. *ISM,* 74).

[18]*IZM,* 84 (cf. *ISM,* 76). J. Verkuyl, *Inleiding in the evangelistiek,* 69-70, gives a brief summary of Bavinck's views on this matter.

derived, is not used in the narrower sense of evangelism, but in a general sense.[19] Nor can the distinction itself be derived directly from the Scriptures. On the one hand Bavinck draws a parallel between evangelism and the preaching of the prophets, of Jesus, and of the apostles to the apostate and strayed among Israel, because that preaching also contained an element of a call to return to a life lived out of the covenant of God. On the other hand he points to the essential difference, namely, that that preaching also always involved a continuing self-revelation of God.[20] There are other objections to a too-facile identification of evangelism with proclamation of the gospel among Jews and of mission with that among unbelievers. First of all, in many cases the NT witnesses were not faced with Jews who had turned their back on the faith of the fathers but rather with those who rigidly clung to that faith.[21] Furthermore, the apostles came in contact with paganized Jews who were farther removed from God than were the gentile converts to Judaism.[22] The work sphere of the church back then thus included all kinds of nuances, and the proclamation of the gospel was in principle understood as one great work, flowing from the one calling of Christ.[23] It is precisely this fundamental principle that must, according to Bavinck, be applied to the missionary task of the church today in mission *and* evangelism: Mission and evangelism both flow from the same calling by Christ and are both expressions of the merciful love that reaches out to all who are as sheep without a shepherd.[24] He adds that in this one calling evangelism even has priority, because it involves people who "live in the same place, who in the past belonged to the same church, who in part still bear the mark of baptism on their forehead and who are therefore to a high degree still our responsibility."[25]

Although from a biblical perspective there is no difference between mission and evangelism, there is a definite difference in approach, since in evangelism we deal with people who sometimes still have knowledge of the covenant and in general still somehow have awareness of the Christian message.[26] These people have a greater responsibility to respond to the gospel, and the proclamation will have to be brought to them "with greater emphasis and force. . . . They can be addressed from within the covenant and exhorted to turn back to Him

---

[19]Cf. *IZM,* 83 (*ISM,* 74-75) and "Zending en evangelisatie," 3.

[20]Cf. *IZM,* 83 (*ISM,* 75) and "Zending en evangelisatie," 3.

[21]Cf. "Zending en evangelisatie," 13.

[22]Cf. *Ibid.,* 3.

[23]Cf. *Ibid.,* 4.

[24]Cf. *IZW,* 84 (*ISM,* 76).

[25]"Zending en evangelisatie," 19.

[26]Cf. *ibid.*

on whom they turned their back."[27] At the same time, this difference should not be unduly exaggerated.

Bavinck then makes a distinction between the objective meaning of the covenant and that which people still know about it subjectively. Even though individuals belong to the "seed of the believers," they themselves can have "so broken away from all religious conviction" that it is scarcely possible to call them to account concerning the covenant, wrote Bavinck, adding, however, that it "is altogether incorrect to think that all those who have strayed have turned their backs deliberately on the church. Innumerable people have never been in a church and know virtually nothing of the basic truths of the gospel."[28] Besides this problem of increasing estrangement from the Christian faith in the West, the church is often faced with virulent prejudices in evangelism and mission, "a deep-seated distrust of Christianity, both in the East and in the West, as a result of all manner of negative experiences people have had with Christianity."[29] As de-Christianization progresses, due to "the process of secularization and the emphasis on pragmatism in our modern world," evangelism will increasingly acquire the character of missionary work. Bavinck was well aware of and closely followed the process of the degeneration of the West into a mission field.[30] And this development, he contended, bore methodological consequences, namely, that the point of departure for mission in the West must be found in secularized reality, with a view to finding a way to confront that reality, if only gropingly, with the message of the gospel—a message that concerns on the one hand "all the questions of the human heart," yet on the other hand is "not according to man." This means that one must always work, via the word that judges and redeems, toward conversion as a break with the past and a new beginning.[31]

1.4. Summary

At the end of this discussion we return to Bavinck's question: to what extent do "Mission among unbelievers and Muslims," "Mission among Jews," and "Evangelism" belong to the essence of mission? We can draw the following conclusions.

The Islamic peoples are included in the missionary mandate in the same way as are other non-Christian peoples. Although this view is defensible in

---

[27] *IZW,* 83 (cf. *ISM,* 75). In this connection Bavinck points out that Paul "in his preaching to the Gentiles ... is milder, more searching, more cautiously probing than when he faces the children of the Covenant."

[28] *IZM,* 83-84 (cf. *ISM,* 75-76); "Zending en evangelisatie," 19, 13.

[29] Cf. *IZM,* 84 (*ISM,* 76) and "Zending en evangelisatie," 35.

[30] *De mens van nu,* published posthumously, is a telling testimony of this, cf. esp. 38-47.

[31] "Zending en evangelisatie," 43.

principle, it is open to question to what extent it can be maintained in practice.[32]

By declaring that since its official rejection of Jesus as the Christ Israel has become a nation among the nations, the proclamation of the gospel among the Jews is obviously part of mission. When Bavinck speaks of "the nations" in the definition of the essence of mission, this is inclusive of Israel. The only difference is that God's immutable promises concerning Israel give the call to mission to this nation a special emphasis. In this way Bavinck aligned himself with an earlier perspective that was current in the RCN until the 1950s and that tended toward 'displacement' theology,[33] which has since been radically altered.[34] Without denying the missionary calling of the church in relation to Israel, it must be said that in light of Rom. 9-11 the church's relationship to Israel is more mysterious than its relationship to other nations: the missionary relationship is different ("grafted into the same tree"), the missionary method is at the very least more modest ("stimulating to jealousy"), the missionary *kairos* is more hidden ("hardening until the fullness of the Gentiles has come in"), and the missionary fruit is more promising from the start ("all Israel shall be saved").

The answer to the question to what extent the work of evangelism belongs to the essence of mission is twofold: there is an essential agreement between mission and evangelism in that both are rooted in the *missio Dei*; and there is an essential difference with respect to the theological position of the object (outside or inside the covenant). However, Verkuyl rightly states that, due to the steady advance of secularization, for Bavinck the boundaries between mission and evangelism gradually faded.[35] His thinking in this respect was closely aligned with the missiological development of that era, which at the 1963 World Mission Conference in Mexico City led to the concept of "Mission in six continents." Bavinck himself did not refer to this, however.

2. The Goal of Mission

The discussion Bavinck devotes to the goal of mission is brief.[36] The content is not very surprising, because he closely aligns himself with the threefold goal of mission

---

[32]At present this matter is once again the focus of much discussion within the RCN. Cf. H. Mintjes, 157ff.

[33]Cf. G. J. van Klinken, 463.

[34]Cf. J. Verkuyl, *Inleiding in de nieuwere zendingswetenschap*, 186, for example, who submitted that because Jews and Christians are included in the same covenant of God, not only the *method* of witness employed by Christians among Jewish people but also the entire *relationship* between them must be dialogical.

[35]J. Verkuyl, *Inleiding in de evangelistiek*, 69-70, discusses Bavinck's view on the relationship between mission and evangelism under the term "synchronization."

[36]Cf. *IZW*, 157-161 (*ISM*, 155-159), *ZWN*, 27-28, 41. J. Verkuyl, *Inleiding in de evangelistiek*, 38, incorrectly states that Bavinck has written "extensively" on this topic.

formulated by Voetius: *conversio gentilium, mohammedistarum et judaeorum* (conversion of unbelievers, Muslims, and Jews), *plantatio ecclesiae aut ecclesiarum* (planting of the church or of churches), and *gloria et manifestatio gratiae divinae* (glorification and revelation of the divine grace).[37] In *ZWN* Bavinck does not yet mention Voetius. He refers to the declarations of the Synod of Middelburg (1896), where the goal of all mission is formulated as "glorification of God's Name," which is "manifest most clearly there where it [the work of mission] leads to the salvation of lost people" but is achieved also "even where it leads to hardening of the heart."[38] He then adopts almost verbatim[39] the opening sentence of J.C. Gilhuis' 1940 study on the missionary task of the church:

> We understand mission to mean the spiritual labor the church must carry out at the command of Christ, to proclaim the gospel among non-Christian nations, to plant His Church, and thus to claim the whole life of those nations to the glory of God's Name.[40]

This may mean that Bavinck did not really study Voetius's missiology, or H.A. van Andel's study of Voetius, until a later stage.

Bavinck interprets the threefold goal formulated by Voetius in his own way, by stating that they are three aspects of the one mighty purpose of God, namely, the coming and spread of the Kingdom of God. "That coming of God is about his glory, his greatness, and his grace. That coming includes the spread of the church over the whole earth. And that coming is realized in the conversion of sinners."[41] Bavinck examines the three aspects in this order (which is formally the inverse of that of Voetius's), which is also the order in which they are discussed here.

In this section of *IZW* (1954) Bavinck also discusses the relationship of church and nation, accommodation, and *possessio*. These topics fit in my opinion better under the approach to mission and the praxis of mission. In the present work they are therefore discussed under those headings. [See section 8.1]

2.1. The Glory of God

In the OT we find, according to Bavinck, the continual longing among Israel that the name of YHWH will receive honor among the nations (Num. 14:16; Ps. 72:17; Ps. 83:19; Hab. 2:14; Ez. 38:23). On the one hand Bavinck acknowledges that this longing does not always stand in a missionary perspective: "Only extremely rarely does the tone of compassion for those who are lost find expression in ancient Israel

---

[37]Cf. H.A. van Andel, *De zendingsleer van Gisbertus Voetius*, 141-150.

[38]*ZWN*, 41. Cf. Extract from the *Acta of the Generale Synode de* GKN (Middelburg, 1896), 22.

[39]Cf. *ZWN*, 41.

[40]J.C. Gilhuis, *De zendingstaak der kerk*, 7; Bavinck wrote a preface to this study and thus was well acquainted with it.

[41]*IZW*, 157-58 (cf. *ISM*, 155).

…"[42] But on the other hand he reads Ez. 38:23 ("I will show my greatness and my holiness, and I will make myself known in the sight of many nations. Then they will know that I am the Lord") as expressing the goal of mission. More persuasive than his citing of these Bible texts is his pointing to the basic OT pattern, which inseparably joins the eschatological revelation of God's Kingdom and the glorification of YHWH on earth: "all harsh dissonants of the alarming play that we call world history will resolve themselves, and all shall end in that sublime symphony of the Kingdom of the Most High."[43] Bavinck, incidentally, does not further substantiate this thesis on the basis of scriptural data, stating only that all "the prophets of the Old Testament speak, each in his own key, of the indescribably great outcome of God's mighty works."[44]

In the NT also, according to Bavinck, what matters in the coming of the Kingdom is worldwide praise to God. "Certainly," he writes, "the Kingdom includes peace, salvation for all who partake of it, but that is not where the primary accent lies; the accent falls much more on the fact that it is the Kingdom of God," which one day will be "the only safe haven, the only rest."[45] In support of this view, Bavinck mentions only two Scripture references that refer to the eschatological breakthrough of the Kingdom, viz., Eph. 1:10-11 and 1 Cor. 15:24-25, 28.

With this approach Bavinck shifts the *gloria Dei* rather one-sidedly to the future. It is precisely his view—which agreed with that of Voetius[46]—that in essence the glorification of God takes on form in the realization of Christ's salvation in human lives that could provide perspective for the provisional realization of the *gloria Dei* in the present.

Striking is further that in *IZW* Bavinck no longer makes any reference to the declarations of the Synod of Middelburg, which state that the glorification of God's Name as the highest goal of missionary work is accomplished in two ways: when the message is accepted and when it is rejected. Apparently he now—without mentioning this shift—aligned himself entirely with H.A. van Andel, who concluded that Voetius applied the principle of *gloria et manifestatio gratiae divinae* (glorification and revelation of divine grace) exclusively to the *collectio et salus electorum* (gathering together and salvation of the elect).[47]

---

[42]*IZW*, 158 (cf. *ISM,* 156).

[43]*IZW*, 158-159 (cf. *ISM,* 156-157).

[44]*IZW*, 159 (cf. *ISM,* 157).

[45]*IZW*, 159-160 (cf. *ISM,* 157).

[46]Cf. H.A. van Andel, *De zendingsleer van Gisbertus Voetius*, 150.

[47]Cf. H.A. van Andel, *De zendingsleer van Gisbertus Voetius,* 150, who shows the difference between the thinking of Voetius and that of the Synod of Middelburg. Cf. also J. Verkuyl, *Contemporary Missiology,* 184, who maintains that Voetius "put all his emphasis on the glory of God who was disclosing his liberating grace and on the praise which was due him for extending that grace." J. Klapwijk's supposition, 16-17, that Bavinck here "disposes of" judgment is untenable: Bavinck merely follows Voetius's lead. J. Kruidhof, 11ff., provides a

2.2. Church Planting

The second goal, which serves the first, is the spread and planting of the church as the provisional manifestation of the Kingdom of God:

> Christ himself already said that in the present dispensation he will build his *ecclesia*, his church, on the *petra* of the confession that he is the Christ (Matt. 16:18). . . . The main point is that we see that, in preparation of the ultimate glorious coming of the Kingdom, God gathers a church for himself from all parts of the world.[48]

In the church believers experience a renewed fellowship with God and with one another:

> All the various divisions and contrasts that have such far-reaching significance in daily life in this world are no longer of any value [in the church], there is "no Greek or Jew, circumcised or uncircumcised, barbarian, Scythian, slave or free," because "Christ is all, and is in all" (Col. 3:11).[49]

Later Bavinck described this renewed fellowship as pneumatocentric.[50]

This goal of *plantatio ecclesiae* transcends that of the conversion of human beings, because "an essential element of all true salvation is solidarity with others."[51] He argues this point on the basis of the NT data only, without any reference to the OT. The church is the body of Christ into which everyone who believes is incorporated (Eph. 1:23), or—using a different metaphor—a building, a temple into which believers are fit (Eph. 2:20-22).[52] Mission is therefore called to give concrete shape to the formation of congregations and the establishment of churches.[53] This necessity is underlined by the biblical reality that only we, "together with all the saints," are able "to grasp how wide and long and high and deep is the love of Christ, and to know this love that surpasses knowledge (Eph.

---

more nuanced analysis by referring to the limited place judgment as ultimate condemnation of unbelief occupies in Bavinck's theology.

[48]*IZW*, 160 (cf. *ISM*, 158). Cf. also *GGNT*, 676, where Bavinck states that "in these 'last days' the Kingdom of Christ reveals itself as *ekklesia*, as Church."

[49]*IZM*, 160 (cf. *ISM*, 158).

[50]Cf. *IGHG*, 87ff.

[51]*IZW*, 161 (cf. *ISM*, 159).

[52]*IZM*, 160 (cf. *ISM*, 159). Cf. *ZWN*, 28: "In his work Paul also addresses individuals, but he nevertheless immediately keeps the larger goal in mind: the establishing of churches of Christ. He views the convert immediately as a member of the church as the body of Christ, the church that will spread over the whole world."

[53]*IZM*, 160 (cf. *ISM*, 158). *ZWN*, 27.

3:18-19).[54]

Bavinck is at variance with his own view of the nature of mission when he expresses himself in such strongly ecclesiocentric terms that he limits the coming of the Kingdom of God to church planting. It is all the more surprising that Bavinck presents this in *IZW* (1954), since he himself, in his earlier *ICNCW* (1948), criticized a too-one-sided ecclesiocentrism: "Others have described the purpose of the missionary enterprise as the planting of the Church, the *plantatio ecclesiae*. But does not the church have within itself the irresistible imperative to subject the whole of its environment to the will of God? Is it not her constant desire to set God's will as a norm in science and art, in politics and social relationships? Is there not latent in the church a permanent tendency to proclaim the Kingdom of God in this world?"[55] This passage shows that he did indeed have an eye for the broader objective: although salvation is not realized apart from the church, neither should it be realized only *in* the church. It would appear that in de *IZW* (1954) Bavinck, without further reflection, adopted the ecclesiocentrism of Voetius.[56]

2.3. Human Conversion

Necessarily implicit in the expansion of the church lies the third goal: the conversion of people everywhere. Without explicitly providing a foundation for this goal on the basis of the OT and/or NT witness—perhaps because it is obvious—Bavinck describes the matter itself as follows: "A complete letting go of the old, of the servitude to sin, and a giving oneself with heart and soul to Christ—that is conversion viewed from a human perspective. The event itself is naturally infinitely greater and richer. It is a being torn away from the 'power of darkness' and a being 'brought … into the kingdom of the Son he loves' (Col. 1:13). It is a being incorporated into Christ and thereby being buried with him in his death and being raised to a new life. It is a radical change, so that one becomes a "new creature": "the old things passed away; behold, new things have come" (2 Cor. 5:17)."[57] Reaching this goal thus very clearly involves a work of God, which he does in people's lives and in which we may be involved as "coworkers with God."[58] It is precisely this theocentric point of departure that again and again provides the motivation to fulfill the missionary mandate with expectancy.

2.4. Summary

Bavinck uses a formulation of goal that is derived from Voetius, a formulation that defines the goal primarily doxologically (or theocentrically), ecclesiocentrically,

---

[54]*IZM*, 161 (cf. *ISM*, 159).

[55]*ICNCW*, 31.

[56]For this ecclesiocentrism of Voetius, cf. J. A. B. Jongeneel, "Voetius' zendingstheologie," 145.

[57]*IZW*, 161 (cf. *ISM*, 159).

[58]*IZW*, 160 (cf. *ISM*, 159).

and soteriocentrically and that also has an eschatological orientation. The connection with what he has said about the essence of mission is obvious.

However, his discussion as a whole would have gained in consistency if Bavinck had thought through the threefold goal more fully from the perspective of the central concept of the coming Kingdom of God—in other words, if he had more clearly correlated ecclesiocentrism and basileiocentrism. Given his earlier statement on the topic in *ICNCW* this would have been logical. It would have provided a closer correlation between the essence and goal of mission, especially the Christological aspect, than is now the case. Furthermore, he could have indicated more clearly the tension inherent in the connection between the second and third goal, between 'already' and 'not yet.'

Finally, the question can be raised cautiously whether in the framework of a Reformed missiology the duality of the glory of God, as it was expressed at Middelburg (1896), can simply be ignored.

3. Missionary Approaches

In *IZW* a chapter on the approaches to mission follows immediately after the chapter on the biblical foundation of mission. In our discussion of Bavinck's view on missionary approach we will follow the main methodological and theological lines he himself drew. The first of these is the primacy of theology as well as the importance of other disciplines to this reflection. In line with Voetius, Bavinck adduces four questions essential to any reflection on missionary approach: to whom, by whom, when, and where the message is brought. He demonstrates the biblical legitimacy of these interrogatives and further elaborates them from the perspectives of ethnology, anthropology, sociology, and psychology.[59] Next, we trace the biblical-theological argumentation[60] he used in support of his proposed twofold understanding of approach: that in the broader *comprehensive* sense, and that in the narrower *kerygmatic* sense. After this, these two forms of approach are discussed in the order just mentioned. Bavinck prefers this order because proclamation is, in his view, always a piece of something bigger. He writes that in the course of missionary history there was a common "naive misapprehension" that all that mattered was proclamation; it was only later that the realization began to grow that proclamation is a portion of a much larger, "far more encompassing" whole, of which "the kerygmatic approach constitutes only a limited part."[61] The treatment of the kerygmatic approach can also be seen as an introduction to the next chapter in this study, dealing with elenctics.

It is important to note that Bavinck's reflection on missionary approach took place squarely in the era of decolonization. He gradually became more and

---

[59]Cf. *IZW*, 21, 88ff. (*ISM*, 6, 82-87).

[60]From a systematic perspective this argumentation fits better in the section dealing with the biblical foundation of mission; but since there is a clear development in Bavinck's line of reasoning respecting the comprehensive approach, it is being dealt with here because a discussion of this development fits better in the present context.

[61]*IZW*, 93 (cf. *ISM*, 87), cf. also *ZWN*, 48, where Bavinck states "that word and deed must continuously support one another."

more aware that this seismic shift in international political relations necessitated a new way of thinking about as well as a fresh implementation of missionary approach. In this connection he wrote:

> For the time being we still find ourselves in an interim period, the period not infrequently referred to as the period of postcolonial cramp, the cramp that comes from ruptured relationships. . . . But in the meantime the new world-era, with its threats and its opportunities, is beginning to take shape slowly. And in that new era mission will have to determine the route it's going to take. Indeed we are already busy working on that.[62]

The question can rightly be raised why, nevertheless, so much attention is given to a missionary approach that in certain respects has had its time. There are two reasons: first, to present a complete insight into Bavinck's missionary theology, and second, because Bavinck gives us principles that are worth being taken into consideration in every renewed missiological reflection occasioned by a changing context.

Finally, it may be noted that Bavinck's missiological frame of reference moves back and forth between the declarations of the 1896 Synod of Middelburg and the theme of the comprehensive approach that had been under discussion since the 1928 International Missionary Conference in Jerusalem. Beyond that his dialogue with third parties was limited.

3.1. Two Fundamental Concepts with Respect to Approach

3.1.1. The Primacy of Theology

In *IZW* Bavinck emphatically points out that we must be careful about trying to derive a practical missionary approach directly from the Bible. It would indicate shortsightedness, for example, simply to apply Paul's method unreflectively to the present.[63] Paradoxically this could even lead to an *un*biblical approach, because failure to take adequately into account the ever changing circumstances in which the missionary mandate is to be fulfilled could result in the *de facto* abrogation of the basic principles of missionary approach found in Scripture.[64] Bavinck wants to search out these principles and use them both as guideposts to and as boundary markers for an appropriate approach to mission,[65] adding, however, that this enterprise requires "great caution," because though we can extract "rich treasures"

---

[62]"Het Vasco da Gama-tijdperk." The extent to which Bavinck himself began to engage in this new reflection will be discussed below in section 3.4.

[63]*IZW*, 85 (cf. *ISM*, 79-80).

[64]Cf. *IZM*, 85-86 (*ISM*, 80), where Bavinck also states that facile conclusions drawn from apostolic missionary methods have proved to be "foolish" in contemporary situations.

[65]Cf. Herman Bavinck, "De zending in de Heilige Schrift," 30, who states that the Scriptures have not been given to us to "repeat verbatim, but in order that we might assimilate them thoughtfully and apply them in daily life."

from the biblical data, we cannot simply conclude from these what is required of us "in our time and under the circumstances in which we find ourselves."[66] It appears that he had become even more cautious here than he was in *ZWN*, where, following Roland Allen, he still adduced the method followed by the Apostle Paul as model for the approach to mission, though there, too, he warned against a simple, direct application of the Pauline method to the modern missionary situation.[67]

At the same time Bavinck protests against the idea that missionary approach involves only anthropology, ethnology, sociology, and psychology.[68] He firmly rejects this kind of secularization of the missionary method and states that, on the contrary, the "what" and the "how" of the approach to mission are inextricably linked. It is definitely not the case that theology provides the answer as long as we look at the *content* of missionary work, but that other disciplines become determinative when it comes to the *manner* of that work.[69] The content strongly determines "what we must do and what we definitely must not do."[70] This becomes all the more clear when we realize that the "what" does not involve only theory but rather a speaking by God himself (2 Cor. 5:20).[71] The work of mission is in principle a meeting "between the living Christ ... and people imprisoned in all kinds of foolish thoughts."[72] The approach must therefore be at all times an expression "of his love, of his unfathomable mercy. The *how* must be such that Christ recognizes himself in it."[73] Although Bavinck only mentions this in passing, he puts forward the incarnation as the most cardinal argument: "The revelation of God never kept floating somewhere at a distance, has never come down to us as a general truth, but has entered into our history, has taken on bodily form 'and dwelt among us.' Because the incarnation of the Word is the heart of revelatory history,

---

[66]"De zendingsmethode van Paulus," 99.

[67]Cf. *ZWN*, 20ff.

[68]Though Bavinck mentions no names here, it is possible that he was thinking of B. Gutmann's *Volksorganische* method (with respect to approach mission should take its cue from indigenous culture), and C. Keysser's *Volkspaedagogische* method (the method of mission should be derived from the indigenous context), both of which he challenged; cf. *IZW*, 124, 138, 163 (*ISM*, 119, 135, 161) and *ZWN*, 183, 186-187.

[69]*IZW*, 85-86 (cf. *ISM*, 80).

[70]*IZM*, 87 (cf. *ISM*, 81).

[71]Cf. *BBO*, 7-15, where Bavinck, albeit in a very different context, developed this idea in a masterly manner.

[72]*IZW*, 87-88 (cf. *ISM*, 82).

[73]*IZM*, 88 (cf. *ISM*, 82).

revelation always has the character of a living, concrete encounter."[74]

How does theology relate to anthropology, ethnology, sociology, and psychology?[75] On the one hand theology gives these disciplines ample room to function because it is convinced that there are no

> abstract, incorporeal, and ahistorical sinners [but only] concrete sinners, whose sinful life is, among other factors, determined by various cultural and historical factors, by poverty, hunger, superstition, tradition, chronic illness, tribal customs, and a thousand other things.[76]

On the other hand, theology limits the use and application of these disciplines. With a reference to Karl Barth[77] Bavinck says that theology will always "raise an admonishing finger and warn that the purity of the gospel must not be sacrificed to the desire to come as close to one's audience as possible."[78]

3.1.2. A Two-fold Approach

Bavinck calls the assumption that in the approach to mission everything revolves only around proclamation a "naive illusion"[79] Both in the light of Scripture and from praxis it appears that the missionary approach is always involved with the totality of existence. The kerygmatic approach is always preceded by and ever accompanied by the comprehensive approach, which finds expression in individual behaviors and in collective forms of assistance and development.[80] A clear development can be discerned in Bavinck's understanding of theological motivation.

In ZWN. Bavinck furnished a brief account of the theological argumentation in support of the position that the missionary approach is always proclamation in both word and deed. He first points to the incarnation of the Word:

---

[74]*IZM*, 89 (cf. *ISM*, 83). It is surprising that Bavinck mentions such an essential theological argument only in passing. It may show that he was often more the "practical" than the "dogmatic" missiologist.

[75]In *IZW* Bavinck does not mention sociology, but in a review of Eugene A. Nida's book *Message and Mission* it is clear that he took it into account. For this review see "Hoe de boodschap verder gaat: Sociologische aspecten in de verbreiding van het evangelie."

[76]*IZW*, 87 (cf. *ISM*, 81).

[77]K. Barth, "Die Theologie und die Mission," 189-215. My impression that Bavinck argues against Gutmann and Keysser (see note 67 above) is supported by this reference to Barth, who in this article also criticizes Gutmann and Keysser. Cf. also T. Yates, *Christian Mission in the Twentieth Century*, 49ff.

[78]*IZW*, 86 (cf. *ISM*, 80).

[79]*IZW*, 93 (cf. *ISM*, 87).

[80]Cf. *IZM*, 93-95, 98-121 (*ISM*, 87-89, 90-120) and *ZWN*, 45-46, 49-50.

"The Word did not become a 'discourse' or an 'argument,' but it became 'flesh,' that is, it appeared in our midst in truly human, living form."[81] The gospel is one witness to this, because Christ did not only embody the love of God with words but with his life. It is therefore in the nature of the Gospel that word and deed support one another. Proclamation of the gospel always implies incarnation of the message "in a life of readiness to help and of compassion."[82] He clearly indicates that it is incorrect to view these actions as merely preparatory to the proclamation. Thus the hospital is not only "the gateway to the church" but it also has "value in and of itself." All deeds are a "demonstration of charity" and are "a sermon in themselves."[83] At the same time Bavinck resists the notion that it would be sufficient to perform Christians deeds. It must always remain clear that in the demonstrating of love it is the love of Christ that is shown.[84] The deeds must never be divorced from the Word, since it is only through the Word that the deeds can be understood in their true significance.

In *MZW* Bavinck provided an interesting theological account of the significance of the Kingdom of God as the dominant motif in the history of revelation.[85] Although this is not a missiological work and the missionary approach is therefore not directly dealt with, Bavinck outlines here for the first time the ideas that are explained in more detail in later position statements in missiological publications such as *ICNCW* and the *IZW*. It is therefore appropriate to include here a summary of this account in the form of an excursus.

The idea of the Kingdom of God is the underlying motif that dominates the whole of creation.[86] From the beginning it is cosmic in nature and implies a perfect harmony, "because each moment in the great edifice of creation is at its most fundamental level oriented toward the one goal that binds everything together, reverend obedience toward the will of the Almighty.[87] The Kingdom is not intended to be static but dynamic: "contained in that Kingdom was from the beginning a call to flourish, to perfection, to an unfolding of all seeds and powers that were concealed in the whole."[88] The Kingdom realizes itself,

---

[81]*ZWN*, 48.

[82]*Ibid.*

[83]*Ibid.*, 53.

[84]*Ibid.*, 49.

[85]*De mensch en zijn wereld*, 47-66. Hints of this development are found earlier, cf. "De komst van het Godsrijk," 6-13.

[86]*De mensch en zijn wereld*, 47-49. Here Bavinck points specifically to the Psalms in which this is expressed: 95:3-5; 33:9; 19:3; 103:19-22.

[87]*ZWN*, 49.

[88]*Ibid.*, 50.

therefore, in history, in which humanity, in turn, plays a decisive leading role, because man is not only a subject of the king but also "co-regent" and "viceroy" in his cultural task (Gen. 1:28-29; Ps. 8:4-7).

But this development is disturbed by sin. Bavinck distinguishes in sin a priestly element that involves a withdrawing from fellowship with God, and a kingly element that involves a breaking out of God's all-encompassing governance, through which "the whole world order has been thrown into disarray."[89] This degeneration of humanity to a continual dissonant (Jer. 8:7) had the immediate consequence that because of him the earth was cursed (Gen. 3:17), and creation subjected to futility (Rom. 8:20), "lest man, who wants to be king, live in a world that, as a glorious Kingdom of God, wants to subject itself only to God."[90] The world in all its interrelationships now falls in the grip of demonic powers and is marked by "deterioration, crumbling, splintering, enmity, opposition, meaninglessness, darkness, and death.[91] Human work no longer is service to God but merely a "struggle for life,"[92] which is marked by meaninglessness and purposelessness, as described especially in the book of Ecclesiastes. How clearly Bavinck saw this is apparent in the following citation:

> Man can do tremendous things, he can penetrate into the deepest mysteries of creation, but all this has no longer meaning, he can no longer build a harmonious world, he cannot undo the brokenness of the world.... All this increasingly strengthens his drive toward self-preservation, his need to brace himself against all disappointments and discouragements, and his strong desire for compensation.[93]

But God has held on to the plan of the Kingdom, and its formation (new birth) has remained the deepest motif of world history. Bavinck mentions several aspects:

1. The coming into being of the Kingdom in history is underlined by the fact that a large part of the Bible consists of

---

[89]*Ibid.*, 51-52.

[90]*Ibid.*, 53.

[91]*Ibid.*, 53-55. Bavinck points out that this demonic drama cannot be fathomed but that it is, according to, e.g., Lk 4:39 and Mk 4:39 (where fever and storm respectively are *rebuked*) an everyday reality.

[92]This term is not Bavinck's but summarizes what he writes in *ZWN*, 55.

[93]*ZWN*, 56.

historical books, in which history continually derives its meaning from the acts of God as a realization of the Kingdom idea.[94]

2. In the existence of Israel the Kingdom of God receives a prefiguration. Israel was both church and nation at the same time, it united in itself the priestly and kingly aspects, and is therefore called a "priestly Kingdom" (Ex. 19:6).[95] The national aspect implied that Israel was continuously involved in political entanglements and that it continued to exist despite battle and opposition. This may be viewed as the history of the Kingdom in "symbolic forms." That this is how Israel also viewed itself, is evidenced by the continually reviving expectation of the Messianic era, in which God would unite all nations under his scepter (Zech. 14:9; Isa. 25:6-12).[96]

3. The coming Kingdom of God is realized in Jesus Christ. "Even as the sin of Adam fragmented the world, so that world is brought together and united in Jesus Christ," who not only as Priest restores man to fellowship with God, but also as King "restores his salvific rule in this degenerated world."[97] This Kingdom, brought nigh in Christ (Matt. 3:2, 4:17), must be understood as cosmic and universal (Eph. 1:9-10; 1 Cor. 15:24-28).[98]

4. The Kingdom of God, which existed in the primeval age, will through all fragmentation and division become fully realized in the end times. Until then it is "near" or "coming." This eschatological character is emphasized continually in both the OT and the NT.[99]

5. Everything else, such as the covenant of grace, is subordinate to this eschatological perspective. "The ultimate goal of our life can never be that we personally may enjoy God again and be redeemed in him, but ... that we once again take our place in the broad context of the Kingdom of God...."[100]

6. The coming of God's Kingdom involves two realities that are inextricably intertwined, "temple" and "palace," i.e., the priestly and the kingly.

---

[94] *Ibid.*, 60.

[95] *Ibid.*, 60, where Bavinck also points out that temple and palace were adjoining, and that Zion was the name for both.

[96] *Ibid.*, 60-62.

[97] *Ibid.*, 58-59.

[98] *Ibid.*, 57, 59-60.

[99] *Ibid.*, 57.

[100] *Ibid.*, 58.

The temple is the primeval age that always remains a reality, and it is at the same time the end time, the signpost to the paradise of God and to the streams of living water. . . . There is Adam, who returns with bowed head to the tree of life on the basis of God's grace in Jesus Christ. . . . The King has the Kingdom of the primeval age behind him and the Kingdom of the end lies before him, on the far horizon. He stands between beginning and end, in the midst of the terrible struggle of God's Kingdom in the world.[101]

Bavinck describes the latter as the "dramatic tension of world history," in which the Kingdom of God has the empire of man as its counterpart.[102] Although the empire of man, because of the collective sinful will, is an inherent impossibility, a utopia that does not have staying power as history attests, humanity tries to rebuild it again and again with a determined, demonic anger against God (Ps. 2:2) in order "to recover the lost unity."[103] "The history of God's Kingdom is therefore not a quietly babbling brook ... it grates over and over against the manifestations of the empire of man, and it points moment by moment to the finale of world history, the great Day of the Lord."[104]

This excursus makes clear what was for Bavinck the most important biblical-theological criterion for a missionary approach that encompasses the whole of existence. Especially the fact that he understood the coming of God's Kingdom Christocentrically and emphasized the inextricable link between the priestly and kingly aspects of the Messiah is of great significance. This safeguards the balance between the vertical and horizontal dimensions of salvation. But what is absent in this valuable perspective is the prophetic aspect, the preaching of the gospel of the Kingdom of God (Mk 1:14). It would have resulted in an even better balance between the kerygmatic and comprehensive sides of the approach if he had taken this aspect into account.[105]

In *ICNCW* Bavinck himself placed the above view in the perspective of the missionary approach.[106] Over against all secularization of the idea of the Kingdom of God in the past (*corpus christianum*) and the present ("the Kingdom of God as

---

[101] *Ibid.*, 65-66.

[102] *Ibid.*, 62.

[103] *Ibid.*, 63.

[104] *Ibid.*, 65.

[105] Cf. also C. Graafland, "Theologische hoofdlijnen," 108-109

[106] Cf. *ICNCW*, 27-41, a separate chapter devoted to this question under the title "The all-embracing missionary task."

an earthly realm with a political program and incorporated in an earthly state"[107]), he also points out emphatically that the Kingdom of God must never be divorced from the church as the community of believers that lives from the reconciling work of Christ. "She [the church] realizes that he alone can acknowledge and obey Christ as King who has accepted Him as Priest and Redeemer, and who has found in His sacrifice the renewal of life."[108] At the same time the church has "within herself the inextinguishable urge to become the Kingdom of God."[109] Bavinck bases this argumentation on Mt. 28: "It is noteworthy that the missionary command in Matthew 28 follows upon the declaration of Christ Himself that all power in heaven and on earth has been given unto Him. The missionary message should never be abstracted from the authority of Christ."[110] The Priest is also the King:

> Jesus is Lord of all life: that is the message [the church] proclaims in every situation, [she] is continually aware that the Lord has made her a savoring salt, permeating the whole of human life. Therefore she can never come to rest; she is always striving and laboring to impress upon everything the seal of the will of God.[111]

The church has on that account a theocratic tendency, whereby it looks back to "the Kingdom of David and Solomon" and forward to "the eternal Kingdom of Jesus Christ."[112]

It must be clearly noted here that Bavinck carefully distinguishes this notion of 'theocratic tendency' from the totalitarian character of non-Christian religion. Over against that which is totalitarian he speaks of the nature of the Christian faith as the root (*radix*) of life: the whole of life stands under the critique of this root. This radical impact does not entail the elimination of existing culture, but rather a renewal of that culture.[113] Bavinck is pleading here, thus, for a careful enculturation of the content of the Christian faith.

> The new culture which thus develops out of the root of faith in Christ is not a universally uniform one. The plant of new life will have a character corresponding to the soil in which it grows. . . . Every country, every people, also every race has its own cultural dispositions and the gospel does not disturb them, but

---

[107]*Ibid.*, 33-37.

[108]*Ibid.*, 37.

[109]*Ibid.*, 36.

[110]*Ibid.*, 30.

[111]*Ibid.*, 28, 37.

[112]*Ibid.*, 37.

[113]*Ibid.*, 29.

rather takes possession of them and stimulates them.[114]

In *IZW* Bavinck does not present such an in-depth theological reflection on the Kingdom of God as dominant perspective. Nevertheless, it is clear that the preceding reflection forms the foundation for Bavinck's vision on the (comprehensive) approach, for it is striking that Bavinck here emphasizes that the deeds "stand in the closest relationship with the kingship of God or the Kingdom of heaven" and "belong to the new world order, in which God will reveal his kingly power in this world."[115]

Bavinck further points out that the multifaceted ministry of Jesus, and the actions of the apostles that broke new ground, confirm that in the missionary approach it is never only the renewing of the heart but also a renewing of societal life.[116] The ministry of Jesus is an indivisible whole of words and deeds (cf. Acts 1:1, where Luke writes that the gospels are "about all that Jesus began to do and to teach"). Bavinck writes: "Where Jesus comes, the demons flee, the storm stills, the fever yields, a new morning rises over this world ravaged by curse and misery"; he views Jesus' miracles as signs that illustrate, support, and confirm proclamation and argues that confirmation of the gospel by wonders and signs continues to be important in and for present-day missionary praxis.[117] And even though the breakthrough of the Kingdom of God has been postponed, in this era of delay—in which the missionary mandate is in force— "something of the light of the Kingdom of God" is already visible because of the accompanying signs (cf. Matt. 10:7-8) and the power of the gospel that is active in everything.[118]

3.2. The Comprehensive Approach

3.2.1. The Essence of the Comprehensive Approach

In Bavinck's definition of the comprehensive approach he openly distances himself from the declarations of the Synod of Middelburg on this subject. There the essence of this approach, that was seen as consisting specifically in providing education and medical help, was described as a necessary preparation for the missionary task proper, the proclamation of the gospel. This was stated plainly by the Synod: "It must be kept in mind, however, that all of this is preparation and the means to an end, but not mission."[119] This perspective led to a distinction between 'primary ministry,' which is understood to consist of the ministry of the Word and

---

[114]*Ibid.*, 29. Bavinck refers to Augustine, here, who states in his *De civitate Dei* that the heavenly city makes its pilgrimage in this world, not destructively but constructively.

[115]*Ibid.*, 96.

[116]*Ibid.*, 97-98.

[117]*Ibid.*, 96-97.

[118]*Ibid.*, 97.

[119]*Extract from the Acta der Generale Synode* (Middelburg, 1896), 34.

the sacraments, and 'subsidiary' or 'supplemental ministries,' such as education and medical help. This terminology clearly expresses the subordinate function of practical missionary service in relation to the proclamation of the gospel. Bavinck criticized this view and terminology.

Although he was convinced that deed must always find its incentive and justification in word, Bavinck maintained that these two entities constitute an indivisible whole and cannot properly exist separately in missionary practice. He expresses this by speaking of *core ministry* and *ancillary ministries*.[120]

Bavinck clarifies his position by distinguishing it from the concept of *comprehensive approach* that was introduced at the 1928 IMC Conference in Jerusalem. This concept was defined as follows: "Man is a unity, and ... his spiritual life is indivisibly rooted in all his conditions—physical, mental and social. We are therefore desirous that the program of missionary work among all peoples be sufficiently comprehensive to serve the whole man in every aspect of his life and relationships"[121] This led to the concept of a four-dimensional missionary approach, in which gospel proclamation, education, medical care, and social-economic aid stand side by side on equal footing. Bavinck criticizes this view particularly because of its anthropological foundation (the starting point for the argument is the "unity of man") as well as its materialistic foundation (it posits that the spiritual life of man is "rooted in all his conditions"), adding that "It would be different if [Jerusalem] had limited [itself] to the statement that spiritual life is interwoven and interconnected with all of life's circumstances, so that every change made in the former bears necessary consequences for all of life."[122] He calls the four-dimensional approach, when viewed in a biblical-theological light, "extremely misleading" because "Christ only commanded us to preach the gospel to all nations."[123] The missionary approach, he contended, is primarily one-dimensional, although this implies of necessity a change of existence in all its dimensions.[124] In this connection he once again clearly describes the relationship between core ministry and ancillary ministries: "...all other ministries only have meaning to the extent that they clarify, concretize, and give focus to that one thing: the preaching of the gospel."[125] Elsewhere Bavinck extensively discusses the values and boundaries of a comprehensive approach, emphasizing the fact that we can speak of a renewal of the totality of life only if we do so from the clear perspective of the

---

[120]*ZWN*, 53-54. He already used these terms in *Ons Zendingsboek* (1941). It is difficult to explain why he did not employ them in *IZW*, in which he clearly rejected the terminology advanced by Middelburg.

[121]*Jerusalem Series VI. The Christian Mission in Relation to Rural Problems*, 287.

[122]*IZW*, 114 (cf. *ISM*, 108-109).

[123]*IZM*, 114 (cf. *ISM*, 109).

[124]*IZM*, 115 (cf. *ISM*, 109).

[125]*Ibid.*

atonement.[126]

The principle of core ministry and ancillary ministries, introduced by Bavinck in *ZWN*, was further grounded and developed by Bavinck's student A.G. Honig,[127] Later, nearly a decade after Bavinck's death, Honig reiterated this precept as follows:

> Choosing for Christ has consequences that touch all expressions of our life in all areas. There is no participation in Christ without separation from the powers in society, in politics, and in the distribution of the goods in this world, powers that oppose Christ's Kingdom of justice.[128]

Bavinck in turn made use of Honig's work in his critique of the "comprehensive approach" in *IZW*.

Bavinck devoted little attention to any further ecclesiological clarification of the core and ancillary ministries. He poses the question, but does not answer it.[129] All he says about it is in an indirect comment in a different context: "There is no room in missionary work for a multiplicity of activities. ... This consideration leads to making a distinction between the "official" missionary ministry, as it takes place in the sending out of missionaries, and the spontaneous, non-official proclamation of the gospel as it occurs through believers, whether individually or in organizational contexts. The missionary task is so broad and so encompassing that it cannot remain limited to the actions of the church in its institutional form but is realized spontaneously in all of life and in the free or organized activity of the believers."[130] Here he appears to integrate (without attribution) the fundamental notion formulated by A.G. Honig, who distinguishes (with Kuyper) between the church as institution, which in consequence of its special offices is responsible for the core ministry, and the church as organism, which via organizations is responsible for ancillary ministries.[131] At a later stage an indirect statement shows that he welcomed the institution of what came to be known as 'world diaconate.'[132]

3.2.2. The Content of the Comprehensive Approach

Bavinck sees four non-official ancillary ministries, clustered around the official core

---

[126]Cf. *ICNCW*, 175-183

[127]Cf. *Bijdrage tot het onderzoek naar de fundering van de zendingsmethode der 'comprehensive approach' in het Nieuwe Testament.*

[128]*De Heerschappij van Christus en de zending*, 62.

[129]Cf. *IZW*, 121 (cf. *ISM*, 116). He did not keep his promise to return to this point later.

[130]*IZW*, 76 (cf. *ISM*, 68).

[131]A.G. Honig, *Bijdrage*, 82ff.

[132]*IGHG*, 103: "The diaconate is gaining entirely new perspectives; we are beginning to speak of world-diaconate."

ministry of the proclamation of the gospel, which are grounded in the mercy of God and provide an embodiment of the preaching of the Kingdom of God. Herewith he abandons the narrower interpretation of Middelburg (1896), which limited itself to medical and educational ministries, and follows Honig's view: "In any event, the demarcation that has up to now existed in the implementation of the missionary task is fundamentally unacceptable."[133]

Medical ministry. In medical aid the condescending love of God for suffering humanity is made visible and faith in all magical means of healing is shattered. Any materialistic understanding of this aid must be opposed by carrying out medical help in gratitude to God for skills received and by trusting in God's blessing.[134]

Educational ministry. Education is intended to promote the growth and development of people and should also contribute to the replacement of a pagan view of life with a biblical one. What must be prevented is that a pragmatization of education and science will cause people to lapse into an a-religious attitude.[135]

Literature ministry. Via theological, devotional, journalistic, and narrative literature faith can be deepened and made concrete and all of life can be brought under the salutary influence of the gospel.[136]

Social-economic ministry. The intent is that the relationships in family and society are corrected on the basis of the Bible and that via agrarian and economic renewal poverty is combated and conquered. Material prosperity, however, may never be divorced from spiritual renewal.[137]

What is striking here is that Bavinck, as indicated by his repeated warnings, was extremely fearful of the danger of the secularization of these ministries.[138] He sees this danger as being rooted in the fact that the Western believer always has the tendency to live dualistically, standing with one foot in the gospel and with the other in the agnostic or even godless culture.[139]

3.2.3. The Method of the Comprehensive Approach.

Bavinck did not discuss the method of the comprehensive approach as such, but he

---

[133] A.G. Honig, *Bijdrage*, 92.

[134] Cf. *ZWN*, 58-61 and *IZW*, 119-120 (*ISM*, 114). Cf. also "De medische dienst in het geheel van het zendingswerk," 7ff. and "Wat heeft het medische werk te maken met den godsdiensten van den inlander," 15ff.

[135] Cf. *ZWN*, 61-62, *IZW*, 120 (*ISM*, 114), "De zending en haar diensten," 83, 91, 99, 107.

[136] Cf. *ZWN*, 44-45.

[137] Cf. *ZWN*, 46, 186-89 and *IZW* 120 (*ISM*, 115).

[138] Cf. *IZW*, 106-113 (*ISM*, 100-7), where Bavinck insistently argues against an unthinking transmission of Western culture.

[139] Cf. *IZM*, 120 (*ISM*, 115).

incorporated it here and there in his argument as a whole. From this we can deduce the following. Bavinck rejects a methodology based on the anthropological principle of the "unity of man," which is implicit in the comprehensive approach. The methodology of the missionary approach must be determined by the theological principle that Christ taught his followers "to take the whole person seriously," so that the realization of all-encompassing redemption can never be detached from the proclamation and continuing effect of the gospel.[140]

> Every line the church draws always begins from the inside, is extended by means of the change in our personal life, originates in Christ. That is a very difficult and thankless message in the midst of a world that wants so much to achieve salvation by other means, but also this truth the church may not disguise.[141]

Thus the "dangerous dualism" that always threatens a comprehensive approach can be challenged. The application of scientific methods brings with it the danger that we bring people

> into the spiritual emptiness of a scientific worldview, in which God is at best tolerated as something one is free to believe in, but is no longer seen as the heart of all phenomena, as the Light of all light and the Salvation of all salvation.[142]

Bavinck applied this line of thinking concretely to the question of world peace. On the one hand he applauded the "peace movement in the church," but on the other contended that the

> Church can never become a kind of international organization [along the lines of, say, the Marxist International] that wants to achieve peace from the outside, by means of motions and compromises. In the final analysis world peace, the fraternity of the nations, belongs to the category of all the things that will be given to us as well (Matt. 6:33) if we seek first the Kingdom of heaven with all our strength and full commitment.[143]

All this does not mean, however, that in the praxis of mission the ancillary ministries cannot precede or simultaneously encompass the core ministry.[144]

In this connection Bavinck also distances himself from the ethnological approach of Bruno Gutmann[145] and Christian Keysser,[146] who, with their *volksorganische* and *volkspaedagogische* missionary method respectively, defended each in his own way (on the basis of the tribal or national-cultural context) a

---

[140]Cf. *IZM,* 116 (*ISM,* 112).

[141]"Drie grote vragen: De vraag naar de verlossing," 184.

[142]*IZM,* 117 (cf. *ISM,* 112).

[143]"Drie grote vragen: De vraag naar de verlossing," 181.

[144]Cf. *IZM,* 93-95, 125 (*ISM,* 87-89, 121).

[145]Cf. *Gemeindeaufbau aus dem Evangelium.*

[146]Cf. *Eine Papuagemeinde.*

comprehensive approach in the sense of collective Christianization.[147] Although for psychological and sociological reasons he wants to deal cautiously with the fact of kinship,[148] he finds in the Scriptures reason to argue for an ethnic approach.[149] This implies not only an extreme reticence toward the idea of "collective Christianization," it also means, *mutatis mutandis*, that in mission the renewal of a society must never be divorced from the conversion of the individual and church planting.[150]

Bavinck is further of the opinion, referring to J. Merle Davis,[151] that the sending church must be careful in this comprehensive approach not to assume too much responsibility and for too long. Practically speaking this level of involvement cannot be sustained, because it will in the long run exceed the financial means of the sending church. And it is incorrect in principle because it hinders the independent development of the younger churches.[152]

3.2.4. Summary

Bavinck's reflection on the comprehensive approach—in which he distinguishes between core ministry and ancillary ministries and grounds their interrelationship theologically in the all-encompassing significance of the Kingdom[153]—constitutes not only a critique of the one-sided position taken by the Synod of Middelburg but also an essential contribution to Reformed and evangelical missiology, arriving at a balanced relationship between word and deed in biblical perspective.[154] It is striking that Bavinck nowhere refers to Abraham Kuyper's well-known adage that Christ's kingship in every area of life must be proclaimed, even though this probably helped shape Bavinck's view.

Earlier in this study it was pointed out that the christocratic (and/or diaconal) aspects in Bavinck's definition of the essence of mission remained underexposed. The importance that Bavinck himself attached to them, as indicated above, merely underscored this inconsistency.

---

[147]Cf. *ZWN*, 183; *IZW*, 124 (cf. *ISM*, 119-20).

[148]Cf. *IZW*, 161ff (*ISM*, 159ff).

[149]Cf. *IZM*, 122-23 (*ISM*, 116-18).

[150]Cf. A.G. Honig, *Bijdrage*, 91: "The goal may not be the religious Christianizing of society [but] is ... solely to place people before the Christ and thus to move them to faith."

[151]Cf. Davis, *New Buildings on Old Foundations*.

[152]Cf. *IZW*, 105 (cf. *ISM*, 100).

[153]C.H. Koetsier, 74, summarizes Bavinck's position with the term *integral mission*.

[154]Cf. the evangelical missiologist J.R.W. Stott, 25.

3.3. The Kerygmatic Approach

3.3.1. The Essence of the Kerygmatic Approach

Bavinck uses the concept of *encounter* to characterize the essence of the kerygmatic approach[155]—an encounter between preacher and hearer, in which a confrontation takes place between the word of God and the person. Bavinck makes it clear that this encounter has theological, psychological, and pedagogical components. In order to investigate these he considers it necessary to be aware first of the image of man in biblical perspective, i.e., "a biblical anthropology."[156] In *IZW* he summarizes his thinking on these matters, which he developed in other publications and which were discussed extensively in an earlier chapter of the present study. The crux is that man in his deepest essence is a rebel. This integral core of being human hides behind all cultural-religious "shells."[157] From this standpoint there are three phases that make the kerygmatic approach an existential encounter.

In the first place, we must truly *see* the person we encounter, in the sense of seeing through him. "Again and again we read in the gospels that Jesus 'looks at' or 'sees' an individual, and in each case this means that he sees through all disguises and penetrates to the one thing that controls the entire life of that individual."[158] The missionary worker is called to come to recognize, by careful exploration, the deepest intentions that lie hidden in the cultural and religious life of people: What does man do with God and why does he do this?

Next, a stance of *loving accommodation* is essential. This means that, having come to recognize the deepest motivation of the other, we try to approach him or her with patience, in "true awareness of our collective guilt before God" and, standing in Christ, sincerely desiring "to do for the other what Christ has done for me."[159]

Finally, this solidarity must result in an *encounter* in which the Word of God is active both in judging and in liberating.

Such an approach must take place not only collectively in proclamation, but also and especially individually, in conversation.[160] Bavinck summarizes the essence of the encounter in a striking comparison: we are not mail delivery persons who have done our job "when we simply have spoken the good word." Rather, we are envoys who as *chargés d'affaires* must look after Christ's business among the

---

[155]*IZW*, 125 (cf. *ISM*, 121).

[156]Cf. *IZM*, 126 (*ISM*, 122).

[157]Cf. *IZM*, 127-128 (*ISM*, 122-123).

[158]*IZM*, 130 (cf. *ISM*, 126).

[159]*IZM*, 130-131 (cf. *ISM*, 126-127).

[160]Cf. *IZM*, 132 (*ISM*, 128). According to Bavinck individual conversation was also the core of Paul's missionary work.

nations, taking care especially to practice the love (*agapē*) of Christ.[161] Bavinck did not provide a more detailed definition of missionary preaching.[162]

3.3.2. The Content of the Kerygmatic Approach

Bavinck is brief on this point, because the content of preaching is a given: the message of grace in Jesus Christ. Of course that message has a number of aspects—such as announcing judgment, exhortation, call to conversion. And preaching can take different forms—such as witnessing (*marturein*) as in a court proceeding, proclamation (*kerussein*) of Christ's kingship, and instruction (*didaskalein*) through the unfolding of the Scriptures. But central to preaching is the bringing of the good news (*euaggelizein*) of the salvation of God in Christ Jesus.[163]

In this connection Bavinck does not state explicitly how he understands that message of God's salvation in terms of its content.[164] But it is evident that hermeneutically he stands within the Reformed tradition.

3.3.3. The Method of the Kerygmatic Approach

From the Scriptures we cannot say more about methodology than that it involves "great flexibility." Especially the person of the preacher ("through whom") and the nature of the audience ("to whom") play an important role, which means that the kerygmatic approach is to a large extent determined psychologically. The only truly fundamental starting point is that the witness must do full justice to the Gospel of Christ: it must be brought out in the clearest possible way. Starting from this principle, one may employ various complementary methods in practice.

Nevertheless, in defining the essence of the kerygmatic approach Bavinck, following Hans Schärer,[165] expressed a preference for what he called the "ascending" or "confrontational" method," by which he meant a gradual unfolding of the biblical witness that takes as its point of departure the religious, ethical and philosophical concepts and suppositions of those being addressed and then confronts these thoughtways one by one with the message of Christ.[166] He substantiates this choice by critiquing four methods as to their theological and

---

[161] *IZM*, 132-133 (cf. *ISM*, 128-129).

[162] Cf. J.A.B. Jongeneel, *Missiologie*, 2, 263-265.

[163] Cf. *IZW*, 133-34 (cf. *ISM*, 129-30).

[164] The heading "The Content of Preaching," *IZW*, 133; (cf. *ISM*, 129), does not cover the content of the section to which it refers, which is more methodologically focused.

[165] In *Die Missionarische Verkündigung auf dem Missionsfeld.*

[166] Cf. *IZW*, 135-136 (*ISM*, 130-131).

psychological merits.[167]

The *antithetical* method. This method, the oldest in the history of mission, seeks—from a classical apologetic perspective, which saw an important point of contact in reason—its strength in an attack on other religions with a view to demonstrating via rational argumentation the error of the religious ideas in question as opposed to the truth of the Bible. Bavinck not only rejects such a point of contact, rooted purely in reason, on theological grounds, but also from a psychological perspective sees no benefit in this approach: it leads to "hot heads and cold hearts."[168]

The *sympathetic* method. This method, starting from a positive theological appreciation of the non-Christian religions, aims at linking Christianity as much as possible with the existing local religion, by terming (apparent) points of agreement with the Bible 'elements of truth,' thus evoking sympathy on the part of the audience. The gospel is interpreted as the fulfillment of all imperfect religious striving. Bavinck recognizes the psychological advantages of this method, but he radically rejected it on theological grounds and explicitly opposed the views of William E. Hocking (USA)[169] Vengal Chakkarai (India),[170] and Toyohiko Kagawa (Japan).[171] Every religion is in principle a changing of the truth into a lie (Rom. 1:25) and there is therefore "an unbridgeable gap between all non-Christian religions and the gospel."[172]

The *thetic* method. This method, championed by Karl Barth and in more nuanced form by Hendrik Kraemer and others,[173] wants to avoid the twin shoals of the methods mentioned above and make an direct unfolding of the biblical message its starting point. The exposition of the revelation in Jesus Christ must evoke faith and as it were spontaneously uncover that which was wrong and sinful in earlier ideas. Theologically this method has the advantage that the Word of God is central and that it is immediately clear that this a new message.[174] At the same time Bavinck objects to this method. From a psychological perspective this method does not lead to a genuine encounter, because it does not adequately take into account

---

[167]In *ZWN*, 65-73, Bavinck briefly discusses all four of these methods, whereas in *IZW*, 136-156 (cf. *ISM*, 131-152), he does not mention the first two but discusses in detail the latter two of them.

[168]*ZWN*, 65-66.

[169]Cf. *IZW*, 140 (*ISM*, 135). See Hocking, *Rethinking Mission*, 1932.

[170]Cf. *IZW*, 138 (*ISM*, 134). See Chakkarai, *Jesus the Avatar*, 1926.

[171]Cf. *IZW*, 151 (*ISM*, 146-147). See Kagawa, *The Religion of Jesus*, 1931.

[172]*ZWN*, 66-68. Cf. also *IZW*, 138ff (*ISM*, 134ff).

[173]Cf. "Het probleem der 'Anknüpfung' bij de evangelieverkondiging," in: Woudenberg, 59-60; Barth, "Die Theologie und die Mission in der Gegenwart"; Kraemer, *The Christian Message in a Non-Christian World*.

[174]Cf. *ZWN*, 68 and *IZW*, 146 (*ISM*, 142).

"the one to whom" one speaks, with the result that the message cannot adequately resonate in the life of the hearers.[175] Furthermore, he agrees with the theological objection raised by Walter Freytag, who pointed out that of necessity our terminology must always be tied in with the conceptual world the audience is familiar with.[176] But if this is done without further stipulation and without a profound confrontation of the new with the old, then it implicitly leads to a reinforcing of syncretistic tendencies.[177] Finally, this method has the methodological problem as to the sequence in which the biblical themes must be proclaimed in a way that will make the message to some degree comprehensible to the audience.[178] The thetic method as an unfolding of the gospel is according to Bavinck possible only at a later stage.[179]

The *confrontational* method. On the basis of his criticism of the preceding method, Bavinck opts for what he called a grappling or confrontational method, which he considers to be more responsible, both theologically and psychologically. His starting point is the Pauline model of approach,[180] in which he distinguishes six guidelines: first, non-Christian religion is a *turning away from God*; second, it even has a *demonic character* (1 Cor. 8:4; 10:19-20); third, at the same time, every religion is based on the datum that *God has spoken*, no matter to what extent that revelation is kept submerged in lies (Acts 14:17; 17:26-27; Rom. 1:19); fourth, this implies an attitude toward the religious ideas that is both *respectful and critical* (Acts 17:23; 19:37); fifth, missionary proclamation presents *no strange God* but rather explains who is in truth the One who has revealed himself (Acts 14:16-17; 17:23); sixth, formally *familiar forms of expression* are used, while the content of each concept is given a *new meaning* (Acts 17:28).[181]

The confrontational method is in principle *kerygmatic*, but in practice *dialogical* in nature. This method

---

[175]Cf. *ZWN*, 69 and *IZW*, 153 (*ISM*, 149).

[176]Cf. *IZW*, 144, 153 (*ISM*, 139, 149). Cf. Freytag, *Die junge Christenheit im Umbruch des Ostens*, 229-236, who shows Paul faced the same problem in his use of Greek concepts.

[177]Cf. *IZW*, 146 (*ISM*, 142).

[178]Cf. *IZM*, 147ff (*ISM*, 143ff). Bavinck argues for "toeing the line" of revelation history when using this method.

[179]Cf. *IZM*, 147 (*ISM*, 142-143).

[180]It is not clear whether Bavinck made use here of R. Allen, *Missionary Methods: St. Paul's Or Ours*. Bavinck does not refer to Allen, who wrote, e.g., that in light of Paul's method much can be said for preaching Christ "with a sympathetic knowledge of the belief of those to whom we preach" and basing "our appeal on the common truth which we hold together with our hearers." At the same time he rejected an approach via reason: "It is another thing to spend our time philosophizing when we might be preaching Christ," (90).

[181]Cf. *ZWN*, 69-71.

is not antithetic, for it does not seek its power in ridicule. . . . Nor
is it sympathetic, for it does not view paganism as a precursor of
the gospel. . . . Finally, it is also not thetic, because it attempts to
come as near as possible to the life and thought of those to whom
the message is being presented.[182]

"Missionary work," Bavinck stated, "is in practice always discussion and cannot be
anything but discussion."[183]

Bavinck sees three advantages in this method: (1) *pedagogical-psychological*, because "attention is engaged from the start, which makes hearts
more receptive for what is to follow";[184] (2) *practical-psychological*, because
demonstration of respect for and effort to take serious account of the cultural-
religious thoughtways and practices of the people among whom one is working can
break down prevailing suspicions of Western feelings of superiority;[185] and (3)
theological, because the message of Christ is not something

that just drops down out of the blue from a strange world. . . .
[But rather] the old is exposed to the light, plumbed in its depths,
laid bare with respect to its fundamental motifs. And then
suddenly the tremendous word of Christ intervenes, laying bare
and judging. . . . A breach [in the old] becomes visible, and
before long the content of the call to conversion takes on a
concrete, well-defined shape.[186]

Bavinck realized, of course, that in all of this, time and place play an
important role. For example, in situations in which religion has been replaced by
science and technology, this kind of 'reaching back' to religious consciousness and
concepts would not only be practically impossible but would also have the wrong
effect psychologically.[187]

3.3.4. The Point of Contact

The question of whether there is such a thing as a point of contact is inextricably
bound up with the position one takes on the mater of missionary approach, and
therefore has already been answered implicitly in the preceding sections.

------

[182]*ZWN*, 71.

[183]"Het evangelie en de andere godsdiensten," 54.

[184]*IZW*, 136 (cf. *ISM*, 131).

[185]*IZW*, 137 (cf. *ISM*, 133) Here Bavinck even writes, "That prompts us,
perhaps occasionally more than we can justify theologically, to take note of what
lives in the hearts of our hearers and to take our point of departure, not in what we
have to say but in what they think and believe."

[186]*IZM*, 136-37 (cf. *ISM*, 133).

[187]*IZM*, 137-38 (cf. *ISM*, 133-34). Bavinck writes, "For they can
experience it as an attempt on our part to push them back again toward a religion
they so recently and with so much passion turned their back on."

Nevertheless, it obviously needs to be dealt with explicitly as well. Bavinck himself addressed this issue at length, owing to his awareness of its extreme importance and the variety of theological implications it bears: actually, the question of the point of contact constitutes the quest for the proper theological assessment of non-Christian religion.[188] Following up on what has been said in the chapters on general revelation and religious consciousness above, Bavinck's views on the matter of point of contact need to be explained.

Following Johannes Witte,[189] Bavinck made a distinction between substantive and formal contact between Christianity and other religions, arguing that formal engagement with non-Christian religions is unavoidable but substantive engagement with them is impossible.[190] The rejection of a substantive or material point of contact is based on the theological starting point that the non-Christian religion taken as a whole constitutes a turning away from God, a replacing of the truth with a lie. If there are things in other religions that look well-matched or compatible with Christian faith, in the end they always prove to be *apparent* similarities.[191] In the formal point of contact lie three moments, the first of which is theological, the other two, practical.

In the first place, we encounter in every non-Christian religion "vague and general intuitions" that have their origin in the revelation of God. It is these intuitions that make a missionary approach possible. Contrary to what Karl Barth contended, mission is not something that takes place "in a void" (*ins Leere*).[192] For God has not left himself without witness (Acts 14:15-17). And it is precisely this fact which constitutes "the great point of contact available to the church for use in her work in service of the gospel."[193] God's prior involvement makes it possible to bear witness to God. Bavinck was in basic agreement with Hendrik Kraemer that generally speaking points of contact in other religions can be established only by way of antithesis, which "is not meant as a negative way of condemnation, but as a deeply positive way of dealing realistically with the dialectical reality" of human religion.[194] This meant for Bavinck that religious awareness may be understood as a point of contact only to the extent that it is an answer to earlier revelation of God: "the only thing revelation fastens onto is revelation."[195] But there is a beginning point, a point of departure for the missionary and evangelist:

---

[188]Cf. "Het probleem der 'Anknüpfung,' " 59.

[189]Cf. J. Witte, Die Christusbotschaft und die Religionen.

[190]Cf. "Het probleem der 'Anknüpfung,' " 61-64.

[191]Cf. *ibid.*, 61; "Het evangelie en de andere godsdiensten," 67; *IZW*, 138-139 (*ISM,* 134-135).

[192]K. Barth, "Die Theologie und der Mission in der Gegenwart," 197.

[193]*IZW*, 140 (cf. *ISM,* 136), cf. *RBCG*, 119.

[194]H. Kraemer, *The Christian Message in a Non-Christian World*, 139:

[195]"Het probleem der 'Anknüpfung,' " 67.

Yes, the preacher of the gospel has a starting point. He does not open the dialogue between God and his listeners: he merely opens a new chapter. He [does] not [have] a point of contact in human reason or human virtue, but in God's work and God's mercifulness. That is the beauty of the missionary task.[196]

Second, the missionary approach cannot escape adopting a variety of existing words and expressions that are used to indicate the "intuitions" mentioned above. Only thus can we make ourselves understood. "Paul and the other apostles did not hesitate to use numerous highly specific words and expressions from Hellenistic culture," such as *logos* and *soteria*, "which were, of course, loaded with wrong connotations, in the preaching of the gospel."[197] Bavinck speaks in this context of "stepping stones."[198] The content of these words and concepts is gradually purified by being used in a different context. Although this takes us "along gaping chasms," we may at the same time be assured "that in our preaching the Holy Spirit does his convicting work in the hearts of our hearers."[199] In the missionary context we

> may bank on the mightiness of the truth.... The truth of God has a strong, compelling power, and gives an entirely new meaning to words and thoughts. We cannot openly and freely fulfil our task in the midst of the non-Christian world if we do not have full confidence in the majestic power of God's truth and hence dare to grasp whatever we can find to portray and visualize the riches of God's Revelation in Jesus Christ.[200]

Third, it is necessary that in the forms of expression in which the gospel is presented, we must seek a "very thorough adaptation to the nature and possibilities of the peoples to whom we preach." By way of illustration Bavinck points, for example, to the preference of the Javanese for allegory and late-night conversations.[201] Although there is clear agreement between Bavinck and Kraemer on the last two points, it would be better to speak of affinity rather than influence, since Bavinck already applied this method at an early stage.

In addition to this cultural-religious point of contact (*aanknopingspunt*), Bavinck also speaks of an *existential* point of contact (*aangrijpingspunt*). He uses the latter in connection with developments in the modern world. Where religious

---

[196]*ICNCW*, 110.

[197]"Het probleem der 'Anknüpfung,'" 67.

[198]"General Revelation and the Non-Christian Religions," 54.

[199]*IZW*, 143 (cf. *ISM*, 139).

[200]"Het probleem der 'Anknüpfung,'" 67

[201]"Het probleem der 'Anknüpfung,'" 66. Cf. also "The Problem of Adaptation and Communication," 307-313. Bavinck himself applied this principle very early on in his booklet *Soeksma Soepana* (The Way of the Soul, 1932), in which, as pointed out earlier, he used the metaphor of the *kraton* (the residence of the ruler of Surakarta) to explain the working of the gospel in the human heart.

consciousness crumbles and secularization strikes, whether in the West or the East, an awareness of spiritual poverty, dissatisfaction, emptiness, and fear often sets in. This is not a thirst for Christ, but the Christian witness can tie into these feelings and experiences and use them as a means to penetrate to the deeper need, the need for God. "God can use [this existential condition] in our preaching as a means to lay bare the heart and make it aware of the much greater misery, the deepest ground of all misery, the fact that we are sinners.[202]

3.3.5. Summary

In his reflection on the kerygmatic approach, Bavinck established the mutual relationship between theology and psychology in a balanced and especially biblically responsible manner. He creditably provided direction in the ever-recurring dilemma whether the missionary proclamation to non-Christians must take the existing religious experience (the knowledge of God that is present) as its starting point or the revelation in Jesus Christ. In other words, whether this preaching must be more theocentric or rather more Christocentric.[203] By taking both theology and psychology into account in his reflection on missionary approach, Bavinck avoided a christocentrism without theocentrism as well as a theocentrism without christocentrism, both of which obstruct the true impact of the gospel and lead to syncretism. The position Bavinck took on this matter leaves room for a balanced interpretation of the concept of the so-called point of contact in the form of antithesis.

3.4. Missionary Approach in the Post-Colonial Era

Bavinck was aware that the ongoing decolonization that gathered momentum especially after the independence of India in 1947 called for renewed reflection on the direction of mission in this world. Following Kraemer, who spoke of the end of the Vasco da Gama era, he points out in a 1959 article in *Trouw*[204] that mission will have to find its way within changed and changing political relationships. In the reflection on this reality, two things are central.

In the first place, mission increasingly loses it national character and increasingly acquires a global face: the colonial context within which mission functioned must be replaced by a joint movement of the churches in ecumenical solidarity.[205]

Second, more than ever before this will involve a genuine encounter with the other religions, now that mission no longer can rely on political support and has

---

[202]*IZW*, 145 (cf. *ISM*, 141).

[203]Cf. H. Kraemer, *The Christian Message in a Non-Christian World*, 21-22, who speaks of two irreconcilable poles. Cf. also J.A.B. Jongeneel, *Missiologie*, 2, 265-266.

[204]"Het Vasco da Gama-tijdperk. Wereldhistorische bespiegelingen en de zending."

[205]Cf. also *IZW*, 302 (*ISM*, 305).

lost its position of cultural superiority: "the gospel itself must do it, unprotected," Bavinck writes in *Trouw*. He judges this positively, in spite of the greater missionary efforts this calls for, and speaks of "unheard-of opportunities." He probably refers here to the fact that the emotional barriers and the opportunistic motives for going over to the Christian faith that were part of the colonial enculturation of mission have been cleared away.

A year earlier, in a book review, he already wrote that it is precisely these changes that are a stimulus to once again "grow closer to the biblical view of mission," yes, that we are thrown back on the essence of the missionary calling: to become part of Christ's progress through this world.[206] This implies that missiology, if it is to provide an adequate interpretation of this missionary approach, must become aware once more of its theological starting points and methodological approaches.

Bavinck points to this phenomenon in other articles as well and emphasizes that the church is called increasingly to inculturation as a means of gaining in missionary appeal. If the church is to continue to communicate its message in a time of increasing nationalism, it is methodologically prerequisite that it have a recognizable face in the world in which it operates.[207]

One of the greatest problems, according to Bavinck, is that with the realization of independence many nations have entered an economic, technological, and social revolution that leads to agnosticism and atheism. This minimizes the interest in existential questions.[208] Bavinck is convinced, however, that in the ferment of the times, in which materialism initially crowds out religion, a quest will arise for a new spiritual balance. The church is called to keep its eyes and ears open to proclaim in *this* void the decisive meaning of the gospel.[209] The above-mentioned existential point of contact (*aangrijpingspunt*) can thus become an extremely relevant point of departure for missionary work.

4. Chapter Summary

In looking at the whole, we can draw the following conclusions concerning Bavinck's thinking with respect to the topics dealt with in this chapter.

Bavinck did not reflect to any great extent on the aim or goal of mission, but simply adopted Voetius' definition: the furtherance of the glory of God, the planting of the church, and the conversion of people everywhere.

Bavinck argued—as time went on more and more in terms of the biblical notion of the Kingdom of God—for a dual *modus operandi* in mission: the comprehensive approach (broader vocation) and the *kerugmatic* approach

---

[206]"Opgenomen zijn in Gods grote daden," review of Gustaf Wingren, *Die Predigt*.

[207]"Verkondiging aan de volkerenwereld. De zending," in J. Waterink et al., *Cultuurgeschiedenis van het Christendom 4:359-409*.

[208]*IZW,* 304 (cf. *ISM,* 307).

[209]Cf. *IZM,* 305 (*ISM,* 308). Bavinck saw this happening in India, see "India in transition."and "Nehroe: 'Ja ik ben veranderd.'"

(proclamation), which he characterized respectively as ancillary missionary service and core missionary service. He clearly distinguished his position on the former from the multi-dimensional comprehensive approach advocated by the ecumenical theology of mission (Whitby 1947). With regard to the kerugmatic approach, he rejected the (anti)thetic method on theological and psychological grounds and opted for the confrontational method, to which, on the one hand, he assigned a dialogical character while denying the existence of an existential or material point of contact on the other.

Further, Bavinck maintained that the focal point of church-centered mission is the *basileia*, through which the two elements of missionary approach—the kerygmatic core ministry and the comprehensive ancillary ministries—are bound together in a relationship that is inseparable and irreversible. According to Bavinck the first component of this dual missionary approach is carried out by the church as official institution and the second by the church as organism of believers.

CHAPTER EIGHT

Elenctics

The future of Europe and of the other continents should only be thought of as a dialogue between two powers that remain constant: humanity and Jesus Christ. ("Jezus Christus is dezelfde, tot in eeuwigheid," 38)

1. Introduction

With the advent of the study of religion in the 19th century came a growing need for theological reflection on the relationship between Christianity and other religions, both as underpinning for and in the service of the missionary mandate. The German missiologist Gustav Warneck was the first to emphasize the importance of a specific discipline of missionary apologetics and argued in his *Evangelische Missionslehre* for a separate place for *Missionsapologetik* alongside the history, theory, and method of missions. Julius Richter, a student of Warneck's, attempted to expand missionary apologetics further in his *Evangelische Missionskunde,* in which he devoted a separate section to this field of study. Richter considered missionary apologetics to be an independent branch of theological apologetics, since he viewed it as having its own task aimed more at the displacing of heathenism than the defense of Christianity. He distinguished three foci in the pursuit of missionary apologetics: provision of a theological foundation for the absolute uniqueness of the Christian faith; a comparison of the Christian religion with other religions which clearly demonstrates the superiority of the former; and a historical demonstration of the fact that the Christian faith conquers all other religions. At the International Missionary Conferences in Edinburgh, Jerusalem, and Tambaram these themes were specifically brought up for discussion, with the result that it became an important item in international missionary reflection. In his own way, Bavinck also dealt with the important question of the relationship with other religions. In *RBCG* he was concerned to demonstrate theologically the absolute uniqueness of the Christian faith vis-à-vis the other religions. And in close parallel with the results of this study he devoted a separate section in *IZW* to "missionary apologetics" under the heading "elenctics," a term he rarely used in other publications.[1] Although he conceded that

---

[1] It may be noted here that only a few of Bavinck's students continued use of the term *elenctics*. It was never used by Hendrik Kraemer who employed the then-current, internationally established term *missionary apologetics*: J.Verkuyl, *Contemporary Missiology*, 361-368, speaks in terms of missionary communication

"in terms of the nature of its subject matter" elenctics "is closely related to dogmatics," he was of the opinion that it is "in intent clearly a missionary discipline."[2] And earlier on he had stated that "missiology does not deal primarily with the question of the content of truth but has to do with the secondary question of how we must bring the truth of Christ."[3] He therefore does not classify it under dogmatics, as Kuyper did,[4] but under missionary theology, as Warneck and Richter had done, "in order that the missionary motive that dominates it may not be clouded."[5]

Bavinck calls elenctics the 'discipline of persuasion' (*elenchein*) and understands this as a two-pronged activity: scholarly reflection on the religions and theological reflection on the apologetic approach to the religious person. These two elements of elenctics can be distinguished but never detached from each other: they serve one another, are the two sides of the same coin. This fundamental point of departure forms the basis for the structure of this chapter.

2. The Term Elenctics

The confrontational notion of *elenctics* was first used in a missionary framework by Gisbertus Voetius, who derived it from Titus 1:13: ". . . rebuke (*elenche*) them sharply, so that they will be sound in the faith."[6] He used this term to indicate what he felt to be the need for the refutation and deconstruction of non-Christian beliefs preliminary to the proclamation of the Christian faith and the building of the church. Kuyper revived the term and put it forward as the antithesis to pseudo-religion, alongside polemics as the antithesis to heresy and apologetics as the antithesis to pseudo-philosophy.[7]

In adopting this concept Bavinck linked it to missionary approach: "Elenctics is the discipline that deals with a very special aspect of missionary approach, viz., the direct confrontation of non-Christian religiosity preparatory to calling people to conversion."[8] He states that elenctics does not consist in the first place of a reactive "defense against the dangerous power of non-Christian religiosity" but instead is strongly dominated by the active missionary idea: "it calls . . . the non-Christian religion to account and tries to convince its adherents of sin

---

through dialogue and trialogue.

[2] *IZW*, 234 (cf. *ISM*, 233).

[3] *CPVW*, 10.

[4] A. Kuyper, *Encyclopaedie*, 3, 359ff.

[5] *IZW*, 233 (cf. *ISM*, 232).

[6] Cf. J.A.B. Jongeneel, *Missiology*, 2, 332 and Kuyper, *Encyclopaedie*, 3, 365.

[7] Kuyper, *Encyclopaedie*, 3, 365.

[8] *IZW*, 234 (cf. *ISM*, 233).

and to move them to repentance and conversion."[9]

The term elenctics is derived from the Greek verb *elenchein,* which initially meant to disgrace or to bring shame on someone, and in Attic (NT) Greek acquired the meaning "to prove guilt, to refute," or "to hold someone's sin before him and to challenge him to turn around."[10] Bavinck refers to a number of biblical texts where this word is found.:

Jude 14-15: "See, the Lord is coming with thousands upon thousands of his holy ones, to judge everyone, and to convict (*elenchein*) all the ungodly of all the ungodly acts they have done."

Revelation 3:19: "Those whom I love I rebuke (*elenchō*) and discipline. So be earnest and repent.

John 16:8: "When he [the Holy Spirit] comes, he will convict (*elenxei*) the world of guilt in regard to sin and righteousness and judgment."

1 Timothy 5:20: "Those who sin are to be rebuked (*elenche*) publically, so that the others may take warning."

Matthew 18:15: "If a brother sins against you, go and show him his fault (*elenxon*), just between the two of you."

On the basis of these texts Bavinck concludes that the term *elenchein* means to punish or chastise, but then in the sense that it includes a conviction of sin and a call to conversion, and argues further that the concept as such falls entirely within the ethical-religious sphere.[11]

The texts cited by Bavinck are a limited choice from the many NT occurrences of the word.[12] He selected them on the basis of the subject of the verb *elenchein*: the Lord (in the final judgment and in the present), the Holy Spirit, the office bearer, and the brother. In this way he shows that *elenchein* refers to a human activity and at the same time has a divine dimension.[13]

---

[9] *IZW,* 233 (cf. *ISM,* 232).

[10] *IZW,* 222 (cf. *ISM,* 221); Bavinck quotes here from G. Kittel, 471.

[11] *IZW,* 222-223 (cf. *ISM,* 221). J. Klapwijk, 18-19, states that this conclusion does not do justice to the meaning of the word *elenchein,* arguing that it is primarily a forensic term and that one can only determine from the context whether it includes a call to conversion. But Klapwijk's contention that Bavinck's interpretation of *elenchein* is 'off the rails'is too strong, for in most of the texts—and elsewhere in the NT—the unmasking does indeed include a call to conversion.   One must guard against a one-sided emphasis on the forensic character of the concept. Cf. here also *Theologisches Begriffslexikon zum NT,* 2, 1095.

[12] Cf. A. Schmoller, 159, who lists nineteen NT references.

[13] It is striking that Bavinck does not mention Titus 1:13 in this connection, the text that inspired Voetius to introduce the term *elenctics.* Given that "office bearer" is its subject, one would think that Bavinck would have preferred this verse over 1 Tim. 5:20.

3. Biblical Foundation of Elenctics

For Bavinck the pursuit of elenctics is a biblical matter, not only because of the use of this term in numerous texts, but much more so because the Bible itself is in principle an elenctic book. "The Bible," he writes,

> is a missionary book in a very remarkable sense of the word. It is a missionary book because it is constantly in discussion with the Gentile outlook upon life, . . . because it continuously addresses the Gentile. It never overlooks the deeply rooted tendencies of self-deification that are so essential in heathenism. It takes account of the fascinating power of heathenism, and is always endeavoring to break its spell.[14]

Writing concerning magical-mystical thinking, Bavinck contended that "The whole Bible constitutes one tremendous witness against this magic and all false mysticism, which seeks a union with God that does not recognize the immeasurable chasm that separates sinful humanity from God the Holy."[15] And in his missiological handbook he reiterated this conviction: "The Bible is from first page to last one immense defense against paganism, against the paganizing tendencies within Israel itself, in short, against the degeneration of religion."[16] Bavinck clarifies this by means of concrete narratives from the OT, almost every part of which "is full of valuable indications" respecting matter, and when we turn to the NT "we soon notice that this part of the Bible, too, is continuously in conflict with the deepest motives of heathenism."[17] Thus the beginning of Genesis is one great protest against self-deification. And the story of Samson, the story of the Ark captured by the Philistines, the plagues in Egypt, and the recorded miracles of Jesus—each is a testimony against magical-mystical thinking.[18] In missionary praxis, as Bavinck experienced himself, the elenctic character of the Bible surfaces again and again.

> Every Gentile who does not read the gospel superficially but with the full attention of his heart will sooner or later make the wonderful discovery that Jesus is different, that His power is different from all other types of power in the world, because the

---

[14]*ICNCW*, 132.

[15]*CMO*, 115.

[16]*IZW*, 245 (cf. *ISM*, 245). Cf. also *CTM*, 29ff., where Bavinck again emphasizes the elenctic nature of the Bible by pointing out five fundamental differences between it and other holy books: in the Bible God is not identified with the creation; the kingdom of heaven rather than the cosmic order is central; ethical norms lie embedded in a relationship of love; progressive salvation history replaces the cyclical view of history; and the resurrection of Christ creates a new age and promises the "restoration of all things."

[17]*ICNCW*, 126, 128.

[18]*Ibid.*, 125-133.

power of Jesus is identical with His self-sacrificing love.[19]
In short, missiology, according to Bavinck, can never avoid the matter of elenctics, because *elenchein* is inherent in the biblical message itself. Bavinck summarizes his thinking on this issue as follows.

> It [the Bible] is a book for the Church . . . and it is at the same time a book for the world. . . . In the Bible God is wrestling with the world, persuading, reproving, admonishing, beseeching the various peoples of the world to accept the truth and be reconciled to God. . . . This book passes a verdict upon our unbelief and our ungodliness and our unrighteousness. . . . But this same book is a source of gladness to those who believe in the redeeming work of our Lord and Savior.[20]

4. Auxiliary Disciplines of Elenctics

For Bavinck the foundation of elenctics lies in the message of Scripture and, directly related to this, in the biblical assessment of the non-Christian religions.[21] However, in order to to gain a clear understanding of non-Christian thought and life, with an eye toward *elenchein*, one needs to consult various disciplines that fall outside the theological curriculum.[22] Bavinck mentions a number of these disciplines as follows.

History of religions. This discipline attempts to trace the developments of the various religions as to their origin, development, and mutual influence. Besides mutual influences among non-Christian religions there are, according to Bavinck, also indications of "a certain special-revelation radiation" at work among the other religions via Israel and the Christian church.[23] Bavinck writes that "standing on the foundation of faith in the Scriptures, we cannot but observe—even though it cannot be demonstrated scientifically—that the history of humanity began with the service and worship of one God, the Creator of heaven and earth."[24] Nevertheless, it would be a misunderstanding to assume and wrong to imply, he states, that all religions, including Christianity, have sprung from the same root. Such a position "would not do justice to the shattering impact of the Fall on

---

[19]*Ibid.*, 132.

[20]*Ibid.*, 139-140.

[21]*IZW*, 17 (cf. *ISM*, xxi).

[22]*Ibid.*, 234 (cf. *ISM*, 233). Bavinck's handling of these disciplines shows clearly that, the fact that they fall outside theology does not mean that there are no mutual ties between them and the theological disciplines. On one side they must be pursued in their own right in light of biblical revelation, on the other they concretize and intensify missiological reflection.

[23]*IZW*, 237 (cf. *ISM*, 236).

[24]*Ibid.*, 235-236 (cf. *ISM*, 234-235).

religious life" and would lead to the "creation of wrong assumptions."[25] Accordingly, he emphatically rejects any idea that the academic study of the history of religions could be pursued without consideration of the historical-religious and *heilsgeschichtliche* developments depicted in the Bible. Rather, he assumes that the latter will be confirmed by the former.[26]

Religious studies. This field of study engages in empirical investigation of the various faith traditions. The study of religion, as well as the history of religions, belong under the humanities rather than under theology.[27]

Psychology of religion. This subject area seeks to determine to what extent religion as a phenomenon can be explained psychologically and which psychological phenomena are an integral part of the various religions, with an eye to discovering the deeper backgrounds of these traditions. Here again he points out emphatically that it is not psychology but theology that has the final word. Although it is true that "many expressions of religious life are connected with other psychological phenomena and must be viewed in connection with them," it is clear from Scripture that standing behind every religion is "the inexpressible mystery of God's involvement with fallen humanity." Moreover, Scripture also provides an "extremely important guideline" for this area of study, viz, that "the unwillingness to acknowledge God lies hidden as the deepest psychological motivation" in every religion. "All psychological investigations in the realm of religion must take this divinely revealed datum into account."[28]

Phenomenology of religion. This branch of knowledge studies and compares phenomena that the various religions have in common and seeks to discover what is essential in these phenomena. Again, Bavinck is convinced that the results of this research will manifest agreement with the biblical data. In this connection he writes:

> Remarkably, it is becoming increasingly apparent that humanity has returned again and again to the same ideas, the same attitudes. . . . We discover the same processes, the same symptoms of degeneration all over the world; humanity appears to be, in spite of radical differences, a unity in a much deeper sense than we generally think.[29]

Philosophy of religion. This discipline has the task of processing the results of religious studies along philosophical lines and hence occupies itself with matters such as the essence, the taxonomy, and the uniqueness of the religions. The objectivity of this philosophical reflection depends on whether it takes as its starting point the authority outside and above us: God's Word. In discussing the question of the essence of religion, Bavinck writes:

> It is clear, that this first question of the philosophy of religion

---

[25] *Ibid.*, 235 (cf. *ISM*, 234).

[26] *Ibid.*, 235-236 (cf. *ISM*, 234-235).

[27] *Ibid.*, 238.

[28] *Ibid.*, 238 (cf. *ISM*, 237).

[29] *Ibid.*, 239 (cf. *ISM*, 238).

already runs into endless difficulties. Who will actually decide what religion is? This is why also the philosophy of religion must begin by listening to God's Word. God alone can tell us what religion is. [30]

In his development of the elenctic approach, Bavinck frequently dealt with these ancillary disciplines, as is apparent from the abundance of publications by others which he cites and interacts with[31] and the number of short publications he himself wrote on this matter.[32]

5. The Divisions of Elenctics

Bavinck splits elenctics into three divisions: general (or historical) elenctics; special elenctics; and phenomenological elenctics.[33]

General elenctics views religious life in its historical development and takes this as the starting point for its argument. Religious life is characterized by an ever-recurring process of degeneration and regeneration. If we see behind this history both the action of the God who reveals himself and the reaction of man who responds, then the history of religious appears to be in the final analysis one great wrestling "of God with man who dreams on in sinful self-deception."[34] This history as such is a call to conversion and surrender to the one, true God.[35] In a separate chapter in *IZW* Bavinck provides a sample of general elenctics from four perspectives: God and the cosmos; God who is pushed and withdraws into the background; God and the moral world order; God and the primeval ocean.[36]

Although Bavinck and Kuyper are closely related in their thinking on this point, they also appear to differ. Bavinck does not share Kuyper's position that in the development of religion one finds not only the negative element of sinful disruption, but also the structural presence of the positive element of "common grace." This powerful working of common grace is the reason why much that is beautiful and good is found in the various religions "like grains of gold in the sand

---

[30]*Ibid.*, 240 (cf. *ISM*, 239). Bavinck says,

[31]He mentions, especially in *CMO, RBCG,* and *IZW* a variety of publications by others from which he draws.

[32]Het primitieve denken; *De godsdienst van Java*; Het hindoeïsme; *De psychologie van de Oosterling*; Berg en zee als mystiek-religieuze grootheden; *Phaenomenologische classificatie der religieuze structuren*; Uitkomsten der studie van buitenbijbelse religies; De absoluutheid van het Christendom.

[33]Cf. *IZW*, 244-246 (*ISM*, 243-244).

[34]*IZW*, 244-245 (cf. *ISM*, 243).

[35]Cf. *Ibid.*, 245 (*ISM*, 244).

[36]Cf. *Ibid.*, 248-272 (*ISM*, 247-272).

on the shore.[37] Bavinck does not reject this possibility entirely: "We may say that by the grace of God repression and substitution do not always succeed."[38] Yet he generally follows Kraemer's much more radical approach on this point,[39] as is demonstrated by his contention that "superficial study leads to the notion that there is a striking level of similarity [between extra-biblical and biblical customs and ideas], but deeper reflection shows that great dissimilarity lies hidden in the similarity."[40]

Special elenctics looks at one specific religion and tries to understand it historically, psychologically and phenomenologically as well as theologically. Armed with this knowledge it is possible on the basis of the Scriptures to convict people of sin and to call them to conversion in the context of mission.[41]

Phenomenological elenctics reflects on a specific phenomenon that is found in several religions, for example, prayer, sacrifice, mysticism. The point is then, "to investigate," on the basis of what the Bible teaches regarding these phenomena, "what the nations have made of [them] and then to call people to account and repentance.[42] Bavinck himself was primarily occupied with the phenomenon of mysticism. His most important publication in this area is *CMO*.[43]

6. The Starting Point of Elenctics

In apologetics, reason is often made *the* starting point for showing the inherent untenability of non-Christian thought. In the early church the logos or *ratio* was considered to be a reflection of the Logos, and hence was viewed as the ally of the Christian faith and as weapon in the battle against all myth-based religion (cf. Justin Martyr). This view was systematized in the Roman-Catholic tradition (cf. Thomas Aquinas). Reason was seen as the source of natural knowledge of God, the gateway to the Christian faith. By means of an appeal to reason, it was thought, it should be possible to convince people that there can be only one God, that there must be justice, and a life after this life. This rational approach was considered necessary: initially any appeal to the Bible would be futile, since it would not be acknowledged as God's revelation by those who did not believe. Only after reason has made its case with compelling power and a first dawning of the light had been

---

[37]Kuyper, *Encyclopaedie*, 3, 453.

[38]*CBTM*, 203. Cf. also *ICNCW*, 96-97, where he gives a striking example of this.

[39]Cf. H. Kraemer, *The Christian Message in a non-Christian World*, 137ff.

[40]*IZW*, 229 (cf. *ISM*, 228).

[41]*Ibid.*, 245 (cf. *ISM*, 244).

[42]*Ibid.*

[43]Other Publications in this field are: "Berg en zee als mystiek-religieuze grootheden"; "Mythos en logos"; a series of articles on mysticism in *GW* 6 (1952); and "Het evangelie en het mystiek levensgevoel."

achieved could the biblical revelation be used as point of departure. The supernatural truths, which were above the reach of reason but in and of themselves not unreasonable, could then be taught from the Bible.

Bavinck points out that Calvin was the first to view this natural knowledge of God in an extremely negative light.[44] Even the most sophisticated thinkers are "worse than obtuse and blind" in their thinking about God,[45] and any sparks of light "are extinguished before they emit a brighter radiance."[46] Calvin subjected the ability of reason to such a charge of critique that reason itself could no longer serve as the starting point in apologetics. "It is nevertheless remarkable," Bavinck writes, "that missiology in the churches of the Reformation remained captive to the ideas" of earlier Roman Catholic theology,[47] and refers in this connection in particular to Voetius.

Voetius, making explicit reference to Thomas Aquinas, states, "We are of the opinion that it is very beneficial not to begin with an exposition of the truth of our faith, but with a refutation of paganism, and to do this with the help of the natural light reason."[48] He continued with a metaphor: "They who plant the faith follow herein the example of gardeners, who first remove the weeds and only then entrust the seed to the cleared ground."[49] In conjunction with this he states further that they who are sent to developed nations must be philosophically trained.[50] An additional argument for taking reason as the point of departure is, according to Voetius, the fact that the Scriptures are not acknowledged by non-believers as revelation from God.[51] Neither is Kuyper, who "willfully" followed Voetius,[52] entirely clear on this point, according to Bavinck. He feels that Kuyper gave too much credit to philosophical argumentation in the refutation of pseudo-religion,

---

[44]Cf. *IZW*, 225 (*ISM*, 224).

[45]J. Calvin, *Institutes* 1.5.12.

[46]*Ibid.*, 1.5.14.

[47]*IZW*, 226 (cf. *ISM*, 225).

[48]"Putamus expeditissimum esse, si incipiatur non a demonstratione veritatis fidei nostrae, sed a refutatione Gentilismi, idque ex ratione ac lumine naturali." G. Voetius, *Disputatio*, 637. Cf. H.A. van Andel, *De zendingsleer*, 172-173.

[49]H.A. van Andel, *De zendingsleer*, 173.

[50]G. Voetius, *Politica*, 334-335. Cf. H.A. van Andel, *De zendingsleer*, 173-74.

[51]H.A. van Andel, *De zendingsleer*, 172. This applies to gentiles (*gentiles*) and Muslims (*Muhammedistae*). In addressing Jews (*Judaei*) one can give proof from the OT of the legitimate claims of the Christian faith.

[52]J.A.B. Jongeneel, *Missiologie*, 2, 332.

inferring this from the fact that Kuyper speaks of demonstrating "the intrinsic untruth" of the non-Christian religions, the "falsification of the tradition of Revelation," and the "abnormal and sinful development of the natural knowledge of God.[53] It is true, as already indicated, that Kuyper holds the view that due to "common grace" much good is found in non-Christian religions. But Kuyper also relativizes philosophical argumentation to a considerable extent. In any case, it is clear that for him the center of gravity of *elenchein* lies in the revelation of God: sinners can be convinced of the error of their ways, he writes, only "if the Light (*Phoos*) beams from Christ into the darkness (*skotia*), and if they, who were given over 'in the sinful desires of their hearts,' are seized by the mercies of God."[54]

When Bavinck comes to defining his own position, he emphatically points out once again that the concept of *elenchein* is of a religious-ethical nature and that it can therefore never refer to persuasion by means of philosophical argumentation. He states that the early apologists, who so strongly embraced the Johannine concept of Logos, could have discovered precisely in the Gospel of John that "coming to the truth" is a religious matter: "People loved darkness instead of light" (John 3:19).[55] Furthermore, it is much too simplistic to view the aberrations in the religions as lapses of reason that can be corrected by means of philosophical arguments. "The matter is much more serious. The rational life of man is too closely intertwined with his instinctive passions, with his emotional and volitional life for reasonable arguments to be able truly to change him."[56] Behind folly lies rebellion against God. The deliberations of reason come to nothing, because people "suppress the truth by their wickedness" (Rom. 1:8).[57] Bavinck acknowledges that the prophets of the OT "in their elenctic attack against idolatry occasionally use rational argument."[58] But—referring to Isaiah 44, where the prophet pillories the foolishness (*nebalah*) of idolatry—he immediately points out that the cutting edge of their argument always consists of the prophetic unmasking of wrong,.[59] In short, reason can provide auxiliary elenctic service here and there, but it can never be the point of departure. Bavinck already pointed this out as early as 1927:

> Wherein lies the uniqueness of Christianity? In this, that it takes
> the misery, the bankruptcy of life much, much more seriously...
> than any other religion. Do we have enough when we know the
> truth, when the road to salvation is outlined for us? No, because
> we don't follow that road. No matter how well I know what I
> must do, there is a power in me that always pushes me toward

---

[53] A. Kuyper, *Encyclopaedia*, 3, 446.

[54] *Ibid.*, 449.

[55] *IZW*, 227 (cf. *ISM*, 226).

[56] *Ibid.*, 229-230 (cf. *ISM*, 228).

[57] *Ibid.*, 230 (cf. *ISM*, 228).

[58] 227-228 (cf. *ISM*, 226).

[59] *Ibid.*

evil.... This misery is not only grounded in the intellect, in ignorance, in error.[60]
At the same time Bavinck knows full well that we cannot simply make the Bible our point of departure, because "the revelation of God in Jesus Christ is not known nor believed" by the non-believer.[61] On the basis of these considerations it is possible to discover a threefold point of departure in Bavinck.

In the first place, Bavinck points out that every human being is within reach of God's general revelation.[62] In addition to the fact that all religions are a response to this revelation, they are also continually unmasked to some extent by it. Before the missionary arrives with his elenctic argument, God has already been there with his truth, so that what can be known of God in any way is plain to them (Rom. 1:19). In addition to the fact that the truth is continually repressed and replaced, it also makes people inwardly restless. "There is deep in the heart of man, also in that of those who adhere to non-Christian religions and believe in them, a very vague awareness that one is playing a game with God and is always secretly busy running away from him."[63] Bavinck declares that the elenctic argument must tie in with this conversation that is constantly being carried on between God and man, and that it must appeal to people's existential insecurity. He puts this in striking language: "This is the only chink in the Goliath-armour of pseudo-religion, where the shepherd boy with his stone—if God guides his hand—can hit people."[64] Starting from "these basic acknowledgments the [elenctic] conversation can begin. . . . In his heart of hearts man has a vague sense that he is trying to fool God and that he is guilty before God."[65] If there is indeed such a thing as a point of contact, it lies in the *psychē* rather than in the *ratio*.

In the second place, The missionary is called "to bring, in obedience to [God's] command, the message of him who alone is the Way and the Truth and the Life."[66] According to Bavinck, the revelation of God in Jesus Christ must stand at the center of the elenctic approach,[67] so that the unmasking of untruth takes place in the light of the truth and through that man discovers his true colors before the face of God. The point of prophetic-elenctic argument is to make plainly clear that religious striving ultimately involves "revolt against the one true God ... self-deification, pulling God down to the world, and the horrifying attempt to make God

---

[60]*LV*, 88.

[61]*IZW*, 228 (cf. *ISM*, 227).

[62]*Ibid.*, 228 (cf. *ISM*, 227). For a detailed discussion of Bavinck's view on this matter, see chapter 4 above.

[63]*Ibid.*, 229 (cf. *ISM*, 227).

[64]*PPRAO*, 19.

[65]*CBTM*, 200-201.

[66]*CMO*, 104

[67]Cf. *IZW*, 232 (*ISM*, 231).

subservient to oneself."[68] He stresses that the fact that the unbeliever does not yet assent to the revelation of God constitutes only an *apparent* contradiction, "because we have to do with a God who reveals himself to every human being, even though that person stubbornly suppresses that revealed truth in unrighteousness."[69] In other words, man is not being addressed by God for the first time, even though he is not initially aware of it. In a certain sense, the unknown God is known. And for Bavinck, direct confrontation with the biblical message is eminently possible because, as already indicated, he views the Bible itself as elenctic in nature. He writes:

> [The Bible] is a book that every Gentile can read and when he
> reads it he feels refuted by it. It is as if this Bible were written
> for him; every page of it is full of weighty wisdom, a wisdom that
> is wonderfully adjusted to his specific needs. Nobody who reads
> the Bible can escape from its appeal.[70]

In the third place, Bavinck points to the decisive importance of the Holy Spirit as the subject of *elenchein*. "The Holy Spirit himself creates the starting point, he awakens in man that deeply hidden awareness of guilt. . . . The Holy Spirit uses the word of the preacher and the Spirit himself creates in man's heart the receptivity that allows the word to enter."[71] Elenctics as a purely human undertaking would be, according to Bavinck, "a rather hopeless affair." The Spirit, however, makes us powerful in Christ.[72] The message of the bearer of good news

> has only one powerful weapon, namely, that its messengers know
> that if they bring it obediently and honestly, trusting in God's
> help and in his Spirit, it will somehow touch the heart of man. ...
> Then the engines of repression are stopped, as it were, and only
> then he sees clearly who he himself is, and who God is.[73]

Bavinck's point of departure in elenctics is not anthropocentric but clearly *theocentric* in a Trinitarian sense: he mentions a theological, a christological, and a pneumatological aspect. In *elenchein* the conversation that God the Father carries on with every human being reaches its decisive and critical climax in the confrontation with the Word (Christ) and through the witness of the Holy Spirit. Philosophical argumentation renders good services in that process but it can never truly lead to conversion because religious aberrations do not simply involve errors in thought but rather secret flight from God.

> It [elenctics] must always try to understand the motives that are
> hidden behind all this. That will often sound mercilessly hard,
> and people will frequently rebel against elenctic witness. And

---

[68] *Ibid.*, 227-228 (cf. *ISM,* 226).

[69] *Ibid.*, 232 (cf. *ISM,* 231).

[70] Cf. *ICNCW,* 133.

[71] *IZW,* 230 (cf. *ISM,* 229).

[72] *Ibid.*, 230, 232 (cf. *ISM,* 229, 231).

[73] *CBTM,* 206.

yet the elenctic word will have to be the decisive word, spoken
with unflagging longsuffering and tact.[74]
This plainly demonstrates that for Bavinck a *psychological* approach is at least as
important in the elenctic encounter as philosophical argument.

7. The Essence of Elenctics

On the basis of the material delineated above, Bavinck defines elenctics as the
discipline "that unmasks all false religion as sin against God and calls people to the
knowledge of the one, true God." Humans do occupy an important place in this
process of persuasion as instrument in God's hand, but the decisive role is played
by God Himself, that is, the Holy Spirit. "The Holy Spirit is actually the only
conceivable subject of this verb [*elenchein*], because conviction of sin transcends
all human capability."[75]   Bavinck thus embeds the cooperative human share in
elenchein in the Trinitarian action of God. This emerges clearly when he writes:

> The knowledge that the Holy Spirit is the true author certainly
> has not been given to us to absolve us from responsibility for
> taking our labors fully seriously. On the contrary, the Holy Spirit
> demands from us true commitment to the task he imposes on us,
> and . . . then he will use us as tools in his hand.[76]

To the extent that man is the subject in *elenchein*, what is necessary—in
addition to "a clear perception of the deepest stirrings of the soul that find
expression in religion"—is a "considered knowledge of that religion." Responsible
theological inquiry cannot do without the knowledge derived from the study of
religions.

8. The Methods of Elenctics

Because of the variety of religions involved, there can be no single,
generally valid elenctic method, according to Bavinck. Even for one particular
religion no fixed method can be developed because *elenchein* "in fact can only be
practiced in living contact with the adherents of other religions."[77]   Any
systematized elenctic approach carries the danger of doing injustice to the living
person, because in practice we never deal with 'Islam,' but always with *a* Muslim
and *his* or *her* Islam. "In other words, elenctics as a discipline can never render
superfluous the delicate probing for the religious secret of an individual and what
it is that fills his whole existence."[78]   Sound gospel proclamation, he writes,
"demands that we take the object of our work fully seriously in our thoughts and our

---

[74]*IZW*, 272 (cf. *ISM,* 271).

[75]*IZW*, 223 (cf. *ISM,* 222).

[76]*IZW*, 230 (cf. *ISM,* 229).

[77]*IZW*, 242 (cf. *ISM,* 240).

[78]*Ibid.*

efforts."[79] Initially, therefore, the elenctic approach has more the character of exploration than proclamation.

But this does not mean that it is impossible to establish some basic methodological principles. In *AWW* Bavinck attempts to extract these principles from the Scriptures, turning for this purpose to an examination of especially the method followed by Paul. The first thing that strikes him is that Paul "was fully cognizant of what lived in the hearts of the people of his time."[80] In *IZW* he draws the conclusion from this that "elenctics must commence with a careful and unhurried scrutiny of the religion with which it is dealing."[81] This examination must be as objective as possible, and in order to guarantee objectivity, Bavinck advises against "focusing on manifestations of degeneration in the religion one studies, but to view it especially in its noblest forms."[82] And for this, elenctics gratefully makes use of the building blocks provided by the disciplines of the phenomenology and history of religions.

Next, Bavinck points out that "through all the glitter of paganism" Paul "saw its hollowness."[83] Bavinck applies this to elenctics, stating that objective examination of religion must be followed by an "attempt to penetrate into the psychological depths that form its background."[84] It is not enough to know what a person's religion teaches. It is also necessary to find out how he or she experiences it: "What is this person doing inwardly with God?"[85] This investigation requires that, besides the psychology of religion, we also consider the biblical witness, for "the Bible supports us at every step by what it teaches us concerning the human heart in its cunning attempts to seek God and simultaneously evade him."[86]

It is armed with this knowledge that *elenchein* proper can begin. Following Hans Schärer,[87] Bavinck speaks of "a slow, probing approach, whose purpose is always to genuinely encounter" people of other religions."[88] Bavinck considered this to be the Pauline approach:

The apostle experienced the preaching of the gospel as a difficult

---

[79]*CPVW*, 12.

[80]*AWW*, 121.

[81]*IZW*, 243 (cf. *ISM*, 241).

[82]*Ibid.*

[83]*AWW*, 122.

[84]*IZW*, 243 (cf. *ISM*, 242).

[85]*Ibid.*

[86]*Ibid.*, 246 (cf. *ISM*, 244).

[87]Cf. H. Schärer, *Die missionsarische Verkündigung*, passim.

[88]*IZW*, 243-244 (cf. *ISM*, 242).

> task, as we can see throughout his letters. The difficulty was not
> that he was ashamed of it ... But every step of the way he
> realized how extremely difficult it is to make the unsearchable
> riches of the love of Christ clear to people who do not know what
> sin and lostness are.[89]

Nevertheless, Bavinck descries in this searching elenctic approach of Paul's a primary structure, an architectonic line that provides direction. This basic schema consists of the following elements: first, Paul speaks about the living God in contradistinction to the idols; then, he points eschatologically to the day of judgment, in which the risen Christ is presented as Judge of the world; and finally, he proclaims redemption, through the crucified Christ who is the Savior of the world.[90] It must be emphasized that Bavinck was not advocating a chronological scheme of 'law and gospel' for the elenctic encounter. On the contrary:

> When it is said that first the Law must be preached to the
> Gentiles and the Mohammedans and then the Gospel, we would
> not want to separate these two so sharply from each other,
> because on the mission field it becomes clear again and again
> that often the majesty of the Law is only clearly understood in the
> light of the gospel.[91]

In the Pauline schema of elenctic witness the cross of Christ is not the starting point; it is, however, the focal point of that witness.[92] This fits with Bavinck's earlier assertion that the best means "by which we can make the distinction felt deeply and radically" is to "place the East before the holy figure of Christ."[93] In summary Bavinck writes:

> In the marketplaces of the cities of Asia Minor and Greece, Paul,
> driven by the Holy Spirit, preached to convict the world of sin,
> of justice and of judgment, with a view to creating an
> opportunity, through this semonizing, [for people] to uncover
> something of the mystery of grace, through the cross of Jesus
> Christ, our Lord.[94]

> On the one hand, the method Paul used can give direction to missionary
approach in our day. This is a big jump chronologically, but not actually, according to Bavinck. Man has not changed, the message is the same, and there are striking

---

[89] *AWW,* 129. Bavinck terms Paul's call in Col. 4:3 for the church's intercession for an opened door a telling sign of his humility.

[90] *Ibid.*, 124-129. Bavinck adduces this schema from what Paul writes in 1 Thess. 1:9-10 and from his speeches in Lystra (Acts 14) and in Athens (Acts 17), and sees it confirmed in Acts 16:31, 19:37, 20:20ff, 24:24-26 and 26:20.

[91] "De zending nu!"

[92] *Ibid.*, 128. Bavinck refers here to 1 Cor. 2:1-2 and 2 Cor. 5:20.

[93] *CMO,* 228-229.

[94] *AWW*, 152. It is clear that Bavinck's reading here of John 16:8ff is more impressionistic than the product of careful exegesis.

parallels between Hellenistic culture and present-day cultures.[95] On the other hand, we must learn from Paul's elenctic approach that "the central content of the gospel was expressed topically in relation to the world of those days."[96] And that must also be our concern today. It is not enough for us to "indiscriminately follow the missionary methodology of the first preachers of the gospel."[97] Bavinck avows that in searching for the appropriate elenctic approach in a concrete situation, it is incumbent upon mission to make grateful use of the knowledge, wisdom and experience native Christians—assuming there are any—can contribute to the development of that approach. The best way of finding out how the solid wall of world views can be breached, so that Christ can enter in, is by "investigating how the gospel is appropriated in the 'Younger Churches,' [by searching out] which concepts provided them with a first foothold, [by ascertaining] how the gospel is reflected in their spirits and minds."[98]

Bavinck stressed many times that in the elenctic situation we must never stand *above* but always *next to* the other. The more we get to know "the deepest stirrings that are hidden behind many foolish and childish arguments," the more we recognize ourselves. We were (and are) fleeing from God and pushing him aside in a similar albeit it much more cunning way. Bavinck then states, "In all your elenctic efforts" you can view things from "the vantage point of your own life, in which God's grace has done its miraculous work" despite the stubborn "recalcitrance of your own heart, and in which he still continues" to work miracles "with infinite patience." Elenctics, he avers, "is possible only on the basis of that true self-knowledge that is kindled in our hearts by the Holy Spirit,"[99] and, he adds, "One must know oneself and the recesses of one's own heart thoroughly to be able to engage authentically in elenctic witness."[100] From this he concludes: "When you stand thus before the other person, who is bound in another religion, it is not difficult to engage him in a conversation. [Standing before the other in this way] you will not have to launch endless intellectual arguments in order to break through the entanglements of his or her thinking."[101] Here emerges the heart-to-heart conversation, in which there is no room to reproach one another for anything, for in this dialogue which becomes a trialogue the Holy Spirit convicts us together of the same sin.[102] Elenctic witness "must be given without any pride. ... It is God's

---

[95] *CPVW*, 11.

[96] *AWW*, 148

[97] *CPVW*, 12.

[98] *Ibid.*, 14, 16, 17.

[99] *IZW*, 223 (cf. *ISM*, 222).

[100] *IZW*, 272 (cf. *ISM*, 272).

[101] *IZW*, 231 (cf. *ISM*, 230).

[102] Cf. *IZW*, 230 (cf. *ISM*, 229-30), Bavinck refers here to Kuyper, *Encyclopaedie*, 3, 449.

message to all of us, without distinction of race and people,"[103] and "there is no more humbling work in the world . . . , for one realizes every moment that the weapon he points at the other has wounded him" as well.[104] By taking this stance, which for him is decisive, Bavinck achieves full integration of the elenctic point of departure he advocates into his elenctic method. The elenctic message, he writes, "cannot wrap itself in philosophical arguments, it cannot 'prove' anything, it cannot be 'logical' in every respect."[105] By the grace of Jesus Christ we have "more powerful means" at our disposal; according to a word of Paul: "My message and my preaching were not with wise and persuasive words, but with a demonstration of the Spirit's power" (1 Cor. 2:4).[106] This message, Bavinck states, "has only one powerful weapon, namely, that its messengers know that if they bring it obediently and honestly, trusting in God's help and His Spirit, it will somehow touch the heart of man."[107] The powers and efforts of the missionary witness, thus, are in and of themselves of little avail in the elenctic situation: "Repudiation is easy, flattery is also easy, but challenging with understanding, witnessing convincingly, that is difficult. The envoy of Christ can do this only when the same Spirit who convicts the world works in him."[108]

From the preceding it is apparent that Bavinck attaches great value to dialogue in both the exploratory and the proclamation phase of the elenctic approach, and that it may therefore be said that in Bavinck's thought *elenchein* bears a dialogical character. The concept of "dialogue" is even used once in *CBTM*: "It [the church] cannot avoid dialogue with them [temple and mosque]. It is not sufficient merely to witness, because [the church] will somehow have to say what it thinks of those other religions.[109]

9. Complicating Factors for Elenctics

Bavinck regularly points out three problems that confront elenctics in practice. There is the ever-recurring problem of syncretism which is inherent in non-Christian religious thinking. And there are the two typically 20th-century problems of nationalism and secularization, which lead to religious renewal and religious decay.

9.1. Tendency toward Syncretism

Bavinck calls attention to the manifestation of a strong tendency toward syncretism

---

[103] *CBTM*, 205-206.

[104] *IZW*, 272 (cf. *ISM*, 272).

[105] *Ibid*, 206.

[106] *IZW*, 231 (cf. *ISM*, 230).

[107] *CBTM*, 206.

[108] *AWW*, 187.

[109] *CBTM*, 199.

everywhere among the nations. This makes the preaching of the gospel more difficult, because it is "much easier to work among people who resist [the gospel] antithetically than among people who say yes to everything but understand [what they hear and see] along syncretistic lines."[110] Already in his first elenctic study, *CMO*, Bavinck illustrates this by showing how much certain aspects of the gospel "appeal to and fascinate"[111] the Javanese, to the extent that they tend to "give Jesus a place of honor, provided that they are allowed to interpret him in the Eastern spirit and thus to recognize Eastern ideas in him."[112] This even goes so far that when the radical difference between Christian faith and Javanese mysticism is emphasized, "a knowing smile" will often appear on the face of the listener, because "he thinks he understands Christianity much better than does the Western preacher."[113] This has a paralyzing effect, and Bavinck continued to be extremely fearful of this danger. In his final publication, *CBTM*, he writes: "It is very well possible that the opposition the Church meets is not as dangerous as the seeming recognition it receives from the syncretistic movements."[114]

Following Kraemer,[115] Bavinck declares this syncretistic tendency to be inherent in the religious cosmic thinking that underlies many religions. The naturalistic apperception of life and of the world leads to totalistic thinking. World and life constitute a unity (macrocosm and microcosm). While it is true that the cosmos is classified in contrasting relationships (e.g., light and darkness), these contrasts are essentially merely apparent, because together, in their connectedness, they constitute the whole and represent the divine. This classification finds expression in a polytheistic religious outlook. The gods of the various nations have different shadings, but they are identical in essence. "Syncretism can grow without hindrance" in the soil of this holistic monism and its implicit relativism.[116]

This syncretistic tendency arises from the idea that all religion is "an external, imperfect, human approach to the one inexpressible truth of God, which is exalted above all things,"[117] and it is reinforced in two ways. In the first place

---

[110]"Syncretisme als zendingsprobleem," 11.

[111]*CMO*, 209.

[112]*Ibid.*, 216.

[113]*Ibid.*

[114]*CBTM*, 199.

[115]Cf. H. Kraemer, *De wortelen van het syncretisme* (1937). Bavinck, "Syncretisme als zendingsprobleem," 12, says "this study [has increased] our understanding of syncretism."

[116]"Syncretisme als zendingsprobleem," 12-13.

[117]"Christus en de wereld van het oosten," 230.

through "the sin of the missionaries" in the past,[118] who—due to a lack of theological knowledge, or out of respect for the religious tradition they encountered and false modesty—have often gone too far in mixing the Christian and the non-Christian traditions.[119]   Once this has happened, an elenctic call to conversion becomes extremely difficult, because the listeners have the idea that they have mastered the Christian faith.[120] In *OKZK* Bavinck implicitly inveighs against the growing relativizing tendencies in the missiological world:

> Mission is possible only from the standpoint of faith in an absolute revelation of God that is valid for all times and people. As soon as I deny that revelation there is no longer a place for mission. As soon as I relativize the truth of God I no longer can find the courage to bother other people with my thoughts. Only when I stand in the certainty that God himself has spoken can I urge others to listen, even as I myself have listened.[121]

Second, nationalism fosters spiritual self-awareness. When it comes to science and technology, "the West is gladly acknowledged as master, but it is extremely difficult for the East to be open to learning from the West about those things with which the East has occupied itself for so many centuries."[122] The West is too godless and too materialistic and the East has produced religious ideas that are too valuable for this.[123] As a result it is difficult for people in the East simply to condemn their own religious past and "to begin anew with Christ."[124] At most there is a preparedness to find a synthesis between their own spiritual heritage and the gospel.[125] Bavinck mentions Mahatma Gandhi as example of this stance: "Gandhi confessed that he also regarded Jesus as a manifestation of God, but not as the only one," and refers to Gandhi's well-known statement: "I don't place him

---

[118] *Ibid.*, 229.

[119] Cf. *ibid.*, 229-230 and "Syncretisme als zendingprobleem," 14-15, where Bavinck refers, in this connection, to the well-known missionary C.F. Andrews, who wrote in a reaction to Tambaram in 1939: "The inclination in Hinduism to bring all religions into harmony with one another is to be preferred by far over the rough and fanatical way in which many Christians condemn other religions." To support his view theologically Andrews quotes the words of Jesus, "Whoever does the will of God is my brother and sister and mother" (Mark 3:35).

[120] "Christus en de wereld van het oosten," 233-234.

[121] *OKZK*, 9.

[122] *CMO*, 230.

[123] *Ibid.* Cf. also "Syncretisme als zendingsprobleem," 13.

[124] *CMO*, 230-231.

[125] "Syncretisme als zendingsprobleem," 13.

[Jesus] upon a solitary throne."[126]

With his fundamental opposition to syncretism and his rejection of the notion that a syncretistic Christendom can function as a kind of transitional phase, Bavinck is more nuanced than Karl Hartenstein, to whom he refers in this context, but he allows for the latter as a practical possibility.[127] God's conversation is not infrequently long-drawn, and *elenchein* is often a long-term undertaking. Thus he can state, with an eye to developments in Asia, that "the word of Christ has become a force in the world of the East," but God "has not yet reached the end of his talk with the peoples of Asia."[128] In this struggle the church is called to make clear "the profound distinction between all that the East has said and thought about God, and what Christ has shown us of God."[129] And even when people have accepted the Christian faith God's conversation with them continues: it is "especially when we speak to those who have already come to the gospel of Christ" that we feel "that we must carefully and cautiously give instruction concerning that which separates the subtleties of the East from the thoughts of the gospel."[130]

9.2. Religious Renewal and Decay

Through the process of civilization an ever-widening gap emerged in the Third World between teachings and life, between religion and culture, between ancient religious ideas and new scientific insights. Bavinck writes: "They all went through a certain crisis in the preceding century when they came into contact with Western civilization. . . . The old traditions simply could not be maintained as before, and the leaders were compelled to chart new courses."[131] The result was that in Islam as well as in Hinduism and Buddhism a process of revitalization began to take place. There was a movement to reinterpret ancient religious views and practices and integrate them into modern life in such a way that it would be energized by them.[132] This, combined with nationalistic ambitions, gave a powerful impetus to religious self-awareness. According to Bavinck, this revitalization constitutes a reinforced blockade against the message of the gospel.[133] Added to this is the fact that the church by maintaining such "metaphysical suppositions as the virgin birth of Jesus," which it must do if it wishes to hold on to the message of the Gospel, is

---

[126]*CBTM*, 198-199.

[127]"Syncretisme als zendingsprobleem,"19.

[128]"Christus en de wereld van het oosten," 233-234. Cf. also *CMO*, 231.

[129]*CMO*, 107.

[130]*Ibid.*

[131]*CBTM*, 196. In *De strijd op het derde front*, 9-11, Bavinck gives a brief overview of the search for "new sources of power in the old faiths."

[132]*Ibid.*, 197.

[133]*Ibid*, 196-197.

said to 'lag behind' the supposed 'developments' in thinking taking place in this so-called 'enlightened age.'[134] Besides, (Western) Christianity is viewed as "having been the cause of sharp disputes and even of religious wars and persecutions in those parts of the world where it was the dominating power."[135] It has such a tainted past that in the eyes of many it is "the least suitable agency to guide men to a new aeon and a new world."[136]

This puts *elenchein* under enormous pressure. Nevertheless it remains an inescapable task to confront the world with the unmasking message of God's grace in Christ. The focus hereby is on four points, all with a spiritual charge: obedience to God, honesty toward the world, humility because of Christianity's tainted past, and faith despite the recalcitrant present. This fundamental existential attitude is entirely characteristic of Bavinck.

More problematic even than the religious revitalization is, according to Bavinck, religious decay. Almost prophetically he begins already before World War II to point out that a great spiritual vacuum is developing. Religious awareness and experience are undermined worldwide by scientific, technological, and economic developments. That which was experienced as mystery appears to be measurable. Fear of, and independence from, the divine powers have given way to medical knowledge and human controllability. Education and development have broken open the walls of the self-contained life and placed it under the aegis of progress. This means on the one hand an enrichment for the mind, but on the other hand it causes an impoverishment in religious life and experience. The divine gives way to the secular. This process of secularization with its godless and normless tendencies is the bitter fruit of Western expansion[137] Western culture has had a revolutionizing and disintegrating impact on religious thought and concepts.[138]

Bavinck realizes that the absence of a religious frame of reference seriously impedes *elenchein*. Nevertheless, he was initially still rather optimistic. In 1937 he wrote:

> In the ferment of this modern era the Younger Churches are beginning to realize that they are not fulfilling their obligation if they remain on the sidelines. They feel that they share responsibility for the fate of their people and their surroundings. And the world around them is also beginning to ask for help, beginning to stretch its hands toward anyone who has something that might be held on to. . . . If we stand in the fervent conviction that Jesus Christ can answer all the needs in the life of the world, it goes without saying that we will watch the developments of these things very attentively. . . . We see it happening, around us and in us; we see it happening in the West and in the East. . . .

---

[134]*Ibid.*, 197.

[135]*Ibid.*

[136]*Ibid.*, 198.

[137]*De strijd op het derde front*, 5-9.

[138]*PO*, 24.

> The more terrible the vacuum and the more serious the call for
> sources of new power becomes, the deeper God bends over
> toward all who call and seek. For he is the Power and the Life
> and the Truth.[139]

Bavinck thus expected keenly that the missionary church would be able to speak the saving word at that critical moment of the time in which he lived.[140] "When I think of what would happen if in Japan or China or India a living, Christian church would grow into a force within the whole life of the nation," he wrote, "I don't really know what could be expected. . . . I believe that miraculous things would then become possible."

Although Bavinck never lost this faith, his optimism gradually waned. In 1942 he wrote:

> If we could bring that revelation [of God in Christ Jesus]
> disencumbered from Western culture, we would have been
> entrusted with a much simpler task than we have now, preaching
> the gospel in the East at the very time the entire East is in the
> process of being permeated so greatly by Western culture.[141]

Bavinck clearly recognizes here that *elenchein* becomes much more difficult in the context of a crumbling religious awareness, since in that kind of situation there is no point of address. Thus Bavinck concludes in 1948:

> If there has ever been a moment in world history that in our
> opinion must be viewed as extremely unfavorable for the spread
> of the gospel in the East, this is it. Both they who bring the
> gospel and they who hear it find themselves in extremely perilous
> circumstances; there is virtually no time for quiet reflection on
> the truth of God, for earnestly seeking the peace of God.[142]

Closely related to this, Bavinck concludes *IZW* (1954) by stating that the "core of all problems" for the future of mission consists in the fact that religious questions are pushed into the background.[143] At the same time, something of his earlier hope remains:

> It is to be expected . . . that the present whirl of developments .
> . . will break sooner or later, and that then the quest for inner
> stability, for a philosophy of life, for permanence will come to
> the fore with overpowering force. Will that be the great hour in
> which God will show us his miraculous works?[144]

It appears from several of Bavinck's publications that against the background of spiritual vacuum, *elenchein* increasingly gives way in Bavinck's thought to the

---

[139]*De strijd op het derde front*, 11-15.

[140]*Ibid.*, 14.

[141]*PO*, 25.

[142]"Christus en de wereld van het oosten," 211.

[143]*IZW*, 304 (cf. *ISM*, 307).

[144]*IZW*, 305 (cf. *ISM*, 309).

verbal proclamation of Christ as the Way, the Truth, and the Life.[145] It is a witnessing in which we are "more powerless than ever before" and are entirely thrown back "on the last resources of power that are available to us: the firm confidence that God is King and that prayer is able to accomplish much."[146]

In connection with his discussion of the relation of elenctics and secularization it must also be mentioned that Bavinck points to the negative impact on *elenchein* brought about by the fact that the Christian West itself has been suffering for a long time from secularizing tendencies that have led toward spiritual decay.[147] Western Christianity is therefore scarcely able to "provide the Oriental with elevated ideas concerning the religion that has been dominant in the West."[148]

10. The Fundamental Significance of Elenctics for Mission

In the light of Bavinck's missionary theology (specifically his *theologia religionum* and his definition of mission) it is evident that for him elenctics is the core of all missionary work: mission without elenctics is an impossibility. For this reason it fully deserves a permanent place in missiological reflection, in Bavinck's opinion.[149] "In the struggle of the present time, when from all sides new, spiritual powers throw themselves upon us, it can be important for us to enter more deeply into elenctics."[150] In this perspective elenctics is not static but must move and develop with the times.

He also explicitly resists a form of missionary theology from which elenctics has disappeared on the grounds that all religions are in principle assumed to be of equal merit. He is firmly convinced that such a theology, which he sees practiced with regularity in history, attacks the very raison d'être of mission.[151] Mission is and remains a task given by God to the church, "to proclaim with holy joy, in the midst of a world in the grip of the evil one, the call to confession of sins and conversion, the call also to faith in Jesus Christ."[152] It must not degenerate "into an exchange of spiritual experiences, a mutual influencing of one another, and

---

[145]Cf. *Christus en de wereldstorm*; *Het raadsel van ons leven*; and "Christus nu."

[146]*IZW*, 306 (cf. *ISM,* 309).

[147]*RBCG*, 77. "Christus en de wereld van het oosten," 210.

[148]*CMO*, 232.

[149]*IZW*, 247 (cf. *ISM,* 246).

[150]*IZW*, 247 (cf. *ISM,* 246).

[151]*RBCG*, 149-156.

[152]*IZW*, 247 (cf. *ISM,* 246).

a strengthening of the spirit of brotherhood."[153] Bavinck's judgment of this kind of missiology sounds emotionally charged: missionary theology of this nature stems, he states, from an "appalling lack of prophetic faith."[154]

The extent to which he himself emphasized the fundamental significance of elenctics right up to the end of his life is apparent in the conclusion of his final missiological publication, where he writes:

> God is different, totally different from the way we human beings have imagined Him in our religious fantasies. In Jesus Christ alone, the *Logos*, the Word, we hear His voice and see His image. This must be the witness of the Church when it comes into contact with other religions....This message concerning the Kingdom is to a certain extent an unmasking—it reveals the very deep process of repression and substitution and makes us ashamed of what we have done with God. This message is revealing, as it shows what goes on in man and in the world, and what God's intention is for all things, and for man, to, His deputy on earth.[155]

11. Chapter Summary

The concept of elenctics was introduced by Voetius and adopted by Kuyper as the method "that unmasks all false religion as sin against God and that summons people to come to the knowledge of the only, true God." Following in the footsteps of Voetius and Kuyper and influenced by Kraemer, Bavinck reflected independently on elenctics and was the first to give this notion a new shape and to put it on an equal footing with the other aspects of Reformed missionary theology. This placed Bavinck in the company of Gustav Warneck and Julius Richter, whose Protestant missiology had already given *Missionsapologetik* the status of an independent discipline.

In contrast to Kuyper, who viewed elenctics as a component of dogmatics, Bavinck subsumed this branch of study as missionary apologetics under theology of mission. This is why he dealt with elenctics in his missiological handbook, *IZW*, as one of the three principal subdivisions of missiology alongside theory of mission and history of mission.

It is not only on the grounds of his biblical-theological understanding of other religions that Bavinck pointed to the necessity for *elenchein* (refutation, persuasion); he also provided a direct biblical warrant for it by demonstrating that persuasion is intrinsic to the biblical message itself. *Elenchein* can never take place in the absence of through knowledge of the other religions and for that reason requires to take full account of the disciplines of the history, psychology, phenomenology and philosophy of religion.

Bavinck took great exception to the theological tradition that considers the *ratio* to be the starting point of *elenchein*. It is incorrect to think that non-Christian religion is characterized mainly by dislocations of thought which can be set right by

---

[153]*RBCG*, 155.

[154]*CMO*, 232.

[155]*CBTM*, 205-206.

means of rational arguments, for this thought enshrouds human rebellion against God. Rational arguments have a supporting role to play in *elenchein*, but the elenctic point of departure lies *au fond* in the revelation of God, the prophetic witness through which the Holy Spirit convicts the heart. However, this prophetic witness by no means hangs in the air, according to Bavinck, since in his view it is formally consistent with both the unceasing conversation between God and humankind at the level of general revelation as well as with people's religious response to that revelation. What this comes down to methodologically is the need to acquire accurate knowledge of the other religions through systematic reflection and genuine encounter so that it will be possible, aided by a biblical analysis of the phenomena, to engage in appropriate witness, understood as prolongation of the dialogue between God and the human person. There is no fixed biblical missionary method. Each situation requires inventiveness, in respect of which the indigenous churches are in a good position to point the way. But the proper elenctic stance *is* set: the Christian witness never stands above but always beside the other.

The thing that most characterizes Bavinck's view is that it subordinates the *rational* aspect to the *theological* and *psychological* dimensions of the elenctic method of missionary witness. In full conformity with his definition of mission, Bavinck defines *elenchein* theocentrically, while emphasizing at the same time that from a human perspective the elenctic approach must be thoroughly informed by empathy and tact. And indeed one is struck by the spirituality and humaneness of the manner in which he himself engaged in elenctics. Pieter Holtrop correctly points to a "subtle difference" between Kuyper and Bavinck: in Kuyper's view elenctics was to be used to address especially the religious *system*, in Bavinck's to address the religious *person*.[156] In all this the question can be raised whether Bavinck allowed enough room for the element of judgment in elenctics with reference to those who persist in their resistance. In view of the multiple aspects of the meaning of the word *elenchein*, much can be said for viewing this element of judgment, too, as an essential facet of elenctics.

Critically speaking, Bavinck's failure, within the framework of *IZW*, to provide anything more than a brief account of his *theologia religionum* can only be considered to be a shortcoming. He does refer to his earlier publication, *RBCG*, in regard to this subject, but a statement of the main features of his fully developed views on this matter would have been more appropriate. This would have made *IZW* as whole more valuable and given it more permanent significance.

In light of the biblical witness, to the extent that this witness is understood as exclusive revelation of God, the place Bavinck claims for elenctic reflection within missionary theology is absolutely justified and necessary. Anyone who considers elenctic witness to be superfluous and wants to understand mission especially—or even exclusively—as dialogue[157] must remember what Verkuyl has written: if it is true that missionary witness is redundant "then the Bible is wrong and the missionary mandate which is found in all four Gospels and is fulfilled in the works of the apostles is based on a mistake." A *theologia religionum* that implies this, argues Verkuyl rightly, represents nothing less than a "boycott of the Spirit-

---

[156] P.N. Holtrop, 163.

[157] This thinking has figured quite strongly in some quarters of the WCC. Cf. D.C. Mulder, "Dialoog als zending," 137-145.

driven calling of the church."[158] The continually raised suggestion[159] that this exclusively dialogical approach represents a newer, deeper understanding is not only incorrect from an historical perspective[160] but also remains theologically untenable. In short, the pursuit of elenctics as interpretive reflection on the biblically grounded notion and reality of trialogue[161] remains an essential task of the Christian church in the fulfillment of its missionary calling in the world.

Elenchein constitutes an essential focal point in missionary reflection and practice. And is particularly pressing now that the church everywhere finds itself confronted with syncretistic tendencies, and immersed in societies that are becoming ever more thoroughly secularized and at the same time increasingly multireligious.

Though the term elenctics was initially adopted by some of Bavinck's students, and although it does not suffer from any lack of clarity, it has not found a place in international missiological literature.[162] Other terms such as missionary apologetics and dialogical approach have more currency in contemporary missiological discourse.

---

[158]J. Verkuyl, *Inleiding in de nieuwere zendingswetenschap*, 485.

[159]Cf., e.g., G. Bouritius, 171.

[160]Historically this view was widely held *before* Tambaram (1938) and was challenged by Kraemer's deepened theological reflection at and after Tambaram.

[161]This term, used by J. Verkuyl, *Inleiding in de nieuwere zendingswetenschap*, 492-493, is expressive of Bavinck's intent. The term reflects the formulation adopted by the IMC in Mexico City in 1963: "Our intention in every human dialogue should be to be involved in the dialogue of God with men and to move our partner and our self to listen to what God in Christ reveals to us and to answer Him" (cf. *Witness in Six Continents*, 147).

[162]The British evangelical J.R.W. Stott, 66ff., does use this term, and the German Lutheran missiologist K.W. Müller, 415-451, refers to Bavinck in calling for new reflection on elenctics.

CHAPTER NINE

Practical Missionary Theology

> When there is confidence that all desire heartily to serve Christ
> and to proclaim his name, then there is already a ready basis for
> discussion. Much will have to be left to the development of the
> young churches themselves. (*IZW*, 205)

1. Introduction

Bavinck's missiological reflection was rooted in his missionary work, and his mission theory was developed especially with an eye to missionary praxis. Driven by this practical outlook, he regularly brings up concrete issues with which he was directly or indirectly confronted in his missionary work. It would do Bavinck as missiologist an injustice if were to limit ourselves to an analysis of his systematic reflection without discussing this practical focus.

  This chapter deals with four practical missionary matters that occupied Bavinck rather intensively: the integration of the Christian faith in existing culture; the relationship between the so-called "older" and "younger" churches, ecumenicity; and the racial problem. The order in which these points—which cover the entire missionary period in Bavinck's life—are discussed is more or less chronologically determined. In the prewar years, in missionary service in Java, he was confronted with the first of these issues, even though he did not write much on it until later in his career. In the postwar era of decolonization, when as professor of missiology he was closely involved in the process leading toward the independence of the 'mission churches,' he gave full attention to the second matter. This was also the time in which the growth of ecumenical relations that had been taking place during the previous fifty years reached its zenith in the establishment of the World Council of Churches in 1948. He became interested in the third issue in the 1950s, when he came into contact with discrimination and apartheid as a result of his visits to South Africa. Finally, the question will be raised to what extent Bavinck's theological points of departure had an impact on in his practical reflection.

2. *Possessio:* Claiming Culture for Christ

From the very beginning Bavinck was deeply convinced of the fact that in mission a struggle with culture takes place, marked by religious as well as political and social factors. As early as 1934 he wrote a study on Christ and the mysticism of the East, the opening sentences of which are characteristic of his thinking on this matter.

> Eastern Asia is in our days the site of an immense crisis. There
> all those spiritual powers that have ruled for centuries are at
> work. There, in our age, is also the immense power of Western
> culture, of secularism, the power of technology, of dominion over
> matter, of atheism and materialism, . . . of nationalism, . . . the
> powerful striving for self-identity. And in the midst of that
> maelstrom of spiritual movements the gospel, too, penetrates the
> world of the East.[1]

In what follows it will become clear how in this confrontation Bavinck chose a
position between isolation and accommodation by means of the key concept of
possessio (take possession of).

2.1. *Possessio* as Theologically Sound Starting Point

Bavinck pointed already at an early stage to the profound difference that always
exists between the content of the Christian faith and the religiously charged cultural
values of the various peoples. Thus he writes in *CMO*, "Christianity is something
unique, something that differs from all human ideas."[2] It is therefore impossible
simply to adopt indigenous thoughts and customs, experiences and reflections. At
the same time Bavinck was deeply aware that the message of the gospel can only
be brought adequately if that takes place in the context of and in confrontation with
that other culture, and that the church only has a future when the Christian faith and
life find embodiment in that culture. Thus he wrote, for example:

> Many young churches have in their whole way of life stayed as
> closely as possible to what the Mission modeled, and thereby
> have distanced themselves rather strongly from their own cultural
> milieu. A major objection to this—fully understandable—attitude
> is that in this way little essential confrontation takes place
> between the new Christian principles and the ancient, non-
> Christian heritage. Thus paganism is displaced, but it is not
> conquered. And that which is displaced will sooner or later
> reassert its power over people's hearts. That is why such a
> confrontation cannot be evaded without doing damage, and why
> the young Christian church must sooner or later come to a new
> reflection on its relationship to the milieu in which it matures.
> Only thus can the church arrive at a way of life that is open to
> and renews the unique character of a people. The Christian
> community must never remain 'alien' in its environment; it must
> become 'indigenous' without surrendering its essence.[3]

Bavinck places this missionary task in eschatological perspective: in this way "the

---

[1] *CMO*, 5-6.

[2] Ibid., 109.

[3] "Verkondiging in de volkerenwereld," 405-406. In this article Bavinck
gives a concise overview of how mission has increasingly come to understand the
necessity of this process.

Kingdoms will bring their splendor into the City of God."[4] This delineates the field
of tension within which missionary praxis constantly moves: on the one hand we
must guard against syncretistic tendencies, while on the other hand we must be
careful not to create an unbridgeable gap.[5] In a 1944 lecture on syncretism as a
missionary problem, he attempts to lay out a negotiable passage between these two
dangerous rocks. He describes syncretism as "a deformity, i.e., a spontaneous,
natural fusion of religions, through which they join to form a holistic religious
complex in which the original boundaries can no longer be traced with clarity."[6]
Proceeding from this definition he goes on to say that "the urge to naturalize
Christianity is in itself not syncretism," but *possessio*. This is the first time he uses
the term,[7] and he defines it in the following terms: the Christian faith takes hold of
a people in that people's own thought forms and examines those forms critically in
the search for an indigenous expression in liturgy, architecture, life style, social
relationships, philosophical and theological reflection. And he adds in this
connection:

> We have to do here with the phenomenon of the neutrality of the
> mental functions. Thinking as such is neutral; whether I think
> linearly or intuitively or visually or emotionally does not bring
> me nearer to the kingdom of God, nor does it lead me farther
> away from it. The gospel grips me in my own mode of thought
> and wants to be confessed by me in that mode of thinking.[8]

The task of mission is to monitor this process: mission collaborates in the
effort to ensure "that among the various peoples the gospel strikes roots as deep as
possible, is naturalized as intensively as possible, without allowing it to fuse with
native pagan ideas and modes of expression."[9] In this context he agrees in principle
with Karl Hartenstein, who rejected the notion that syncretism should be viewed as
an intermediate religious stage (*religiöses Durchgangsstadium*): "Syncretism is not
an intermediate step, but rather something final, closed, truly a new religion."[10] At
the same time Bavinck refines this position by stating that in practice such a
syncretistic intermediate step is often unavoidable:

> We cannot conceive of anything other than that a period of
> intense syncretization is coming, throughout the East. . . . The

---

[4]"Christendom en cultuuruitingen," 45.

[5]*IZW*, 171 (cf. *ISM*, 170).

[6]"Syncretisme als zendingsprobleem," 17.

[7]Insofar as I have been able to determine, Bavinck himself introduced this
concept.

[8]"Syncretisme als zendingsprobleem," 18.

[9]Ibid., 19.

[10]K. Hartenstein *Die Mission*, 62: "Der Syncretismus ist keine
Durchgangsstufe, sondern irgendwie etwas Letztes, Geschlossenes, wirklich eine
neue Religion."

first Christian church also experienced such a period. What is
essential is that the Christian Church in those countries [of the
East] must first have understood the voice of Christ so
profoundly that it can meet this syncretic impulse and come to
confession of the true faith.[11]

He develops this issue further entirely along these lines in *IZW*, strikingly in the
chapter on the goal of mission. Although that is questionable from a systematic
standpoint, it shows that for him this issue is definitely not incidental but rather
constitutes a core problem.

He begins his discussion with an explicit rejection of Roman Catholic
missionary practice, as expressed specifically by Johannes Thauren, who from the
perspective of the theological notions concerning nature and grace always argued
for a far-reaching *accommodatio* (accommodation).[12] Over against this, Bavinck,
following Kraemer,[13] points to the all-pervasive character of sin and the all-
encompassing character of the non-Christian religions, which in the Reformed
perspective gives rise to a much greater apprehension concerning the idea of
accommodation.[14] In fact, he considered the concept of accommodation to be
essentially unusable, because it implies too strongly the thought of mutilation or
denial of the gospel. Although he acknowledges here again that from a practical
perspective accommodation is inescapable, he nevertheless maintains theoretically
that this must never be more than a means to an end, that ultimately all things must
receive new connotations through the gospel. Terminologically he sees this goal
best expressed in the concept of *possessio*, which he further defines with the help
of a reference to a statement by Heinrich Frick: who wrote with the use of
indigenous language in mind: "We are therefore never dealing with simplistic
adaptation, but with an adaptation that simultaneously means radical change."[15]
Bavinck applies this thought to all areas that involve *possessio*.

Although Bavinck holds this position on principle, he points at the same
time to two factors that must keep one from taking too extreme a position. In the
first place the fact must be taken into account that in the midst of all degeneration
there are, thanks to God's involvement, also valuable cultural elements. "

There is still such a thing as conscience, that wondrous thing of
which Paul speaks with such amazement (Rom. 2:14-15). In the
moral realm, in the judicial sphere, and in various other areas we
frequently encounter unimagined and unexpected values. The

---

[11]"Syncretisme als zendingsprobleem," 19.

[12]*IZW*, 171-182 (cf. *ISM*, 169-179).

[13]H. Kraemer, *The Christian Message in a Non-Christian World*, 135:
"Every religion is an indivisible, and not to be divided, unity of existential
apprehension."

[14]*IZW*, 175 (cf. *ISM*, 173).

[15]Cf. *ibid.*, 182 (*ISM*, 179), n. 20, "Wir haben es hier also nie mit glatter
Anpassung zu tun, sondern mit einer Anpassung, die gleichzeitig Umbruch
bedeutet."

cultures we encounter on the mission field are, in a sense, indivisible structures, but they nevertheless show here and there a curious fissure. . . . [This is why] we can never charge headlong at paganism with an inflexible theory.[16]

And in *ICNCW* (75-77) Bavinck not only states that the degeneration of religious cultures has limits, but adds pointedly that denying that fact would make the missionary approach in principle hopeless: "Then preaching is in itself utterly impossible because it finds no words that can be used as vehicles of truth."

The second thing that must be taken into account in this connection is that through the centuries many cultural peculiarities have lost their original religious connotations and have for all intents and purposes been secularized. Bavinck then concludes: ""In practice we thus can take a more lenient position vis-à-vis the customs of the nations, than our Reformation perspective would seem to demand," and with this in view he thinks it advisable, following Heinrich Frick, to apply the criterion of 'core-proximity' to morals and customs: "To what extent are these customs still clearly noticeable within the sphere [of the core or essence] of pagan thought?" He adds that though in practice "it will not always be easy to apply this criterion, . . . we do have here a possibility in hand to examine practical reality [or religious traditions] calmly and soberly. [17]

2.2. *Possessio* as Sound Missionary Practice

Bavinck emphasizes on the one hand that the principle of *possessio* does justice to the principle of biblical-theological teaching, while on the other hand he shows repeatedly that application of this principle fully allows for other factors that are encountered in the work of mission. In the first place, *possessio* allows for the practical factor. One can do nothing but use the existing language, in which all kinds of concepts such as grace, sin, God, redemption are known but have a different content. Following Frick, who posits that using the native language requires a conversion of the language to Christ,[18] Bavinck says:

> Each time the [gospel] is preached in a different language, to a different people, it has to transmute a variety of words, as it were, and give them new content. [The gospel] does not find anywhere in the world a ready language that fits completely and absolutely like a garment.[19]

Second, *possessio* takes psychological factors into account. Too much emphasis on the Western cultural heritage and Western theological achievements can cultivate feelings of inferiority and ultimately lead to a strong need to compensate for this Western domination. Such reactions can be prevented if the indigenous heritage is embraced in a balanced manner and a native Christian style

---

[16]*Ibid.*, 176 (cf. *ISM*, 174).

[17]*Ibid.*, 177 (*ISM*, 174-175).

[18]H. Frick, *Christliche Verkündigung*, 24.

[19]*CMO*, 109.

and Christian theology[20] are evolved. Bavinck added, from his own experience, that in some instances this remained a very sensitive issue: missionary efforts to foster the integration of indigenous culture into local Christian life was sometimes "interpreted by the younger Christians as a disguised effort to keep them 'in their place,' to deny them the riches and strengths of Western life."[21]

Third, *possessio* allows for the sociological factor. There are quite a few customs and practices that have, besides religious connotations, also a social function. Indigenous Christians end up in social isolation if they let go of these customs all at once and thereby sever their social ties. This is unwise. To the extent that this is possible, indigenous mores and customs must be maintained on the basis of the criterion of core-proximity mentioned above.[22]

Fourth, *possessio* does justice to the *missionary* factor. From a missionary perspective it is fatal if becoming a Christian seems to be identical to adopting Western ways of living. By doing this, young churches build a wall of misunderstanding and distrust around themselves. What matters is that they search, in continuity with the overall lifestyle of the existing social environment, for their own forms in which to express the new life in Christ, in order to build bridges to the non-Christian environment. Mission is called to stimulate this process in every way possible.[23]

2.3. Examples of *Possessio*

2.3.1. Initial Steps Toward a Contextual Theology

In presenting a number of practical illustrations of *possessio* for which Bavinck argues, I begin with the most important one: theological inculturation or contextualization. Although these concepts were not yet used in Bavinck's day, he continually raised the issues by them. He was convinced of the necessity of working everywhere toward the development of an indigenous theological framework closely connected with the categories of thought and imagination of standing religio-philosophical traditions and also in confrontation with actual social contexts.

As for the relationship Bavinck posited between existing heritage and the gospel, he wanted initially to make congenial use of indigenous images and concepts to express the Christian view. A typical example of this is his well known publication *Soeksma soepana* (The way of the soul), in which Bavinck, as beginning missionary, made an attempt to interpret the gospel with Javanese images. But Bavinck saw that what was involved was more than just a (homiletic) exercise in translation. This is already apparent in *CMO*, in which he states:

---

[20] As early as 1933 Bavinck was arguing (in *De Opwekker* 78, 457-465) for the development of a Javanese dogmatics.

[21] Cf. *IZW*, 182 (cf. *ISM*, 179-180) and "Syncretisme als zendingsprobleem," 19-20.

[22] *IZW*, 178-180 (cf. *ISM*, 175-177).

[23] *IZW*, 179-182 (cf. *ISM*, 176-179).

> We are well aware that there in the Dutch East Indies and also on Java an indigenous Christian theology will have to grow, into which the struggle with Islamic mysticism and Hinduism is, as it were, incorporated. It is true that the fostering of such a theology is a work, not of years, but of centuries, but the seeds of such a theology must be scattered now, so that these seeds can, under God's blessing and in his time, sprout and bear fruit.[24]

In *Soeksma soepana* itself he tries to scatter some of this seed, by confronting the mystical view of the world and life with the biblical view and to point out "what separates the delicate subtleties of Eastern thought from the ideas of the gospel."[25] He indicates very clearly that he does not want to import and impose Western theological formulations:

> We cannot outline beforehand the lines along which Eastern thinking about Christ will develop. There are far too many factors that can influence that process. Also, it will still require very much intellectual work before the broad lines can be drawn that run from the gospel to all areas of life and searching.[26]

Rather than this prior determination of Eastern theology by the West he calls for exactly the opposite: the Western churches must consciously take a step back because there are moments when only the indigenous church has the understanding to articulate the decisive theological words.

> Our theological discussion is of the utmost importance for the church in the East and that church listens to it with bated breath. But in the end it is that church that has to formulate its own answer, find its way through the tangle of questions that com to the surface. We can never adequately understand the thoughts that occupy our brothers in the East, the problems that creep up on them. And even if we were able to do so, the answer we would give could never provide full satisfaction because it would not be an answer that grew out of their own heart.[27]

Bavinck sees two possibilities in this process. On the one hand there is the danger of darkening the truth of the gospel, because in a more or less syncretistic manner the message of the gospel is identified with ideas from the religious heritage. He presents a number of clear examples of this in ICNCW, in which he discusses "indigenous conceptions of Jesus."[28] On the other hand these religious elements can, if continually placed under the critical test of the Bible that purifies them, light up the truth of the gospel all the more. As early as 1934 Bavinck closed one of his publications *CMO* with the significant words:

> And when before long a flowering church will have arisen in the

---

[24]*CMO*, 107. Cf. also *CPVW*, 17-18.

[25]*CMO*, 6, 107.

[26]*CMO*, 231.

[27]"Christus en de wereld van het Oosten," 241.

[28]*ICNCW*, 157-167.

world of the East, then Christ will perform miracles there. The Asian has gifts and strengths that make him extremely suited to grasp the meaning of the gospel. After all, his heritage makes him more strongly convinced of the omnipresence of the divine in all matters of daily life and he will therefore also be better able to see in all aspects of life the hand of Christ. He is not as far removed from mystery as we are, and therefore Christ can do great things there. The Asian is better able to listen than we are, he is able to wait more quietly for the voice of God and to surrender himself in greater passivity to God. But above all, the Asian values external things such as money and possessions, honor and name less highly than we do, and he is more aware that the form of this world is passing away. And now, in addition, the gospel of Christ will show him that we must not hold the world in contempt . . . , but that same gospel will also admonish him to look up and to expect that unshakable Kingdom that will one day appear and towards whose coming we all reach with yearning."[29]

Thus the mystical view of life is not only subject to the critique of the gospel, but also makes a contribution in and through this process to a deeper and better understanding of the gospel.

Bavinck continuously emphasized that theology must be correlated with the social context. In the midst of existing oppressive structures and developments, such as nationalism, the advance of technology, and secularization, the church and theology are called to fulfill a prophetically critical task, by means of which they will develop a unique, contextualized face.[30] They may never join liberating and restorative movements without further consideration, but must always think things through thoroughly, all the way to Christ, the final arbiter of good and evil, right and wrong. In 1960 Bavinck stated this view as follows: "The problem of transition is essentially not merely a social or economic or political problem, but it has a religious background. A people can only find its future if it finds God."[31]

2.3.2. Integration of Manners and Customs

In *IZM* Bavinck points to a number of ever-recurring areas of life where *possessio* can be applied: rituals connected with marriage, agriculture, death, initiation, feasts, and the organization of the worship service.[32] In his discussion he merely sets out some pointers to give direction, in the awareness that each situation calls for its own approach and that the 'younger churches' must break new ground in their own

---

[29]*CMO*, 232.

[30]*IZW*, 169-170 (cf. *ISM,* 167-169). Cf. also *ZWN,* 186-189, where Bavinck speaks positively of the influence of social problems in Japan on the development of theology.

[31]"India in Transition," 37.

[32]*IZW*, 182-193 (cf. *ISM,* 179-189).

context. He writes, "When men and women among them stand up full of the holy Spirit, believers who live close to Christ and close to their own people, then solutions can be found that are fully satisfying."[33] Again, it is clear that for Bavinck *possessio* is not a peripheral matter but a task of eminent importance. "It will prove to be of immeasurable significance when the young churches on the mission field increasingly find their own forms of being, in which something of the old cultural heritage is retained yet faith in Jesus Christ is not compromised in any way."[34] Bavinck's application of *possessio* can be further illustrated in terms of two concepts with which Bavinck explicitly dealt: *tribal solidarity* and *Circles of five*.

Where it is still found, Bavinck points out, the tribal relationship is very strong. This is due specifically to its religious roots. The tribe is viewed as the microcosm that stands in a magical relationship with the macrocosm. The whole of society is regulated, socially, ethically, and economically on the foundation of this deep conviction. Characteristic features of tribal solidarity are collectivity and (implicitly) the absence of individuality or personal responsibility. Self-deification and magic determine norms and values.[35] Although Bavinck recognizes many positive elements in this tribal collectivity, he nevertheless distances himself from Bruno Gutmann, who elevates it to something given in creation that must be preserved at all costs. Bavinck criticizes Gutmann's position as follows:

> God certainly has created man as a being who must live in relationships and who can only live in the full sense of the word in those relationships. But that does not mean that tribal connections as they actually exist, in which individual responsibility is generally completely dissolved in the mores of the tribe, may also be viewed as an expression of God's intention. There are, in fact, weighty reasons to imagine that they constitute an extremely dangerous overloading of the meaning of community and in this way form a threat to spiritual and moral life.[36]

Nevertheless, Bavinck argues that the tie with the tribe should not simply be severed. He supports this with two arguments. First, due to a lack of individual responsibility, a premature severing of the link with the tribe and the resultant loss of the protective function of tribal mores could have disastrous results.[37] Second, such a break can easily lead to isolation, so that the church blocks the very roads that would enable it to realize its missionary calling toward the other members of the tribe.[38] At the same time tribalism as a whole is subject to critique by the

---

[33] *IZW*, 194 (cf. *ISM*, 190).

[34] *Ibid.*

[35] *ZWN*, 182-184; *IZW*, 162ff (cf. *ISM*, 160ff).

[36] *IZW*, 164 (cf. *ISM*, 162); cf. B. Gutmann, *Gemeindeaufbau aus dem Evangelium*, 87.

[37] Cf. *IZW*, 163-164 (cf. *ISM*, 161-162).

[38] Cf. *ZWN*, 182-185. *IZW*, 168 (cf. *ISM*, 166-167).

Christian faith: "The preaching of the gospel will have to repeat without any hesitation to those who live by tribal loyalty alone the ancient words, "leave your country and your people."[39] The old religious roots must be severed and communal solidarity must find its foundation in Christ, customs must be grafted onto the gospel, and a correct relationship between individuality and collectivity must be fostered.[40] Bavinck emphasizes here also that this is a long-term process, because "the tree of paganism cannot be felled with one stroke."[41]

During his work on Java, Bavinck at one point came up with an example of creative *possessio* by establishing the above-mentioned Circles of Five,[42] which proved to be a great success at the time. The number 'five' has played a very important role in all Javanese thinking and feeling since ancient times onward. In Javanese culture this number indicates a measure of plurality that at the same time constitutes a unity: "The Javanese recognize five senses, the Javanese week consists of five days, the world consists of five points of the compass (the four compass points plus the zenith), the hand has five fingers, etc."[43] In order to give the work of Bible study groups a new impetus, Bavinck made use of this sacred number. His intent was to create indissoluble units by establishing such groups of five people. That unity found expression especially in brotherhood and mutual trust. Other Javanese customs and the language of symbols, to which Javanese society is so attached, were also adopted to allow for optimal functioning of this work with small groups. At the quarterly joint meetings of the Circles of Five participants sat in a large circle around candle holders set up in the shape of a cross, which pointed to their salvation in Christ and the necessity of spreading this light everywhere.[44] Furthermore, stress was laid on five essential elements of the life of faith: faith in the Lord, love of neighbor, worship of God, pursuit of joy, battle against sin.[45]

2.4. Summary

Bavinck was always deeply aware that mission is more than preaching the gospel in order to save souls and establish churches. As is already implicit in its use of a foreign language, mission entails from the very outset a confrontation with existing culture. Mission has a mandate to critically assimilate existing culture and to root Christian theology and praxis in that culture in light of the gospel. This inculturation of the gospel also has a variety of social components that must be

---

[39] *IZW*, 165 (cf. *ISM*, 163):

[40] Cf. *ZWN*, 185-186 and *IZW*, 124-125 (*ISM*, 119-120).

[41] *IZW*, 125 (cf. *ISM*, 120).

[42] Cf. "Jeugdwerk: De kringen van 5," 353-363; these Circles of Five have already been discussed in more detail in chapter two above, *quod vide*.

[43] *Ibid.*, 355.

[44] *Ibid.*, 358.

[45] *Ibid.*, 360.

thought through thoroughly, all the way to Christ, the ultimate critical authority. Bavinck's choice of the term *possessio* to describe this process was a well considered one. *Possessio* bears, much more than does the concept of *accomodatio*, a critical quality with respect to existing culture. That Bavinck also valued the religious heritage of the East, is evident from his conviction that a critical processing of this heritage can also yield enrichment of Christian understanding.

Furthermore, it appears that his theological reflection was linked to a strong sense of realism: due to the recalcitrant nature of practical reality, *possessio* will always consist, from a practical point of view, of a process full of syncretistic tendencies which must be overcome slowly but surely. What is also striking is the extent to which, in working out the significance and implications of *possessio*, he takes practical, psychological, and social factors into account, alongside theological motifs. The continuity between Bavinck's systematic thinking and practical reflection is evident: both the theological assessment of non-Christian religions and cultures, on the one hand, and the missionary calling of the church to foster the embodiment of the kingdom of God among the nations, on the other, receive equal attention in his work.

The term *possessio* has dropped from general use in missiological literature and reflection in favor of more common concepts such as "inculturation" or "contextualization." This does not imply, however, that the principle expressed by the notion of *possessio* should be surrendered and exchanged for a concept of contextualization which—on the basis of an appeal to the incarnation as an adaptation to human categories—allows for a dynamic but uncritical integration of existing religio-cultural and socio-political patterns with the life and work of the church." Both the incarnation of the Word and incorporation into the Christian communion by means of baptism speak a more critical language, which underlines the theological legitimacy of Bavinck's approach.

Finally, it must be said that Bavinck's sanguine expectation regarding the progressive Christianization of culture—an anticipation which was very common in Western Christian circles during the second half of the 19th and the first half of the 20th century—today sounds unrealistic and unduly idealistic. But it should be added immediately that Bavinck's high hopes on this score were attended by a healthy degree of soberness begotten of his realistic outlook. Thus he wrote, for example:

> The surging power of communism, the secularization of life, the political and social tensions found throughout the world make it impossible to expect quick results. We will have to think in terms of longer time spans if we are to remain reasonable. Nevertheless, there are signs everywhere that make us hopeful for the future. . . . One thing needs to be stated immediately and emphatically, however. Due to its nature the Christian community has an immeasurable head start over its surroundings. In a world in which religious values are wearing away, in which old ideas and concepts are being uprooted, and in which the supreme pressure of a secularized, godless culture is being felt more strongly with the passing of each day, the Christian community has a foundation of faith, an inner conviction about life, a new view of man and the world. It continues to grope and stammer, but it also contains potential of infinite scope. . . . In the regions of the younger churches in Asia and Africa, America and Australia,   a new chapter in the cultural history of

Christianity is beginning to be written.[46]
Today one speaks with much more restraint due to the ongoing marginalization of the church. Nevertheless, it is to be hoped that the deepest motif of this expectation—the faith that Christ works through his church in salutary ways—will enduringly vitalize his church. The church's prayer, "Thy Kingdom come," given by Christ himself to his disciples, does not have to lose in fervency.

3. The Relationship between 'Older' and 'Younger' Churches

This section will be limited to a brief sketch of the practical-theological principles Bavinck applied to the question of the relationship between Western and so-called 'mission churches.'

3.1. The Period before the Second World War

In his book on mission and the ecumenical movement in the 20th century[47] A. Wind describes how from the 1920s onward the Western churches began to work more and more clearly for the independence and equality of the so-called younger churches in Asia and Africa. The well-known 'three-self formula' introduced in the middle of the 19th century by two leading missionary leaders—the American, Rufus Anderson (1796-1880), and the British, Henry Venn (1796-1873)—to express what they envisaged as the ideal missionary policy, began to play a renewed role during this period. Missionaries and mission executives once again began to advocate the view of Anderson and Venn that mission should bend its best efforts to foster self-supporting, self-governing, and self-propagating or self-extending indigenous churches. In the practical-theological reflection that took place at and after the International Missionary Conferences in Jerusalem in 1928 and in Tambaram in 1938, colonialist relationships came under increasing criticism and were ever more explicitly and sharply renounced. This development was accelerated by World War II, when many younger churches had of necessity to make do without leadership and support from the Western churches. At the 1947 International Missionary Conference in Whitby, Canada, the term "partnership in obedience" was introduced to denote the ideal relationship between the 'older' and 'younger' churches.[48] This concept evinced the conviction that 'younger' churches should function as independently as possible and in any case have equal standing with the 'older' churches, with a view to the joint fulfilment of their common missionary mandate in the world. Bavinck's reflection on this relationship gained momentum particularly after the Second World War, when ecclesiastical and national developments on the mission field of the RCN compelled him to deal with the problem. In those years he attempted, especially through the agency of a series of articles in a denominational weekly, to help guide the move toward independence of the 'younger' churches and to defend the changing relationships within the arena of the rather critical rank and file of the church. From this developed a practical-theological reflection that found formal expression in his 1954 missiological

---

[46]"Verkondiging aan de volkerenwereld," 408-409

[47]A. Wind, *Zending en oecumene in de twintigste eeuw*, 1, 150.

[48]*Ibid.*, 168.

handbook, *IZW*.

3.2. Changing Relationships after 1945

Until World War II the RCN, in spite of the relative independence of their daughter churches,[49] had a leading role in the spiritual, business, and financial affairs of these churches. But three closely related factors caused an irreversible change in this relationship.[50] In the first place, the contact between the RCN with their daughter churches on Java and Sumatra, which for a variety of reasons had already become increasingly limited since the beginning of World War II, was severed altogether as a result of the Japanese occupation. The indigenous Christians were now more than ever called to assume responsibility for their life and work. The churches managed this quite well during the war, and when, after the occupation, contact was reestablished, the indigenous churches were unwilling to simply surrender the independence they had gained. They had learned to provide leadership, establish policy, and develop activities.

Second, the growing nationalism that in these years became more radical, did not bypass the Christian church. The desire to be free from foreign domination had also grown within the Indonesian churches. Dutch colonial rule was increasingly perceived as oppressive, as an infringement of people's rights that was fundamentally unacceptable, certainly from a Christian perspective. This sentiment, of course, also had repercussions in the attitude of the indigenous churches toward the Western churches. Any Western involvement in ecclesiastical matters was interpreted as a form of disguised imperialism. Political and ecclesiastical relationships thus were often intertwined and difficult to disentangle.

Third, it had become apparent that the indigenous church during the time when it was left entirely to its own devices had gained in popularity among their own people. Until then, the Christian church had been seen as something Western and therefore stood at the margins of society. The expectation was that it would barely survive without support from the West. But when the opposite happened and the church most definitely appeared to be an indigenous matter, confidence slowly began to grow in the Christian community and it became more integrated into society. Thus the church became, more or less spontaneously, a greater missionary force in the predominantly Islamic society of Indonesia. Because of these developments the indigenous churches did not want to continue in the old pattern. Thus, at the ground-breaking 1947 Kwitang conference in Jakarta, after much mutual distrust had been dispelled, a new relationship was launched. The most

---

[49]This Reformed principle of the relative independence and fundamental equality of churches had already been strongly emphasized by Voetius (cf. Jongeneel, "Voetius' zendingstheologie," 136) and reiterated at the synod of Middelburg, as follows: "Since each local church, also on Java, is complete within itself and stands directly under King Jesus, the sending church, in her role of mother church, may support and advise but must never arrogate any authority to itself over such a church. The Javanese church is coordinate with, not subordinate to us." Cf. *Uittreksel uit de Acta der generale synode van de GKN*, 37.

[50]Cf. a series of articles by Bavinck in *GW* between 1945 and 1948. For further data concerning the tensions, and developments in these relationships, see T. van der End, *Gereformeerde zending op Sumba 1859-1972*.

important decision was that leadership and responsibility in all areas was placed fully in the hands of the indigenous churches, although the Western churches were asked to provide, to the extent that this was necessary, intellectual, missionary, and financial support. This put the Western churches in a radically different position. They had to exchange their leadership role for an attitude of service and assistance.

In his usual irenic manner, Bavinck constantly tried to create understanding for this situation among the rank and file of the church and to promote a positive attitude. This was far from simple, however, because political and ecclesiastical affairs were closely intertwined in the Netherlands too. The most important question that emerges here is: What moved Bavinck to take this position? Was he prompted only by the need to make the best of the inevitable or did principle also play a role? The answer can be found in what he wrote at the end of 1945:

> As we all see immediately, this [new relationship] constitutes a very far-reaching change. A situation that, according to our plans, we would not encounter until many years hence has suddenly become a fact. And I want to add immediately, a fact that we must accept."[51]

This statement shows clearly that, although there is a measure of willingness to be guided by circumstances, his attitude was inspired by much more than anything like expedience. Apparently other, deeper motivations would in the end have led to the same development in his thinking. Circumstances merely speeded up the process.

3.3. A Biblically Sound Perspective

Bavinck wanted to deliberate the relationship between older and younger churches from a biblical perspective. In doing so he clearly realized that when looking for principles in the Bible the differences in conditions then and now must be taken carefully into account.[52]

On the one hand Bavinck points out "that Scripture is completely ignorant of the distinction between older and younger churches."[53] Although the New Testament of course speaks of individual congregations, the church is understood especially in a mystical sense as the body of Christ and is therefore seen as "a mighty, unbreakable unity: 'one Lord, one faith, one baptism; one God and Father of all, who is over all and through all and in all' (Eph. 4:6)"[54] This means that in principle there is no basis for a distinction between older and younger churches or for a measure of authority of the former over the latter. "Each church that is closely

---

[51]"Nieuwe orientering in ons zendingswerk."

[52]"De zendingsmethode van Paulus en die van ons," *HZB*, 39 (1951): 99. Bavinck here points out by way of example that we can learn something from the way in which Paul dealt with the churches that had been founded, but he adds, "if people want to imitate [this] indiscriminately, I am suddenly once again very skeptical."

[53]*IZW*, 195 (cf. *ISM*, 191).

[54]*IZW*, 195 (cf. *ISM*, 191-192).

tied to Jesus Christ and listens to his voice," he wrote, "is as such a member of the body of Christ, is one with all other churches wherever they may be, and is called to fulfill its own charge independently.[55]

On the other hand, however, Bavinck sees that the apostles, especially Paul, did not consider their task accomplished as soon as they had established a local congregation. Even after elders were appointed to give leadership to the life of the local churches, Paul continued to care in many ways for these young, as yet not mature, congregations:

> He wrote letters to and regularly visited [them], gave all kinds of advice [to them], not infrequently in the form of an explicit command, he counseled, advised, and encouraged the elders—in short, he continued to watch over such a church as a father watches over his children. That concern for the churches he mentions as one of heaviest burdens he has to bear (2 Cor. 11:28).[56]

In all of this, Bavinck adds, one must take into consideration that Paul did not follow this method by virtue of a mandate from a sending church or mother church—for example, Antioch—but by reason of his apostolic office. "As apostle, that is to say as one sent by Jesus Christ, he had the authority to do these things, by virtue of the guidance that was given him day by day by the Holy Spirit."[57] It was therefore not another church that persisted in exerting a measure of authority over younger congregations, but Jesus Christ himself, who through his servants continued to guide and direct these younger and weaker churches.[58]

The preceding shows that the situation then and the situation now differ too much to draw direct conclusions from the New Testament for missionary praxis today. It is possible, however, to extrapolate some fundamental insights.

In the first place, older churches must not in any way assume an authoritative or paternalistic role with respect to younger churches. This implies that they will never allow their mutual relationship to be manipulated by political norms, but must always formulate their relationship according to their own needs and strengths. That being the case, the nomenclature 'older church' and 'younger church' must be used exclusively as a chronological designation.[59]

Second, the 'mother' church, whenever this is considered necessary and desirable, must fulfill a serving role in the building up of the 'daughter' church. Three dangers must always be kept in mind here: that the sending church assumes too much of a dominant role and too little of a dependent position; that it takes too many responsibilities out of the hands of the younger church; and that it considers

---

[55]*IZW*, 198 (cf. *ISM,* 194-195).

[56]*IZW*, 198 (cf. *ISM,* 195).

[57]*IZW*, 196 (cf. *ISM,* 193).

[58]Cf. *IZW*, 198 (*ISM,* 194).

[59]Cf. *IZW*, 210-212 (*ISM,* 198-199).

itself indispensable for too long.[60] The serving function of the mother church could be realized, according to Bavinck, especially in the areas of theological training, Christian literature production, reflection on the challenges posed by a changing society, and missionary work.[61]

Bavinck gave separate attention to what was then the most sensitive issue: the serving function of the older churches in the carrying out of the missionary task by the younger churches. He considered the idea that missionary work continues primarily to be the responsibility of the Western churches not only indefensible on principle but also unwise from a practical standpoint. In light of the Bible the indigenous churches have from the very beginning a missionary task with respect to their own surroundings. Referring to Eph. 6:15, Col. 4:5 and 1 Peter 2:9, Bavinck writes that in the letters of the apostles "it is always considered a perfectly normal and self-evident matter that the congregation, and even every member of a congregation is active as a missionary."[62] And viewed practically, the indigenous churches should even be given a leading role in the execution of the missionary mandate, because they stand literally and figuratively much closer to their own people.

> The mother church lies somewhere over there, far away, in Europe or America; it consists of Western people, whites, people of a particular culture and of a particular level of development. The young church is on the mission field, in the turbulence, in the midst of the bitter struggle between Christ and Satan.[63]

At the same time, Bavinck argued, the mystical unity of the church as the Body of Christ warrants and requires that Western and indigenous churches carry out their missionary task side by side.

> It was not at all strange that Timothy, who came from Lystra in Asia Minor, was sent out by Paul to do important work in Corinth, for although Lystra and Corinth may be far apart and belong to entirely different worlds, the churches in the two cities are one in Christ. Even very fundamental differences, such as race, language, and culture, lose their compelling force when it comes to the unity in Christ"[64]

In this connection Bavinck argued for the principle of *partnership in obedience* articulated in Whitby in 1947, adding: "Perhaps this is putting it too weakly. The two churches are more than partners, they are one and the same church."[65] The notion that the older churches no longer have a missionary task but have been

---

[60]Cf. *IZW*, 200-201 (*ISM*, 197-198) and also "Samenspreking met de kerken in Java," 399 and "Wat kunnen wij nu nog voor Indonesie doen?" 235.

[61]Cf. *IZW.*, 218-221 (*ISM*, 214-217).

[62]*IZW.*, 208 (cf. *ISM*, 205-206).

[63]*Ibid.*, 209 (cf. *ISM*, 206).

[64]*Ibid.*, 209 (cf. *ISM*, 206-207).

[65]*Ibid.*, 210 (cf. *ISM*, 207).

relegated solely to helping the younger churches is, like the question as to who actually has the greater responsibility, no longer relevant. The churches must not compete with one another but cooperate from the catholic perspective in service of their one King.[66]

In this vision lies for Bavinck the motivation to react positively to the developments in the churches in Indonesia. Independent of changing political structures—and thus whether in a colonial or a post-colonial situation—churches must practice this biblical way of dealing with one another, always keeping the building up of the kingdom of God clearly in view. This central principle, used as point of departure, provides the element of action in reaction to circumstances with a theological foundation. Putting a brake on the accelerating tempo of developments, turning back the clock, would only lead to great distrust on the part of the indigenous church toward the RCN, Bavinck stated, and would result in a clouding of the relationship and a severing of good ties between them and *thereby do damage to the building and spread of the Kingdom of God.*[67]

4. Ecumenicity

In the sequel Bavinck's evaluation of the ecumenical movement, which had been gaining ever-increasing momentum since the 1910 International Missionary Conference in Edinburgh, will be reconstructed on the basis of an impression he wrote of the inaugural meeting of the World Council of Churches in 1948,[68] and particularly his later views on ecumenicity and the pragmatic necessity of ecumenical efforts as reflected in a 1954 essay and in two additional works, which came out in 1948 and 1954 respectively.[69]

4.1. Positive Assessment of the Ecumenical Movement

The establishment of the World Council of Churches (WCC) in 1948 caused considerable discussion within the RCN regarding the position it should take with respect to joining the ecumenical movement as it came to expression in both the Dutch Ecumenical Council of Churches and the WCC.[70] At the RCN Synod of 1946 a majority of delegates rejected membership,[71] because it was felt that the

---

[66]Cf. *Ibid.*, 210-211 (*ISM,* 207-208).

[67]Cf. "Aan de vooravond van de samenspreking met de Javaanse kerken," 381.

[68]"De vergadering van de Wereldraad van Kerken."

[69]"Apostoliciteit en katholiciteit," *OKZK,* and *IZW.*

[70]The following data are taken mostly from A. Wind, *Zending en oecumene in de twintigste eeuw,* 1, 208-210.

[71]The synod took its lead from the 1930 synod, where the decision was taken to forgo participation in the ecumenical movement for fear of ecclesiastical relativism and a blurring of boundaries. J. van den Berg, "De gereformeerde kerken

Basis adopted by the WCC—"The World Council of Churches is a fellowship of churches which confess the Lord Jesus Christ as God and Saviour"—left too much room for various interpretations, particularly given the WCC participation of churches with liberal leanings. A minority, however, argued for critical solidarity with the WCC, but an attempt to move the 1949 RCN synod in this direction failed. of this second option. In a 1948 article a prominent RCN commentator, S. Zuidema, contended that it was exactly in the diversity among the churches that the justification for the establishment of the WCC was to be found,[72] and that it was precisely on the grounds of the Basis of the WCC that the RCN should engage positively in dialogue with the ecumenical movement. "Just as it would be glorious if we no longer needed hospitals because there was no more illness," he wrote, "so it would be an answer to prayer if there were no need for an Ecumenical Movement because there was only one, true church."[73] And Bavinck moved along similar lines. The article he wrote in 1948 on the inaugural assembly of the WCC reveals a great personal affinity for the ecumenical idea. The following quote, with which he begins his reflections, shows the extent to which the assembly touched an ecumenical chord in him:

> It was in itself already a great joy to see, hear, and meet various great figures from the 'world church'. . . . One felt oneself instantaneously caught up in the world movement, and that in itself was already a tremendous event. . . . In fact, now and then this conference evoked, in spite of all its shortcomings, apocalyptic thoughts and emotions. Such emotions are of course always to some degree dangerous. . . . Nevertheless, a conference such as this is capable of opening up perspectives that raise great expectations."[74]

Bavinck then discusses the significance of the WCC. He observes that "the reality of the 'world church' is difficult to deny" and means by this that the "different churches in various countries of the world affect and influence one another in many ways and stand together in a single immense struggle with the problems of this age."[75] He considers it to be of essential importance to discern this reality: "One may shudder at the thought, or one may be as happy as a child with

---

en de oecumenische beweging," 9-22, presents a good overview of developments up to 1960. He points out that the RCN did not withdraw from ecumenical cooperation as such. At the same synod the decision was taken to join the International Missionary Council by way of the Dutch Missionary Council. The reason adduced for joining the IMC was remarkable: because it did not have a foundational statement, no doctrinal conflict could develop.

[72]Zuidema, 5.

[73]*Ibid.*, 6-7.

[74]"De vergadering van de Wereldraad van Kerken," 274.

[75]*Ibid.*, 275.

it, but I don't think that one can deny these facts."[76] Bavinck sees the WCC as a substantiation, a concrete embodiment and intensification of existing interchurch relationships.

> The various spiritual movements that flow through the churches are brought into contact with one another at such conferences [as the inaugural meeting of the WCC], they are combined in a single focus. They challenge one another, they are weighed against one another, they interpenetrate. In short, a process of fermentation takes place that sometimes continues for many years.[77]

It therefore reflects, in his view, "a gross lack of understanding of the supranatural character of the church" to condescendingly look down on the WCC.[78] In view of the web of mutual relationships that exists among churches, of which the RCN—whether consciously aware of it or not—is also a part, Bavinck considers it irresponsible to stay on the sidelines. "I must give vent to a complaint," he wrote in this connection:

> I fully acknowledge all objections that can be raised against such a World Council of Churches, but it deeply grieves me that our voice has not been heard there. That we have not collaborated in the preparations, in the reports, and that we did not participate in the discussions. ... There are among us certainly people with something to say in this worldwide context, but because we stand on the outside we have no way to make our voice heard.[79]

In addition, Bavinck was of the opinion that in light of the Christocentric Basis of the WCC there is more to be said for than against participation, all the more so because the WCC has no pretensions of being a super church, but rather an organization that allows the participating churches to retain their own interpretations of Christian faith and life. This latitude is not only its weakness but also its strength. On the basis of the faith that the truth of God's Word will manifest itself to be stronger than all forces of doubt and unbelief, and on the basis of the promise that Christ himself will bring his work to completion, we do not have to avoid dialogue with others but on the contrary are allowed to seek it.[80]

Despite this passionate plea, the RCN remained on the sidelines. It was not until the synod of 1963 that the RCN became affiliated with the WCC. The question as to how Bavinck viewed this move must remain unanswered because he never expressed himself on it, very likely because his health at that time had already deteriorated too much for him to react adequately to it.

---

[76] *Ibid.*, 275.

[77] *Ibid.*, 276.

[78] *Ibid.*, 276.

[79] *Ibid.*, 277. Bavinck states almost dramatically, "The names of men such as Barth, Kraemer, Van Dusen, Merle Davis are known far into China and Japan, in India and Africa. But of our existence no one knows."

[80] *Ibid.*, 279-282.

4.2 Fundamental Reflection on the Ecumenical Idea

In 1954 Bavinck published a substantial practical-theological essay in a volume on the apostolic church in which he reflected further on the ecumenical movement.[81] Bavinck commences this composition, which clearly shows his fundamental position,[82] by pointing out that catholicity was already understood in the Early Church as an essential ecclesiastical characteristic, as is shown by the Apostolic and Nicene Creeds. The church has always viewed catholicity as a quadripartite concept, comprising: an *ecumenical element*—united with Christ as head, the church as Christ's body constitutes an indissoluble unit; a *missionary element*—in light of the all-encompassing nature of the atonement in Christ the Church is destined to spread among all nations; an *apologetic element*—in contradistinction to sectarianism the church preserves the totality of the truth intact; and a *holistic element*—given the totality of redemption, the church leads humanity in an all-encompassing manner and heals its ills.[83] On the significance of the concept of catholicity Bavinck states: the church's "unity and its global perspective are . . . both contained in this one word."[84]

In light of the Reformed confessions, the ecumenical and the missionary or apostolic aspects of catholicity were especially relevant for Bavinck. For example, the Heidelberg Catechism, Question and Answer 54, states concerning the holy catholic church that "the Son of God from the beginning to the end of the world, gathers, defends, and preserves to himself by his Spirit and word, out of the whole human race, a church chosen to everlasting life, agreeing in true faith." And the Belgic Confession of Faith declares that "this holy Church is not confined, bound, or limited to a certain place or to certain persons, but is spread and dispersed over the whole world."

Next Bavinck points out on the basis of church history that the church until far into the nineteenth century fell seriously short with respect to both of these aspects: it evidenced far too little apostolic zeal and it too readily accepted its divisions. However, in the second half of the nineteenth century a change began to take place. A growing awareness of the apostolic calling and, along with this, a great increase in missionary praxis soon laid bare the painful and paralyzing reality of ecclesiastical disunity. This led to new ecumenical endeavor that found concrete expression in the conferences of the International Missionary Council, convened from 1910. It was not so much distress over confessional diversity as the practical necessity of cooperation that brought churches and missionary societies together. "At this stage of ecumenical thinking," Bavinck concludes, the perception of

---

[81]"Apostoliciteit en katholiciteit."

[82]Which is closely related to that of H. Bavinck in *De katholiciteit van christendom en kerk*. Cf. also J. Veenhof, "Honderd jaren theologie aan de Vrije Universiteit."

[83]"Apostoliciteit en katholiciteit," 218.

[84]*Ibid.*, 219.

"missionary urgency was strongly predominant."[85]

Gradually the ecumenical process gained in depth. Thus, in addition to concerning itself with the question of missionary urgency, those involved in the ecumenical movement also began to reflect on the differences in confession, church organization, and liturgical practice. From the time of the Stockholm conference in 1925 and the Lausanne conference in 1927, the ecumenical movement traveled along two channels, Life and Work and Faith and Order, which in time joined together to form the WCC.[86] Although these two branches of the new ecumenical body established in 1948 often continued to pursue their own ways in terms of consultation reflection and backing, they were nevertheless brought into close relationship with one another in the WCC.

There was a legitimate fear, according to Bavinck, that the ecumenical dialogue could easily get bogged down in interminable otiose discussions and thus come to a dead end. Only the continual awareness of the church's apostolic calling in this world would "lead the church as a whole to greater unity and solidarity."[87] Citing various reports of international conferences and other publications, Bavinck states that the insight that the ecumenical and apostolic elements of catholicity are theologically interrelated and cannot exist apart from one another in praxis was deepened and broadened in these years.[88] Bavinck makes it clear that on the one hand he heartily endorses these ecumenical developments, and on the other that he intends to follow them critically.

Bavinck stresses the *theological* grounds for ecumenicity by pointing out that the catholicity of the church is founded on "the work of Christ, who as the one Lord involves the whole earth in his redemptive work."[89] It is therefore of utmost importance to the church to be both one and global, "that is, ecumenical in the full sense of the word."[90] He states emphatically that whatever differences in race, nationality, or national character there may be, they can never be of essential significance, because new birth in Christ is a phenomenon so radical that it places the church in a new order of being, in which all erstwhile forms of partition have been removed or at least have lost their divisive power. He points here to Eph. 2:15-16: "His [Christ's] purpose was to create in himself one new man out of the two [Israel and the Gentiles], thus making peace, and in this one body to reconcile both of them to God through the Cross."[91]

Furthermore he adduces the *practical-missionary* motive for ecumenical relations and cooperation by saying that in the whole conception of the highly

---

[85]*Ibid.*, 222.

[86]*Ibid.*, 219-224.

[87]*Ibid.*, 228.

[88]*Ibid.*, 224-228.

[89]*Ibid.*, 232.

[90]*Ibid.*, 233.

[91]*Ibid.*, 233-35.

advocated relationship between unity and apostolicity "lies a natural, self-evident truth," and anyone who has observed "the movement of church life in the last number of decades is deeply touched by the fact that again and again catholicity and apostolicity search for one another and need one another."[92] On the battlefront of confrontation with the demonic powers of modern life, churches come to grasp and experience their fundamental unity on a deeper level, while innumerable more minor distinctions recede into the background. Rejection of every form of ecumenicity can exist only by virtue of an ecclesiastical contentedness that does not grasp that we live in an "apocalyptic age," in which the fundamental content of the faith is at stake.[93]

Though up to this point Bavinck was positive in his approach to the ecumenical movement, his tone becomes more critical when it comes to the question of truth. It is this inescapable point that makes the whole issue much more complex, "more complicated and more insoluble."[94] He points out that the question of truth does not come peeking around the corner only after the joint fulfillment of the apostolic mandate has resulted in the establishment of formal ecumenical relations and discussions about confession, liturgy, and church order commence, but that this question calls for discussion from the very beginning. Bavinck expresses this process as follows: "As soon as one strives to realize catholicity more concretely, no matter in what organizational form, suddenly the great differences in confession, liturgy, and church government come to the fore as a serious obstacle."[95] The apostolic mandate immediately implies the question of truth, because this mandate must be understood as including not only the call to missionary work but also the obligation to remain faithful to the apostolic witness as the foundation on which the church stands (cf. Eph. 2:20) and to the unabridged preaching of this witness today. Apostolicity implies "a believing acceptance of the apostolic witness," and it is therefore impermissible "to trivialize the question of truth in any way when speaking of the apostolate."[96]

Although Bavinck is fully convinced that many differences among the churches will and may be relativized on the frontline between church and world, he is no less convinced that there must be unequivocal clarity concerning the core content of the apostolic *kerygma*. "The church can only be truly catholic when it accepts in faith the word of the apostles and passes this word on to the present generation in our day alive and with power."[97] But he was not altogether confident that this was adequately recognized in the WCC. He appreciated the positive

---

[92]*Ibid*, 228; cf. 239

[93]*Ibid.*, 230.

[94]*Ibid.*, 235.

[95]*Ibid.*, 238.

[96]*Ibid.*, 236, 242.

[97]*Ibid.*, 239; he added an important observation here to the effect that exercise of "the apostolate constrains us to pursue a new, fresh reflection on the message of the apostles."

intentions of the ecumenical movement, but seriously questioned whether the WCC did not all too readily gloss over the differences in interpretation of the adopted core confession. Do people and churches in the WCC "really mean the same thing when they state and acknowledged that Jesus is Lord?"[98] He emphatically points out that more must be said with regard to the Basis of the WCC if there is to be genuine mutual recognition and a true ecumenical relations among churches.[99]

He also questions the way in which a distinction is made between the central truth ("Jesus Christ as God and Savior") and the so-called 'more peripheral' truths (such as the view of Scripture, the doctrine of creation, and the theology of the sacraments). In Bavinck's opinion care should be exercised in making a distinction of this nature, because "the whole truth of the revelation of God presents itself to us as a 'living, organic whole." He makes an important distinction of another kind here, however, namely, between that which presents itself objectively as truth and what people and churches understand it to mean subjectively. Even though the core of the gospel is fully accepted, these subjective interpretations can evince large lacunae or differences. However, insufficient clarity is not an obstacle to, but rather a stimulus for ecumenical solidarity.[100] He wishes to take into consideration that due to all kinds of factors there may remain differences of opinion on details:

> We may take into account that one person—because of his
> upbringing as well as his aptitude, position, studies, and all kinds
> of other factors—undoubtedly has more problems with the
> struggle against modern, secularized thinking than another, so
> that we must not presume to judge too readily.[101]

But even taking that into account, the decisive question remains whether there is an "essential and heartfelt preparedness to be obedient to the word of Jesus Christ" or whether "the apostolic witness is received extremely critically and with many reservations," in which case ecumenical "dialogue is obstructed and we gradually lose the possibility of striving together toward a more authentic mutual encounter in Jesus Christ.[102] Ecumenicity then becomes a problem because the lack of recognition of essential commonalities also makes mutual acknowledgement impossible.

Elsewhere Bavinck points out that it is incorrect to legitimate internal church divisions by means of pretty concepts such as pluriformity or plurality of the church. By speaking of pluriformity the notion is created that all that is involved are differences in external forms, with the result that the much deeper differences in confession are camouflaged and ignored. And in reality the introduction of the

---

[98] *Ibid.*, 237.

[99] *Ibid.*, 238. Bavinck refers, for example, to the proposal of the Norwegian churches, who urged the addition of the phrase "according to the Scriptures" to the Basis.

[100] *Ibid*, 239 and 239-241.

[101] *Ibid.*, 241.

[102] *Ibid.*

concept of plurality puts paid to the fundamental unity of the church. In point of fact these terms do nothing but veil an essential lack of catholicity.[103] All this shows that Bavinck, like Herman Bavinck before him, assumed an ambivalent stance with respect to ecumenicity: he searched for the unity that is offered while wanting to preserve the truth that has been given.

Despite this ambivalence, Bavinck nevertheless draws a clear conclusion from his reflection:

> Because the church is catholic, that is, has a global destiny, it must also be apostolic, must turn itself to face the world. . . . And while it thus busies itself apostolically, it becomes more deeply aware of its catholicity in the sense of the fundamental unity of all believers in Christ Jesus. . . . In this process the question of truth forces itself on the church. Only when it dares to face this question humbly and courageously ... [will] the Spirit, the one Spirit of Jesus Christ, found it more and more firmly in the faith and in this way make the church an ever more fit instrument in the hand of the one Lord, who in mercy stretches his hands out toward the misery of the world in which, trembling, we now stand and struggle.[104]

This passionate plea for true ecumenicity, which will bring blessing to the church and salvation to the world, shows that ultimately it is not Bavinck's critical reservations but his faith in the work of the Holy Spirit to lead his church in all truth that has the final say.

4.3. The Practical Necessity of the Ecumenical Efforts

Especially on the mission field and in the younger churches Christians must bend their very best efforts toward the realization of mutual cooperation and unity. In addition to the biblical summons to unity, which is the deepest and decisive motive for seeking it,[105] Bavinck mentions three other motives that should spur missionaries and local believers on to engage in ecumenical activity. In the first place, it is viewed as a sign of inner weakness and as proof of lack of credibility when churches and mission organizations work separately and compete with one another.[106] Next, it is irresponsible simply to export the divisions that have evolved in the course of history and to impose them on newly founded churches, or to tie then permanently to that past.[107] And finally, many younger churches have a pressing need for closer mutual solidarity, on the one hand to be able to better recognize one another in the one faith, and on the other in order to attain a stronger

---

[103]Cf. *IZW*, 203 (*ISM*, 200)

[104]"Apostoliteit en katholiciteit," 242.

[105]Cf. *OKZK*, 40.

[106]Cf. *IZW*, 203 (*ISM*, 200).

[107]Cf. "Apostoliciteit en katholiciteit," 229.

position in the world in which they live.[108] Bavinck then points out three avenues by which divisions can be done away with as much as possible and unity can be promoted.

First, the sending churches are called to enter into dialogue with one another, in order to arrive at the maximum cooperation possible in carrying out the missiological task. Not only should they arrange an allocation of territories to avoid any form of competition, but differences between them should also be discussed. If agreement can be reached in broad lines via such a platform, the foundation will have been laid for growth in mutual trust, missionary cooperation and the formation of one church on the mission field. This cooperation should include the search for agreement on such practical things as Bible translations, hymnals, and liturgies.[109] Bavinck writes that this necessity for cooperation does have limits:

> If a given church were to come to the conclusion that the mission that works nearby does not in fact preach Christ but rather proclaims a kind of idealistic humanism under the guise of Christian words and that that mission tramples underfoot the most fundamental doctrines of the Christian church, then it will be very problematic to engage in any kind of cooperative consultation with that mission.[110]

Second, the younger churches can establish mutual contact with each other when called at a given moment to take an appropriate confessional stance vis-à-vis the world in which they live. While younger churches will, as a matter of course, initially adopt the confessional standards of the 'mother church' as a guideline, they will gradually feel the need to formulate a confessional statement of faith of their own, one that is appropriate to the needs and challenges of their situation.[111] And when this need arises, the local churches can engage in joint reflection on the problems posed by the powers they have to contend with and be of mutual service in considering a pertinent timely response to the questions with which they are confronted.[112]

In the third place, the older churches must in no way hinder the younger churches which are striving for unity, but rather advise and stimulate them as much as possible toward this goal. When only reservations are expressed and this guidance that seeks to serve is withheld, the danger exists that younger churches sooner or later will reach for a unity that is undesirable.[113] In the process of unification the following deserve special attention: liturgy, church order, and confession. Bavinck's thinking here is in keeping with the common ecumenical

---

[108]Cf. *OKZK*, 41 and *IZW*, 205-6.

[109]Cf. *IZW*, 204-205 (*ISM,* 201-202).

[110]*IZW*, 205 (cf. *ISM,* 202).

[111]Cf. *Ibid.*, 206 (*ISM,* 203-204).

[112]Cf. *Ibid.*, 206-207 (*ISM,* 203-204), *OKZK*, 44-45, and "Theologie in het verre Oosten," 179.

[113]Cf. *OKZK,* 45 and *IZW*, 205 (*ISM,* 202-203).

points of discussion.

Although for Bavinck the liturgical question is not the most important one, he nevertheless thinks that it can be divisive, which means that it is an unavoidable topic for discussion. The goal is to find liturgical models that on the one hand are not indiscriminate imitations of Western patterns and practices, but which on the other are not infected by pagan ideas.[114]

Matters are more complicated in the area of church order. It is important to understand that things which have developed historically should not be made absolute, Bavinck writes, but various matters of church order must always be weighed and laid down in the light of Scripture. He was clearly quite optimistic about possibilities in this area: the search for appropriate forms of church order "is a glorious and delightful task ... provided we have the conviction" that everyone involved in this task is concerned to "be obedient to the Word of God."[115]

The confessional issue is the most difficult one of all. On the one hand, if there is agreement on the essential points of the gospel, it is sometimes easier to find one another in the non-Western world than in the West. The more detailed points of disagreement that are divisive in the West are often below the horizon in the East. It is fruitless to raise these more peripheral confessional issues and to demand agreement on them as well. It is better to leave such matters to the discretion of the younger churches themselves. On the other hand existing confessional differences must not be trivialized. Where the truth is trifled with for the sake of unity, it "is impossible to become truly one."[116] In Bavinck's view there were clearly "circumstances, also on the mission field, where division is better than unity. That is always the case when the truth of God's Word is sacrificed to a human search for unity" for unity's sake alone.[117]

4.4. Summary

In his reflection on the relationship between the older and the younger churches, Bavinck took political involvements and psychological sensitivities fully into account. Appealing to the basic biblical-theological principle that churches are equal, he also consistently advocated both growth toward autonomy on the part of younger churches and mutual missionary cooperation. He did not, however, move in a new direction; rather, he further elaborated and gave practical focus to the ecclesiological views of the 1895 Synod of Middelburg, where, in continuity with Voetius, the necessity of younger-church independence had been clearly established. He also openly aligned himself with the idea of "partnership in obedience" that emerged from 1947 IMC conference in Whitby. Furthermore, his thinking on older-younger church relations evidences a clearly observable consistency between theory and praxis: in his definition of mission, Bavinck describes mission as the work of the *church* and speaks of incorporating people into

---

[114]Cf. *OKZK*, 42.

[115]*Ibid.*, 42-43.

[116]*Ibid.*, 43.

[117]*IZW*, 206 (cf. *ISM,* 203).

the *fellowship* of those who expect the coming of the Kingdom. Implicit in the concept "church" is the notion that all churches jointly—and consequently each church individually—have a missionary task. And the concept "fellowship" implies the equal position and mutual serving function of the churches.

In view of current relationships between the older and the younger churches, Bavinck's plea is outdated. Nevertheless, the biblical principles he adduces retain their significance as warning and protection against any form of imperialism in the relationship between churches.

Bavinck held a nuanced position in respect of the ecumenical movement. Basing himself on biblical teaching concerning the catholicity and apostolicity of the church he warmly supported ecumenism on the national and international level. This was entirely in line with the open attitude he himself always maintained toward theologians and missiologists outside the RCN. On the other hand, he maintained a critical reserve with respect to ecumenical efforts by positing the question of truth as decisive criterion for judging the success or failure of ecumenism. Unlike the majority in the RCN he refused to reject ecumenical encounter out of hand, but on the contrary wanted to engage in the ecumenical movement. Bavinck's *ambivalence* with regard to ecumenism, it must be noted, had nothing to do with *equivocation*. Behind his ambivalence lay the basic conviction that was so characteristic of Bavinck, namely, the exclusive prerogative of Scripture to determine Christian thought and action: the right of the ecumenical movement to exist is anchored in Scripture, and Scripture forms the basis for true ecumenicity. Johannes van den Berg was right in characterizing Bavinck as a catholic-Reformed thinker.[118]

Bavinck's view on the pursuit of ecumenism has not lost its relevance for today. Given the developments in the WCC there is from a biblical perspective no less reason for apprehension than when Bavinck expressed his concern. The idea is still common among some that with a "*minimum* of foundation a *maximum* of outward cooperation"[119] can be achieved.[120] The question of truth deserves full attention. At the same time, it is especially Christians with a Reformed orientation who can learn from Bavinck today that the biblical call to unity must not be surrendered too quickly and certainly not out of hand, but must rather be held onto until the bitter end because of its apostolic (missionary) dimension. It is precisely the basic Reformation principles, which inform Bavinck's ecumenical outlook, that will stimulate churches of Reformed origin to participate in ecumenical encounter: the principle of *sola* and *tota Scriptura*, which points only to the Scriptures as sacred and not any theological tradition, and therefore creates room for dialogue; the principle of *sola fide*, which expresses the expectation, hope against hope, of the continual working of the Spirit; and the principle of *sola gratia*, which precludes pride and calls believers to the humble service of their fellow human beings, i.e., to

---

[118]"De wetenschappelijke arbeid van Professor Dr. Johan Herman Bavinck," 41.

[119]Cf. K. Deddens and M. K. Drost, *Balans van het oecumenisme*, 10.

[120]At the conference of the WCC in Canberra (1991) syncretistic elements were clearly in evidence—which were, incidentally, forcefully opposed

impart to others the blessings with which they have been blessed.[121]

5. The Problem of Race

Because of his missiological expertise, Bavinck regularly spent time and lectured in South Africa from the 1950s on. This exposed him quite directly to the racial problem there and to the politics of apartheid.[122] This confrontation led to reflections on the problem of race in general, which found expression in a 1956 publication on this problem (*RPW*), and more specifically on the complex situation in South Africa, about which he regularly published articles in various periodicals, especially in *GW*.[123]

5.1. The Absence of Racial Problems in the Bible

In *RPW* Bavinck points out that the Bible is not only ignorant of the word *race* but also lacks any reference to the concept as such. The lines of demarcation between the nations are not drawn exclusively on the basis of their descent.[124] In the OT laws it is striking that Israel must treat strangers (non-Israelites) trueheartedly, no matter who they are (cf. Exod. 12:38; Deut. 10:18-19). Strangers have the same legal standing as Israelites, based on the pregnant argument "I am the Lord your God" (Lev. 24:22). In the subsequent history of Israel life-or-death battles are sometimes fought with nations that are racially related to Israel. In the prophetic writings all kinds of races appear to fall within the compass of God's mercy (cf. Isa. 18:17; 19:25; 45:1; Zech. 8:23).[125] When the separation of Israel from the nations is mentioned, it is never motivated by a difference of race or culture; rather, it is a command from God, that in Christ is abolished (Eph. 2:14-22).[126] The oft-used appeal to the curse on the son of Ham (Canaan) as an argument for assuming or

---

[121]Cf. P.J. Visser, "Een gereformeerde? Aller dienaar!" 42-45.

[122]It is not impossible that Bavinck indirectly had come into contact with this issue before, given the fact that Abraham Kuyper had already written a considerable amount about the political and social relationships in South Africa.

[123]The most significant of these articles and some sections from *Het rassenvraagstuk* were collected by J. van den Berg and published with brief notes in *Een geheel andere waardemeter* (1972). Van den Berg emphasizes that Bavinck's contributions to the reflection on the situation in South Africa are clearly dated. It was "a time in which many hoped that an open dialogue about the apartheid question with and in the South African churches might lead to a new, creative vision, to a change that would be the harbinger of a different relationship between the races in that part of the world" (10).

[124]*RPW*, 5. Bavinck mentions that Moses married an Ethiopian; overruling Miriam's displeasure at this, God takes Moses under his protection.

[125]*RPW*, 6.

[126]*Ibid*, 8.

positing an eternal inferiority of all non-Semitic and non-Caucasian nations is entirely incorrect from a biblical-exegetical standpoint.[127]

The NT speaks nowhere "of any reserve toward other races." Any differences disappear utterly in Christ: Greek and Jew, circumcised and uncircumcised, barbarian and Scythian, slave and free are one in him (cf. Gal. 3:28; Col. 3:11).[128]

The Scriptures, therefore, are ignorant of any distinctions between superior and inferior nations. Israel, too, is a nation like the other nations and owes its special position strictly to God's electing love. What matters in the biblical-theological perspective on the nations is their unity in Adam, whereby the emphasis falls on shared sinfulness and the universal nature of salvation in Christ (cf., e.g., Rom. 5:12-21).[129] The fact that the Bible has no knowledge of a racial problem does not mean, however, that one cannot speak to this issue from Scripture. "If there is one problem that must be viewed and also be judged from the perspective of faith in Christ, then it is certainly this issue."[130]

5.2. The Reality of the Problem of Race in History

Although biblically humanity constitutes a unit, from an anthropological perspective it represents a great diversity. Bavinck, following Albert Drexel, defines the concept *race* as "a sum of individuals who are linked together by a set of hereditary characteristics."[131] Three main races can be distinguished: Caucasoid, Mongoloid, and Negroid, each of which contains many varieties. Bavinck did not venture to explain the origin of these varieties.[132] Rather, as theologian he seeks to interpret this variety. He sees it as an enrichment, willed by God, that reflects the fullness of being human in the image of God. From this perspective he emphasizes the need for mutual communication, with a view to fostering the sharing of complementary human qualities, gifts and strengths.

Through the centuries there have been continual feelings of superiority and

---

[127]*Ibid.*, 7. Bavinck contends that all that can be derived from the available data is a temporary political relationship (servitude) between Canaan's descendants and the descendants of the other two. In doing so he plainly distances himself from A. Kuyper, who argued in *Lectures on Calvinism* that Shem and Japheth "have been the sole bearers of the development of the race" and that "no impulse for any higher life has ever gone forth from the third group." J.M. van der Linde. discusses this issue at great length in *Over Noach en zijn zonen*, but nowhere mentions Bavinck.

[128]*RPW*, 7.

[129]*Ibid.*, 8-9.

[130]*Ibid.*, 9.

[131]A. Drexel, 12. Bavinck thinks here of differences in skin color, hair growth, facial expressions, and build, as well as disposition and temperament.

[132]*RPW*, 11. He does point out that many factors, such as climate, way of life, and cultural development, have also been of influence.

inferiority going back and forth between the races.[133] Bavinck gives three causes for such feelings. First, there is a tendency to measure others against one's own cultural attainments; anyone who does not measure up to these is considered inferior. Second, directly related to the first cause is the frequent lack of interest in and respect for someone else's culture. Third, it is often forgotten that if it is at all possible to speak of a higher level of civilization and development, such a civilization would have to be viewed as a product of God's favor and should be cause for engaging in active service of others rather than seen as something that points to or proves the superior quality of a people (race) or provides grounds for self-aggrandizement.[134]

Next Bavinck points out that the racial problem has become increasingly more complex because it nearly always coincides with social, economic, political, cultural, and religious differences that have accentuated differences between people. His description of these issues shows the extent of his concern with and understanding of the complexity of this problem.[135]

The result of all this has been that sharp tensions have developed and deep distrust has grown, especially toward white Westerners. Bavinck foresaw catastrophic consequences taking place in his own day, unless efforts were made toward a new foundation "for authentic trust on both sides."[136] He sees the fulfillment of this spiritual and moral project as an important task for the church of Jesus Christ. "This may be called one of the greatest issues facing the church at this moment in world history."[137] Drawing on his own missionary experience he points out that more is involved in the alleviation of racial tension than the creation of equal living conditions alone: what is needed is a changed attitude. According to Bavinck the key question for Christians is: "How does Christ want us to act in these [racial] relationships? What motives should guide us and what must be our goal?" And he adds, "One thing is certain from the outset. We will have to examine ourselves with ruthless honesty and we must not hesitate to draw the consequences from that examination. We will have to stand before God in openness and find our

---

[133]*Ibid.*, 13-14. Bavinck refers here to two statements made at Jerusalem 1928: D.T. Jabavu from Africa said there that "many white Christians do not treat blacks as people who have a fully fledged personality"; and Miss V.N. Tilak from India stated, "We Indians have only limited contact with white people, and then we say, 'Oh, he is an American,' or 'Oh, he is an Englishman!' In such expressions our often unconscious feeling of superiority is expressed in a very subtle way."

[134]*Ibid.*, 14-17. Bavinck points in this connection to the beneficent effect of the gospel on people's thinking and life, and states further that there is no scientific basis whatsoever for thinking that one race has more potential than another.

[135]*Ibid.*, 20-32.

[136]*Ibid.*, 17. Bavinck writes, "If no spirit of rapprochement and a desire to meet one another in a new way begins to grow among the various races, the future of humanity looks dark."

[137]*Ibid.*, 18.

way out of the labyrinth by listening reverently to Him."[138]

5.3. The Race Problem from the Perspective of the Gospel

In *RPW* Bavinck points out that in the past, attempts have been made to establish guidelines for the relationship between the races, but that these have often functioned in a faulty manner. Thus, from the beginning of the colonial period there was talk of a moral-religious *sense of calling* on the part of the Western imperial powers vis-à-vis the colonial regions. But this so-called sense of calling was frequently permeated by a longing for power and wealth and served as a cover for maintaining one's own position of leadership, it was, in other words, very often lacking in loving willingness to truly serve the other.[139]

The same holds for the much-used term *guardianship*. Guardianship was acceptable, Bavinck thought, as long as it was naturally and reciprocally acceptance by all parties involved, and so long as it retained a temporary character and did not become an end in itself.[140] Bavinck was also very decisive in his rejection of any self-willed or self-serving interpretation of the *providence of God*. The fact that God has willed diversity does not legitimate conduct that cultivates diversity by means of violence and according to one's own norms. That kind of behavior is tantamount to assuming God's role as Master of providence."[141]

Instead of the above-mentioned tainted and incorrectly interpreted concepts, Bavinck opts for the biblically-based concept of *equality*.[142] The Bible bears witness to equality in the sense "that before [God] we all count as sinners, who can be saved only by his grace."[143] Bavinck refers here to Col. 3:25, which states that with God there is "no partiality." As deepest theological motif for any reflection on race relations he cites the incarnation of Christ, "who emptied himself and became neither Westerner nor Easterner, neither white nor black, but *human*."[144] This equality becomes visible in the Christian church especially in the celebration of the Lord's Supper. Equality in principle, however, would be "a cheap manifestation" if it finds concrete expression only in church relationships. It must make itself felt in all kinds of other human relationships as well.[145]

Although Bavinck does not ignore the biblical aspect of the *uniqueness* of

---

[138]*Ibid.*, 32.

[139]*Ibid.*, 33-38

[140]*Ibid.*, 38-40.

[141]J. van den Berg, *Een geheel andere waardemeter*, 97-101.

[142]Bavinck, *RPW*, 41, correctly point out that this concept must never be understood as absolute but always as relative.

[143]*Ibid.*, 41.

[144]*Ibid.*, 53.

[145]*Ibid.*, 40-43.

the nations and the enriching diversity implicit therein, he opposes on principle any attitude in which equality is threatened or curtailed on the grounds of that so-called uniqueness.[146] For Bavinck the core of the far-reaching racial problem is religious, that is, a direct result of the sinful pride of people. Accordingly, he contends that the most important key to solving the problem lies in an attitude that is sanctified by Christ, an attitude which helps people to rediscover each other as fellow human beings and encourages them to let love for neighbor determine their actions.[147] Or in Bavinck's words:

> There does not exist in this world a single substitute for that
> wondrous thing the Bible calls love. Paul would say, even if I
> were to give a hundred million dollars to build homes for people
> of another race and schools and athletic fields and had not love,
> I would gain nothing.[148]

In light of the preceding it is clear that Bavinck assigns a pioneering role to the church and to mission[149] to reflect on the principles of, and practical approach to, this problem of race. In this reflection they must let themselves be guided above all by the biblical notions concerning the Kingdom of God. It is not correct to interpret this kingdom along exclusively eschatological lines and in this way turn it into a provisional entry in the ledger sheet of grim and recalcitrant world events. In the awareness that the Kingdom has come in Christ, church and mission know that the last things (*eschata*) are fully underway and that relationships that have developed historically must be exposed to the pressure of the ever-new Kingdom dynamic. This must, of course, be done with a due sense of realism, but reality must never be elevated to a normative position. Church and mission must not rest until the perspective on reality that takes the kingdom of God as its norm has been realized.[150]

5.4. Summary

In his reflection on the race problem there was always only one norm for Bavinck: the gospel. On the one hand he did not want to say *more* than the gospel does, which made him modest in his opinions on practical-political measures. This modesty was furthermore strengthened by a level-headed understanding of the

---

[146]*Ibid.*, 43-47. He points out that, because of deeply rooted distrust, too strong an emphasis on uniqueness is interpreted as an attempt to keep certain groups of people from advancing culturally. Conversely, peoples who have acquired independence (and equality) begin very naturally to take note once again of that which is unique to them.

[147]*Ibid.*, 52-54.

[148]*Ibid.*, 51.

[149]In *OKZK*, 8, Bavinck emphatically points out that mission owes its right to exist to the assumption that the nations are "of one blood" and that God is the God "of the entire earth."

[150]J. van den Berg, *Een geheel andere waardemeter*, 97-101.

complexity of the problem: the intertwining of political, social, economic, and psychological factors prompted him to take a cautious approach. On the other hand he did not want to say *less* than the gospel. This meant that he was decisive in testing fundamental attitudes behind practical policies: every attitude that was not in line with the biblical principle of equality had to be condemned. And in this the church had to fulfill a pioneering role. He was convinced that where this essential equality was the underlying assumption, it would have a beneficial effect on the political, social, economic, and ecclesiastical structures.

From the preceding it appears that Bavinck consistently wanted to give concrete shape to his theological principle that the gospel renews all relationships. By calling especially the church, i.e, Christians to account with respect to this responsibility, he also maintained the principle that the horizontal dimensions of salvation are not unrelated to its vertical dimension. This approach, in which modesty and decisiveness go hand in hand, is reminiscent of the way in which Paul critiqued the social relationships of his day. Although Bavinck himself never explicitly referred to Paul in this connection, it is not impossible that he did have the Apostle's example in mind, since it was important to him that the manner of approach, too, always be grafted onto the Scriptures, in the conviction that this would yield the most fruitful way of operating in the world.

6. Chapter Summary

The material presented above has shown that there is a great consistency between Bavinck's systematic reflections and practical applications. Bavinck's missionary theology had its origin in praxis and was oriented toward praxis. Nowhere in his work is it possible to find a discrepancy between theory and practice, on the contrary, they are regularly interwoven. In fact, the distinction made in this volume between systematic and practical missionary theology has something of an inappropriate flavor when applied to Bavinck.

This chapter was devoted to an examination of the practical outcome of his systematic thought in four areas: the integration of Christian faith in existing culture; the relation between the 'younger' and 'older' churches; ecumenics; and the race issue.

Bavinck was always deeply aware that mission is more than proclamation of the gospel alone: from the very onset it is also a confrontation with the culture in which it takes place, a fact already implied by its use of foreign languages. It is incumbent on mission to undertake a critical appropriation of culture in the light of the Gospel and to foster the firm implantation of Christian theology and practice in the various cultures of the world. This inculturation of the gospel also has many societal components, which must be critically thought through down to the final principle, Christ himself. In line with his views relating to theology of religion Bavinck used the term *possessio* to designate this process of inculturation, a notion which holds title to a far greater critical capacity with respect to religion and culture than does the concept of *accomodatio*. At the same time, he expressed appreciation for the religious heritage of existing cultures: its critical appropriation can lead to the enrichment of Christian thought and tradition. Furthermore, it is evident that he coupled his theological reflection with a strong sense of reality: owing to the refractoriness of things the way they are, *possessio* can only be understood, practically speaking, as a process in which syncretistic tendencies must slowly but surely be won over. Moreover, one is struck by the extent to which Bavinck employed practical, psychological and social motifs in addition to theological themes in formulating his missiology.

In reflecting on the relationship between the 'older' and 'younger' churches Bavinck reckoned fully with political intricacies and psychological sensitivities. Further, taking his lead from the foundational biblical-theological principle that churches are equal, he persistently appealed for the emancipation of the 'younger' churches and for missionary cooperation among all churches. In this he not only followed the 1895 Synod of Middelburg but also linked up with the idea of *partnership in obedience*, one of the themes of the 1947 International Missionary Conference held in Whitby, Canada. Moreover, his thinking on this matter evinces a clear consistency between theory and practice: Bavinck defines mission as the activity of the *Church* and speaks of the incorporation of new believers into the *koinonia* of those who await the coming of the Kingdom. In the concept *Church* lies enclosed the idea that all churches together have and consequently every church separately has—a missionary task. And the notion *community* implies the parity of the churches and their obligation to mutual service.

With respect to ecumenics Bavinck assumed an ambivalent stance. On the one hand he warmly advocated—on theological and missiological grounds, *viz.*, the catholicity and apostolicity of the church—the development of ecumenical relations at both the national and international level. On the other hand he maintained a critical reserve by adducing the question of truth as decisive criterion for judging ecumenical success or failure. Unlike the majority in the Reformed Churches in the Netherlands at that time, however, Bavinck did not employ this criterion as a means of dismissing ecumenical encounter in advance but, quite the opposite, as a spur to engagement in ecumenical affairs. Beneath this ambivalent position lay the fundamental conviction, so characteristic of Bavinck, that Scripture has final authority in all things, including ecumenics and ecumenical relations.

In his treatment of the race problem there was one sole norm for Bavinck: the gospel. On the one hand he did not wish to say anything *more* than the gospel, which led him to exercise restraint in judging practical political matters. This modesty was moreover strengthened by a sober awareness of the complexity of the problem of race: to his mind the interlacement of political, social, economic and psychological factors required a cautious approach. On the other hand he did not want to say anything *less* than the gospel. This meant that he insisted on the necessity of testing the primary attitude and governing assumptions behind practical policy in the area of race relations: any prior stance or belief which ran counter to the biblical principle of equality was to be condemned, and in this the church should play a leading role.

In general it can be concluded that Bavinck's work is generally marked by a pronounced consonance of systematic reflection and practical application. At the same time his theological approach is harmoniously linked to his psychological sensitivity and sober sense of reality. This is not to be construed as opportunism: in imitation of Christ he sought to serve the cause of God and his fellow human beings as effectively as possible.

CHAPTER TEN

Concluding Postscript

In this final brief recapitulatory chapter, attention is briefly drawn to three matters respecting the development, content, and significance of Bavinck's missiological oeuvre, *viz.*, the originality of his thought, the continuity and discontinuity evident in his missionary theology, and the question of the relevance of his writings as this comes to expression in the form of references to them in the works of others.

1. The Originality of Bavinck's Missiology

Properly speaking, the whole of Bavinck's missiology can be qualified as original. As the first missionary theologian of the Reformed Churches in the Netherlands he offered a biblical examination of the fundamental questions with regard to the Christian missionary calling and task. Though his thinking and writing was in thorough keeping with the Protestant tradition in general and the Reformed tradition in particular, he also made singular contributions to both the theological grounding and formulation and the deepening and broadening of existing missionary principles and themes. Nevertheless, it must also be pointed out in this regard that despite his emphasis on the necessity of a "patient listening to the Bible," he himself did not always engage in careful, detailed biblical exegesis. Thus, his work did not represent so much an apex as it did a powerful and authoritative beginning in the cultivation of the discipline of missiology from a Reformed perspective. Bavinck's freshness and independence of thought are more clearly evident in that which characterizes his theology in general and in the way in which he developed a number of particular topics and issues.

In general his originality is shown by the way in which he integrated theological reflection with a psychological approach, based on his deep conviction that the Bible is a thoroughly psychological book. He put a great deal of effort into careful analysis of the psychological reality of theological verities. By means of this method he was able in a truly phenomenal way to fathom and portray human religious response to divine revelation. On one side, this is illustrated by his description of the religious phenomena of non-Christian traditions. In *CMO*, for example, he provides a sharp analysis of the psychological tendencies present in the mystical sense of life, and in *RBCG* and *CBTM* he develops an original morphology of religious consciousness. And in all of this one feels a constant tension: Bavinck is fascinated by mysticism and the reality of religious consciousness while at the same time giving substantive expression, on the basis of observed psychological processes, to his theological judgment that vis-à-vis God man is in deepest essence a rebel on the run. The *grandeur* of religious man constitutes at one and the same time his *misère*. On the other side, his psychological approach manifests a spiritual (affective) edge: Bavinck seeks to ascertain in both mission (the elenctic encounter) and pastorate what takes place in the human heart once God's Word takes hold in it through the operation of the Holy Spirit. This urge to get to the bottom of the mystery of (religious) man never stood on its own in Bavinck's work, however, but was always meant to serve the high purpose by which he had been seized, namely the communication of the gospel in as adequate a way as possible. As A. Pos wrote, Bavinck's efforts to arrive at a psychological understanding of man were directed toward the discovery of the roots of resistance in the human heart to true life with and service of God.[1] This psychological sensitivity was also an important determining factor in the development of his views in the area of practical missionary theology. It was precisely this psychological enrichment of theology that gave Bavinck's missiology the distinctive character and content which differentiated it from other missionary theologies of his time. The topical significance of Bavinck's missiological thought is grounded more in this original psychological approach than in his biblical reflection. It is primarily due to this approach that his works can be said to belong to the category of modern classics[2] and that they retain their importance in the present post-Christian era in which 'religious feeling' is once again a thriving preoccupation within the general population.[3]

Bavinck's originality is further certified by the contributions he made in five distinct theological areas, each of which demonstrates that he not only built upon the Protestant, Reformed and ecumenical traditions, but that he was also an independent thinker.

As the first Reformed missiologist Bavinck provided a Trinitarian interpretation of general revelation. This form of revelation, he argued, is theocentric in origin, christocentric as to content, and pneumacentric with respect to its effectua-tion. This is a very crucial point that begs further theological reflection, certainly when it comes to its missionary implications.

Bavinck also developed an entirely original morphology of religious consciousness,[4] consisting of what he called five "magnetic points": a sense of belonging to the whole, a sense of transcendent norms, a sense of the governance of existence by a providential or destining power, a sense of the need for redemption, and a sense of relatedness to a higher or supreme power.

On the matter of the relationship between word and deed in mission, the 1896 Synod of Middelburg employed the distinction between 'primary' and preparatory 'secondary' missionary tasks or ministries, according to which 'deed' was not considered to be an essential part of the missionary calling. Using biblical arguments, Bavinck rejected this traditional position, calling for the institution of a new set of concepts. He preferred to speak of the kerygmatic 'core missionary task,' consisting of the preaching of the gospel, and companion 'auxiliary

---

[1]Cf. "Leven en werk van Dr. Johan Herman Bavinck," p. 2.

[2]Cf. J. Verkuyl, "Woord vooraf," p. IX.

[3]Cf. R. van Woudenberg, *J.H. Bavinck: Een keuze uit zijn werk*, p. 31.

[4]Cf. J. Verkuyl, "Woord vooraf," p. XIII, and H. Kraemer, *Religions and the Christian Faith*, pp. 79-81.

missionary ministries,' consisting of life-renewing deeds, all of which he subsumed under the single term 'missionary proclamation.' Though Bavinck stood for a broad, comprehensive understanding of mission, he carefully distinguished his own position from the notion of 'comprehensive approach' espoused by the ecumenical movement.

Though the discipline of elenctics was not originated by Bavinck—this concept was already employed by Voetius and Kuyper—he did inject it with new life.[5] It is especially in this area of missionary apologetics that Bavinck's heart lay: he was convinced that elenctics constituted the nerve center of all missionary and pastoral work. In fact, in *ICNCW* he argues that the Bible itself is an elenctic book from beginning to end. He pleads for a thorough and careful cultivation of this discipline with the help of the information and knowledge accumulated in the area of religious studies. The work of persuasion (ἐλέγχειν) necessarily consists of a combination of theological, psychological and spiritual aspects: theological because religious conviction is not brought about by means of rational argumentation but rather through the operation of the Holy Spirit, psychological because persuasion entails an effort to discover what the other has done with God, and spiritual because ἐλέγχειν leads to salutary results only in the absence of any feelings of Christian superiority and in the humble awareness on the part of the one who is engaging in witness that the elenctic weapon is pointed first of all at him- or herself. With this, Bavinck offers a concept of dialogical encounter which reveals its Reformed origin and is thoroughly Christian as to content.

Possessio (taking into possession) is the term Bavinck uses to express what today is called the inculturation of the Christian faith and the contextualization of the gospel. He did not choose this word by chance or default but purposely. It conveys both his theological conviction that religion in its totality constitutes defection from God and his psychological persuasion that the old must, as it is emptied, be filled anew. Behind his insistence that the teaching and life of the church must become indigenized lay the conviction that such inculturation would have far-reaching beneficial effects on local Christian theology and religious experience.[6] And his view that the indigenous church itself must have a definitive say regarding this process shows that any thought of the 'superiority' of the Western church and its theology were totally alien to him.

2. Continuity and Discontinuity in Bavinck's Missiology

2.1. Continuity

Bavinck's missiology , and especially his *biblical* missionary theology, evinces a great measure of continuity. One thinks here in particular of the Trinitarian, ecclesiological, eschatological and doxological themes that run as *leitmotivs* through his writings. His thought is rooted in the central Voetian missionary goals and motives adopted at the Synod of Middelburg in 1896: conversion of the human

---

[5]Cf. J.A.B. Jongeneel, "Voetius' zendingstheologie," p. 121, and R. Fernhout, "Van elenctiek naar dialoog," pp. 9-17.

[6]Cf. A.G. Hoekema, *Denken in dynamisch evenwicht*, p. 195, who points to the pioneer role Bavinck played in the encouragement and promotion of *theologia in loco*.

person, the planting of the church, and the Glory of God. It is within this frame of reference that Bavinck's thought and work assumed deeper and broader dimensions as time went on. This development was fueled not only by his biblical reflections but also by his adoption of elements primarily from Protestant and secondarily from ecumenical missionary theologies. This receptivity to outside influences did not, however, lead to any truly fundamental shifts in his thinking. As J. van den Berg has pointed out, "he [Bavinck] transposed these influences into the musical key of his own experience."[7] In only one case did his ongoing reflection lead him to depart from the positions taken by the Synod of Middelburg, namely, the question of the relationship between word and deed referred to above.

Bavinck's missionary theology is characterized throughout by an ardent elucidation of ideas without a great deal of scientific display. On the one hand this demonstrates the weakness of his missiology but on the other its strength: it is not theological abstraction that typifies Bavinck's missiological endeavors but rather spiritual involvement in the worldwide work of God in mission. His classroom lectures, too, were shot through with this unconditional commitment and outspoken loyalty to the gospel of Christ, which greatly inspired many of his students.[8] And this spiritual dimension constitutes one of the most important factors imparting lasting value to his missionary theology.

2.2. Discontinuity

There are two points in Bavinck's missionary theology that display discontinuity. First of all, one notices this in the development of his theology of religion (*theologia religionum*) and secondly, in an increasing concentration on the Kingdom of God in his writings.

At the beginning of his missiological career Bavinck's view of the religious life of man in general and of non-Christians in particular was strongly influenced by his insights in the area of the psychology of religion. At that time he was of the opinion that a relationship existed between Christian faith and the general religious feelings experienced by human beings, with the result that he was not only critical but also appreciative of this omnipresent religious sense. He characterized religious consciousness as a genuine search for and simultaneously a running away from God or, conversely, as flight from and at the same time a reaching out toward God. Later on, in consequence of his involvement in preparations for the 1938 World Missionary Conference in Tambaram and under the influence of Hendrik Kraemer's book, *The Christian Message in a Non-Christian World*, Bavinck moved from an approach largely conditioned by psychology of religion to a more clearly theological position, which he further developed within a distinctly Reformed frame of reference. Though psychology continued to figure in Bavinck's thought, after Tambaram it began to play an increasingly subordinate role in his missiology.

The second point of discontinuity in Bavinck's work has to do with the change of emphasis on the notion of the Kingdom of God. In an article published in 1978 one commentator stated that "the Kingdom of God occupied a limited and

---

[7]"De wetenschappelijke arbeid van Professor Dr. Johan Herman Bavinck," p. 41.

[8]Cf. A. Pos, "Leven en werk van Dr. Johan Herman Bavinck," pp. 25-24.

small place" in Bavinck's missionary theology.[9] But this judgment needs to be qualified. In 1961, toward the end of his missiological career, Bavinck himself spoke of the concept of God's Kingdom as "that almost always forgotten chapter of doctrinal theology," which is nevertheless "one of the most dominant ideas when we are dealing with missions."[10] Though the notion of the Kingdom may have received little attention in Bavinck's earlier reflection, in his later work it functioned more prominently. It may be said that the increasing advertence to the theme of the Kingdom of God in Bavinck's reflection went hand in hand with a growing interest in it in theology in general and in ecumenical missiology in particular. The first signs of a shift in his thinking on this matter were furnished by his 1948 publication, *ICNCW*. In this book the emphasis on church-planting as the goal of mission is expanded to include the broader perspective of the provisional realization of the Kingdom, and in later publications Bavinck placed greater emphasis on this notion than he did before. Further, though his missiological handbook, *IZW* (*ISM*), is clearly ecclesiocentric in terms of its organization, it also has a *basileia*-centric cutting edge. Notwithstanding these emphases, however, Bavinck never developed a thoroughgoing interpretation of Reformed missionary theology from the perspective of this biblical concept of the Kingdom.

3. Relevance of Bavinck's Missiology

3.1. In the Netherlands

Through his publications and classroom work Bavinck exerted a great deal of influence in the Netherlands. In the seminal work of the generation of missiologists following Bavinck, including J. Blauw, J. Verkuyl, A.G. Honig Jr., and others, missiology has evolved to a greater or lesser degree along the lines established by Bavinck.

In his book, *Goden en Mensen* (Gods and Humans) Blauw placed Bavinck's relational approach to religious consciousness in a new theological framework, namely that of man as image of God. For Blauw religions are a-priori signs that God looks after humankind and that man belongs to God. At the same time, like his teacher, Blauw recognizes the ambivalence of human religious response to God. That Verkuyl consciously chose to develop his thought against the background of Bavinck's missionary theology is already clearly shown by the Dutch title of his own missiological textbook: *Inleiding in de nieuwere zendings-wetenschap* (Introduction to the Newer Science of Mission). For Verkuyl the most important themes of Bavinck's missiology are the latter's *theologia religionum* and by extension his views on elenctics, which Verkuyl incorporates into his discussion of what he calls 'trialogue.' With respect to the theology of mission, Verkuyl enlarges upon Bavinck's understanding of comprehensive approach by defining the essential task of mission in terms of the vertical and horizontal dimensions of the Kingdom of God. Honig appropriated and built upon Bavinck's thought in much the same way as did Verkuyl. In his books dealing with, among other things, religious phenomena and the core meaning, scope and significance of the proclamation of salvation Honig refers repeatedly to Bavinck.

---

[9]C. Graafland, "Theologische hoofdlijnen," p. 106.

[10]"Theology and Mission," p. 63.

Finally, in the contemporary generation of older and younger Reformed and Roman Catholic scholars and academics in the Netherlands there are many in the area of missiology and also other disciplines, such as philosophy and systematic theology, who, in one way and to one degree or another, have been influenced by Bavinck in their work.[11]

3.2. Outside the Netherlands

At the international level Bavinck exerted some influence through his foreign contacts, foreign students, travels, guest lectureships and English-language publications, most notably in Indonesia, North America and South Africa at institutions of theological education.[12] Nevertheless, he has remained generally unknown outside his native country. There are hardly any references to his work in missiological publications appearing after the 1960s in countries other than the Netherlands. Exceptions to this are the English evangelical theologian John R. Stott and the German Lutheran missiologist Klaus W. Müller, who have made affirmatory references to Bavinck's ideas, particularly those dealing with elenctics.

4. Closing Word

Analysis of Bavinck's relevant works shows no evidence that any radical changes occurred in his missiological thinking throughout the years. A comparison of his first introduction to mission, *Ons zendingsboek* (1941), with *IZW* (1954), which mark roughly the period of his tenure as professor of missions, does not show any fundamental shifts. Johannes van den Berg, however, rightly determined that a *progression* can be observed:

> The horizon widens, the insight into the relationship between phenomena continually deepens, new threads are continually added to the pattern; but through all of this the course of his thinking, both formally and substantively, is characterized by a striking continuity.[13]

One can refer here specifically to Bavinck's deepened biblical-theological reflection on the foundation and essence of mission; to his continuing reflection on the

---

[11]These include, among many others, the following (in alphabetical order): M.E. Brinkman, A. Camps, J.D. Gort, C. Graafland, S. Griffioen, P. Holtrop, J.A.B. Jongeneel, H. Mintjes, D.C. Mulder, K. Runia, J. van den Berg, A. van Egmond, C. van der Kooi, J.J.E. van Lin, R. van Rossum, H. Visser, H.M. Vroom, A. Wessels, R. van Woudenberg, and the present writer.

[12]Among missiologists outside the Netherlands who have been influenced in one way or another by Bavinck are (in alphabetical sequence): G.H. Anderson (USA), D.J. Bosch (SA), H.R. Boer (USA), J.H. Boer (Canada), M.L. Daneel (Zimbabwe), H. Dekker (USA), J.J.F. Durand (SA), R. Greenway (USA), Anne-Marie Kool (Hungary), J.N.J. Kritzinger (SA), P. Meiring (SA), G.C. Oosthuizen (SA), E.D. Roels (USA), W. Saayman (SA), W.R. Shenk (USA), P. Tuit (USA), C. Van Engen (USA), and A.F. Walls (Scotland).

[13]J. van den Berg, "De wetenschappelijke arbeid van Professor Dr. Johan Herman Bavinck," 41.

relationship between church and Kingdom of God, and, closely related to that, between word and deed; and to the incorporation of his religio-theological insights into his reflection on missionary approach.

Bavinck tried to present within the Reformed context a thorough, biblical reflection on mission. He unquestionably succeeded. Yet all work is human, and although on the one hand he has provided us with valuable insights, at times his exegetical work and theological reflection bore a rather fragmentary character. It is not impossible that this was related to the fact that he engaged in missiology not only as a scholar but also with the passion of a missionary. His method of work probably also explains his limited use of documentation as well as the fact that even within the theoretical framework of *IZW* he sometimes discussed missionary praxis in too much detail. But along with these critical marginal notes on his work method we must also draw attention to its positive side, namely, the fact that his theoretical study of mission never stood on its own in isolation but was always pursued in the service of missionary praxis, with a view to the expansion of the Kingdom of God—a basic concern that will always be indispensable for any meaningful missiology.

The preceding does not detract from what others have concluded, namely, that Bavinck did pioneering work in the development of a missionary theology from a Reformed perspective by deepening it biblically and broadening it in terms of content.[14] Because of their biblical grounding his insights deserve continued attention. Verkuyl correctly noted that the missionary framework in which Bavinck developed his missiological principles dates back to a past (colonial) era, and on that account their implementation as envisaged by Bavinck can not be adopted indiscriminately. They do, however, constitute a basis for fresh reflection on mission in a changed and changing world.[15] Bavinck himself was in any case a convinced proponent of this ongoing reflection, which he saw as a missiological application of the Reformation principle *reformata, semper reformanda*.[16]

The final conclusion of this study is that Bavinck's missionary theology clearly retains its relevance for the present time. It represents an excellent point of departure for the further development of a Reformed theology of mission and *theologia religionum*, which could, in turn, constitute a substantial contribution to contemporary missiological discourse. One of the closing sentences of Bavinck's missiological handbook, *IZW*, reflecting both his realistic faith and his buoyant spirituality, is as fresh and applicable as when he wrote it:

> When we look at the world of our day, we must take clear-eyed account of the immense resistance [to the Gospel] which manifests itself everywhere. But we may also rejoice to note that

---

[14]Cf. A. Pos, "Leven en werk van dr. John Herman Bavinck," 24; J. van den Berg, "De wetenschappelijke arbeid van professor Dr. Johan Herman Bavinck," 39; J. Verkuyl, *Inleiding in de nieuwere zendingswetenschap,* 65; C. Graafland, "Theologische hoofd-lijnen," 63.

[15]J. Verkuyl, *Inleiding in de nieuwere zendingswetenschap*, 65-66.

[16]Cf. *ZWN*, 223 and *IZW*, 303-306 (*ISM*, 306-309). Bavinck points to the need of continuing reflection in various articles as well.

time and again, often at totally unexpected moments, by God's grace doors are opened that offer access to a new, hopeful future.[17]

---

[17]*IZW*, p. 305, (cf. *ISM*, p. 308).

Bibliography

1. Primary Sources (in chronological order)

J.H. Bavinck's Books, Monographs, and Addresses

Der Einfluss des Gefühls auf das Assozationsleben bei Heinrich von Suso, Erlangen, 1919.
Zielkundige opstellen, 1925, Bandung.
Inleiding in de zielkunde, Kampen (1926), second revised and enlarged edition prepared by A. Kuypers, Kampen 1935.
Levensvragen, Magelang, 1927.
Persoonlijkheid en wereldbeschouwing, Kampen, 1928.
De tien geboden, Magelang, 1932.
Hoe kunnen wij den Heere Jezus vinden?, Magelang, 1933.
Christus en de mystiek van het Oosten, Kampen, 1934.
Menschen rondom Jezus, Kampen, 1936.
De strijd op het derde front, Zeist, 1937.
Geschiedenis der Godsopenbaring II: Het Nieuwe Testament, Kampen, 1938.
Jezus als zielzorger, Baarn, 1938.
Christusprediking in de volkerenwereld, Kampen, 1939.
De boodschap van Christus en de niet-christelijke religies: Een analyse en beoordeling van het boek van dr. Kraemer, The Christian message in a non-Christian world, Kampen, 1940.
Het raadsel van ons leven, Kampen, 1940.
Alzoo wies het woord: Een studie over de voortgang van het evangelie in de dagen van Paulus, Baarn, 1941.
Ons zendingsboek, no place name, 1941.
Het probleem van de pseudo-religie en de algemene openbaring, no place name, no year, bound separate issue of an article that appeared in *Orgaan van de Christelijke Vereeniging van Natuur- en Geneeskundigen in Nederland,* 1941, 1-16.
De bijbel het boek der ontmoetingen, Wageningen, 1942.
De psychologie van den Oosterling, Loosduinen, 1942.
De toekomst van onze kerken, Bruinisse, 1943.
Het primitieve denken, critical review of Lévy Bruhl, *Les fonctions mentales,* and K.Th. Preuss, *Glauben und Mystik im Schatten des höchsten Wesens,* stenciled address delivered at the missionary conference, Bilthoven, 1943.
Christus en de wereldstorm, Den Haag, 1944.
De zegen van den arbeid, Den Haag, 1944.
Hoofdmomenten uit de zendingsgeschiedenis en andere referaten, stenciled manuscript, Putten, 1944.
Herinneringen aan het laatste oorlogsjaar 1944-1945, unpublished stenciled manuscript located in the Bavinck family archives.

Zending in een wereld in nood, Wageningen, 1946; fourth enlarged version, Wageningen, 1948.
Leven bij den bijbel, Den Haag, 1946.
De mensch en zijn wereld, Baarn, 1946.
De godsdienst van Java, stencil, no place name, 1947.
Onze kerk zendingskerk, Kampen, 1948.
The Impact of Christianity on the Non-Christian World, Grand Rapids, 1948.
Religieus besef en christelijk geloof, Kampen, 1949.
Het woord voor de wereld, Baarn, 1950.
In de ban der demonen, Kampen 1950.
En voort wentelen de eeuwen: Gedachten over het boek der Openbaring van Johannes, Wageningen, 1952.
Menschen rondom Jezus, Kampen, 1952.
Inleiding in de zendingswetenschap, Kampen, 1954.
Het rassenvraagstuk: Probleem van wereldformaat, Kampen, 1956.
Religies en wereldbeschouwingen in onze tijd, Groningen, 1958.
Flitsen en fragmenten, Kampen, 1959.
Verslag van prof.dr. J.H. Bavinck betreffende zijn reis naar Suriname in opdracht van de Sticusa, 1960 (located in the Center for the Historical Documentation of Dutch Protestantism from 1800 Onward, Free University, Amsterdam).
Ik geloof in de Heilige Geest, Den Haag, 1963.
Wij worden geroepen, Wageningen, 1964.
The Church Between the Temple and Mosque, Grand Rapids, 1966.
Stille tijd in vrije tijd: Evangelisch weekboek, Kampen, 1966.
De mens van nu, Kampen, 1967.
Religieus besef en christelijk geloof, reprinted with a foreword by J. Verkuyl and enlarged with *Algemene openbaring en de niet-christelijke religies* (translation of "General   Revelation and the Non-Christian Religions" [1955] by R. van Woudenberg), Kampen, 1989.
De absoluutheid van het christendom, Bandung, no year.

Co-authored works

Inkeer en uitzicht; een woord voor deze tijd, with C.B. Bavinck, Kampen 1940.
Het geloof en zijn moeilijkheden, with J.H. de Groot and M.J.A. de Vrijer, 1940.
De christen en zijn moeilijkheden, with J.H. de Groot, M.J.A. de Vrijer and K. Dijk, 1941.
Salve Rex, with H. Kraemer and K.H. Miskotte, 1941.

J.H. Bavinck's articles in books, journals and magazines

"Iets over de psychologie der religie," *Gereformeerd Theologisch Tijdschrift,* 28 (1927, 1928), 341-346. Also published in R. van Woudenberg (ed.), *J.H. Bavinck: Een keuze uit zijn werk,* Kampen, 1991, 32-36.
"Een woord van verweer tegen prof. Hoekstra en prof. Waterink," *Gereformeerd Theologisch Tijdschrift,* 28 (1927, 1928), 544-552. Also published in R. van Woudenberg (ed.), *J.H. Bavinck: Een keuze uit zijn werk,* Kampen, 1991, 37-45.
"Christendom en cultuuruitingen," *De Macedoniër,* 36 (1932).
"De crisis van het zendingsonderwijs in Indië," *De Macedoniër,* 36 (1932), 97-101, 129-133.

"Jeugdwerk, de kringen van 5," *De Macedoniër*, 37 (1933), 353-363.

"Is het christendom absoluut?" *Horizon*, 1 (1934, 1935), 265-272.

"Zijn alle godsdiensten gelijk?" *Horizon*, 1 (1934, 1935), 297-302.

"Het christendom als absolute religie," *Horizon*, 1 (1934, 1935), 329-233.

"Het dertigjarig jubileum van de Opleidingsschool te Djokjakarta," *De Opwekker*, 81 (1936), 488-491.

"Het geloof waaruit de kerk leeft," *De Opwekker*, 82 (1937), 520-547.

"Drie grote vragen, De vraag van den mensch en zijn plaats; De vraag der openbaring; De vraag naar de verlossing," *De Macedoniër*, 42 (1938), 82-91, 97-104, 178-184.

"De cultuur-wijsgerige studiekring," in: *Het Triwindoe-Gedenkboek Mangkoe Nagoro*, Part 7, Surakarta, 1939, 9-13.

"Berg en zee als mystiek-religieuze grootheden," *Almanak van het studentencorps aan de VU*, Amsterdam, 1939, 133-144.

"Het probleem der 'Anknüpfung' bij de evangelieverkondiging," *Vox Theologica*, 11 (1939, 1940), 105-111. Also published in R. van Woudenberg (ed.), *J.H. Bavinck: Een keuze uit zijn werk*, Kampen, 1991, 57-69.

"Jezus Christus is dezelfde...tot in eeuwigheid," in: A.G. Barkey Wolf, J.H. Bavinck, A.K. Straatsma, *Gisteren en heden Dezelfde en tot in eeuwigheid*, Den Haag, 1939, 30-46.

"Veel vragen en één antwoord," *De Standaard* (May 25, 1940).

"Worden wij weer primitieve menschen?" *Horizon*, 7 (1940, 1941), 306-312.

"Christus nu," in: J.H. Bavinck, H. Kraemer, K.H. Miskotte, *Salve Rex*, Den Haag, 1941, 7-35.

"Zending en cultuur," in: *Indische dag,* a collection of addresses, Heemstede, 1941.

"Phaenomenologische classificatie der religieuze structuren," *Vox Theologica*, 13 (1941, 1942), 28-32.

"Het evangelie en de andere godsdiensten," *Het Zendingsblad*, 39 (1941), 148, 164, and 40 (1942), 3, 35, 52, 67.

'De zending en haar diensten," *Het Zendingsblad*, 40 (1942), 83, 91, 99, 107, and 41 (1943), 28, 44, 51, 59.

"De komst van het Godsrijk," in: *Militia Christi*, addresses delivered at the 20th gathering of the Association of Reformed (Gereformeerde).Men's Societies, 1942, 6-13.

"Mythos en logos," *Almanak van het corpus studiosorum in academia campensi 'Fides Quaerit Intellectum,'* 51 (1943), 55-66.

"De medische dienst in het geheel van het zendingswerk," and "Wat heeft het medische werk te maken met den godsdienst van den inlander," in: *Voordrachten op de conferentie voor medici en verpleegsters in augustus 1944 te Voorburg*, stenciled collection of conference addresses, Baarn, 1944, 7-8, 15-18.

"Het hindoeïsme en syncretisme als zendingsprobleem," in: J.H. Bavinck, *Hoofdmomenten uit de zendingsgeschiedenis en andere referaten*, stenciled manuscript, Putten, 1944, 7-10.

"Nieuwe oriëntering in ons zendingswerk," *Gereformeerd Weekblad*, 1, 23 and 24 (1945), no pagination.

"Mijn oordeel over de Nederlandsche Volksbeweging" and "Dupliek," in: W. Schermerhorn (ed.), *Christelijk-nationale en humanistische wilskracht in de Nederlandsche Volksbeweging*, Amsterdam, 1945, 3-5, 52-53.

"De zending nu!" foreword in *Historisch Document*, a reissue of the address on mission delivered by A. Kuyper in Amsterdam in 1890, no place name, 1945; also incorporated in the bound 43rd volume of *Het Zendingsblad*.

'Op weg naar een nieuwe zendingsstrategie," "De jonge kerken moeten het doen," "De taak der oudere kerken," "Zendingswerk onder leiding der jonge kerken," "Zending en cultuur," "Het vraagstuk der aansluiting," "Zending in een veranderende wereld," "Aan de vooravond van de samenspreking met de Javaanse kerken," "Samenspreking met de kerk op Java," *Gereformeerd Weekblad,* 2 (1946), 82, 91,107, 116, 133, 169, 189, 381, 399.

"Het eerste gebod," in: Th. Delleman (ed.), *Sinaï en Ardjoeno, Het Indonesische volksleven in het licht der tien geboden,* Aalten, 1946, 21-45. Also published in R. van Woudenberg (ed.), *J.H.Bavinck: Een keuze uit zijn werk,* Kampen, 1991, 88-109.

"De deur op een kier," "Het moeilijke gesprek," "Kunnen wij nog met vrucht in de zending werken?" "Onze zendingsvelden opgenomen in grotere verbanden," "Centralisering in het zendingswerk," "Het vraagstuk van de decentralisatie in de zending," "Wijde perspectieven," "De breedheid van de zendingstaak," "Waar liggen de grenzen van de zendingstaak," *Gereformeerd Weekblad,* 4 (1948), 84, 93, 108, 115, 131, 147, 163, 179, 195, 227.

"Christus en de wereld van het Oosten," in: F.W. Grosheide *et al., Christus de Heiland,* Kampen, 1948, 208-242.

"De vergadering van de wereldraad van kerken," *Bezinning,* 3 (1948), 273-282.

"Review of J.C. Hoekendijk, *Kerk en volk in de Duitse zendingswetenschap,*" *Nederlands Theologisch Tijdschrift,* 3 (1949), 304-306.

"Theologie in het verre Oosten," *Gereformeerd Weekblad,* 4 (1949) 179.

"Zendingsbegrip en zendingswerkelijkheid," *De Heerbaan,* 2 (1949), 1-8.

"Pinksterverlangen in de volkerenwereld,"and "Hebben wij de Heilige Geest ontvangen?" in: G. Brillenburg Wurth, J.H. Bavinck, P. Prins (eds.), *De Heilige Geest,* Kampen, 1949, 7-20, 437-452.

"Toekomstverwachtingen voor ons zendingswerk," "Onze gemeenschappelijke taak," "Wat kunnen wij nu nog voor Indonesië doen?" *Gereformeerd Weekblad,* 5 (1949), 178, 214, and 5 (1950), 235.

"De jonge kerk en het cultureel erfgoed," *De Heerbaan,* 3 (1950), 327-330.

"Overal, behalve in Israël," *Gereformeerd Weekblad,* 6, 44 (1951), no pagination.

"Verkondiging aan de volkerenwereld, De zending," in: J. Waterink *et al., Cultuurgeschiedenis van het christendom,* Part 4, Amsterdam-Brussels, 1951, 359-409.

"Uitkomsten der studie van buitenbijbelse religies," in: J. Waterink *et al., Cultuur geschiedenis van het christendom,* Part 5, Amsterdam-Brussels, 1951, 368-377.

"De zendingsmethode van Paulus en die van ons," *Het Zendingsblad,* 49 (1951), 99.

"De kerk, zendingskerk," *Het Zendingsblad,* 50 (1952), 20.

"Kerk en Zending," *Het Zendingsblad,* 50 (1952), 100.

"Het vraagstuk spitst zich toe," in: J.H. Bavinck and G. van Veldhuizen, *Mens of robot,* Den Haag, 1952, 5-47.

"Mystiek," "Geloven en kennen," "Mystiek dus niet–wat dan wel?" *Gereformeerd Weekblad,* 7 (1952), 313, 329, 361. Also published in R. van Woudenberg (ed.), *J.H. Bavinck: Een keuze uit zijn werk,* Kampen, 1991, 110-144.

"Indrukken van Zuid-Afrika," *Gereformeerd Weekblad,* 7 (1952), 141, 150, 164, 174, 180, 189, and 8 (1953), 219.

"Protestantisme," in: *Ontmoeting der levensovertuigingen, Inleidingen gehouden op de Zomerschool*, no place name, 1954, separate pagination for each article.

"Het rassenvraagstuk in Zuid-Afrika," *Anti-Revolutionaire Staatkunde*, 24 (1954), 257-269.

"Apostoliciteit en katholiciteit," in: *De apostolische kerk*, theological essays presented on the occasion of the centenary of Kampen Theological Seminary, Kampen, 1954, 218-242.

"Nieuwe uitzichten in het zendingswerk," in: *Gespannen verwachting*, a publication of the Association of Reformed (Gereformeerde) Girl's Societies, 1955, 10-16.

"General Revelation and the Non-Christian Religions," *Free University Quarterly*, 4 (1955), 43-55. Also published in Dutch translation as "Algemene openbaring en de niet-christelijke religies," in J.H. Bavinck, *Religieus besef en christelijk geloof*, Kampen, 1989, 192-209, and R. van Woudenberg (ed.), *J.H. Bavinck: Een keuze uit zijn werk*, Kampen 1991, 70-87,

"The problem of adaptation and communication," *International Review of Missions*, 45 (1956), 307-313.

"Het evangelie en het mystisch levensgevoel," farewell lecture, Kampen, October 5, 1956, *De Heerbaan*, 9 (1956), 157-165. Also published in R. van Woudenberg (ed.), *J.H. Bavinck: Een keuze uit zijn werk*, Kampen, 1991, 145-153.

"Religie en het christelijk geloof," *Bezinning*, 12 (1957), 61-71.

"Hendrik Kraemer als denker en medewerker," *De Heerbaan*, 11 (1958), 84-96. Also published in R. van Woudenberg (ed.), *J.H. Bavinck: Een keuze uit zijn werk*, Kampen 1991, 158-171.

"Bijbel en ras," *De Heerbaan*, 11 (1958), 53-70.

"Harrenstein als oecumenische gestalte," *Uitzicht*, 5 (1959), 160-164.

"Het Vasco da Gama-tijdperk, Wereldhistorische bespiegelingen en de zending," *Trouw*, (September 12, 1959).

"India in Transition," *Free University Quarterly*, 7 (1960), 26-37.

"Hoe de boodschap verder gaat: Sociologische aspecten in de verbreiding van het evangelie," *Trouw* (July 10, 1961).

"Theology and Mission," *Free University Quarterly*, 8 (October 1961), 59-66

"Nehroe, 'Ja ik ben veranderd,'" *Trouw*, (November 24, 1962).

"Die Gereformeerde Kerk van Suid-Afrika en die Sending," *Pro Veritate*, 3, 2 (1965), 1ff.

"Artikelen over de rassenproblematiek en Zuid-Afrika," in: J. van den Berg, *Een geheel andere waardemeter*, Amsterdam, 1972.

"De religie en de ontwikkelingsproblematiek," in: *Problematiek van de ontwik-kelings-landen*, published by the Foundation for International Cooperation of Dutch Universities and Colleges, no place name, no year, 21-36.

Archives and Interviews

The central archives of the Reformed Churches in the Netherlands (GKN), housed partly in the Netherlands National Archives in Utrecht and partly at the Central Offices of the Uniting Protestant Churches in the Netherlands, Utrecht.

The archives of the Gereformeerde Kerk in Heemstede.

The archives of the Gereformeerde Kerk in Delft, housed in the municipal archives of Delft.

The archives of Kampen Theological Seminary, largely housed in the municipal archives of Kampen.
The J.H. Bavinck archive in the Center for the Historical Documentation of Dutch Protestantism from 1800 Onward, Free University, Amsterdam.
Interviews with family members, C.B. Bavinck (son), M.H. Bavinck-Bonda (daughter-in-law), G.M. Popma-Bavinck (daughter), H.J. Bavinck and B. Bavinck (nephews).
Interviews with others who knew J.H.Bavinck personally, J. van den Berg, J. Verkuyl, A.G. Honig jr., J. v.d. Linden, D. Bakker, M.J. Richters-Hessels, L.J. Wolthuis.

2. Secondary Sources (in alphabetical order)

Specific

Bakker, F.L. "In memoriam prof. dr. J.H. Bavinck," *Algemeen Handelsblad* (June 24, 1964).
Breukelaar, W. "Berichten over werkzaamheden van J.H. Bavinck," *Het Zendingsblad*, various issues and years.
Haak, C.J. "De elenctiek van J.H. Bavinck en zijn actualiteit voor de moderne missiologie," theme issue, J.H. Bavinck 100 jaar na zijn geboorte, *GMO Bulletin*, 5 (1996), 31-84.
Kievit, J. *Tussen Clemens en Barth, De visie van J.H. Bavinck op de religies*, Th.M. thesis, Free University, Amsterdam, 1987.
Klapwijk, J. *Vervagend oordeel, Genade en oordeel in Bavincks Inleiding in de zendings-wetenschap*, Curaçao, 1988.
Kruidhof, J. "Fundering van de zending, Over de ernst van de werkelijkheid," theme issue, J.H. Bavinck 100 jaar na zijn geboorte, *GMO Bulletin*, 5 (1996), 7-30.
Pos, A. "Bij het sterven van prof. dr. J.H. Bavinck," *Trouw* (June 24, 1964).

Pos, A. "In memoriam prof. dr. J.H. Bavinck," *Centraal Weekblad*, 12, 27 (1964), no pagination.
Pos, A. "Leven en werk van Dr. Johan Herman Bavinck," in: J. van den Berg *et al.* (eds.), *Christusprediking in de wereld*, Kampen, 1965, 7-26.
Ridderbos, H.N. "In memoriam prof. dr. J.H. Bavinck," *Gereformeerd Weekblad*, 20 (1964), 2.
Rullmann, J.A.C. "Bij het overlijden van prof. dr. J.H. Bavinck," *Nieuw Rotterdamsche Courant* (June 24, 1964).
Slagboom, J. *J.H. Bavinck als zendeling*, Apeldoorn, 1985.
van den Berg, J. "Prof. Bavinck 40 jaar in het ambt," *Centraal Weekblad*, 9, 28 (1961), no pagination.
van den Berg, J. "De wetenschappelijke arbeid van Professor Dr. Johan Herman Bavinck," in: J. van den Berg *et al.* (eds.), *Christusprediking in de wereld*, Kampen, 1965, 27-42.
van den Berg, J. *Een geheel andere waardemeter, Beschouwingen van Prof. Dr. J.H. Bavinck over het rassenvraagstuk en Zuid-Afrika*, Amsterdam, 1972.
van den Berg, J. "The legacy of J.H. Bavinck," *International Bulletin of Missionary Research*, 7, 4 (October 1983), 171-174.
van Woudenberg, R. "Dr. Johan Herman Bavinck (1895-1964), Theoloog van Woord en antwoord," in: R. Woudenberg (ed.), *J.H. Bavinck: Een keuze uit zijn werk*, Kampen, 1991, 7-31.

Verkuyl, J. "In memoriam prof.dr. J.H. Bavinck," *De Heerbaan*, 17 (1964), 93.

Verkuyl, J. "Prof. dr. J.H. Bavinck," in: J. Verkuyl, *Inleiding in de nieuwere zendingswetenschap*, Kampen, 1975, 60-66.

Verkuyl, J. "Woord vooraf," in: *Religieus besef en christelijk geloof*, enlarged with *Algemene openbaring en de niet-christelijke religies*, Kampen, 1989, ix-xix.

Visser, P.J. *Geen andere naam onder de hemel, De missiologie van Johan Herman Bavinck*, Th.M. thesis, University of Utrecht, 1987.

Visser, P.J. "De openbaring Gods in missiologisch perspectief, De visie van J.H. Bavinck op de relatie tussen Gods openbaring en de niet-christelijke religies," in: J. van der Graaf (ed.), *Een vaste burcht voor de kerk der eeuwen*, essays presented to K. Exalto, Kampen, 1989, 166-190.

General

Algra, A. *De Gereformeerde Kerken in Nederlands-Indië / Indonesië (1877-1961)*, Franeker, no year.

Algra, H. *Het wonder van de negentiende eeuw*, Franeker, 1979.

Allen, R. *Missionary methods, St. Paul's or Ours?* Londen, 1912.

Allen, R. *The Spontaneous Expansion of the Church and the Causes Which Hinder It*, Londen, 1927.

Anonymous. "God in de internationale politiek," *Koers*, 26, 23 (1995), 4.

Arndt, W.F. and F.W. Gingrich. *A Greek-English Lexicon of the New Testament and Other Early Christian Literature*, Chicago, 1960.

Baas, H. *Van Baarn tot Leusden, 40 jaar Zendingscentrum 1946-1986*, Leusden, 1986.

Bailey, C. *Epicurus, The Extant Remains*, Oxford, 1926.

Bailey, C. *Titi Lucreti Cari*, Vol. I, Oxford, 1972.

Bakhuizen van den Brink, J.N. and W.F. Dankbaar. *Handboek der kerkgeschiedenis*, Vol. 4, Den Haag, 1968.

Bakker, F.L. "Enkele gegevens over de Opleidingsschool te Djokja," *De Macedoniër*, 40 (1936), 257-264.

Bakker, W. (ed.). *De Afscheiding van 1834 en haar geschiedenis*, Kampen, 1984.

Bakker, W. (ed.). *De Doleantie van 1886 en haar geschiedenis*, Kampen, 1986.

Balke, W. *Heel het Woord en heel de Kerk, Schetsen uit de geschiedenis van de vaderlandse kerk*, Kampen, 1992.

Barth, K. "Die Theologie und die Mission in der Gegenwart," *Zwischen den Zeiten*, (1932), 43-65.

Barth, K. *Het christelijk openbaringsbegrip*, translation of *Das christliche Verständnis der Offenbarung* by H.C. Touw, Nijkerk, no year.

Barth, K. *Kirchliche Dogmatik*, Vol. I.2, Zürich, 1969.

Barth, K. *Church Dogmatics*, Vol. I.2, tr. By G.T. Thomson and H. Knight, Edinburgh, 1956.

Bassham, R.C. *Mission Theology 1948-1975, Years of Worldwide Creative Tension, Ecumenical, Evangelical, and Roman Catholic*, Pasadena, 1979.

Bauer, W. *Wörterbuch zum Neuen Testament*, Berlin-New York, 1971.

Bavinck, C.B., et al. *Ons aller moeder*, no place name, 1926.

Bavinck, C.B. *Welke zijn de oorzaken van het kerkelijk-gescheiden leven der Gereformeer-den in Nederland*, Aalten, 1921.

Bavinck, C.B. *Gaat in tot Zijne poorten met lof*, farewell sermon, December 2,

1930, Rotterdam.
Bavinck, H. *De katholiciteit van christendom en kerk*, Kampen, 1888.
Bavinck, H. *De offerande des lofs*, Kampen, 1901.
Bavinck, H. *De zekerheid des geloofs*, Kampen, 1901.
Bavinck, H. *Gereformeerde dogmatiek,,* Vols. 1, 2, 3, Kampen, 1906, 1908, 1910.
Bavinck, H. "De zending in de Heilige Schrift," in: H. Beets, *Triumfen van het kruis*, Grand Rapids, 1914, 7-30.
Bavinck, H. *Beginselen der psychologie*, Kampen, 1923.
Bavinck, J. *Stemmen des heils*, no place name, 1863.
Bavinck, J. *De Heidelbergse Catechismus in 60 leerredenen verklaard*, Vols. 1, 2, Kampen, 1903.
Bavinck, J. *Feeststoffen I, II en III*, Kampen, 1909.
Beker, E.J. and J.M. Hasselaar. *Wegen en kruispunten in de dogmatiek*, Vol. 1, Kampen, 1978.
Bergema, H. "Over de beteekenis van de kennis der Javaansche cultuur voor het verstaan van de Javaansche levensvisie," *De Macedoniër*, 36 (1932), 257-268.
Bergema, H. *Rondom Israël*, Kampen, 1957.
Berkhof, H. "Emancipatie, secularisatie en de zending van de kerk," in: J.D. Gort and H.J. Westmaas (eds.), *Zending op weg naar de toekomst*, essays presented to J. Verkuyl on the occasion of his retirement, Kampen, 1978, 166-177.
Berkouwer, G.C. *Dogmatische Studiën, De algemene openbaring*, Kampen, 1951.

Bertram, G. "θεοσεβής, θεοσέβεια," in: Gerhard Kittel (ed.) *Theological Dictionary of the New Testament*, Vol. 3, Θ–K, translated by Geoffrey W. Bromiley, Grand Rapids, 1972, 123-128.
Blauw, J. *Goden en mensen, Plaats en betekenis van de heidenen in de Heilige Schrift*, Groningen, 1950.
Blauw, J. *Gottes Werk in dieser Welt, Grundzüge einer biblischen Theologie der Mission*, München, 1961.
Blauw, J. "Rijmloos, Overwegingen bij het thema 'evangelie en religies,'" in: J. van den Berg *et al.* (eds.), *Christusprediking in de wereld*, Kampen, 1965, 111-132.
Boersema, J.A. "Een halve eeuw zending van de Gereformeerde Kerken (Vrijge-maakt) tegen de achtergrond van Middelburg 1896," *Documentatieblad voor de geschiedenis van de Nederlandse zending en overzeese kerken*, 3, 2 (1996), 51-70.
Bosch, D.J. *Witness To the World*, Londen, 1980.
Bosch, J. *Figuren en aspecten uit de eeuw der afscheiding*, Goes, 1952.
Bouquet, A.C. *The Christian Faith and Non-Christian Religions*, Londen, 1958.
Bouritius, G. "Interreligieuze dialoog," in: H. Schaeffer (ed.), *Handboek godsdienst in Nederland*, Amersfoort, 1992, 167-179.
Bremmer, R.H. *Herman Bavinck als dogmaticus*, Kampen, 1961.
Bremmer, R.H. *Herman Bavinck en zijn tijdgenoten*, Kampen, 1966.
Brillenburg Wurth, G. and W.A. Wiersinga. *Het evangelie in een ontkerstende wereld*, Kampen, 1953.
Brinkman, M.E. *De theologie van Karl Barth, Dynamiet of dynamo voor christelijk handelen, De politieke en theologische controverse tussen nederlandse barthianen en neocalvinisten*, Baarn, 1983.
Broekhuis, J. *Oriëntatie in de godsdienstwetenschap*, Zoetermeer, 1994.
Brouwer, K.J. *Zending in een gistende wereld*, Amsterdam, 1951.

Brunner, E. *Natur und Gnade*, Tübingen, 1934.
Brunner, E. *Der Mensch im Widerspruch*, Zürich, 1941.
Buskes, J.J. *Hoera voor het leven*, Amsterdam, 1960.
Calvin, John. *Institutes of the Christian Religion*, Vol. 1, translated by Ford Lewis Battles, Philadelphia, 1960.
Calvin, John. *Institutie*, translated by A. Sizoo, Delft, 1931.
Calvin, John. *Verklaring van de bijbel, Romeinen*, Goudriaan, 1972.
Chakkarai, V. *Jesus the Avatar*, Madras, 1926.
Clemen, C. *Der Einfluss des Christentums auf andere Religionen*, Leipzig, 1933.
Christelijke Encyclopedie, Vol. 5, Kampen, no year.
Dana, H.E. and J.R. Mantey. *A Manual Grammar of the Greek New Testament*, New York, 1960.
Dankbaar, W.F. "Het apostolaat bij Calvijn," in: W.F. Dankbaar, *Hervormers en humanisten, Een bundel opstellen*, Amsterdam, 1978.
Daubanton, F.E. *Prolegomena van protestantsche zendingswetenschap*, Utrecht, 1911.
Davis, J.M. *New Buildings on Old Foundations, A Handbook on Stabilizing the Younger Churches in Their Environment*, New York-Londen, 1947.
Deddens, K. and M.K. Drost. *Balans van het oecumenisme*, Enschede, 1980.
Dee, J.J.C. *K. Schilder, Zijn leven en zijn werk*, Vol. 1, Goes, 1990.
de Vos, H. *Het christendom en de andere godsdiensten*, Nijkerk, 1962.
Dibelius, M. *Paulus auf dem Areopag*, Heidelberg, 1939.
Drexel, A. *Die Völker der Erde*, Vol. 1, no place name, 1947.
"Edinburgh to Melbourne," theme issue, *International Review of Mission*, 67, 267 (July, 1978).
Endedijk, H.C. *De Gereformeerde Kerken in Nederland*, Vol. 1, Kampen, 1991.
Esser, B.J. *De Goddelijke leiding in de zending*, Rotterdam, 1914.
Esser, B.J. "Ambt en kerkelijke positie der missionair-predikanten in de Gereformeerde Kerken en de opleiding daartoe," *De Macedoniër*, 37 (1933), 97-112.
Fernhout, R. "Van elenctiek naar dialoog," in: R. Bakker, R. Fernhout, J.D. Gort, A Wessels (eds.), *Religies in nieuw perspectief*, essays on interreligious dialogue and religiosity presented to D.C. Mulder on the occasion of his retirement, Kampen, 1985, 9-17.
Freytag, W. *Die junge Christenheit im Umbruch des Ostens*, Berlin, 1938.
Freytag, W. "Mission im Blick aufs Ende," *Evangelisches Missions Zeitschrift*, (1942), 321-333.
Frick, H. *Christliche Verkündigung und vorchristliches Erbgut*, Stuttgart-Basel, 1938.
Gilhuis, J.C. *De zendingstaak der kerk*, Kampen, 1940.
Gilhuis, J.C. *Ecclesiocentrische aspecten van het zendingswerk*, Kampen, 1955.
Goodall, Norman. "Towards Willingen," *International Review of Mission*, 41 (1952), 129-138.
Goodall, Norman (ed.). *Mission Under the Cross, Addresses Delivered at the Enlarged Meeting of the Committee of the International Missionary Council at Willingen in Germany, 1952*, London, 1953.
Gort, J.D. and H.J. Westmaas (eds.), *Zending op weg naar de toekomst*, essays presented to J. Verkuyl on the occasion of his retirement, Kampen, 1978.
Gort, J.D. "The Contours of the Reformed Understanding of Christian Mission," *Mission Focus*, 7, 3 (September 1979), 37-41. Also published in enlarged form as "Contours of the Reformed Understanding of Christian Mission, An Attempt at Delineation" in *Calvin Theological Journal*, 15, 1 (April

1980), 47-61, and in *Occasional Bulletin of Missionary Research*, 4, 4 (October 1980), 156-162.

Gort, J.D. "Buitenkerkelijken als randkerkelijken," in: J.M. Vlijm (ed.), *Buitensporig geloven, Studies over 'randkerkelijkheid'*, Kampen, 1983, 137-152.

Gort, J. D. "Van Edinburgh 1910 naar San Antonio 1989, Een doorlopend verhaal," *Wereld en Zending*, 18, 4 (1989), 359-365.

Graafland, C. "Theologische hoofdlijnen," in: C.A. Tukker (ed.), *Gij die eertijds verre waart: Een inleiding tot de gereformeerde zendingswetenschap*, Utrecht, 1978.

Graafland, C. "De bijbelse fundering van het zendingswerk," in: C.A. Tukker (ed.), *Gij die eertijds verre waart: Een inleiding tot de gereformeerde zendingswetenschap*, Utrecht, 1978.

Grolle, J.H. *Gesprek met Israël*, Den Haag, 1949.

Grosheide, F.W. "Beginselen der Gereformeerde Evangelisatie," in: *Handboek voor Gereformeerde Evangelisatie*, Kampen, no year.

Grosheide, F.W. *Kommentaar op het NT, De Handelingen der Apostelen I*, Amsterdam, 1942.

Gutmann, B. *Gemeindeaufbau aus dem Evangelium, Grundsätzliches für Mission und Heimatkirche*, Leipzig, 1925.

Hadiwyono, H. *Man in the Present Javanese Mysticism*, Baarn, 1967.

Handboek van de Gereformeerde Kerken in Nederland, 22 (1910), Goes, 1910.

Harnack, A. von. *Dogmengeschichte*, Vol. 1, Tübingen, 1909.

Harnack, A. von. *Mission und Ausbreitung des Christentums in den ersten drei Jahr-hunderten*, Vol. 1, Leipzig, 1924.

Hartenstein, K. *Die Mission als theologisches Problem, Beiträge zum grundsäßlichen Verständnis der Mission*, Berlin, 1933.

Hartenstein, K. "Heidentum und Kirche," *Evangelisches Missionsmagazin*, 80 (1936), no pagination.

Hartveld, G. "De vraag van Lessing, Wie van de drie?" *Rondom het Woord*, 21 (1979), 21-29.

Hastings, J. (ed.). *Encyclopaedia of Religion and Ethics*, no place name, 1909.

Hepp, V. *Dr. Herman Bavinck*, Amsterdam, 1921.

Hocking, W.E. *Rethinking Missions, A Laymen's Inquiry After One Hundred Years*, New York-Londen, 1932.

Hoekema, A.G. *Denken in dynamisch evenwicht, De wordingsgeschiedenis van de nationale protestantse theologie ca.1860-1960*, Zoetermeer, 1994.

Hoekendijk, J.C. *Kerk en volk in de Duitse zendingswetenschap*, Amsterdam, 1948.

Holsten, W. *Das Evangelium und die Völker, Beiträge zur Geschichte und Theorie der Mission*, Berlin-Friedenau, 1939.

Holsten, W. *Das Kerygma und der Mensch, Einführing in die Religions- und Missions-wissenschaft*, München, 1953.

Holtrop, N. "Van Middelburg tot aan de einden der aarde," *Documentatieblad voor de geschiedenis van de Nederlandse zending en overzeese kerken*, 3, 2 (1996), 160-170.

Holtzmann, O. *Neutestamentliche Zeitgeschichte*, Tübingen, 1906.

Honig jr., A.G. *Bijdrage tot het onderzoek naar de fundering van de zendingsmethode der 'comprehensive approach' in het Nieuwe Testament*, Kampen 1951.

Honig jr., A.G. *De heerschappij van Christus en de zending*, Kampen, 1973.

Idenburg, J. et al. *Evangelische benadering van de mens*, Delft, 1953.

Jongeneel, J.A.B. and E. Klootwijk. *Faculteiten der godgeleerdheid, theologische hoge-scholen en de derde wereld*, Leiden, 1986.

Jongeneel, J.A.B. (ed.). *Ganges en Galilea, Een keuze uit het werk van Stanley J. Samartha*, Kampen, 1986.

Jongeneel, J.A.B. "Voetius' zendingstheologie, De eerste comprehensieve protestantse zendingstheologie," in: J. van Oort *et al.*, *De onbekende Voetius*, Kampen, 1989.

Jongeneel, J.A.B. "De zendingstheologie van F.E. Daubanton," *Nederlands Theologische Tijdschrift*, 44 (1990), 288-307.

Jongeneel, J.A.B. *Missiologie*, Part 1, Zendingswetenschap, Part 2, Missionaire theologie, Den Haag, 1991.

Jongeneel, J.A.B. "De missie volbrengen," in: W. Aantjes *et al.*, *Gereformeerden en het gesprek met de cultuur*, Zoetermeer, 1991, 191-201.

Jongeneel, J.A.B. "Missie en zending," in H. Schaeffer (ed.), *Handboek Godsdienst in Nederland*, Amersfoort, 1992, 573-586.

Jonker H. and E.S. Klein Kranenburg. *Bijbel en ervaring*, Zoetermeer, 1991.

Joosse L.J. (ed.). *Leren hoe hij wand'len moet, over woord en daad in de zending*, Goes, 1992.

Kagawa, T. *The Religion of Jesus*, Londen, 1931.

Kamphuis, J. *Zien in de toekomst*, Groningen, 1979.

Karrer, O. *Het religieuze in de mensheid en het christendom*, Bilthoven, 1939.

Keysser, C. *Eine Papuagemeinde*, Kassel, 1929.

Kinghorn, J. (ed.). *Die NG Kerk en apartheid*, Johannesburg, 1986.

Kinnamon, M. and B.E. Cope, *The Ecumenical Movement: An Anthology of Texts and Voices*, Geneva / Grand Rapids, 1997.

Kittel, G. *Theologisches Wörterbuch zum Neuen Testament*, Vol. 2, Stuttgart, 1935.

Koetsier, C.H. *Zending als dienst aan de samenleving*, Delft, 1975.

Kok, J. *Meister Albert en zijn zonen*, Kampen, 1984³.

Korff, F.W.A. *Het christelijk geloof en de niet-christelijke godsdiensten*, Amsterdam, 1946.

Kraemer, H. *Kerk en zending*, Den Haag, 1936.

Kraemer, H. *De wortelen van het syncretisme*, Den Haag, 1937.

Kraemer, H. *Blijvende opdracht*, Den Haag, 1941.

Kraemer, H. *Communicatie*, Den Haag, 1957.

Kraemer, H. *Godsdienst, godsdiensten en het christelijk geloof*, Nijkerk, 1958.

Kraemer, H. *The Christian Message in a Non-Christian world*, Grand Rapids, 1969.

Kraemer, H. *Waarom nu juist het christendom?*, Nijkerk, 1960.

Kraus, H.J. *Biblischer Kommentar, Psalmen*, Vol. 2, Neukirchen-Vluyn, 1966.

Kuitert, H.M. *In rapport met de tijd*, Kampen, 1990.

Kuyper, A. *Lectures on Calvinism: Six Lectures Delivered at Princeton University, 1898*, under the auspices of the L. P. Stone Foundation).

Kuyper, A. *Het Calvinisme, Zes Stone-Lezingen in October 1898 te Princeton gehouden*, Amsterdam-Pretoria, no year.

Kuyper, A. *Encyclopaedie der Heilige Godgeleerdheid*, Vol. 3, Kampen 1909.

Lambooy, J. "De methode van de elenctiek van het heidendom," *De Macedoniër*, 43 (1939), 38 ff.

Lekkerkerker, A.F.N. *De prediking van het NT, De brief van Paulus aan de Romeinen*, Vol. 1, Nijkerk, 1971.

Liddell, H.G. and R. Scott. *A Greek-English Lexicon*, Oxford, 1958.

McCracken, G.I. *St. Augustine, The City of God Against the Pagans*, Vol. 2, London- Cambridge, Massachusetts, 1963.

Mintjes, H. "In de lijn van Abraham, Honderd jaar Gereformeerde Kerken en de Islam," *Documentatieblad voor de geschiedenis van de Nederlandse zending en overzeese kerken*, 3, 2 (1996), 140-159.

Mulder, D.C. "Dialoog als zending," in: J.D. Gort, H.J. Westmaas (eds.), *Zending op weg naar de toekomst*, Kampen, 1978, 137-145.

Mulders, A.J.M. *Missiologisch bestek: Inleiding tot de katholieke missieweten-schap*, Hilversum-Antwerpen, 1962.

Müller, K.W. "Elenktik, Gewissen im Kontext," in: H. Kasdorf and K.W. Müller (eds.), *Balanz und Plan, Mission an der Schwelle dritten Jahrtausend*, Festschrift presented to George W. Peters on the occasion of his 80th birthday, Bad Liebenzell, 1988.

Muller, Richard A. *Dictionary of Latin and Greek Theological Terms Drawn Principally from Protestant Scholastic Theology*, Grand Rapids / Carlisle, 1985.

Nauta, D. (ed.), *Biografisch lexicon voor de geschiedenis van het Nederlandse protestan-tisme*, Vols. 1, 2, Kampen, 1983.

Neill, S.C. *A History of Christian Missions*, Harmondsworth, 1964.

Neill, S.C. *Christian Faith and Other Faiths*, Londen, 1968.

Neill, S.C., G.H. Anderson and J. Goodwin (eds.), *Concise Dictionary of the Christian World Mission*, London, 1971.

Neurdenberg, J.C. *Proeve eener handleiding bij het bespreken der zendingsweten-schap*, Rotterdam, 1879.

Nida, E.A. *Message and Mission, The Communication of the Christian Faith*, New York, 1960.

Norden, E. *Agnostos Theos, Untersuchungen zur Formengeschichte religiöser Rede*, Leipzig, 1913.

Oepke, A. *Das neue Gottesvolk*, Stuttgart-Basel, 1938.

Oepke, A. "εἰς ," in: Gerhard Kittel (ed.), *Theological Dictionary of the New Testament*, Vol. 2, Δ–Η, translated by Geoffrey W. Bromiley, Grand Rapids, 1964, 420-434.

Otto, R. *Das Heilige*, Breslau, 1922.

Pol, D. *Midden-Java ten Zuiden*, Hoenderloo, 1939.

Pol, D. "Vorstenlanden,' in: *Christelijke Encyclopedie*, Vol. 5.

Pos, A. "Oosterse theologie," *De Heerbaan*, 8 (1955), 159 ff.

Reichelt, K.L. *Der Chinesische Buddhismus, Ein Bild vom religiösen Leben des Ostens*, Basel, 1926.

Rienecker, Fritz. *Sprachlicher Schlüssel zum Griechischen Neuen Testament*, Giessen-Basel, 1960.

Reinhard, J. "Wandlungen im Missionsdenken der letzten 50 Jahre," *Evangelisches Missions Zeitschrift* (1943), 175 ff.

Richter, J. *Evangelische Missionskunde*, Vols. 1, 2, Leipzig, 1927.

Ridderbos, H.N. *De komst van het Koninkrijk*, Kampen, 1985.

Ridderbos, J. *Strijd op twee fronten, Schilder en de gereformeerde elite in de jaren 1933-1945 tussen aanpassing, collaboratie en verzet op kerkelijk en politiek terrein*, Vols. 1, 2, Kampen, 1994.

Runia, K. *Het evangelie en de vele religies*, Kampen, 1990.

Schärer, H. *Die Begründung der Mission in der katholischen und evangelischen Missions-wissenschaft*, Zürich, 1944.

Schärer, H. *Die missionarische Verkündigung auf dem Missionsfelde*, Basel, 1946.

Schippers, R. *De bronnen van een oecumenisch ethos*, Kampen, 1951.

Schleiermacher, F.D.E. *Über die Religion, Reden an die Gebildeten unter ihren Verächtern*, Hamburg, 1958.

Schleiermacher, F.D.E. *Der christliche Glaube, Nach den Grundsätzen der evangelische Kirche im Zusammenhange dargestellt*, Berlin, 1960.

Schlunk, M. *Paulus als Missionar*, Gütersloh, 1937.

Schmidlin, J. *Katholische Missionslehre im Grundriss*, Münster, 1923
Schmidlin, J. *Einführung in die Missionswissenschaft*, Münster, 1925.
Schmoller, A. *Handkonkordanz zum Griechischen Neuen Testament*, Stuttgart, 1973.
Schürer, E. *Geschichte des jüdischen Volkes im Zeitalter Jesu Christu*, Vol. 3, Leipzig, 1898.
Schuurman, B.M. *Over alle bergen*, Den Haag, 1952.
Schweitzer, A. *Die Mystik des Apostels Paulus*, Tübingen, 1930.
Seesemann, Heinrich. "παροξύνω, παροξυσμός," in: Gerhard Friedrich (ed.), *Theological Dictionary of the New Testament*, Vol. 5, Ξ–Πα, translated by Geoffrey W. Bromiley, Grand Rapids, 1970, 857.
Smit, W. *De Islam binnen de horizon, Een missiologische studie over de benadering van de islam door vier Nederlandse zendingscorporaties, 1797-1951*, Zoetermeer, 1995.
Stellingwerf, J. *De Vrije Universiteit na Kuyper, De VU van 1905 tot 1955, een halve eeuw geestesgeschiedenis van een civitas academica*, Kampen, 1987.
Stott, J.R.W. *Zending in de moderne wereld*, translation of *Christian Mission in theModern World*, (Eastbourne, 1975), Goes, 1978.
Sundkler B.G.M. and A. Fridrichsen. *Contributions à l' étude de la pensée missionaire dans la Nouveau Testament*, Uppsala, 1937.
Thauren, J. *Die Akkomodation im katholischen Heidenapostolat*, Münster, 1927.
Tigchelaar, J.J. "Liefde in daden," in: C.A. Tukker (ed.), *Gij die eertijds verre waart: Een inleiding tot de gereformeerde zendingswetenschap*, Utrecht, 1978.
Uittreksel uit de Acta der generale synode van de GKN, Middelburg, 1896.
van Andel, H.A. *De zendingsleer van Gijsbertus Voetius*, 1912.
van Andel, H.A. "De Conferentie op de Olijfberg," *De Macedoniër*, 33 (1929), 64-75.
van Baal, J. *Ontglipt verleden, Verhaal van mijn jaren in een wereld die voorbijging*, Vol. 2, Franeker, 1989.
van Beek, *et al. De Afgescheidenen en hun nageslacht*, Kampen, 1984.
van den Berg, A.J. *De Nederlandse Christelijke Studenten-Vereniging 1896-1985*, Den Haag, 1991.
van den Berg, J. "De Gereformeerde Kerken en de oecumenische beweging," in: W.F. Golterman and J.C. Hoekendijk (eds.), *Oecumene in 't vizier*, essays presented to W.A. Visser 't Hooft on the occasion of his 60th birthday, Amsterdam, 1960, 9-22.
van den Beukel, A. *De dingen hebben hun geheim*, Baarn, 1991.
van den Toren, B. *Breuk en brug, In gesprek met Karl Barth en postmoderne theologie over geloofsverantwoording*, Kampen, 1995.
van der End, T. *Gereformeerde zending op Sumba 1859-1972, Een bronnenpublicatie*, Alphen aan de Rijn, 1987.
van der Linde, J.M. *Gods wereldhuis*, Amsterdam, 1980.
van der Linde, J.M. *Over Noach en zijn zonen, De Cham-ideologie en de leugens tegen Cham tot vandaag*, Utrecht-Leiden, 1993.
van der Linde, S. *Zending naar gereformeerd beginsel*, Huizen, 1946.
van der Woude, A.S. "God en de goden in het Oude Testament," *Rondom het Woord*, 21 (1979), 3-11
Van Dusen, H. *Het Christendom in de wereld*, Amsterdam, 1948.
van Eck, J. "In gesprek met het heidendom," *Wapenveld*, 42 (1992), 131-135.
van Klinken, G.J. *Opvattingen in de Gereformeerde Kerken in Nederland over het*

Jodendom, Kampen, 1996.
van Koppen, C.A.J. *De geuzen van de negentiende eeuw, Abraham Kuyper en Zuid-Afrika*, Wormer, 1992.
van Leeuwen, A.T. *Hendrik Kraemer, Dienaar der wereldkerk*, Amsterdam, 1959.
van Leeuwen, C. *De prediking van het OT, Amos*, Nijkerk, 1985.
van Lin, J.J.E. *Protestantse theologie der godsdiensten, Van Edinburgh naar Tambaram, 1910-1938*, Assen, 1974.
van Niftrik, G.C. *Een beroerder Israëls. Enkele hoofdgedachten in de theologie van Karl Barth*, Nijkerk, 1949.
van Roon, A. *Prediking van het NT, De brief van Paulus aan de Efeziërs*, Nijkerk, 1976.
van Ruler, A.A. *Theologie van het apostolaat*, Nijkerk, 1953.
van 't Hof, I.C. *Op zoek naar het geheim van de zending, In dialoog met de wereldzendingsconferenties 1910-1963*, Wageningen, 1972.
van Woudenberg, R. "Christelijk exclusivisme en religieus pluralisme," *Nederlands Theologisch Tijdschrift* (1994), 275-290.
van Woudenberg, R. "Waarheid en haar adjectieven," *Radix*, 21 (1995), 32-46.
Veenhof, J. "Honderd jaar theologie aan de Vrije Universiteit," in: M. van Os and W.J. Wieringa (eds.), *Wetenschap en rekenschap, 1880-1980, Een eeuw wetenschaps-beoefening en wetenschapsbeschouwing aan de VU*, Kampen, 1980.
Veenhof, J. "Geschiedenis van theologie en spiritualiteit in de Gereformeerde Kerken," in: M.E. Brinkman (ed.), *100 jaar theologie, Aspecten van een eeuw theologie in de GKN, 1892-1992*, Kampen 1992.
Verkuyl, J. *Zijn alle godsdiensten gelijk?* Baarn, 1953.
Verkuyl, J. *Inleiding in de nieuwere zendingswetenschap*, Kampen, 1975.
Verkuyl, J. *Contemporary Missiology: An Introduction*, Grand Rapids, 1978.
Verkuyl, J. *Inleiding in de evangelistiek*, Kampen, 1978.
Verkuyl, J. *Gedenken en verwachten, Memoires*, Kampen, 1983.
Verkuyl, J. "De spanning tussen westers imperialisme en kolonialisme en zending in het tijdperk van de 'ethische koloniale politiek,'" in: J. de Bruijn (ed.), *Een land nog niet in kaart gebracht, Aspecten van het protestants-christelijk leven in Nederland in de jaren 1880-1940*, Amsterdam, 1987.
Verkuyl, J. *De kern van het christelijk geloof*, Kampen, 1992.
Versteeg, J. "De bijbelse fundering van het zendingswerk," in: C.A. Tukker (ed.), *Gij die eertijds verre waart: Een inleiding tot de gereformeerde zendingswetenschap*, Utrecht, 1978.
Verstraelen, F.J., *et al.* (eds.) *Oecumenische inleiding in de missiologie, Teksten en kon-teksten van het wereldchristendom*, Kampen, 1988.
Verstraelen, F.J., *et al.* (eds.). *Missiology, An Ecumenical Introduction, Texts and Contexts of Global Christianity*, Grand Rapids, 1995.
Visser, P.J. "Bijbelse taxatie van niet-christelijke religie" in: A.G. Knevel, *Jezus de enige weg*, Kampen, 1991, 59-65.
Visser, P.J. "Confrontatie met niet-christelijke religie," in: A.G. Knevel, *Jezus de enige weg*, Kampen, 1991, 66-70.
Visser, P.J. "Een gereformeerde? Aller dienaar!" *Kontekstueel*, 6, 5 (1992), 42-45.
Voetius, G. *Disputatio de Gentilismo*.
Voetius, G. *Politica Ecclesiastica*, 4.
Voetius, G. *Tractaat over de planting en planters van kerken*, translation of *De plantatione ecclesiarum*, Groningen, 1910.
Vroom, H.M. *Geen andere goden? Christelijk geloof in gesprek met Boeddhisme, Hindoeïsme en Islam*, Kampen, 1993.

Vroom, H.M. "Van antithese naar ontmoeting," *Gereformeerd Theologisch Tijdschrift*, 91, 3 (1991), 122-137.

Warneck, G. "Die moderne Weltevangelismus-Theorie," *Allgemeine Missions-Zeitschrift*, 24 (1897), 305-325.

Warneck, G. *Evangelische Missionslehre*, Vols. 1, 2, 3, Gotha, 1894-1905.

Warneck, G. *Die Mission im Lichte der Bibel*, Gütersloh, 1907.

Warneck, J. *Paulus im Lichte der heutigen Heidenmission*, Berlin, 1913.

Wernle, *Paulus als Heidenmissionar*, Tübingen, 1909.

Wessels, A. "Op weg naar een contextuele missiologie," in: R. Bakker *et al.*, (eds.), *Religies in nieuw perspectief*, Kampen, 1985, 109-136.

Wessels, A. *En allen die geloven zijn Abrahams geslacht*, Baarn, 1989.

Wessels, A. "Biblical presuppositions for and against syncretism," in: J.D. Gort *et al.*, (eds.), *Dialogue and Syncretism: An Interdisciplinary Approach*, Grand Rapids, 1989, 52-65.

Wielenga, D.K. *De akker is de wereld*, Amsterdam, 1975.

Wiersinga, H.A. *Zendingsperspectief in het Oude Testament*, Baarn, 1954.

Wiersinga, H.A. *Bijbel en zending*, Baarn, 1955.

Wind, A. *Leven en dood in het evangelie van Johannes en in de Serat Dewarutji, met een elenctische confrontatie*, Franeker, 1956.

Wind, A. *Zending en oecumene in de twintigste eeuw*, Vols. 1, 2, Kampen, 1984, 1991.

Wingren, G. *Die Predigt*, Göttingen, 1955.

Wisse, G. *Mémoires*, Utrecht, 1953.

Witte, J. *Die Christus-Botschaft und die Religionen*, Göttingen, 1936.

Yates, T. *Christian Mission in the Twentieth Century*, Cambridge, 1994.

Zielhuis, L. *Het offermaal in het heidendom en in de Heilige Schrift*, Franeker, 1951.

Zuidema, S.U. "Gereformeerd oecumenisch," *Bezinning* 3 (1948).

Index of Names